ANCIENT INDIAN HISTORY AND CIVILIZATION

ANCIENT INDIAN HISTORY AND CIVILIZATION

Trends and Perspectives

N.N. BHATTACHARYYA

MANOHAR
2026

First published 1988
Reprinted 2021, 2022, 2023, 2024, 2025, 2026

ISBN 978-81-85054-54-4

Published by
Ajay Kumar Jain *for*
Manohar Publishers & Distributors
4753/23 Ansari Road, Daryaganj
New Delhi 110 002

Printed at
Replika Press Pvt. Ltd.

Preface

This book is an introduction to ancient Indian history and civilization; it is intended mainly for non-specialists who want to acquaint themselves with certain aspects of India's past. One may very reasonably raise the question whether there is any need at all to bring out a fresh volume when there is no dearth of excellent works on ancient India. Admitting the validity of this argument it may be pointed out that compared to the popular writings on the histories of other ancient civilizations, similar works on India are few and far between. Moreover, there is always scope for a new perspective and interpretation.

Indian historiography in the modern sense was initiated by our erstwhile British rulers and it was largely characterised by an imperialistic viewpoint and prejudiced outlook. It began with James Mill and was later enriched by a host of historians of whom V.A. Smith was the typical representative. To them "the autocratic king, oppressive and unconcerned with the welfare of his subjects, was the standard image of the Indian ruler. . . . As for actual governing, the underlying assumption was that British administration was in fact superior to any other known to the history of this subcontinent" (Romila Thapar 17). This mentality is reflected even in the monumental *Cambridge History of India* in the first volume of which the Graeco-Roman sources of Indian history have been regarded as more dependable than the Indian sources, the masterworks of Indian art attributed to the Hellenic school, and all cultural attainments, including literary pursuits, have been interpreted in terms of the civilizing mission of the Aryans who came from outside.

Another aspect on which scholarly emphasis was laid was orientalism of which the study of Indology was a part. British orientalism, as David Kopf has tried to show, was to a great extent politically motivated. The intention was to impress upon the minds of educated Indians the belief that their sympathetic rulers were keen on making their subject-peoples self-conscious by bringing to light the forgotten chapters of their cultural heritage. Undoubtedly this paid the rulers political dividends. At the same time, the exploration of the ancient attainments began to create a subtle nationalism among some educated Indians. The discovery of ancient monuments and historical sites, the deciphering of inscriptions, the studies and researches on the ancient texts, the formulation of the concept of Aryan superiority, etc., fired their imagination. They felt the need to have a complete history of India written from a purely Indian point of view; they hoped that this would help to create a sort of national awakening. The name of Bankim Chandra Chatterjee comes to the forefront in this connection—he was probably the first Indian to formulate the nationalistic conception of history and chalk out the lines on which it should be written.

The British historians popularised the concept of Aryanism and the legend that just as in the past the Aryans left their homeland with a civilizing mission, so also their modern counterparts, the British people, had a similar mission to accomplish with the help of their Aryan brethren and collaborators in India. The result was not quite what they expected. The concept of Aryanism was so enthusiastically received by all sections of the Hindus that it became a driving force of Indian nationalism which aimed at restoring the 'glorious Aryan past'.

The second idea which the British historians had tried to imprint on the Indian mind, and with considerable success, was the myth of Indian spiritualism which implied that the Indians did not bother about things temporal, that their mind was always absorbed with higher philosophical thought and that they were completely indifferent to politics, administration, science, technology and other aspects of material advancement. The motive behind the propagation of this myth of Indian spiritualism was detected by some nationalist historians, and they tried to refute it with all sorts of arguments. B.N. Seal wrote a volume on the positive sciences of the Hindus while the history of Hindu chemistry was written by P.C. Ray who was himself a renowned chemical scientist. K.P. Jaiswal's *Hindu Polity* was written to refute the British assertion that India was unfit for parliamentary democractic institutions. In the 'Preface' Jayaswal noted with gratification that the book was cited by Sir Sankaran Nair in his Note to the Government of India's First Despatch of Constitutional Reforms, dated 5th March 1919. The *Modern Review* (March 1919) held R.C. Majumdar's *Corporate Life in Ancient India* to be "a crushing answer to those who are at present struggling to establish against history that self-government is the chartered monopoly of the western nations." The *Amrita Bazar Patrika* (26th February 1919) claimed that "the book will furnish the most convincing reply to the reiterated argument of the Anglo-Indian friends that India was quite unfit for experiment of democratic institutions."

The Department of Ancient Indian History and Culture of Calcutta University, the first of its kind in any of the universities of India, was opened in 1920 by Sir Asutosh Mukherjee with the professed aim of teaching and researching the magnificent achievement of ancient Indian civilization to serve the cause of national awakening. This department attracted scholars from all over India who were encouraged to research and write on different aspects of Indian civilization. The example of Calcutta University was followed by a few other universities, as a result of which numerous books written from a nationalistic outlook were published. The Indian History Congress too was inspired to launch a project to prepare a complete history of India in several volumes. A few volumes have been published but since it is a public body and has to function under many difficulties, the project has not been completed. It goes to the credit of the Bharatiya Vidya Bhavan of Bombay to bring out a complete history of India. In eleven massive volumes, under the general title *History and Culture of the Indian People*, it covers all the aspects of Indian civilization. The first five volumes were published in the fifties and the remaining ones in the sixties under the guidance of K.M. Munshi and the efficient editorship of R.C. Majumdar who devoted thirty years of his life to this task.

The *Cambridge History* model was followed in these volumes

though the perspective was different. A dignified Indian point of view was adopted which was not marred by the spirit of narrow nationalism. This viewpoint was based on facts, verified through fresh research. The experiment was started with the *Dacca History of Bengal* (1943) and in the Vidya Bhavan series it was implemented successfully. In the 'Foreword' of the first volume of the Vidya Bhavan series K.M. Munshi observed:

> To be a history in the true sense of the word, the work must be the story of the people inhabiting a country. It must be a record of their life from age to age presented through the life and achievements of men whose exploits became the beacon lights of tradition; through the characteristic reaction of the people to the physical and economic conditions; through political changes and vicissitudes which create the forces and conditions which operate upon life; through characteristic social institutions, beliefs and forms; through literary and artistic achievements; through movements of thought which from time to time helped or hindered the growth of collective harmony; through those values which the people have accepted or reacted to and which created or shaped their collective will; through efforts of the people to will themselves into an organic unity. The central purpose of a history must, therefore, be to investigate and unfold the values which age after age have inspired the inhabitants of a country to develop their collective will and to express it through the manifold activities of their life.

The Bharatiya Vidya Bhavan series tried to remain faithful to this approach. The countributors were given full liberty to express their own views, even if they went against existing or cherished notions. But the volumes as a whole, notwithstanding their professed objectivity, reflect the culture of the dominant class and equate it with the entirety of the 'Indian way of life'. What has been presented is 'history from above' in which the ruling class has been given greater importance, the social viewpoints of the Dharmaśāstra tradition have been regarded as ideal, the masterworks of art treated from a purely aesthetic point of view ignoring other conditions, and the so-called higher forms of religion and philosophy emphasised. These volumes subscribe to the myth that the ancient civilization of India was homogeneous. The past is interpreted as if it was a single cultural entity. All contradictions are smoothed out and inconvenient facts are ignored.

While there has been no dearth of research works on ancient Indian history, and also of regional studies—and many of such works are indeed valuable for the abundance of historical data contained in them—these books can be handled only by those who have a previous acquaintance with the subject. There are not many books intended for general readers. A.L. Basham's *The Wonder that Was India* (1954) has been extremely popular both in India and abroad. Mainly intended for the Western reader, the book is a good introduction to the study of Indian civilization in its totality. It is a polished work, done by a sympathetic *mleccha*, an epithet by which Basham likes to characterise himself, which emphasises the brighter aspects. In the efficient hands of one having lifelong experience in Indological studies a subtle idealisation is manifested throughout even as the author poses to be critical. By contrast Romila Thapar's *History of India* (1966) is a more objective assessment in which the socio-economic forces determining the characteristics of different political periods have been so outlined as to convey a meaningful significance to the study of Indian history. According to Thapar every economic infrastructure of a given period engenders its own mode of exchange and distribution and builds up its own political, legal, religious and ideological set-up. At the same time geographical, climatic and ecological conditions, and contact with foreign cultures create certain overgrowths which acquire some measure of independent existence. Thapar's insistence on the socio-economic substrata recalls the Marxist viewpoint though the latter has not been specially emphasised in her book. The same also holds good in the case of her *Ancient Indian Social History* (1978).

Marxist historiography in India got off to a limping start in the hands of the political activists whose main purpose was to fit some half-baked data in a preconceived mould. The Bengali version of Deviprasad Chattopadhyaya's *Lokāyata* (1955) which was subsequently written in English (1959) and translated into other languages, was the first credible work on Marxist lines. It attempted to revive and reconstruct the ancient school of Indian materialism and trace its roots to the vast arena of popular cults and rituals, beliefs and practices. Deviprasad has devised a methodology of his own which has found expression in *Indian Philosophy* (1964), *Indian Atheism* (1969), *What is Living and What is Dead in Indian Philosophy* (1976) and *Science and Society in Ancient India* (1977). In all these works, which strictly speaking do not come within the purview of history, he has attempted to identify the class-orientation of ideas and institutions and their transformation in different levels of social hierarchy.

D.D. Kosambi's *Introduction to the Study of Indian History* (1956) has earned scholarly recognition as a Marxist approach to Indian history. He has his own, rather simplified, Marxist definition of history in the Indian context which is, "presentation in a chronological order, of successive development in the means and relations of production." Apart from some thought-provoking suggestions and the isolated handling of certain issues the book is neither comprehensive nor systematic in its treatment of the subject. Perhaps that is why Ingalls remarked: "One cannot refrain from crying out against a view of Indian history which assigns twenty-five pages to the coinage of Magadha, one page to the *Bhagavadgītā*, three lines to Indian mathematics and an universal blank to philosophy." Kosambi is critical of Marx's theory of the immutability of Indian society but he believes that

> India shows extraordinary continuity of culture. The violent breaks known to have occurred in the political and theological superstructure have not prevented long survivals of observances that have no sanction in the official Brahmin works, hence can only have orginated in the most primitive stages of human society; moreover, the Hindu scriptures, even more the observances sanctified in practice by Brahmanism, show adoption of non-Brahmin local rites. That is, the process of assimilation was mutual, a peculiar characteristic of India.

In his subsequent *Culture and Civilization of Ancient India in Historical Outline* (1965), he holds that a "tunnel vision" persists in all disciplines concerned with Indology and that there has always been a "failure to present the main problems of Indian history". He begins with the problems of methodology and lays emphasis on the functional role of the tribal societies in the uneven development of production system. For the study of the material culture and social institutions of the primitive peoples he insists on the prehistoric archaeological findings as the key to the understanding of the process of the transition from food gathering to food production. His comment, that the "cultivated grains, though not classed as artefacts, are as much a product of human activity as pottery", is indeed significant. His views on the Harappan civilization and Aryanism are very much subjective and require to be revised in the light of fresh research. He connects the advent of the historical age and the rise of state powers with changes in the technique of production caused by the introduction of iron implements and at the same time holds that Buddhism and Jainism were ideological reflections of urban development, of urban kingship and city nobles. He deals with the economic factors, especially the role of foreign trade, in the development of the Indian civilization of the Gupta period, and ascribes its decline to the unfavourable foreign trade balance. He thinks that the decline in foreign trade from the post-Gupta period onwards had a counter-impact on the agrarian economy giving rise to a feudalistic pattern.

Like the imperialist and nationalist historians, the Marxist historians are inconsistent, contradictory and divergent in their viewpoints, understanding and interpretation. R.S. Sharma holds that "it may be too much to assert that historical materialism can provide the only scientific approach to the investigation of ancient Indian social structure, but its possibilities are still to be explored, and hence in any future study of ancient Indian society such a line of enquiry cannot altogether be ignored." This reflects an indecisive attitude towards the Marxist approach in sharp contrast to that of Deviprasad or Kosambi. Again there are problems in the application of Marxist principles. For example, D.A. Suleykin's (1954) suggestion of the periodisation of ancient Indian history according to the social formation has been rejected by Kosambi on the ground that, apart from the difficulty of dating and localising the evidence and that of combining and universalising its content, neither in the means of production nor in the so-called stages of social development was there any homogeneity by which such a periodisation is possible. R.S. Sharma has sought to identify seven stages of ancient Indian economy, but these stages cannot be defined well enough so as to constitute different stages of historical development. Again, Kosambi says that in the Indian context there was extension and quantitative growth in production which yielded qualitative changes at different periods of history. But it is doubtful whether qualitative change is possible without an active counterforce within the productive system itself or even whether the caste-oriented traditional technique of production had the propensity of generating such an active counterforce from within. As regards the specific conditions there are also divergences among Marxist historians. While S.A. Dange, R.S. Sharma and D.R. Chanana attribute to India the social form called slavery, Kosambi rejects it outright. There is no agreement among the Marxist scholars on the definition of feudalism in the Indian context. To quote R.S. Sharma: "Just as there are as many definitions of socialism as there are socialists, so also there are as many definitions of feudalism as there are scholars working on the subject."

This brief survey of the changing approaches to Indian history shows how complex the subject is. However the present volume only aims at outlining some general trends of ancient Indian history and civilization. Since its purpose is to convey a meaningful account of the past in relation to the present and to trace and identify certain special features which characterise the ancient history and civilization as a whole, the presentation of certain problems, criticisms and views in regard to historiography cannot be avoided. The present volume has no special theoretical preoccupation. It begins with the prehistoric and protohistoric background of Indian civilization which shows that just as in modern times backward, semi-modern and ultra-modern techniques of production co-exist side by side, so also in the remote past there was uneven development when some regions witnessed the growth of copper-bronze technology while others were still in the food-gathering stage of Old Stone Age cultures. Gradual ruralisation of urbanised settlements, a belated and crippled growth of the Neolithic-Chalcolithic features and the sporadic appearance of Iron Age cultures demonstrate that the process of development did not follow any uniform and orderly sequence. This uneven development was also a feature of the subsequent Vedic age which left two permanent legacies. The material culture and the socio-political institutions, as can be seen from Vedic literature, clearly demonstrate a process of detribalisation and the consequent emergence of various occupational groups which later crystallised into castes and subcastes of various ranks in the Hindu social hierarchy. The other legacy was in the field of ideas which was conserved and elaborated in later philosophical literature.

The difficulties in periodisation have been touched upon. In this work a simple political periodisation has been made which is based upon the traditional model of dynastic importance. However, even this traditional periodisation has a very limited significance because, apart from the Mauryas, there was no ruling dynasty which exerted its influence all over the country. The problem is further complicated by the elaborate growth and survival of regional powers. Instead of presenting details of political history, emphasis has been laid upon the pattern of political development shaped by the emperors, kings and feudatories. Various political theories and systems of administration have been discussed in the fourth chapter. In spite of the existence of a well defined science of polity and the elaborate growth of political institutions of various types Indian society was never a political society. Indian social life could not be designed in accordance with the need of the state. This was due to the prevalence of the typical 'state within the state' or the caste system which demanded absolute allegiance of the individuals to the social groups in which they belonged. There is no separate chapter on economic condition, but facts concerning the economic life are concentrated in the chapters dealing with cities and villages and with the indigenous and foreign accounts. The shifting tensions in urbanisation, production system and the trade balance as may be detected from relevent sources throw significant light on corresponding social mobility and economic changes. In all these chapters certain representative sources are made to speak for themselves. The chapter on temples and images is a survey of the evolution of Indian art. It becomes evident that ancient and early medieval art was essentially religious in character and that the so-called secular elements were an integral part of the all pervading religious canvas in which extra-religious items, even the erotic carvings, could be accommodated without any feeling of inconsistency.

Special emphasis has been laid in this volume on the history of ideas since it is only in this field that we have historical continuity down the ages. These have been discussed under three distinct categories. The first category comprises certain ideas and concepts which are effective in Indian life even today. The ancient attitude towards science has been discussed against the background of the prolonged conflict between the idealistic and materialistic schools. The ambivalence of the Hindu mind as manifest on the one hand by the logical approach towards the concept of God and, on the other, by the acceptance of the *a priori* concept of *karma* as a blind force controlling all walks of human life makes an interesting study. The second category comprises religious ideas. The increasing importance of the Vedānta, especially of its theistic interpretation, which characterised the subsequent religious history of India, has been brought to light. Instead of giving a detailed account of the origin and the development of different religious sects, emphasis has been laid on the turning points. The third category dwells on literary pursuits. Here also instead of dealing with a mechanical history of literature special importance has been attached to the genesis and development of literary ideas: the original pattern, its subsequent modifications, and the gradual sophistication and individualisation. The insistence on the history of ideas arises from the need to stratify the successive phases of evolution through which the ancient Indians passed, not only as seen in their material remains but in their language and literature and other allied features.

The author's thanks are due to Sri Ramesh Jain of Manohar Publications who as an importunate creditor has got the work done and to Mrs. Jasjit Mansingh for editing the manuscript. Because the book mainly deals with the general trends of ancient Indian history and civilization intended for the non-specialists it has not been burdened with footnotes. A select bibliography comprising names of easily available books has, however, been supplied. Despite his best efforts some lapses and blemishes must have crept in this volume for which the author craves the indulgence of his readers.

NARENDRA NATH BHATTACHARYYA

Department of Ancient Indian
History and Culture,
University of Calcutta,
51/2, Hazra Road,
Calcutta 700019

Contents

Preface v

1. THE PREHISTORIC AND PROTOHISTORIC BACKGROUND 1

1. Uneven Development: The Archaeological Evidence. 2. The Stone Age Cultures. 3. Pre-Harappan Neolithic-Chalcolithic Settlements. 4. Urbanism: The Harappa Civilization 5. Post-Harappan Neolithic-Chalcolithic Settlements. 6. Beginning of Iron Age: Associated Graves and Wares. 7. The Aryan Hypothesis in Indian History.

2. THE VEDIC CIVILIZATION AND ITS IMPACT ON THE INDIAN WAY OF LIFE 27

1. The Vedic Literature vis-a-vis the Vedic Tradition. 2. From Tribe to State: Political Evolution in the Vedic Age. 3. Incomplete Detribalisation and the Caste System. 4. Vedic Society and Economy. 5. Religion and World-view: Influence on Later Indian Thought.

3. EMPERORS, KINGS AND FEUDATORIES: A STUDY IN POLITICAL HISTORY 49

1. The Era of Magadhan Ascendency (600-200 B.C.). 2. Aśoka: The Policy of Dharmavijaya. 3. The Post-Mauryan Age: Kings and Feudatories (200-30 B.C.). 4. The Foreign Hordes: Relation between Kings and Clan Leaders. 5. The Kusana Empire: Central Asian Horizon (A.D. 15-176). 6. Regional

Powers (A.D. 100-200). 7. Tribal Principalities and Feudatories of the Pre-Gupta Period. 8. The Imperial Guptas (A.D. 320-467). 9. Disintegration of the Guptas (A.D. 467-570). 10. Feudatories of the Guptas. 11. Deccan in the Gupta Age. 12. Political Fragmentation after the Guptas. 13. Harṣa: The Lord of Uttarāpatha (A.D. 606-46). 14. Deccan and South India: Cālukya-Pallava Rivalry. 15. Struggle for Mastery over Kanauj. 16. The Three Kingdoms: Expansion and Degeneration. 17. Distribution of Regional Powers in Northern India. 18. Regional Powers in the South. 19. Colas under Rājarāja and Rājendra. 20. Western Cālukyas: Someśvara and Vikramāditya VI. 21. Increasing Importance of the Feudatories. 22. Beginnings of the Medieval Period (A.D. 1000-1300).

4. THE POLITICAL SYSTEM: THEORETICAL AND PRACTICAL ASPECTS 111

1. Vedic Concept of the Popular Sanction of Sovereignty. 2. The Buddhist Political Ideas. 3. The Mauryan Policy of Centralisation and Its Limitations. 4. The Kautilyan State. 5. The Post-Maurya State System. 6. Jaimini on King's Land-right: Some Questions Relating to the Hypothesis of a Feudal Structure 7. Socio-Political Ideas as Reflected in the *Manusmṛti*. 8. The Gupta and Post-Gupta Polity. 9. The *Nītisāra* of Kāmandakī. 10. The Economic Perspective. 11. Feudalistic Formations: Extent and Degree.

5. STATE WITHIN THE STATE 143

1. The Caste System: An Introduction. 2. Caste System in the Dharmasūtras and Dharmasāstras. 3. Inconsistencies in the Varṇasankara Theory. 4. Caste and the Reformistic Religious Systems. 5. Hierarchy and Social Position. 6. The Brahmanical

Exploitation: Anatomy of an Exaggeration. 7. The Practice of Untouchability. 8. The Subcastes. 9. A Note on Slavery in Ancient India.

6. CITIES AND VILLAGES 176

1. Uneven Development of Urbanism. 2. The Nature of Urbanisation. 3. Economic Life in Cities and Villages: Evidence of Early Buddhist Literature. 4. Glimpses of Village Life in the *Gāthā Saptaśatī*. 5. Ports and Market Towns: The *Periplus*. 6. Life of the Urban Elites: The *Kāmasūtra* Evidence. 7. Villages and Towns in Post-Gupta Period. 8. Ports and Maritime Trade in Early Medieval India.

7. INDIA IN SOME FOREIGN AND INDIGENOUS ACCOUNTS 197

1. Preliminary Remarks. 2. The Account of Megasthenes. 3. Hieun Tsang's Description of India. 4. Early Arab Accounts on Society and Economy. 5. Medhātithi: Interpreter of Hindu Jurisprudence. 6. Dāmodaragupta and Kṣemendra. 7. Al-Bīrunī's India: *Kitab-ul-Hind*. 8. The *Mānasollāsa*: A Source Book of Contemporary Information. 9. Marco Polo on India.

8. THE IDEOLOGICAL ASPECTS 226

1. Materialism versus Idealism. 2. Attitude towards Science: The Conceptual Aspects. 3. The Concept of God in Indian Philosophical Systems. 4. The Doctrine of *Karma*. 5. Growth of the Theistic Concepts. 6. Appearance and Reality: Two Aspects of Vedānta.

9. RELIGIOUS GLEANINGS 246

1. Towards Theistic Transformation. 2. Hinduism in the Making. 3. Neo-Bhakti Movements

from South: The Nāyanārs and the Āḷvars. 4. Religion of the Merchants. 5. New Theoretical Orientation of the Hindu Sects. 6. Metamorphosis of Buddhism.

10. TEMPLES AND IMAGES 268

1. The Maurya and Post-Maurya Period. 2. The Classical Period. 3. The Early Medieval Period. 4. The Nature and Extent of Patronage. 5. Erotic Art on Temples.

11. LITERARY ASPECTS: SOME OBSERVATIONS 292

1. The Primitive Substratum. 2. The Great Epics: Their Influence on Indian Literature. 3. The Purāṇas: Literature of the Masses. 4. Sophisticated Literature: Some Characteristics. 6. Regional Literature. 6. Indian Literature Abroad.

Select Bibliography 319

Index 325

1

The Prehistoric and Protohistoric Background

1. Uneven Development: The Archaeological Evidence

One of the main reasons for the uneven development which has characterised the history of the Indian people throughout the ages is the peculiar geographical situation of the country where climatic, tectonic and topographical variations have created a number of different regions, each with a distinct character. As a result, different groups of peoples have been confined within the narrow limits of their own distinct cultures. These vary, even today, from community to community and from region to region. Certain regions have advanced far more rapidly than others and the growth of many primitive communities has been retarded by the difficulties of their natural habitat which also explains their uneven economic development.

Although the precise nature of the material culture and social institutions of the early Indians is somehow recorded, it is not possible to trace, identify and document the exact preconditions of the subsequent uneven development. That is why archaeological finds in the field of prehistory and proto-history assume great importance; these may tell us how men of some particular period and area actually lived, and provide the rationale for the type of society that existed and the manner of its functioning. Although archaeology in India has evolved without any specific sophisticated theoretical foundation, and the prehistory of this subcontinent is still at a stage in which the establishment of chronological and sequential relationship between sites and regions has not been fully possible, the efforts of the last fifty years give a fairly clear picture in regard to a good number of areas and cultures which may be of some help in defining the process of social changes.

Archaeological excavations have revealed that in India the transition from food-gathering to food-production and that from rural settlements to urbanism did not follow a uniform and orderly sequence of events. With the end of the three-fold Stone age the course of change varied vastly. In some cases there was reasonable advancement in accordance with the changing productive conditions while in others the development was arrested. The Early and Middle Stone ages correspond roughly to the Lower and Middle Palaeolithic respectively of the archaeological tradition as found in Europe and Western Asia, but in the case of the Late Stone age in India there is some difficulty. This is due to the fact that in India there is no major phase corresponding to the Upper Palaeolithic blade and burin industries of Europe and Western Asia. Although in Andhra, Karnataka, Maharashtra, Bihar, Uttar Pradesh and Madhya Pradesh, there are traces of a blade and burin culture flourishing towards the end of the late-Pleistocene period, these sporadic occurrences have been regarded as a peculiar growth of the existing flake industries and not as an essential part of the three-fold sequence of the Stone age.

In the Indian context, Neolithic conditions are rather complex and are interrelated with the problems of uneven development with which we are dealing. This is due to regional peculiarities caused by local environments and external influences. The number of pure or full-fledged Neolithic sites, characterised by gray wares, polished stone axes and bone tools, is not large. Polished stone tools, occasionally associated with handmade pottery and bones of domesticated animals have often been found below the levels of the first metal-using cultures. But in many cases metals have been found along with polished stones; we come across the use of black-painted red wares, long stone blades and copper-bronze implements which are characteristics of Chalcolithic conditions. Thus the presence of the Chalcolithic elements in the Neolithic and vice versa has made it very difficult to make a sharp distinction between the cultural stages or to say when the Late Stone age cultures developed into the Neolithic and the latter into the Chalcolithic. Because of this overlapping, the term Neolithic-Chalcolithic is sometimes used jointly to explain the Indian situation.

Even this Neolithic-Chalcolithic stage has no uniformity in regard to space and time in the Indian context. It is only in the pre-Harappan occupations of northwestern and western India, which appear to overlap in their latest phases with the Harappa civilization, that an earlier transition into the Chalcolithic may be inferred even as the rest of the subcontinent presents a different picture. While the Harappans were at the zenith of their power and prosperity, in other parts of India Late Stone age cultures prevailed though in some places Neolithic preconditions were apparent suggestive of a settled community life dependent on agriculture and animal husbandry. Many of these cultures coincided with the end of the Harappa civilization, and there was a transition to the metal-using stage, in certain cases under direct Harappan contact but in most cases under the shadow of Harappan influence which, of course, varied from region to region both in extent and in degree. It should be pointed out that copper tools have not been invariably associated with stone tools in the east and their presence in the south is sparse and limited compared to the extent they are found in the sites of northern Deccan and central India.

2. *The Stone Age Cultures*

Early Stone age begins with large assemblages of extremely crude stone implements found practically all over India except in Sind and Kerala. The numerous Early Stone age sites—scattered in the vast region between the Himalayas and the Kaveri from north to south and between the Sabarmati and the lower reaches of the Ganges from west to east—testify to the existence of man in India as far back as the middle-Pleistocene period. In the Punjab and adjoining regions assemblages of implements, suggestive of chopper-chopping and hand axe, have been found. The former, called Sohanian or Soan, has been reported from five successive horizons, each of which also yields pebble tools associated with flake implements. Massive and crude in the earliest phases of the Sohanian, these reveal a progressive refinement in the younger horizons. Partly contemporary with early Sohanian is a series of hand axes of Abbevilleo-Acheulian affinities which occur in profusion at many sites almost all over the country. These sites yield hand axes, cleavers and flake-tools which are reminiscent of assemblages from south and east Africa. In the southern sites bifacial tools predominate. Quartzite forms an important element in the materials from which tools were made. Pebble tools were used for cutting, slicing, smashing, skinning and other purposes. The hand axe, with its different subtypes, was an all-purpose tool. The cleaver with its four types of edges and butts was also used like a hand axe. Chopping tools and flakes were used for skinning and dismembering game, splitting bones and other purposes. Men were nomads who favoured temporary habitation in the foothills, open plateaux, river banks and at the edge of forests where raw materials to manufacture tools and implements were easily available and where they could find plenty of water, game and edible roots and fruits. High altitudes seem to have been avoided and so also very low marshy areas.

The Middle Stone age industries, found all over India except in Kerala, are mostly based on flakes, corresponding in very general terms to the Levallois-Mousterian industries of Europe and Western Asia. The tools are made of smoother materials like agate, chert, jasper, chalcedony, etc., and comprise scrapers, borers or awls, points, small choppers, small hand axes and, rarely, small cleavers. From the viewpoint of technique, typology, stratigraphy and raw material the Middle Stone age has some difference with the preceding one. The tools, principally based on flakes, are comparatively small and could have been used, some after hafting with a bone or wood handle, for wood-work, skinning and hunting. The frequent occurrence of stone tools in river gravels and their absence from cave deposits indicate a nomadic life in the open. No fixed settlement of the Middle Stone age is known in the Indian subcontinent, except the Sanghao cave near Peshawar. Men lived along the banks of the rivers and foothills where raw material was easily available. The economy of the Middle Stone age was also based primarily on hunting and gathering. Tools of this age suggest that there was an increasing degree of specialization in the hunting pursuits. The Middle Stone age belonged to a part of the geological late-Pleistocene period.

The Late Stone age of India, which is technologically comparable to the transitional Mesolithic stage of European prehistory, is characterised by microlithic tools of various shapes fashioned from carefully made parallel-sided blades and also from flakes and chips of stone. Generally, microliths occur on the surface, but in some places they have been found in stratified levels. They belong to the geological Holocene period and may be roughly assigned to c.8000-2000 B.C. The Late Stone age people lived in all sorts of environment, including sand dunes, natural caves and rock shelters. Economically this stage was that of food-gathering inasmuch as the people relied for a livelihood on hunting, fishing and collecting, although some change was under way. For instance, the sites of Langhnaj and Adamgarh contain bones of both wild and domesticated animals which suggests that the economy of the hunters began to be supplemented by pastoralism. The sites of Panchmarhi in Madhya Pradesh, Lekhahia and Baghai Kor in Uttar Pradesh, Bagor in Rajasthan, Langhnaj in Gujarat and Sarai Nahar Rai in the Ganga-Yamuna Doab have yielded burials. The crouching posture in which a number of skeletons have been found leaves no doubt that they were deliberately buried with some tender beliefs regarding the fate of the departed ones. Some of the rock-shelters and caves in Madhya Pradesh and Uttar Pradesh where microliths have been discovered in abundance contain paintings, very often coloured. A few of them may be contemporary with the Late Stone age but the majority seem to belong to later times.

3. Pre-Harappan Neolithic-Chalcolithic Settlements

The term 'Neolithic' implies a stage in the subsequent development of the Stone age cultures in which there was a qualitative change in the manufacture and use of stone tools. This change was often accompanied by ancillary crafts, e.g., the new processes of polishing tools such as axe-heads and hoe-blades, the widespread use of pottery, weaving, etc. In a wider sense,

Neolithic denotes a cultural or economic stage—characterised by the change from hunting to farming economy—when man learnt not only to smoothen his stone tools by different methods but had begun as well to produce his own food, domesticate various animals, make pottery and adopt a settled life instead of moving from place to place in small groups. This new food-producing economy was distinctive of what Morgan called Barbarism marking a great change from Savagery or the food-gathering economy of the Stone ages which was the sole source of livelihood during the major period of human prehistory. Neolithic society had the potential to increase supply and thus to support a growing population. According to Gordon Childe, this was a revolution and it distinguished barbarism from savagery.

But in the Indian context, as has already been pointed out, owing to the geographical diversity and uneven economic development which survives up to the present day, it is difficult to see any uniformity and orderliness in the process of socio-economic change. What Childe has called Neolithic Revolution happened only in a limited area; and it created the preconditions for the rise of Harappa civilization. But in other parts of the subcontinent the process of change was very slow. In most cases, the Neolithic and Chalcolithic settlements of India belong to the late-Harappan and post-Harappan period. Moreover, there was an admixture of Neolithic and Chalcolithic elements and it is very difficult to make a sharp distinction between the two. The Southern cultures are supposed to be more akin to the Neolithic while those belonging to Central India and Deccan have a greater degree of Chalcolithic affinities. Further development of the cultures of the mixed type, in which the Chalcolithic elements predominate, has been observed at numerous sites of Madhya Pradesh, Maharashtra, Rajasthan, Gangetic Doab, Gujarat, Bihar and Bengal. But these cultures cannot be placed earlier than c.1750 B.C.

Among the few settlements of the unmixed type in which metal is absent, reference may be made to those of Baluchistan, specially in the Quetta region, and in the valleys of the Loralai and the Zhob which are evidently pre-Harappan, belonging to the middle of the fourth millennium B.C. In Kashmir, the earliest period of Burzahom, the lowest time limit of which is c.2375 B.C, is characterized by pit-dwellings, polished stone implements, bone tools including awls, needles, points, chisels, harpoons, etc., and handmade pottery. Among the sporadic traces of Neolithic cultures in different districts of Assam and Meghalaya, tools have been collected mostly from the surface. A few have, however, been recovered from the excavated site of Deojali Hading in north Cachar. The finds consist of pottery and stone implements, especially for using on the ground. These cultures have tentatively been assigned to the period between 3000 and 2000 B.C.

The Neolithic village farming and pastoral communities which existed in Baluchistan and the Indus valley as early as the fourth-third millennium B.C. had a quick transition into the Chalcolithic stage. The original character of the assemblages resembled those of Iran and perhaps those of the Ubaidian imprint in Southeastern Iran, but it gradually changed and developed features which eventually culminated in the Harappan urban civilization. Among the important pre-Harappan settlements mention may be made of Mundigak in Afghanistan, Kili Gul Mohammad and Damb Sadat in the Quetta valley, Rana Ghundai in the Loralai valley, Periano Ghundai in the Zhob valley, Anjira in the Surab valley of Central Baluchistan, Kulli-Mehi and Nal-Nandara in South Baluchistan, Amri and Kot Diji in Sind, Kalibangan in Rajasthan, etc. Period I of Kili Gul Mohammad goes back to the beginning of the fourth millennium B.C. while other settlements of Baluchistan have different periods ranging between 3500 and 2000 B.C. The major period of the pre-Harappan settlements of Sind is around c.2700-2200 B.C. while the beginning of Kalibangan I has been assigned to c.2400 B.C.

In the earlier periods of the settlements of Baluchistan we have evidence of houses made of mud brick or hard-packed clay while in the subsequent periods greater sophistication and more compactness are found. In a few cases the transformation of the settlement into a town with massive defensive walls and square bastions of sun-dried bricks is observed. The second aspect of the cultural evolution is indicated by the transition from hand-made to wheel-made, often painted, pottery. This may be amply demonstrated with reference to the sites of Baluchistan where this change in the productive technique took place probably owing to Iranian influence. The pre-Harappan pottery of Amri and Kot Diji is of well-levigated clay, wheel-made and with a ground ranging in colour from pinkish to red, having painted designs in some cases. The pre-Harappan pottery of Kalibangan is light and thin. The third and fourth features are indicated by the transition from blades made of coarse flakes to those made of better lithic elements showing remarkable advance in execution, shape, smoothness and sharpness and by the transition from stone to metallic implements. Among the grave-goods are found pots, copper implements, ornaments of semi-precious stones, etc. Terracotta bulls and Mother Goddess figurines testify religious beliefs. The latter has been found not only in the Zhob valley but also in Kulli and Mehi as well as in Gumla and Hathala. These figurines were connected with primitive fertility concepts based on the equation of natural and human fecundity which found ritual expression in early agricultural communities.

4. *Urbanism: The Harappa Civilization*

A considerable part of the early populace of Baluchistan was formed by a few agricultural and pastoral communities that came to settle in this region from Iran. There was also a parallel influence from Sind and the adjoining regions, which was by no means insignificant. In the subsequent phases there was an overlapping with the Harappa civilization, from Quetta in the north to Las Bela in the south and from the Makran coast in the west to the Khirdhar range in the east. Sutkagendor and Sotka-koh on the Makran coast were Harappan centres which controlled much of the economic life of southern Baluchistan. Dabar Kot in the Loralai valley of northern Baluchistan was also developed into a Harappan settlement. In Sind, at the pre-Harappan settlement of Amri, the successive phases reveal the same process of transformation of the earlier unplanned mud-brick and irregular-sized-brick construction. In Amri II there are traces of a rampart. The later periods of Amri contain important Harappan elements. The pre-Harappan Kot Diji has a defensive wall, well-aligned streets and houses. This settlement was probably occupied by the Harappans. It seems likely that beneath the Harappan occupation of Mohenjodaro and Chanhudaro lay a pre-Harappan culture corresponding to that of Kot Diji or Amri. The same holds good also in the case of Kalibangan in Rajasthan where the pre-Harappan settlement was enclosed by a mud-brick fortification. A pre-Harappan baked-brick drain with two courses has also been found. At Kalibangan there appears already to have been a standardization of brick sizes. Here the process of transition from pre-Harappan to Harappan can clearly be observed.

Remains of Harappa civilization are scattered over an area no less than about half a million square miles and containing more than seventy centres. This area extends up to Sutkagendor to the west on the Makran coast near the border of Iran, Lothal on the gulf of Cambay and Bhagatrav on the Narmada to the south, the Himalayan foothills as far as Manda in Jammu to the north and Ganga-Yamuna region beyond Delhi to the east. Much has been written on the town planning of Mohenjodaro and Harappa, the earliest excavated sites situated respectively in the Larkana district of Sind and in the Montogomery district of Punjab, which is characterised by well-executed roads and lanes, an elaborate drainage system, brick-built buildings of various sizes and shapes and different arrangements for civic amenitites, the two most prominent being the Great Bath at Mohenjodaro and the Great Granary at Harappa. Subsequent excavations at Harappa have revealed evidence of fortification. It appears that after a preliminary occupation of the apparently unwalled settlement the Harappans built a citadel with imposing defences which were reconditioned from time to time. Kalibangan, where traces have been discovered of the remains of massive brick walls around both the citadel and the lower town and where the transition from pre-Harappan to Harappan can be successfully detected, has much in common with Mohenjodaro. At Lothal the town is divided into six blocks, each on a raised platform and separated by roads, the principal one running from north to south. The situation of the famous dockyard with artificial channels for entrance and exit is on the eastern side. The rectangular town also has a massive protective wall.

It has been suggested on the basis of the similarity of the

excavated relics that a strong and centralised authority must have regulated the life and activities of the people over this extensive region and that the cities of Harappa and Mohenjodaro must have served as the twin capitals of the empire. Some hold that concentration of social surplus by a divine monarch or a small priestly caste may be deduced from the strongly-walled citadel unearthed at Harappa. But all this is surmise; nothing definite about the Harappan state system—how it came about and how it was maintained—is known to us. However, certain facts are suggestive. Firstly, the population was heterogeneous and comprised different racial types, the principal ones being Mediterranean, Proto-Australoid and Alpinoid. Secondly, Harappan society was a class-divided society. Within the urban population itself architectural remains reveal that there was a difference of wealth. The rows of mud brick tenements contrast visibly with the spacious two-storeyed houses comprising court-yards, bathrooms, private wells, etc.. which accommodated what may be termed as the Harappan bourgeoisie. Thirdly, there was a rapid growth of professionalism. The cities sheltered a mixed population, the major section of which came from the adjacent villages to seek fortune as craftsmen, artisans and manual labourers. The discovery of a variety of objects for day-to-day use proves that apart from the priests, rulers, traders and agriculturists, there was a network of specialised professions. Fourthly, the uniformity of weights and measures all over the area, the similarity of the seals, the evidence of extensive trade, the common elements in architecture and town-planning and also in art and religion cannot be ignored. All these suggest political, economic and cultural unity of the Harappan civilization and the existence of a functioning state system.

The Harappans were not conversant with the metallurgy of iron. The principal metals for manufacturing tools and other objects were copper and bronze. Four main varieties of metal were prevalent—crude copper, refined copper, tin-bronze, and arsenic-copper alloys. The Harappan bronze has a tin-alloy content often as high as 11-13 per cent. Copper vessels were raised from sheet metal while those of bronze were cast by *cire perdue* method. Gold was used for making ornaments. Gold at Mohenjodaro contains a substantial proportion of silver and is very light in colour. The same may be said about the gold from Lothal. Gold was probably imported from the Anantapur and Kolar districts. There is no dearth of silver objects at Harappa and Mohenjodaro, but these are absent at Chanhudaro and only a few have been recovered from Lothal. The sources of silver were probably Afghanistan, Iran and Armenia. At Harappan sites lead objects are known and lead occurs often as an alloy in copper tools. A large number of ivory objects have been found at Harappa, Mohenjodaro and Chanhudaro, and some at Lothal and Surkotada. Objects made of steatite, etched carnelian beads, lapis lazuli, shells, etc., have been recorded. The variety of materials from which different brands of household and trade objects were manufactured implies a well-knit commercial infrastructure pervading a vast region, transgressing even boundary limits. For steatite, copper, lead, etc., the Harappan craftsmen depended on southern Afghanistan, Rajasthan, Western Baluchistan, the Karadag region of Northern Iran and other places.

No textiles of any description have been preserved, but from the discovery of spindles and spindle-whorls it is evident that spinning of cotton and wool was very common. Dyers' vats indicate that dyeing was practised. Pottery consisted mostly of wheel-made wares, found in many shapes and sizes for daily practical use. Most of the pottery is of pinkish colour with a bright red slip, and when decorated black was used. The majority of terracotta human figurines are those of females, nude except for a narrow girdle round the loins. Animal figures have also been found. Chanhudaro appears to have been a centre for manufacturing toys judging from the large number unearthed there. A few statues have been found which were cut from soft stone. The best is a bust in steatite from Mohenjodaro with well-arranged hair and beard and half-shut eyes. The statue of a dancing girl in bronze reveals a striking anatomical faithfulness. The seals and sealings are of three classes—large intaglio seals of steatite and terracotta, miniature seals or amulets of steatite, and seals of terracotta or faience made from moulds with devices and inscriptions in relief. The script found on the seals has not as yet been deciphered.

The cultural uniformity of the Harappan civilization is reflected not only in town-planning but also in other aspects of social and economic life. Harappan urbanism rested on the capability of producing food on a large scale and the use of rivers which were sufficiently dependable to facilitate transport, irrigation and trade. Apart from the existence of an extensive inland trade, there was also intimate cultural and economic interaction between the Harappan civilization and the West. The Harappan posts of Sokta-koh and Sutkagendor on the Makran Coast and the dockyard of Lothal point to the maritime trade with Iran, Mesopotamia and Western Asia. Circular button-seals and bun-shaped copper ingots have been found both at Lothal and in the Persian Gulf region. Harappan type seals discovered from Ur, Kish, Susa, Lagash and Tell Asmar are also indicative of trade contacts. Some scholars hold that Meluhha mentioned in the early Mesopotamian texts was the same as that of Harappan India. But this identification is doubtful.

Many of the living features of the later Hindu religion and philosophy can be directly traced to Harappan sources. In this connection reference may be made to the principles of Tantrism, the philosophical Sāṅkhya, the practice of Yoga and modern Śāktism. The Mother Goddess figurines, scenes on seals and ritual objects, large stone *liṅgas* and *yonis* seem to be the precursors of Tantric practices, of magic fertility rites that formed the basis of primitive Tantrism, and of the personal deities arising from them. In popular Hinduism *liṅga* and *yoni* (male and female organs) stand respectively for Śiva and Devī, and a prototype of the former is found in the seals unearthed at Harappa and Mohenjodaro. The three-faced male god, seated in the posture of a Yogin on several seals, may rightly be regarded as the prototype of the Indian god Śiva, the consort of the Mother Goddess. In some depictions he is provided with horns on the head, and in one instance surrounded by animals.

The Harappans buried their dead singly in oblong pits in a cemetery outside the township, as has been noticed in Cemetery R-37. There is another cemetery known as Cemetery-H at Harappa proper, but it belongs to a different later culture. Human bones have also been found in the Harappan mounds of A-B, F and J. Forty-one skeletal remains have been discovered at Mohenjodaro. Kalibangan, Lothal, Rupar and other Harappan sites have also yielded burials. At Lothal two bodies were found laid in an embracing posture. Circular graves are found at Kalibangan. In such burials a big urn, along with a few small pots, all without bones but containing human belongings, were placed in a round pit. It is interesting to note that the Harappan graves were comparatively poorly furnished.

Attempts have been made to determine the date of the Harappan civilization through comparison with vestiges of similar architectural and sculptural remains in Mesopotamia and with the Indian type objects discovered in pre-Sargonid and Sargonid sites. On the basis of Indic seals found at Ur, Kish and Tell-al-Asmar, datable from about 2500-2300 B.C., the beginning of the Harappan civilization had been fixed during the middle of the third millennium B.C. The majority of the finds of seals belong to the Sargonid and Isin-Larsa periods indicating, therefore, trade contacts between 2350 and 1770 B.C. Subsequently, by means of radio carbon-dating the total time span of Harappan civilization has been fixed between 2300 and 1750 B.C. This dating also holds good in regard to the Harappan phases of Kot Diji, Lothal and Kalibangan.

Various theories have been put forward to explain the end of the Harappan civilization. Once it was believed that this civilization was destroyed owing to Aryan invasions, but there is no reliable archaeological evidence in support of this view. A good number of post-Harappan cultures, belonging to an inferior category, have been attributed to the Aryans quite arbitrarily. Such contentions have been proved to be meaningless, especially in view of the fact that the myth and reality of the Aryan hypothesis have not as yet been clearly understood, at least in the archaeological sense. Likewise, the flood theory is incapable of explaining the destruction of all the Harappan sites. The same also holds good in regard to the theory of climatic changes. The end of Harappa civilization was not due just to one cause. In India, even in the historical period down to the modern times, we come across desertion, depopulation and ruralization of cities, which is due mostly to ecological, economic and political causes. It is therefore not impossible that under similar circumstances the Harappan cities were deserted and that a considerable section of their inhabitants migrated and settled elsewhere in various parts of this subcontinent, often among comparatively backward communities. It is also not improbable that many such backward communities thus received a fresh fillip, especially in the field of metallic technology, from the Harappan immigrants.

5. Post-Harappan Neolithic-Chalcolithic Settlements

How much of the Harappa civilization survived the disintegration and evacuation of the cities is difficult to say. It is, however, held that a great deal connected with craftsmanship and trade survived as also some aspects of religious beliefs and practices, though not at the same sites. Elsewhere, in particular in Western Asia and Egypt, cultural traits had changed, owing to repeated invasions, migrations and other factors, but the cities remained—at most the centre of gravity shifted from one city to another. The Harappan cities had a different fate. In some cases they were completely deserted while in or near the others we come across the emergence of new, though culturally inferior settlements. Thus at the site of Harappa itself the Cemetery-H culture came into existence. At Amri, Chanhudaro, Jhukar, Mohumjodaro and other sites the Jhukar culture was evolved which was succeeded by another phase at Chanhudaro and at the mound of Jhangar on the other side of the Indus.

Different post-Harappan phases are observed at the sites of Gujarat, especially at Lothal, Rangpur, Rojdi and Somnath, the time-span of the settlements being 1800-1000 B.C. In the case of pottery the appearance of lustrous red ware and white painted black-and-red ware, the antelope and bull motifs and geometric designs shows a departure from the Harappan tradition. The presence of copper tools and stone blades is also recorded. The Ahar culture of the Banas valley in southeast Rajasthan—its three periods covering the time-span between c. 2000 and 1000 B.C.—is characterised by the absence of stone tools and the profusion of copper implements. Ahar pottery is of seven types, the principal one being black-and-red with white embellishment. The site of Gilund, also in the Banas valley, is wider in extent and is characterised by Ahar types of pottery, terracotta figurines, brick-built structures and also a stone blade industry.

Extensive traces of Chalcolithic cultures have been found in the Chambal, Narmada and other river basins of Central India. These had mud huts erected on wooden posts, the walls made of bamboo frames plastered with mud. Brick-built structures, defensive walls, ovens, relics of foodgrains, copper tools and implements, terracotta bull-figurines, etc., have also been found at different sites. At Navdatoli the continuity of sequence from the Stone age to the Chalcolithic period has been traced. The latter has four phases. The first is marked by round and square huts, stone blades, copper tools and a kind of distinctive pottery commonly known as Malwa ware. The second phase is characterised by goblets on pedestals and the third by a distinctive fine red pottery with black-painted decoration known as the Jorwe ware. In the fourth phase a kind of lustrous red ware is found. The second period of Kayatha, datable between c. 1965 and 1675 B.C., has yielded painted black-and-red were recalling links with Ahar. Two other sites in the region, Ávra and Manoti, have yielded a similar type of pottery. The third period of Kayatha belonging to c. 1675 and 1380 B.C. exhibits Malwa and Jorwe types of pottery. The earlier phases of Nagda and Eran have also yielded the Malwa type.

The Chalcolithic settlements of Maharashtra and adjoining regions have many features in common with those of central India. The first phase of Daimabad yields evidence of a ground axe and blade industry, rough black or gray ware and a cemetery recalling features of unmixed Neolithic. In the second phase of Daimabad and the first phase of Prakash, datable between c. 1760 and 1400 B.C., we find the introduction of copper implements and Malwa type of ware. Copper implements have been found at Chandoli, Nevasa, Jorwe, Sonegaon and other sites in which the culture is homogeneous and assigned to c.1375-1050 B.C. Four bronze images have been found at Daimabad. The stone tools from these sites comprise anvil, hammer, polished axe, chisel, ball, etc., and in the case of pottery the Malwa and Jorwe types predominate. Eight residences have been discovered at Inamgaon, the biggest of which is 20 × 12 feet. The biggest residence at Nevasa measures 45 × 20 feet while the ordinary ones are 8 × 7 feet. Traces of weaving have been noticed at Nevasa, Inamgaon and Chandoli.

At Nevasa 131 and at Inamgaon 50 burials have been found. Bahal, Chandoli, Daimabad and Sonegaon have also yielded burials. Some of these indicate a high rate of child mortality. Extended burial is the usual custom. Grave goods have also been found. The exact significance of the terracotta figurines from Nevasa is not clearly known, but Inamgaon has yielded genuine Mother Goddness figurines.

The Neolithic sites in the south include Brahmagiri, Sangankallu, Piklihal, Hallur, Gaurimedu, Maski, Nagarjunikonda, Utnur, Tekkalkota, etc. The earlier phases of these cultures (c. 2300-1800 BC.) are characterised by a development of the ground stone-axe industry and flake or blade tradition often associated with microliths of quartz and chert, and by the evidence of the domestication of cattle as also the introduction of hand made pottery. In the subsequent phases (c. 1800-1500 B.C.) we come across huts raised on round wooden posts with mud floors, polished stone implements comprising axes, adzes, pounders, chisels, etc., with an increase in the number and regularity of stone blades and occasional copper tools, especially at Hallur, Brahmagiri, Piklihal, Maski and Tekkalkota. The sites of Nagarjunikonda, Palavoy, Piklihal, Tekkalkota, Brahmagiri, Hallur, T. Narsipur, Terdal, Kovalli, etc., yield burials. Complete and partial burials seem to have been in vogue and urn burials have also been found.

The process of transition from Neolithic to Chalcolithic is not well defined in eastern India. Chirand, in the Saran district of Bihar, has yielded ground stone and bone tools, shell ornaments and hand made pottery recalling unmixed Neolithic assemblage. The profusion of bone tools deserves special mention. The topmost level of Chirand belongs to c. 1650 B.C. and the lowest to c. 2500 B.C. The site has also yielded terracotta figurines, a black-and-red ware, evidence of mud-built floors and oven, etc. At Sonpur, Vaisali, Maner and Antichok the existence of a black-and-red ware tradition has been traced. A terracotta female figurine with elevated breast has been found at Uriup. Copper bangles and ornaments of semi-precious stones have also been noticed. At Sonpur post-cremation pit-burial and urns containing human bones have been discovered. Kuchai in the Mayurbhanj district of Orissa has yielded a coarse grit-tempered red ware in association with polished stone implements. At Tamluk in the Midnapur district of West Bengal excavations have yielded in the stratified lowest level Neolithic celts and badly fired pottery. At Manisdal copper implements have been found. In the Pandu Rajar Dhibi in the Burdwan district the transition from Neolithic to Chalcolithic and then to Iron age may be observed from the traces of mud and lime-built floors, ovens, stone blades, ground axes, copper implements, terracotta figurines and extended burial found at different levels.

Many Copper Hoard cultures, preceding the Early Iron age, have been discovered in the Ganga-Yamuna Doab region and elsewhere. A distinctive ochre-coloured pottery is associated with many of these cultures. This pottery was first recognised during the explorations at Bisauli and Rajpur Parsu. It has a wide distribution in the Saharanpur district and is found also below the Early Iron age levels of Hastinapur and Ahicchatra. Although the association of this ochre-coloured pottery with the Copper Hoard cultures cannot be ignored, nor can it be said that these two are invariably linked. The difficulty is that the Copper Hoards have not been found in any marked stratified level. Apart from the Ganga-Yamuna Doab, Copper Hoards have been discovered in Bihar, Orissa, Madhya Pradesh, Rajasthan, Sind, Baluchistan, Western Punjab and North Western Frontier Province. As early as in 1821 more than 400 copper objects and about 100 silver objects were found at Gungeria in the Balaghat district of Madhya Pradesh. Various speculations about post-Harappan group migrations, external influences, acculturations, etc., have been put forward by eminent archaeologists with reference to some of these Copper Hoard cultures on the basis of comparative study of the implements and associated pottery. However, these are speculations, notwithstanding their interesting implications, and acceptable conclusions have yet to be formed.

6. *Beginnings of Iron Age: Associated Graves and Wares*

The beginnings of the Iron age in India are also characterised by the process of uneven development. In southern and central Baluchistan, a whole chain of cairn cemeteries has been discovered representing a people who had a uniform cultural level, the manifestation of which may be dated between c. 1100 and 750 B.C. They knew the art of horse riding, the use of iron and handmade pottery. In the Swat Valley the cemeteries located near Timargarha, Thana, Butkara, Loebanr, Katelai and other sites reveal what is commonly known as Gandhara Grave culture. Its first and second periods belong to the Chalcolithic age, the former (c. 1600-1300 B.C.) being characterised by complete inhumations and the latter (c.1200-1000 B.C.) by post-cremation burials in urns. Its third period (900-600 B.C.) belongs to the Iron age which is characterised by post-exposure and post-cremation burials as well as by the existence of iron implements in the graves of the former category. In a cist-burial in the Leh valley of Ladakh a few iron objects have been found. At Burzahom in Kashmir, Asota in North Western Frontier province, Karachi in Sind and certain sites of Uttar Pradesh burials with Megalithic inclination and iron objects have been discovered. At Amreli in Saurashtra the excavated trenches in the habitation area reveal the existence of two cultural complexes. The lower levels belong to the Chalcolithic period and the upper ones to the Iron age.

In north India Iron age occupations are associated with a special type of pottery, commonly known as painted grey ware, which has a wide distribution in Punjab, Rajasthan and the Ganga-Yamuna Doab region. At Rupar in Punjab it is found between the Harappan and the early-historic remains. In the Doab region it has been found in association with iron implements at Panipat, Sonepat, Bagpat, Indraprastha, Alamgirpur Mathura, Noh, Atranjikhera, Ahicchatra, Hastinapur and other sites. These cultures have been placed between c. 1000 and 450 B.C. In the eastern Gangetic region a new type of pottery is associated with the Iron age occupations which is known as northern black polished ware. This is found specially at Rajghat (Banaras), Sonepur, Chirand, Prahladpur, Kausambi and other sites. Its development took place after 500 B.C. Relics of the Iron age have been found at Sravasti in Uttar Pradesh. Buxer in Bihar and Burdwan (Pandu Rajar Dhibi) in West Bengal.

At Somnath in Gujarat, the period IIIB contains northern black polished ware, although period IIIA contains iron implements in association with black-and-red ware. This holds good also in the case of Broach. Nagal and Nagara. At Eran and

Nagda in Madhya Pradesh iron implements have been found in association with black-and-red ware. At Prakash and Bahal in Maharashtra iron implements have been found in association with black-and-red ware below the northern black polished ware level. Such association is also found at Maheswar, Tripuri, Ranjala, Nevasa and other sites. At Kausambi both black-and-red ware and painted grey ware are found along with iron implements.

In peninsular India iron implements have been found in association with a white-spotted black-and-red ware or simple reddish ware. In southern and southeastern India the sites of Sisupalgarh, Dharanikota, Hallur, Arikamedu, Alagorai, etc., as well as the Megalithic burial sites contain iron implements. Although Megalithic graves with Iron age relics are more frequent in the south, these are not rare in northern India as we have noticed above. So far as the southern Megaliths are concerned, we find a strange uniformity in regard to the grave goods, especially in the case of iron objects. It appears that these iron objects had a special manufacturing centre whence these were sent to different sites for depositing in the graves. Among the principal sites mention should be made of Brahmagiri, Jadganhalli, Maski, Halingali, Terdal, Sangankallu, T. Narsipur, Hunnur and Hallur in Karnataka; Sanur, Kunnattur Amrithamangalam, and Paiampalli in Tamil Nadu; Yelleswaram, Nagarjunikonda, Kesarpalle and Pochampad in Andhra Pradesh; Janapani and Khapa in Maharashtra; and Dhanora in Madhya Pradesh.

The beginnings of the Iron age in India have conspicuously been associated with the so-called Aryan migrations. This has yielded a good number of interesting speculations but no tangible result, as we shall see in the next section.

7. *The Aryan Hypothesis in Indian History*

Vedic literature reveals the existence of a composite but uniform civilization constituted by a variety of standardized cultural streams which flourished, especially in Northern India between c. 1500 and 800 B.C. The Vedic language, which later came to be known as Sanskrit after its subsequent refinement, was supposed to belong to the Indo-European or Aryan family.

Sir William Jones in his famous address of 1786 to the Asiatic Society of Bengal pointed out the striking similarity between Sanskrit on the one hand and certain ancient larguages of Asia and Europe on the other. According to him this similarity was due to descent from a common parent language which later came to be known as Indo-European or Aryan. But the concept 'Aryan' was never confined to the exclusive domain of philology. It developed racial, psychological and also political connotations and came to be used to serve a variety of purposes.

Notwithstanding Max Müller's warning that the implication of the term 'Aryan' should not go beyond its purely linguistic suggestivity, Penka and his followers insisted on a racial interpretation, arguing that the original language must have evolved within a particular race, (the Nordics of the Scandinavian region in their opinion), the migration of which into different countries led to the propagation of the language far and wide. Psychological considerations were also there. Since a good number of the so-called 'Aryan' languages belonged to Europe and since Euorpe was culturally superior in many respects to the other parts of the world, the concept 'Aryan' acquired a connotation of superiority. Hence it was believed, and the belief was popular, that in remote antiquity the Aryan' spread in different directions, especially in the Oriental world inhabited by the 'aboriginals', with a 'civilizing mission'. This idea obviously contributed to the cause of imperialism and colonialism: 'White man's burden', in the words of Kipling; or 'thousand years Aryan rule', in the words of Hitler. Again, the concept 'Aryan' had helped the educated and half-educated Indians of the recent past to get rid of their inferiority complex caused by the British rule. The idea that the Indians, especially those belonging to the higher castes, and their British masters were the fruits of the same tree had far-reaching psycho-political consequences, especially when the British used to say 'our Aryan brethren, the mild Hindu'. Conversely, again, the concept 'Aryan' was an inspiring force in the national movement of India, one of the purposes of which was to restore the 'glorious Aryan heritage'.

Starting from the North Pole and Greenland, almost every region of Asia and Europe, including India as well, has been claimed, at different times and on different grounds, by scholars belonging to different disciplines to be the original homeland of the undefined Aryans. Once Germany and its adjoining regions, from Scandinavia in the north to the Danube in the south and the Dniper in the east, were regarded as the cradle land of the early Aryans. More specifically the Danube basin, the coastal region of Sweden, the areas around Lithuania and some other places were suggested by various scholars on grounds other than purely linguistic. It is also to be remembered that India should have a definite place in the controversy relating to the Aryan homeland. The very existence of the *Ṛgveda*, the oldest extant literary production of the Indo-European language, demonstrates that there is no compelling argument against India's claim to be regarded as the cradle land of the Aryans, if their existence was at all a reality.

Among the races of western Asia which have been associated with the Aryans were the Hittites who had routed the older Assyrian colonies from Cappadocia in Asia Minor about 1950 B.C. and ruled over the region till 1200 B.C. Their language was very close to the source–Indo-European, so close that it was sometimes called the sister-language. It has been suggested that the proto-Hittites had separated from the main body of the primitive Indo-Europeans at a time when the palatals had not yet been originated in the basic language. The Mitannis also belonged to the Indo-European family and they established their supremacy in northern Mesopotamia during 1600-1400 B.C. The third important people associated with the Aryans were the Indo-Iranians whose ancestors were supposed to reside about 2000 B.C. in the Pamir region or in the Russian Turkestan area. On the basis of this geographical distribution it was inferred that about 2000 B.C. two branches of the Aryans settled themselves respectively in central and western Asia, one represented by the ancestors of the Indo-Iranians and the other by those of the Hittites and kindred tribes. Thus the original homeland, it has been suggested, should be equidistant from central and western Asia and as such it may be located in some part of South Russia including the Kirghiz Steppes lying to the south of the Urals. It has also been suggested that the early Indo-European vocabulary reveals a steppe-land at the foot of a mountain range. This south Russian homeland theory has been popular among eminent scholars like G.A. Grierson, W. Brandenstein, B.K. Ghosh, R. Hauschild, H. Peake, H.J. Flure, O. Schrader, V.G. Childe and others.

It should be pointed out in this connection that the recommendation of the south-Russian homeland may be regarded as merely a subjective assumption given the camouflage of objective truth. The data underlying such a formulation are much too meagre and flimsy. However, so far as the Indo-Iranians are concerned, the existence of an archaic Indo-Iranian speech form about 1400 B.C. is traceable in the Boghaz-Köi and a few other inscriptions. From these stray records it was concluded that about 1400 B.C. the undifferentiated ancestors of the Vedic Indians and Avestic Iranians lived in Asia Minor (Boghaz-Köi is modern Boghaz-kale in Asiatic Turkey) before their subsequent migrations to Iran and India and that they spoke in a dialect which was not till then fully characterised as Vedic or Iranian. But this has created another problem. If the undivided forefathers of the Vedic tribes were still in Asia Minor about 1400 B.C., and it is not possible to assign for the beginning of the Vedic age any date later than 1500 B.C., then how was it possible for one stream of their descendants to settle in India at least 100 years prior to that date? The *Ṛgveda* must have been composed between c. 1200 and 1000 B.C. by which time the Vedic tribes had been so fully naturalised as to rule out memories of their ancestral home. It contains no reference to an earlier home outside India or to any memory of extra-Indian association. A span of time larger than this was really needed for the Vedic Indians to forget all their previous history before giving final form to the *Ṛgveda*.

So the theory of Aryan migration from western Asia does not stand valid. It has therefore been suggested that the Indo-Iranians were concentrated in what is now known as Russian Turkestan or the neighbouring Pamir region from where they entered Iran and India. But this too is simply a suggestion. The archaeologists, however, insist on an Aryan migration into India from Iran. On the basis of the anomalous objects found at different archaeological sites of central and western Asia and on the evidence of the intrusion of a different type of pottery at certain sites, it has been inferred that about the second millennium B.C. there was turbulence in this vast region and the existing cultures were threatened or destroyed by the invasion of outsiders. These outsiders have been equated, quite arbitrarily, with the Aryans. It must be pointed out here that while archaeology may tell us about the destruction of settlements or the establishment of new ones on the ruins, it cannot identify the peoples concerned with all such changes unless there is other corroborative evidence.

Between 1928 and 1934 M.S. Vats excavated at Harappa a post-Harappan cemetery which came to be known as Cemetery H. It has been suggested by V.G. Childe (1934), B.N. Datta (1936), M.S. Vats (1940), and R.E.M. Wheeler that the Cemetery H culture belonged to the Aryans, who after destroying the Harappans, erected their own settlement on this ruined site. S. Piggott (1950) had suggested that the burnt out portions of Rana Ghundai, Nal and Dabarkot were indicative of planned destruction and the emergence of the Jhukar culture at Amri, Jhukar, Chanhudaro, Lohumjodaro and other sites as well as certain implements found at Shahitump, Mohenjodaro, Kurram and Rajanpur implied an infiltration from the west in Baluchistan and Sind. So far as the first part of Piggott's suggestion is concerned, so little is known about the stratigraphy and chronology of the said sites that it is not possible to say whether the burnings took place at the same time. With regard to the second part of his suggestion, the objects which have been cited are too few to prove anything. Wheeler's view that the founders of the Cemetary H culture destroyed the Harappans about 1500 B.C. can no longer remain valid since the end of the Harappa civilization took place much earlier, around 1750 B.C. Secondly, the Cemetry H culture did not develop immediately after the end of the Harappan settlements. There was a long time-gap between the two. Thirdly, if the Cemetery H culture may at all be regarded as of Aryan inspiration, there should have been a larger area and a greater number of centres of this culture. But apart from two centres at Bhawalpur in Pakistan no trace of this culture have been found elsewhere. The idea of connecting the Aryans with the peoples of Cemetery H culture was challenged by B.B. Lal (1953), A. Ghosh (1962) and G.F. Dales (1964). Since the sixties few have accepted the theory that the Aryans were responsible for the destruction of the Harappan civilization.

In 1927 P. Mitra tried to connect the Aryans with the Copper Hoard cultures of the north and northwest. In 1936 Hiene-Geldern tried to reach the same conclusion on the basis of five copper bronze tool-types found in the Kurram Valley, Punjab, Sind and the Ganges plain and held that these were "brought to India between 1200 and 1000 B.C. by a migration from the South Russian steppes passing through Caucasia and North Persia." Referring to the harpoon-heads and antennae-swords of the Gangetic region he suggested that since these were not found in any stratified context, they should be associated with the Aryans of the northwest. In 1944 Piggott supported this view but later in 1950 he suggested that the tool-types of the Gangetic region belonged to the Harappan refugees. In 1951 B.B. Lal pointed out that there was no basic connection between the Gangetic valley specimens and those found in the west. In 1956 Hiene-Geldern restated his hypothesis on the basis of some extra finds. He attributed the antennae-swords of the Gangetic valley to the Koban culture. But according to D.P. Agarwal, the Copper Hoard cultures of India do not exhibit any mutual link among themselves. Also there is no way to link with the Aryans the copper objects recovered in the 1960s from Khurdi in the Nagaur district of Rajasthan, Mehasana and the Karakoram region. The association of the ochre coloured pottery with the Copper Hoards of the Gangetic and adjoining regions has been previously noted, but it cannot be said that these two are invariably linked up. Nor is it possible to prove that the makers of the ochre coloured pottery were Aryans.

The theory that the Aryans came to India in two waves was popularised by A.F.R. Hoernle (1880), G.A. Grierson (1907), H. Risley (1915) and R.P. Chanda (1916), but it was subsequently rejected by S.K. Chatterjee (1926) and others on philological grounds. However, some archaeologists became interested in the two wave theory. They held that the words *tāmrāyasa* and *kṛṣṇāyasa* used in the Vedas were suggestive of the existence of two classes of Aryans, the copper-using class which came earlier and iron-using class which came later. We have already had occasion to refer to the Gandhara Grave culture (A.H. Dani 1967) and see that graves at Timargarha and other sites of the Swat valley have three periods, the first and second (1600-1300, 1200-1000 B.C.) belonging to the Chalcolithic age and the third (900-600 B.C.) to the Iron age. W. Barnhard took into account a few skeletons, belonging to the first and third periods, and divided them into two physical types, namely, Eurodolicomorph and Leptodolicomorph. He held that these two physical types represented the two waves of the Aryans. Those who came first, in the fourteenth century B.C. had no idea of iron. The second wave around ninth century B.C. knew not only the use of iron but had a different type of burial system as well. The argument is not, however, convincing.

In 1963 H.D. Sankalia tried to associate the post-Harappan Chalcolithic cultures of Central India, Rajasthan, Northern Deccan and Raichur Doab with Iraq and Iran and insisted on their Aryan inspiration. According to him these cultures belonged to the Puranic communities like the Aśmakas, Haihayas, Yādavas and others who were of Aryan stock. G.R. Sharma held that the pottery from Kausambi resembled that of the late-Harappan and post-Harappan Navdatoli, Mehgam, Rangpur and Motamachiala and, taken as a whole, implied an Aryan inspiration here. More interesting is the view of D.P. Agarwal who, in 1966, tried to identify the founders of the Ahar and Gilund cultures of the Banas valley (c. 1800-1200 B.C.) with the Aryans on the basis of pottery and terracotta types. He suggested that the Ahar culture originated as a result of the employment of Harappan craftsmanship by the intrusive west Asiatic Aryans of the first wave and that the painted grey ware people represented the second wave. It is said that the west Asian and Harappan streams of Ahar craftsmanship had an earlier manifestation in Desalpar pottery. The excavated remains of Desalpar IB, which also include bi-coloured cream polished pottery are said to belong to the Aryans who were supposed to have destroyed the Harappan settlements of the Gujarat region, made their own settlements in the Banas valley and spread to the Gangetic divide. Against this hypothesis it may be said that the branding of the Ahar or Banas culture as Aryan and linking it up with Tepe Hissar, Shah Tepe, Anau and other sites in Iran on the basis of superficial resemblances can be nothing more than wishful thinking. This holds good also in the case of the so-called Harappan elements attributed to the Ahar culture.

We have already had the occasion to refer to the wide distribution of painted grey ware culture in the vast region of northern India. This ware was first discovered during the Ahicchatra excavations of 1940-44, but its significance in the archaeological sequence of the upper Gangetic valley was understood in 1950-52 by B.B. Lal, who demonstrated its existence in stratified context at Hastinapur. He identified the makers of the painted grey ware culture with the Aryans. According to him relics of this culture have been found in places mentioned in the *Mahābhārata* in that region which was known as Brahmāvarta or Brahmarṣi-deśa, the most civilized region of the Indian tradition. That is why the users of the painted grey ware should be regarded as Aryans. In the *Mahābhārata* it is stated that after the destruction of Hastinapur, caused by flood, king Nicākṣu shifted his capital further downstream to Kauśambi. Lal's identification of a flood-scar towards the end phase of the painted grey ware period has been considered suggestive in this respect. On the basis of the wide geographical distribution, uniformity and distinctiveness of this painted grey ware culture, Lal interpreted it as intrusive, extra-Indian and Vedic, parallels of which he claimed to have found at Lakhiopir to the north of Karachi, Afghanistan, Shah Tepe in Iran, Hasanlu in Iranian Azarbijan, even at far distant Thessaly. The identification of the painted grey ware peoples with the Aryans, though considered to be reasonable by a few scholars, is not at all convincing. The mere occurrence of the relics of this culture in certain places mentioned in the *Mahābhārata* is not proof of its Aryan origin. According to the literary evidence, sites like Hastinapur, Ahicchatra, etc., should be much older than the seventh or eighth century B.C. as is found through archaeological reckoning. It is probably because of this late date that Wheeler held that the painted grey ware culture belonged to the Aryans of the second wave. This oversimplified explanation does not solve the problem. The excavated sites of this culture, from Punjab in the north to Ujjain in the south, and from Bhawalpur in the west to the Bihar border in the east, are not consistent with the cultural life as reflected in the Vedic texts.

2

The Vedic Civilization and its Impact on the Indian Way of Life

1. The Vedic Literature vis-a-vis the Vedic Tradition

The Vedic literature is a collection of about fifty texts which is divided into four principal categories, namely, Saṃhitā, Brāhmaṇa, Āraṇyaka and Upaniṣad. Besides, a number of subsidiary texts are included in the Vedic literature which are known as the Vedāṅgas. The Saṃhitā is a collection of hymns and verses which contain facts pertaining to all aspects of ancient life in general and rituals in particular. It contains four texts, namely the *Ṛgveda, Sāmaveda, Yajurveda* and *Atharvaveda.* From a strictly philological point of view the *Ṛgveda* was composed between c. 1200 and 1000 B.C. The Brāhmaṇa is a collection of interpretative texts, each of which is connected with a particular Saṃhitā, e.g., *Aitareya* and *Kauṣītaki* with the *Ṛgveda*; *Pañcaviṃśa, Ṣaḍviṃsa* and *Jaiminīya* with the *Sāmaveda*; *Kaṭha, Taittirīya* and *Śatapatha* with the *Yajurveda;* and *Gopatha* with the *Atharvaveda.* The later Saṃhitās and the earlier Brāhmaṇas were composed between c. 1000 and 800 B.C. and the later Brāhmaṇas and the earlier Āraṇyaka-Upaniṣads between c. 800 and 600 B.C. Like the Brāhmaṇas, the principal Āraṇyakas and Upaniṣads are ritual texts connected with the Saṃhitās. There is no hard and fast line of demarcation between the Brāhmaṇas and the Āraṇyakas, nor between the Āraṇyakas and the Upaniṣads, so far as the contents are concerned.

The *Ṛgveda,* among the five recensions of which only the Śākala has survived, is divided into 10 *maṇḍalas* (sections) and

1028 *sūktas* (chapters) which comprise more than 10,000 verses, not all of which were composed by one person or at the same time. The first, eighth and tenth *maṇḍalas* were later compositions. The ninth *maṇḍala* was also a separate collection which was later incorporated into the main body of the *Ṛgveda*. The first attempt to arrange the verses in accordance with their contents was made by Yāska in his *Nirukta* VII. 1.2 in which a threefold division is found, namely, *pratyakṣa* or direct, *parokṣa* or indirect and *ādhyātmikī* or spiritual. Yāska has also referred to as many as 17 commentators on the *Ṛgveda* who flourished before his time and whose interpretations of the older verses varied widely. Modern understanding of the *Ṛgveda* rests primarily upon Sāyana's commentary.

The *Atharvaveda*, earlier called *Atharvāṅgirasa*, has two branches, Saunaka and Paippalāda, and 731 *sūktas* grouped in 20 chapters. A major portion of the fifteenth and the sixteenth chapters is composed in prose. The *Atharvaveda* represents a wider geographical region than the *Ṛgveda*. Glimpses of social life and also the character of the deities and rituals as found in it differ from those found in the *Ṛgveda*. Of the *Sāmaveda* the Kauthuma recension is more widely known than its two other recensions. It has two parts, Ārcika and Uttarārcika, which together have 1810 verses. The verses are composed in *gāyatrī* or *pragātha* metre with the purpose of magical application during the recitals. The *Yajurveda* is divided into two parts, White and Black, the former having only one branch known as the *Vājasaneyī Saṃhitā* and the latter four, namely, *Kāṭhaka Saṃhitā*, *Kapiṣṭhala-kaṭha Saṃhitā* (in fragments), *Taittirīya Saṃhitā* and *Maitrāyaṇī Saṃhitā*. The names of the principal Brāhmaṇa texts have been referred to above. Although the Brāhmaṇas have been suffixed to the Saṃhitās, both classes of literature are different in character. The social and ritualistic aspect of life as reflected in the Brāhmaṇa literature is different from that reflected in the earlier texts. The distinction between the Brāhmaṇas and Āraṇyakas and that between the Āraṇyakas and the Upaniṣads is not very clear. The *Aitareya* and *Kauṣītaki* Āraṇyakas and Upaniṣads are associated with the *Ṛgveda*. The *Āraṇyaka Saṃhitā*, *Āraṇyaka Gāna* and *Jaiminīya-Upaniṣad Brāhmaṇa*, as well as the *Chāndogya* and *Kena* Upaniṣads are connected with the *Sāmaveda*. The *Yajurveda* has three Āraṇyakas, namely, *Kaṭha*, *Taittrīya* and *Śatapatha*, and six Upaniṣads namely, *Kaṭha*, *Taittirīya*, *Maitrāyaṇīya*, *Śvetāśvatara*, *Iśā* and *Bṛhadāraṇyaka*. Like the Brāhmaṇas, the Āraṇyakas and the Upaniṣads are ritual texts, but in some of these texts the genesis of the doctrine of *brahman* or the Universal or Cosmic Self and its identification with *ātman* or Individual Self may be traced.

The Vedāṅga literature is comprised of six different categories. Texts belonging to the Śikṣā (education) category deal with phonetics and other aspects of language. Apart from Śaunaka's *Ṛgveda-Prātiśākhya* and Kātyāyana's *Vājasaneyī-Prātiśākhya* we know about the *Prātiśākhyasūtras* connected with the *Atharvaveda* and *Taittirīya Saṃhitā*. For the students of the *Sāmaveda* there were two digests known as *Puṣpasūtra* and *Pañcavidhasūtra*. Besides, there were Anukramaṇi or glossary-texts, the principal ones being the *Bṛhaddevatā*, *Ṛgveda-sarvānukramṇī* and *Ṛgvidhāna*. No early texts belonging to the Chandas (prosody), Vyākaraṇa (grammar) and Jyotiṣa (astronomy) categories have been found. The *Nirukta* of Yāska, composed about 700 B.C. is an interpretative text of Vedic etymology and conceptions. Texts of the Kalpa category are known as sūtras which are of three kinds—Dharma (laws and norms), Gṛhya (family life, taboos, sacraments and customs), and Śrauta (religious beliefs and rituals). These texts are individually designated after the names of the composers like Āpastamba, Āśvalāyana (from Aśvala), Sāṅkhyāyana, Baudhāyana, Kātyāyana, Hiraṇyakeśī, Pāraskara, Gobhila, Vasiṣṭha, Gautama and others.

The Vedic texts consist of heterogeneous elements contributing to all forms of primitive knowledge, ranging from the brewing of wine to the highest cosmological speculations. Subsequently, however, the Vedic language became obscure; the real meaning and significance of the original passages was forgotten; artificial and imaginary interpretations were invented and the basic contents were overlooked. Eventually the Vedas came to be looked upon as a symbol of spiritual knowledge, a very sacrosanct tradition not to be approached lightly. Thus what came to be known later as the Vedic tradition was different from the actual contents of the Vedic literature. By the term Vedic tradition is meant certain standardized thoughts and social norms which are regarded as the fundamentals of Indian life. The Vedic doctrine of *brahman* has been the subject of Indian philosophical speculation throughout the ages. Although the Vedic rituals have gone out of vogue, certain Vedic sacraments are still followed. In many popular cults of Hinduism some of the Vedic gods are still regarded as the supreme being. Often when some popular deity or cult, even of non-Vedic origin, rose to prominence, it had to receive Vedic sanction before its position could be secured. The Vedic conceptions of the transmigration of soul, *karma* and rebirth are ingrained in the Hindu mind even today. The social rules and norms prescribed in the Dharmasūtras have formed the basis of the legal texts, subsequently known as Dharmaśāstras or Smṛtis, by which the Hindu society is still governed.

2. From Tribe to State: Political Evolution in the Vedic Age

In the Ṛgvedic age there was a tribal organisation of society and a state system in modern sense was not possible. The name Bhāratavarṣa was probably adopted from the Bharata tribes which inhabited the area between the Yamuna and the Sarasvati. They were associated with the Tṛtsus who settled on the eastern bank of the Pāruṣṇī (Ravi). Among other tribes mentioned in the *Ṛgveda* were the Sṛñjayas (of western Uttar Pradesh), Purus and Yadus (on both banks of the Sarasvati), Kṛvis (between the Indus and the Chenab); Druhyus, Turvaśas and Anus (between the Chenab and the Ravi); Matsyas (in the present Alwar-Bharatpur region); Ajas, Śigrus and Yakṣus (between the Yamuna and the Sarasvati); Pakthas, Bhalānases, Viṣāṇins, Alinas and Śivas (in the North Western Frontier Province); Cedis (to the south of the Yamuna); Uśīnaras and Vasas (towards the east of the Yamuna). Pārāvatas (to the south of Yamuna), etc. Among the non-Vedic tribes mention is made of the Kīkaṭas, Kirātas, Caṇḍālas, Parāṅkas Śimyus and others.

The chief political event of the Ṛgvedic age was *dāśarājña* or the battle of ten tribes. It was a battle of the Tṛtsu-Bharatas against the combined force of the five tribes known as Puru, Yadu, Turvaśa, Anu and Druhyu. The latter group was assisted by five smaller tribes known as Alina, Paktha, Bhalānas, Śiva and Viṣānin. The Tṛtsu-Bharatas were victorious under the leadership of Sudās who also defeated the Ajas, Śigrus and Yakṣus. Two earlier leaders of the Tṛtsu-Bharatas were Divodāsa and Pijavana. The former fought against the Purus, Yadus and Turvaśas and also defeated the non-Vedic Dāsa chief Sambara and the Paṇis. The Dāsas against whom the Vedic tribes fought, have been described as *kṛṣṇatvach* (black-skinned), *anāsa* (flat-nosed) and *mṛdhravāc* (evil-tongued). Descriptions of their forts and cities suggest the existence of a settled way of life and a state system. The Paṇis were a non-Vedic community with mainly commercial pursuits. Among the other rival non-Vedic tribes, the Dasyus are described as *akarman* (not performing proper duties), *adevasu* (hostile to the gods), *abrahman* (hostile to priesthood), *ayajvan* (riteless) *avrata* (without sacraments) and *anyavrata* (follower of a different tradition). Among the Vedic tribes, which were mostly pastoral, a regular feature of life was the struggle to acquire cattle wealth, and as such the tribal leadership was necessarily military.

In the post-Ṛgvedic literature the process of the formation of state system can be observed. The older tribes had sunk into oblivion and a number of new tribes had come into existence such as the Sālvas (Alwar), Ikṣvākus (Ayodhya), Kosalas (eastern Ayodhya), Kāśis (Varanasi), Māgadhas (south Bihar), Aṅgas (Bhagalpur), Vaṅgas (Bengal), Vidharvas, Niṣadhas and Kuntis (Madhya Pradesh and Maharashtra), Satvants (between the Ganga and Yamuna but subsequently they shifted to the southwestern direction), Nīcyas, Apācyas, Vāhīkas and Ambaṣṭhas (western India, collectively known as the Pratīcyas), Uttarakurus, Uttaramadras, Mujavants, Mahāvṛṣas, Gandhāris, Bāhlikas, Keśis, Kekayas and Kambojas (northern region, collectively known as the Udīcyas), etc. The names of a few non-Vedic tribes are found such as the Andhras (between the Krishna and the Godavari), Puṇḍras (northern Bengal), Śabaras (Madhya Pradesh and Orissa), Mutivas (on the Musi river near Hyderabad), etc. Among the older tribes the Purus joined with the Bharatas and formed the Kuru kingdom. The Kṛvis and Sṛñjayas merged with the Pañcālas who, along with the Kurus, became masters of the central region of northern India. The

Videhas were also advancing towards statehood in the eastern region.

The word *rājan* or *rājā* in the *Ṛgvedā* denoted a tribal chief and not a monarchical king. References to several *rājās* attending the assemblies can only be explained in terms of the attendance of a number of tribal chiefs at a meeting. In *Ṛgveda* X.34 it is clearly stated that *rājā* is the commander (*ṣenānī*) of the tribe (*gaṇa*) and the first (*prathama*) among the group (*vrāta*). He is the protector of the tribe (*gopa janasya*) and his function was basically that of a war-lord. In the *Ṛgveda* popular assemblies and institutions like Sabhā, Samiti and Vidatha are mentioned. The chiefs went to the Samiti just as they went to the Sabhā (*RV.* IX. 92.6, X.97.6). There are many passages which refer to the distribution of wealth in the Sabhā. One of the words for wealth in the *Ṛgveda* is *vārya*, derived from the root *vṛṇ* meaning 'division' which implies that there cannot be any wealth without its inner propensity of distribution. The *Ṛgveda* I.31.6, I.117.25, III.1.18, IV.38.4, IV.8.1, X.8.85-86, etc. (Cf. *AV*, IV.25.1, V.20.12, etc.) mentions Sabhā as an assembly for distribution of wealth, for secular or religious ends, and war. Sabhā was a place for discussion of public affairs which women also could attend. In *RV* I.167.3 it is said that the woman in the Sabhā utters appropriate sentences needed for the purpose. Elsewhere (III.56.6) it is said that three women who are in conformity with Ṛta come three times a day to attend the Sabhā. The Samiti had the responsibility for war and that is why the tribal chiefs had to attend it: *rājānaḥ samityau iva*. According to *Nighaṇṭu* II.17 the Samiti served as the war council.

Subsequently, however, with the disintegration of the tribal system and the establishment of regular kingship and growth of state power, there was a considerable decrease in the importance and function of these popular assemblies. In the later Saṃhitās and Brāhmaṇas these popular assemblies are rarely mentioned and in subsequent literature there is no mention of them at all. With the development of pastoral economy the Vedic tribes became increasingly aggressive—raids and wars brought in more cattle. As a consequence there was greater demand for military leadership which in turn laid the foundation for the growth of state-power and kingship. This is reflected in the *Ṛgveda* in which the praise of the war-lord Indra surpassed that of all other deities. The *Aitareya Brāhmaṇa* I.1.14 says that state and kingship had emerged from military necessity. The word *udāja*, with its variant *nirāja*, records that the king took a share of war booty. In return for his warlike services the king received the obedience of the people and in particular their contribution to the maintenance of royalty (*Mait. Saṃ.*, I.6.10, *Taitt. Br.* II.7.18.2). The *Śatapatha Brāhmaṇa* V.3.3.12 openly says that the king is the visible representative of Prajāpati because the institution of kingship is essential to put an end to anarchy. The concept of sovereign monarch finds mention in the Brāhmaṇa literature. This sovereignty—apart from conquest—could also be achieved by performing rituals like the Aśvamedha or Rājasūya which were used as graceful methods for securing allegiance of the smaller powers. The institution of kingship was, to a certain extent, deified.

However, it has to be observed that at least in the Brāhmaṇa literature, notwithstanding the usual hyperboles in regard to the institution of kingship, emphasis was laid on the king's election and checks on his power. On the evidence of *Nirukta* II.10 it is known that there were elected kings even in the later Vedic age. Details of rituals like the Aśvamedha, Rājasūya or Vājapeya show that the king had to accept, although symbolically, the fact that he was subordinate to the popular will. It is stated in the *Gautama Dharmasūtra* VIII.1 that the king was the lord of all, but not of the Brāhmaṇas. The latter had an organisation of their own, a 'pressure group' known as the *praiṣad*, to advise the king on different occasions.

Despite ample glorification and rationalisation of the institution of kingship in post-Ṛgvedic literature, the rise of monarchy and state power in different parts of India did not follow an orderly or uniform pattern. In the later Vedic age a few kingdoms such as those of the Kurus or the Pañcālas, existed like islands among the vast network of tribal settlements. The evidence of the Buddhist and Jain texts as well as that of the Purānas also bears this out. In the time of the Buddha there were *mahājanapadas*, or bigger tribal settlements, only a few of which came close to statehood like Kosala, Vatsa, Avanti and Magadha. One should not fail to recall in this connection that almost in every period of ancient Indian history the ruling dynasties in different parts of the country were formed by tribes like the Mauryas, Śuṅgas, Kuṣāṇas, Sātavāhanas and others, and that the territories owned by them gradually acquired the characteristics of a state.

The Indian state system throughout the ages was not sufficiently integrated. This was partly due to the fact that complete detribalisation, the precondition for the growth of some kind of national sentiment, did not occur on a large scale. This semi-detribalisation also explains the existence of an autonomous counter-power, a state within the state, namely the caste system. This was a cluster of well-integrated social groupings commanding absolute obedience from their members. Indian society, as the poet Tagore perhaps rightly understood, was always a civil society which could not be transformed into a political one notwithstanding serious efforts from outside. Even today, the principal obligation of an average Indian individual is to the caste to which he or she belongs.

3. Incomplete Detribalisation and the Caste System

All over the world there is a four-fold social division comprising the intellectual class, the ruling class, the trading class and the working class. These four classes are known in India as the four *varṇas* comprising respectively the Brāhmaṇas, the Kṣatriyas, the Vaiśyas and the Śūdras. The earliest theoretical indication of this four-fold division is found in *Ṛgveda* X 90. But this four-fold division, which is mainly normative, does not explain the structural formation and the functional role of the caste system. In fact, there are thousands of castes and the law-givers, throughout the ages, have tried to bring them into the order of an idealised four-fold system by adopting various methods.

The caste system has several characteristics. First, every caste has a special caste-profession. Second, every caste is endogamous, i.e., a man belonging to a particular caste should marry a woman of his own caste. Third, every caste is autonomous and is guided by its own social laws and customs. Fourth, every caste has a specific status, high or low, in the social hierarchy, with exclusive rights and privileges of its own. It should also be remembered that the highest caste is not always the dominant caste. It is, and it has been, the castes of the middle rank which are the most powerful and influential. Fifth, the number of the castes is ever-increasing. At every period of history one may come across the emergence of new castes, and this process is ongoing. The exclusive area of one caste cannot be encroached upon by another caste, e.g., a barber cannot take the occupation of a washerman. Change of occupation is, however, permitted so far as the higher castes are concerned, e.g., the Brāhmaṇas or the Kṣatriyas can take up the occupation of the Vaiṣyas and the Śūdras. The argument in favour of this change of profession is that not all Brāhmaṇas are born learned enough to teach the Vedas and perform religious rites and not all Kṣatriyas are born strong enough to become administrators or warriors. But when a Brāhmaṇa or a Kṣatriya takes up a lower occupation his social position is lowered to the rank of the Śūdras although he retains his caste identity.

The caste system originated and evolved under diverse historical conditions, one of which was the process of incomplete detribalisation to which we have already had the occasion to refer. The *pañca-kṛṣṭi* of the *Ṛgveda* has been explained by Yāska as the five classes of men; it included the four *varṇas* and the Niṣādas were the fifth—*ni* means down, and *sad* means 'to settle'. Of the eight peoples associated with the Niśādas, as we find in the Rudrādhyāya of the *Yajurveda*, the Vrātas, Puñjiṣṭhas, Śvanins and Mṛgāyus were hunters while the Takṣaṇ, Rathakāras, Kulālas and Karmāras left the tribal fold and settled in Vedic society as members of the lower castes having undertaken the occupations of carpenter, chariot-maker, potter and blacksmith respectively. The working of such a social process of detribalisation by which specific castes are formed on the basis of certain selected or given occupations in the bigger Hindu social hierarchy can be seen in India even today. The commentator Mahīdhara explains the word Niṣāda as it occurs in the *Vājasaneyī Samhitā* as denoting a Bhilla or Bhil. The Buddhist Jātakas describe them as hunters and foresters. The Purāṇas mention the Kirātas, Bhillas, Nahālakas, Bhrāmaras and Pulindas as descendants of the Niṣādas and describe them as black, low-statured, short-armed, having high cheek bones, a flattened nose, red eyes and copper-coloured hair—characteristics still conspicuous among many hill tribes of present-day India.

In Sanskrit literature, tribes of the Vindhyan region belonging to the Niṣāda stock are often called Kirātas, Śabaras and Pulindas. The Kirātas are mentioned in the Puranic lists of Janapadas as dwelling in Udīcya or Uttarāpatha (northern) region and also in the Parvatāśraya or the Himalayan region. The *Periplus* refers to the Kirātas (Kirrhadae) living to the north of Dosarene (Tosali in the Puri-Cuttack region) as savages with flattened noses and also horse-faced and long-faced tribes (cf. the Aśvamukha and Dīrghāśya of the Purāṇas) subsisting on raw meat (Puruṣāda, cf. the term Kravyād, 'eaters of raw flesh' of the *Atharvaveda* and *agrophagoi* of the Greek writers). Ptolemy locates them near the Mount Maiandros, and one branch, the Airrhadoi, lived in the coastal region beyond the mouth of the Ganges. In the *Aitareya Brāhmaṇa*, the Śabaras are classed as Dasyus with the Andhras, who lived in the tract between the Krishna and the Godavari, Pulindas, Mutibas and Puṇḍras. The Mutibas, also called Mucipa and Mubipa, lived in different parts of present Andhra Pradesh while the Puṇḍras or Pauṇḍras in eastern India. The land inhabited by the Śabaras is located to the south of the Vindhyas in the Puranic lists of Janapadas (even today a tribe called Saora is found on the Eastern Ghats) but Ptolemy locates the Śabaras to the north of the Vindhyas. The Pulindas are mentioned along with the Andhras in an inscription of Aśoka. The *Bṛhatsaṃhitā* refers to them especially as a *gaṇa* or tribe. There were several branches of the Pulindas, namely a western branch, a Himalayan branch related to the Kirātas and Ṭaṅganas, and a southern branch. According to the *Kathāsaritsāgara*, the territory of the Pulindas was situated in the Vindhyas on the route which went from Kosambi to Ujjayini. However, the term Pulinda was probably applied to any hunting people; in the Buddhist literature even the wild tribes of Śrī-Laṇkā, like the Veddas, have been identified with the Pulindas. Ptolemy refers to the Poulindai as *agrophagoi*, i.e., a tribe subsisting on raw flesh, roots and wild fruits. The same term was used by Herodotus to describe the Padaeans who dwelt on the western region of the Indus. The classical writers have attributed the term *ichthyophagoi* or eaters of raw fish, to certain Indian tribes.

The present situation is not very different from the past. The tribal population of modern India, numbering almost forty million, still live in the same regions where their ancestors were located by the writers of the ancient texts. These tribes not only speak in different languages, but are also at different stages of economic development. The most primitive among the southern tribes are the Aranadans of the Nilambur forest who have given up their rock shelter habitations very recently and are still at the food-gathering stage, subsisting on vermin, trapped game and certain roots and fruits. The same holds good in the case of the Chenchus of the Nallamallais and in that of the Birhors, Koruas and Hill Marhias of the Central region who depend mostly on food-gathering and hunting for their livelihood. Some of the food-gathering tribes like the Paniyars of Wynad now survive as bonded labourers under powerful peasant communities. Again there are certain tribes like the Muthuvans, Kannikaras, Irulas, Sholagas, Malasers, Kadars, etc., who have combined food-gathering with slash-and-burn and other forms of primitive agriculture.

Some tribes—the pastoral Todas, the agricultural Badagas and the artisan Kotas of the Nilgiri hills—have been able to proceed a few steps further and form a closely knit economic unit. Tribes of the central zone, generally speaking, are on a higher level of development than the southern primitives. Instead of hunting and food-gathering they practice shifting cultivation with the hoe and the axe as implements. The Mundas, Santals, Oraons and other comparatively advanced tribes of the central zone have permanent plough cultivation. Terrace cultivation with irrigation is common among certain north-eastern tribes, and weaving is fairly developed. The Kotas of the Nilgiris are the artisan tribe *par excellence*. In Orissa and Chota-Nagar certain tribes have adopted specialised methods of exploiting the jungles and of exchanging the products for money. The Hos, Mundas, Santals, Bhumijs and similar other tribes have been so completely converted into agriculturists that there is little difference between them and other agricultural castes.

These are only a few examples to show that even in modern

times the backward tribes of India are not at the same level of development. In some cases the tribes disintegrated owing to the change in the mode of production which eventually resulted in the growth of a new society based on a broader social platform. In other cases it was due to pressure from outside. Long ago, Kauṭilya, who was a champion of organised statehood, categorically prescribed that the *saṃghas* and *gaṇas* should be destroyed by any means—war, diplomacy, sabotage, bribery and any suitable corrupt practice—and that the tribals should be cut loose from their kinship bond and engaged in various professions required by the larger society or by the state. They were thus lured to leave their original habitat and settle in villages and were given specific occupations to cater to the needs of broad-based societies. Being dissociated from their environment, they became occupational groups at the first stage and then became transformed into castes of various status under the bigger fold of Hindu society according to the importance of their profession and service. But this detribalisation did not work in one direction only. Many tribes, unable to subsist in their traditional environment, came to villages and towns and settled in bigger localities on the basis of different occupations and eventually became part of the larger Hindu society. In many cases the more primitive ones, especially those belonging to the hunting and food-gathering stage, left their wild shelters, being unable to subsist on their traditional mode of living but since they did not develop any productive-mentality in the economic sense and were unable to find a suitable livlihood, they became beggars, thieves and criminals. Again, while one branch of a particular tribe has been found to have adopted the new mode of life they encountered, the other branch is found to have maintained its traditional way of living. For example, when the food-gathering economy of southern India gave place to the agricultural economy and many tribes were transformed into settled villagers, in remote areas a branch of the Chenchus resisted this change and clung tenaciously to their food-gathering conditions.

The problem of the law-makers of ancient India was to incorporate various such detribalised castes into the framework of the imaginary but idealised four-fold social order or *varṇa* system and to explain and rationalise existence in the prescribed set-up. They tried to solve this problem by inventing the theory of *varṇasaṅkara* or 'mixed-caste', according to which the origin of each functioning caste was attributed to uneven hypergamic or hypogamic marriage. This may be illustrated with reference to the Ambaṣṭhas, a well-known tribe of the Punjab region. After their detribalisation they ware transformed into occupational castes, but their caste status varied due to the kind of occupation they followed in different parts of the country. The law-makers felt the need to give them a place in the social hierarchy and therefore they described them as a mixed caste, born from the union of a Brāhmaṇa male and Vaiśya female. The transformation of the well known regional tribes like the Andhras, Ābhīras, Āvyantyas, Drāviḍas, Licchavis, Khasas, Oḍras, Puṇḍras, Niṣādas, Bhojas, Māgadhas, Vaidehikas, etc., into occupational castes may thus be explained similarly. Although the theory of *varṇasaṅkara* was imaginary and devoid of historical validity, it was successfully used to incorporate, at least theoretically, innumerable castes or subcastes in the given pattern of the four-fold social division. Even the foreign tribes like the Kambojas, Śakas, Cīnas, Pahlavas, Yavanas, etc., were included in the four-fold order and described as degraded Kṣatriyas.

In most cases the tribal background of the castes is amply transparent. Castes like the Kaukkuṭa, Kaivarta, Kṣatṛ, Pulkasa, Meda, Āhiṇḍika, Kārāvara, etc., are described as being descended from the Niṣādas, the well-known general name of the primitive hunting tribes. Likewise ancient tribes like the Ambaṣṭhas, Andhras, Veṇas, Sātvatas, Bhojas, Māgadhas have been described as the ancestors, either in the paternal or the maternal line, of many a known caste. In certain cases the very names of the castes indicate their tribal affiliation. It is only in the professional names of the castes like Ayaskāra (heater of metal), Āśvika (dealer in horse), Gopa (milkman), Carmakāra (leather-worker), Karmakāra (blacksmith), Kulāla (potter), Modaka (confectioner), Takṣan (carpenter), Tantuvāya (weaver), Naṭa, Nartaka (public entertainer), Nāpita (barber), Tailika (oilman), Dhīvara (fisherman), Buruḍa (bamboo-worker), Bhiṣak (physician), Rajaka (washerman), etc., that the tribal identity recedes into the background.

What is suggested here is that in India, especially among the backward communities, the demarcation line between the tribal and the caste system is not very clear because the latter, in reality, is the consequence of detribalisation, a process which is not yet complete. Tribal elements still exist in the structural set-up and functional role of the caste system as also in institutions like village communities, customary laws, folk religions, and oral traditions, etc.

In many cases the disintegration of tribal societies was also affected by external factors, either in the form of a new system of production or that of the enforcement of state power. In the former case, the older techniques of production were never given up completely and new innovations could not be uniformly enforced all over the vast country or adopted spontaneously by all sections of the peoples. In the latter case, state power was never strong enough to transform the uneven and retarded 'civil societies', saturated with tribal elements, in accordance with the absolute need for creating a full-fledged broad-based political society to serve its own ends. The *status quo* thus was maintained through the preservation of all the uneven social formations evolved over space and time.

4. Vedic Society and Economy

The Ṛgvedic economy was predominantly, if not exclusively, pastoral. In fact, out of 10,462 verses of the *Ṛgveda* only 25 refer to agriculture and, significantly enough, 22 out of the said 25 verses belong to the later portions of the *Ṛgveda*. Side by side the importance attached to the possession of cattle is shown in numerous passages. The word *go* denoting the cow, is used as one of the synonyms of *pṛthivī*, the earth. According to the *Nighaṇṭu* II.11 nine other terms were also used to denote the cow. Even in *Ṛgveda* VI.50.11 the gods are invoked as offsprings of the cows, and the poets do not hesitate to compare their songs with the lowing of cows (VII. 32.22, VII. 106.1, IX. 2.2, etc.) or to designate the starry heaven after the term *gāvaḥ* (I. 154.6, VII. 36.1. etc.). Winternitz (I. 64-65) says: "Again and again in the songs and invocations to the gods the prayer for cattle and horses occurs. Also the strife amongst hostile aboriginal inhabitants turns on the possession of cattle. Therefore, too, the old world for 'war' or 'battle' is originally desire for cattle (*gaviṣṭi*). In most extravagant expressions, cows and bullocks are praised as the most precious possessions."

The *Ṛgveda* was composed over a long period of time. Though the class society had already been established, in the *Ṛgveda* there are glimpses of primitive undifferentiated life. There are a few references to equal distribution of produced and conquered wealth but a greater number of passages refer to individual ownership and inheritance. In *Ṛgveda* I.70.10 there is mention of distribution of property among the sons even during the lifetime of the father. The *Taittirīya Brāhmaṇa* III.1.9.4 mentions the story of Manu's distribution of property among his sons. It should be remembered that in pastoral societies the sense of property developed quickly because cattle were the best medium of exchange which could be preserved and multiplied and inreased by wars and raids.

The pastoral economy of the Vedic peoples, when supplemented by agriculture, created conditions for rapid class division which is abundantly testified by the later Saṃhitās and Brāhmaṇas. In the post-Ṛgvedic age the disintegration of the tribal system paved the way for the rise of state power and surplus in the field of production helped to create privileged classes with varying status. This process is amply reflected in the emergence of various professionals in different walks of life. The higher administrative officials were known as *ratnins* or *rājakṛts* (king makers). There was also specialisation in priesthood. The *Atharvaveda* III.5.6-7, *Taittirīya Saṃhitā* IV. 5.4.2, *Vājasaneyī Saṃhitā* XVI.26.28, XXX.5-13, *Kāṭhaka Samhitā* XVII.13, etc., refer to numerous professionals such as artisans, craftsmen and manual workers, besides military men, agriculturists and traders. The production of surplus also prepared the ground for the rise of urban settlements. Trade was facilitated. The word *śreṣṭhī* occurs in the later Vedic literature in the sense of banker or merchant. The word *kusīdī* refers to one who invests capital for interest. The Gṛhyasūtras refer to a ritual called *paṇyasiddhi* for success in trade.

Such changes in the economic field were conducive to a greater degree of social inequality. In *Atharvaveda* IV.2.22 the world *bali* denotes taxation to be paid through cattle or a share of produce. In the Dharmasūtras the king's right to impose taxes has been justified on the grounds of his corresponding duty to protect his subjects. According to some Dharmasūtras (*Baudhāyana* I.10.18.1 and *Vasiṣṭha* I.42) the king is entitled to receive one-sixth of the produce as tax, while *Gautama* X. 24-35 prescribes one-sixth or one-eighth or one-tenth of the land produce, one-fifth of the cattle-wealth or gold, one-twentieth of the commercial goods, one-sixtieth of the raw materials of production and one day's labour of the artisans and toilers. In the *Āpastamba Dharmasūtra* II.10.10.26 exemption from paying taxes is granted to priests, non-professional women, ascetics, students, minors and physically disabled persons.

The greatest pressure of taxation and social injustice fell on the castes belonging to the Vaiśya and Śūdra categories because they were connected more intimately with all sorts of social production. According to the *Aitareya Brāhmaṇa* VII.29.3 the existence of the Vaiśyas depended on the mercy of the Brāhmaṇas and the Kṣatriyas. In social life they had no security and their property could be easily appropriated by the ruling class. The condition of the Śūdras was worse. Even the laws discriminated against them. The Brāhmaṇas were exempt from capital punishment. The murder of a Brāhmaṇa could never be compensated and the murderer had to be tried and punished most severely. The murder of a Kṣatriya, according to the *Āpastamba Dharmasūtra* I.9.24.2-4, could be compensated by offering 1000 cows, that of a Vaiśya by offering 100 cows and that of a Śūdra by offering only 10 cows. The *Āpastamba* II.10.17 openly justifies such discriminatory punishment. There was also discrimination in regard to women; the patriarchal system of inheritance was the rule. The *Śatapatha Brāhamṇa* IV.4.2.13 says (also *Nirukta* III.4) that women cannot be owners of property nor even of themselves. According to the Dharmasūtras, if a man has no son his property will pass on to his *sapiṇḍa* relations, that is brothers and their descendants or father's brothers and their descendants in the male line. If none be available then it would pass on to the *sakulya* relations, i.e., distant cousins in the male line. This tradition of discrimination was followed with greater zeal by the subsequent law-givers who boasted that their injunctions were based solely upon the Śrutis or the infallible Vedas.

5. *Religion and World-View: Influence on Later Indian Thought*

The religion of the *Ṛgveda* is patriarchal, a reflection of the society of the pastoral warriors. The pastoral tribes require greater courage and hardihood than the agricultural, and also an efficient leadership to protect the cattle thus fostering the cult of heroes. The herder in his nomadic life has to live under the scorching heat of the sun, the dreadful thunder, the devastating storms. So his religion is mainly concerned with the sky, in which astral and nature myths, personified as gods and godlings, make their appearance. The supreme being of the pastoral religions is generally identified with the sky-god who rules over other deities like the headman of a patriarchal joint family.

The nature-gods of the *Ṛgveda* are divided into three categories: celestial like Mitra, Puṣan, Viṣṇu, Uṣas, Ādityas, Aśvins, etc.; atmospheric like Indra, Trita Āptya, Mātariśvan, Rudras, Maruts, Vāyu, Parjanya, etc.; and earthly like Agni, Pṛthivī, Soma, etc. In the case of the Ṛgvedic deities one can easily find the working of the process of anthropomorphism. In most cases, behind the human forms, the natural background is clear. That is why the Ṛgvedic deities are also classified as transparent, translucent and opaque. To the first category belong deities such as Uṣas, Agni, Sūrya, Vāyu, Āpaḥ, Dyaus, Pṛthivī, etc., where the natural phenomena can easily be detected. To the second category belong Indra, Varuṇa, Viṣṇu, etc.; in this category anthropomorphism is stronger but the natural background still remains. To the third category belong deities like the Aśvins whose natural beckground has altogether vanished. It is also to be observed that at the initial stages the Ṛgvedic deities had some sort of equality: each deity has been invoked as if he or she is supreme. This equality has been described by Max Müller as henotheism which was perhaps a reflection of primitive tribal equality. Subsequently, however, with the development of class society, there was also discrimination in the status of the gods.

It is also to be observed that in the Ṛgvedic age in particular and in the Vedic age in general, man's attitude towards the deities was not that of surrender and devotion. Men understood the gods as representatives of natural forces, and the praise addressed to them was no more than poetic effusion.

What they really believed was that the natural forces, personified as gods, could be controlled and brought to the task of human welfare through Yajña or ritual. Ritualism must have had its roots in primitive magic which was an illusory technique to make nature work in the service of man. Vedic ritualism—Yajña as it was called—was a development of this primitive magic, the purpose of which was to produce *apūrva*, i.e., what was not previously produced. The Vedic Yajña was not sacrifice, i.e., offering of dear things to the gods. The texts and the commentaries of the Pūrva Mimāṃsā school of Indian philosophy uphold unconditional atheism and at the same time the efficacy of rituals.

In the Vedic literature we come across a kind of progress from crude and unconnected notions to more refined ideas and broader views. There was a steady but multifarious advance from a concrete physical cause to the abstract, ritualistic, theistic, physiological and psychological First Principles. The *Ṛgveda* postulates only water as the primordial element or matter from which others gradually evolved. Hiraṇyagarbha or the Golden Germ is said to have arisen in the beginning from great waters. Elsewhere in the *Ṛgveda* it is stated that waters contained the floating egg from which arose Viśvakarman, the craftsman who fashioned the earth. The conception of the primeval waters recurs in the mythology of the Brāhmaṇa literature which speaks of the waters as having produced after a year's ferment the golden egg from which sprang Prajāpati.

It is in the Upaniṣads that we have the first mention of the doctrine of the five elements. The distinction of the elemental essence or the *tanmātra* and the gross embodiment of substance is suggested. In the later Vaiśeṣika Sūtras the common characteristics of the forms of matter constituting the physical world are described. Of the various properties of the forms of matter, the most important seems to be the inherent causality, that is, the capacity for generating an effect with itself as its cause, like water hardening itself into ice. By nature water is liquid and its capacity of generating different effects is conditional. By nature earth is solid, but under certain conditions it is reduced into atoms or *paramānus*. Earth and water possess motion which generates velocity (*vega*), and the latter once generated in an object produces a series of motions in succession until the object stops due to gravity (*gurutva*). This gravity is absent in fire and air; there is thus nothing to check their movement. These are inseparably connected with the objective world as the necessary conditions of the creative process. Only a substance of wider dimension can hold or support created objects, and that is why *ākāśa*, or space, with infinite extension is needed to hold the objects of limited dimensions.

In the Vedic tradition emphasis is laid upon the association and identification of the human faculties with those of nature, often seeking the source of unity behind all diversity. The earliest attempt to find the common origin of the diverse phenomena of nature in nature itself is found in the Upaniṣads which give a hierarchy of different grades of reality. The idea of *brahmaṇ* has been conceived not only as the essence of cosmic phenomena, but also as that of the organic and mental functions of a human being. After this correspondence was made, the next step was probably to consider the world as really a soul or *ātman*, a universal soul, of which the individual is a microcosm. In the Upaniṣads there are what may be called *saprapañca* (material) and *niṣprapañca* (non-material) views of reality. According to the first view, *brahman*, the term by which the ultimate reality is known in the Upaniṣads, is the ground of the manifestation of the universe, and according to the second, it is the basis of the illusory appearance of the world. In the terminology of the later Vedānta, the universe of the *saprapañca* view is a *pariṇāma* or transformation of *brahman*, while on the *niṣprapañca* it is a *vivarta* or transfiguration thereof.

The *Śvetāśvatara Upaniṣad* mentions some of the most popular theories current in its time in explanation of the origin of the Universe: God (Īśvara), time (Kāla), inherent nature (Svabhāva), destiny (Niyati), chance (Yadṛcchā), elements (Bhūta), female organ (Yoni) and soul or male principle (Puruṣa). The same list recurs in the *Suśruta Saṃhitā* in which the theories of Puruṣa and Bhūta have been dropped and instead of Yoni reference has been made to *pariṇāma* of Prakṛti or the modification of primal matter.

So far as Bhūtavāda or doctrine of elements is concerned we have seen that in the Vedas the visible world is thought of as a product of the five gross elements: earth, water, fire, air and space. But in the course of time it was felt that these gross elements might have come into existence through an organic evolutionary process from such material principles as Prakṛti, Māyā, etc. This original principle, rather the material cause, may itself be a reality possessing all the power necessary to unfold the whole universe out of itself as we find in the Śāṅkhya; or an illusory reality as we find in the Advaita Vedānta or in the Buddhist Mādhyamika and Yogācāra systems; or of the power of the Supreme Being as we find in the later theistic systems. The Svabhāvavādins, however, believe in four elements without counting the space as the fifth, since it is not a subject of direct perception. In the Sāṅkhya-Yoga the five elements are prefixed by the evolutes of Prakṛtī. In the Vaiśeṣika philosophy the five elements belong to the nine substances intended to comprise all corporeal and incorporeal things. The same idea is also found in the Pūrva Mīmāṃsā. Earth, water, fire and air possess colour and tangibility. Space is inferred as the substratum of sound.

Though there are various gods in the Vedic texts invoked on different occasions and praised by the poets, Īśvaravāda, or the idea of an omniscient and omnipotent God creating the world out of his own self, has little place in the Vedic scheme. The gods are subordinate to rituals or Yajñas. There is also reason to believe that the doctrine of *karma* and rebirth, which is fundamental to Brahmanism, Buddhism and Jainism and which is rooted in the Vedas, has something to do with the non-theistic stand. The basis or guiding principle of the doctrine of *karma* and rebirth was probably the agricultural maxim: As you sow, so you reap. An individual's present life is conditioned by his or her deeds of the past life, and the deeds of the present life determine the course of the future. In this cycle of rebirth, caused and conditioned by *karma*, the position of God is redundant. The Upanisadic concept of the identity of the macrocosm and the microcosm—of the universal and individual self, aimed at explaining cosmic and psycho-physical principles—has often been used to suggest that the power of creation belongs to the pure stainless *brahman*, the material and efficient cause which for its own sport develops itself into the world without undergoing the least change. But side by side it has also been demonstrated that the changing and impermanent world cannot be the effect of an eternal and changeless cause.

The conception of Kāla, or time, as the first principle is found in the *Atharvaveda*. The sequence of phenomena observed in creation implies the existence of a factor which is technically known as Kāla. In the Nyāya Vaiśeṣika scheme time is held to be a substance, supersensuous, pervasive and eternal in nature. The same is also held by the Mīmāṃsakas, but the Advaita Vedāntists propose to remove it from the realm of reality. Both Svabhavāvāda and Yadṛcchāvāda reject the idea that nature reveals a divine power working behind it. By Svabhāva is meant the nature of the object, as burning in the case of fire, and the transformation of objects by themselves. By Yadṛcchā is meant the occurrence of the object without any previous plan. It is the doctrine of accidental coincidence. The world-view of the Lokāyatikas was mainly based upon the former doctrine though the latter was not entirely absent in their thought. Niyativāda or the doctrine of fate is not significantly represented in the history of Indian ideas. The last great representative of Niyativāda was Gośāla Maṅkhaliputra of the Ājīvika sect.

The conception of Yoni (female organ, female womb) as the first principle is associated with the primitive cosmogonical belief in sexual dualism. There is reason to believe that the Sāṅkhya conception of Prakṛti in its earlier pre-Vedic stages had a close bearing on the cults, rituals and ideas centering round Yoni or the female organ of generation. The principle of sexual dualism is manifested in the conception of a sky father and an earth mother which pervades many a cosmogonic myth. In the *Ṛgveda*, heaven (Dyaus) and earth (Pṛthivī) are described as universal parents. The idea of Prakṛti in place of the earth evolved in the course of time. This Prakṛti began to be conceived as the germinal productive principle—the eternal mother capable of evolving all created things out of herself but never so creating unless united with the eternal spiritual principle, the Puruṣa.

It may be concluded that the Vedic tradition spawned many of the later ideas dealing with questions concerning the origin, inner nature and purpose of the world which have found theoretical expression in the philosophical literature of India.

Although the Vedic texts erected the framework of concepts and relations to satisfy some emotional and intellectual needs (on the basis of heterogeneous contents), and drew upon a variety of sources, including pre-Vedic and non-Vedic ones, they reveal different world-views based upon material, divine, ritualistic and abstract principles. Even the anti-Brahmanical systems like Buddhism and Jainism derived some of their ingredients from the Vedic tradition, for example, the doctrines of *Karma* and rebirth. The professed atheism of these systems must have also been inspired by Vedic sources, because another atheistic school of Indian philosophy, the Pūrva Mīmāṃsā, which bears certain features in common with Buddhism and Jainism, claims its Vedic origin and its commitment to the Vedas quite frankly. In the Pūrva Mīmāṃsā gods are subordinate beings in relation to the human beings; they can be produced for the sake of human welfare by performing rituals. The same is also held in Buddhism and Jainism in which gods are subordinate to the Budddhas and Jinas, but in these systems the role of ritualism is denied and substituted by a different set of ideas.

3

Emperors, Kings and Feudatories: A Study in Political History

1. The Era of Magadhan Ascendancy (600-200 B.C.)

The next historical period, which is placed between c. 600 and 200 B.C., began with a massive socio-religious movement launched by the Buddha and his illustrious contemporaries when the existing tribal confederacies (*mahājanapadas*) were developing the characteristics of state organisation. In this lay the seeds of the subsequent Magadhan ascendancy. The growth of Magadhan state-power required the annihilation of many a tribal settlement. Bimbisāra of the Haryaṅka clan, who was a contemporary of the Buddha, consolidated the power of the Magadhan state by annexing to it the settlement of the Aṅgas and the Kāśis while his son and successor Ajātaśatru exterminated the tribal confederacy of the Vajjians which comprised nine clans of the Mallas, nine clans of the Licchavis and eighteen tribes of Kāśi and Kosala.

While in the sixth century B.C. eastern India had been undergoing a transition from tribal settlements to statehood, especially under the leadership of Magadha, the frontier tribes of the northwest had a different experience. As a consequence of the Persian invasion certain areas of the Sindhu and Gandhāra region became parts of the Achaemenian empire. Although the Persian hold continued up to 330 B.C. till the Achaemenian emperor Darius III was defeated and his kingdom destroyed by the Macedonian invader Alexander—the Persian grip on the Indian provinces was never so tight as to detribalise the entire population and to introduce an elaborate administrative machinery conducive to the strengthening of the empire. However, here and there under the shadow of the Achaemenian empire a few tribal settlements were transformed into states, the kings of which were allowed to rule independently in lieu of the normal allegiance to the Persian emperors.

The Macedonian invasion led by Alexander was the second foreign invasion. Greek writers wove a halo of romance round the name of Alexander, but his Indian invasion had no permanent result, except that it opened up communication between Greece and India and paved the way for a more intimate intercourse with the west. Alexander divided his Indian conquests into seven satrapies, three of which were given to his Indian assistants. The only tangible consequence of Alexander's invasion was the annihilation of the tribal settlements of north-western India. The new beneficiaries, the Indian princes who helped the invader, could not hold these for a long time and eventually the states of the northwestern region and their tribal dependencies came under the political authority of the Mauryas.

The Haryaṅka dynasty, which under Bimbisāra and Ajātaśatru laid the foundation of a future empire ruled in Magadha between c. 544 and 430 B.C. The next dynasty was that of Śiśunāga and his successor during whose time (430-364 B.C.) Avanti, Vatsa and Kosala were incorporated with Magadha. The third dynasty was that of the Nandas who ruled between c. 364 and 324 B.C. The Purāṇas credit the Nandas for conquering the territories of the Aikṣvākus, Pañcālas, Kāśis, Haihayas, Kaliṅgas, Aśmakas, Kurus, Maithilas, Śurasenas and Vītihotras. There may be some exaggeration in the Puranic statement but from epigraphic evidence it appears that the Nandas did hold sway over the Kaliṅga country as far as the Godāvarī and the Kuntala region which comprised parts of Karnataka and Maharashtra. Greek writers refer to the Nandas as masters of the Gangaridae (peoples of the Gangetic region) and Prasii (Prācyas or Easterners) having all the military might and mastery of a large empire but lacking in strength and popularity.

The Nandas were eventually exterminated by a tribal chief Candragupta (324-300 B.C.) of the Moriya (Maurya) clan of

Pipphalivana. Taking advantage of the unsettled position of the Indian dominions of Alexander after the latter's death, Candragupta made himself master of Punjab and Sind. Around 305 B.C. Seleucus, the successor of Alexander in the eastern part of his empire, tried to regain the lost Greek possessions, but had to purchase peace by ceding to Candragupta territories then known as Aria (Herat), Arachosia (Kandhahar), Paropanisadae (Kabul) and parts of Gedrosia (Baluchistan). The Saurāṣṭra region was under his occupation and there is evidence to show that a considerable portion of the Deccan and south India was under his direct political influence. Thus Candragupta may be regarded as the first empire builder in India. Since Candragupta's son Bindusāra (300-273 B.C.) is not known as a conquerer and since Aśoka's inscriptions credit him only with the conquest of the Kaliṅgas, it may be inferred that the Mauryan occupation of southern India took place during the lifetime of Candragupta.

2. *Aśoka: The Policy of Dharmavijaya*

Aśoka (273-236 B.C.), the next Mauryan king, has been regarded as one of the greatest rulers of human history. Far more than an average enlightened despot this 'greatest of kings', as H.G. Wells called him, was the first founder of a welfare state based on broad-minded principles who declared in emphatic terms that all men were his children. He was the first and last Indian emperor to issue edicts in order to proclaim his ideas of statehood, political principles, the administrative set-up, laws of individual and social behaviour, the gospel of religious toleration and norms of ethics pertaining to society at large. The geographical distribution of his inscriptions shows that except for a few districts of the far South and the Assam region in the east, the rest of India was under his influence. His Rock Edicts, comprising a set of fourteen inscriptions, have been found incised at eight places—Shahbazgarhi, Manshera, Kalsi, Girnar, Sopara, Dhauli, Jaugada and Yerragudi. His Minor Rock Edicts are a set of two inscriptions incised at different places, such as Rupnath, Bairat, Sasaram, Maski, Gavimath, Palkigundu, Gujarra, Arhaur, Amarapuri, Rajula Mandagiri, Yerragudi and Chitaldroog. His Pillar Edicts are a set of seven inscriptions found at Topra, Ambala and Meerut district, Kausambi near Allahabad, Sanchi, Sarnath, Lauriya Araraj, Rampurwa, Nandangarh and Nigliva. Two inscriptions in Aramaic characters have been discovered at Taxila and Jalalabad. A bilingual inscription in Greek and Aramaic and another only in Greek have been discovered at Kandahar. While the distribution of these inscriptions undoubtedly points to his great influence over a vast region, it does not necessarily mean that the entire region indicated by the inscriptions was under his direct rule.

Since Aśoka became a celebrated character in history, Buddhist writers have woven numerous legends around his person to prove the greatness of Buddhism. By doing so, a ruthless Aśoka was transformed into a saintly Aśoka. According to the Sanskrit Buddhist tradition Aśoka was a sadist who got pleasure by torturing and slaying others; he eventually became repentant and was converted to Buddhism by the venerable monk Upagupta. The Pali Buddhist tradition charges him with the killing of his brothers and claims that he had his sins expiated by being initiated into Buddhism by Moggaliputta Tissa. It is difficult, however, to say whether Aśoka was a confirmed Buddhist. He might have been influenced by certain Buddhist ideals, occasionally visited the Saṅgha and patronised the system, but this does not mean that he was really a Buddhist, notwithstanding the claims of later Chinese and Tibetan writers. It is a fact that the Third Buddhist Council was held at Pāṭaliputra during his time at which a programme had been adopted to depute missionaries to different countries outside India. As the king, Aśoka must have extended his patronage to make the council of grand success, but this does not prove that Aśoka was a part of it particularly in view of the fact that the council was of the Theravādins. It is not plausible that a king like Aśoka who preached the doctrine of religious toleration should have any sectarian affiliation.

By the eighth year after his coronation Aśoka had exterminated the Kaliṅgas. It was not unusual for the head of a powerful state to occupy the adjacent tribal territories and recast the tribal societies in the service of the state as a policy of expansion—a policy which has been neatly outlined by Bhīṣma in the *Mahābhārata* and Kauṭilya in the *Arthaśāstra*, both of whom have categorically observed that the existence of the *saṅghas* or *gaṇas*, i.e., tribal systems, is always a threat to the ideals of a state. The universal experience is that detribalisation takes place in two ways—internally due to different socio-economic conditions and externally due to onslaught from neighbouring state power. Like his predecessors—Ajātaśatru or Alexander or Candragupta—Aśoka also followed the second way which was natural for any aspiring king. But there was the problem of tribal resistance. The Vajjians fought tooth and nail against Ajātaśatru; Alexander was stubbornly resisted by the tribals. The extermination of the Kaliṅgas was achieved at a very high cost. Aśoka has himself stated in his Rock Edict XIII: "One hundred and fifty thousand were therefrom captured, one hundred thousand were there slain, and many times as many died." Evidently this carnage could not have been one-sided.

It is against this background that Aśoka's policy of *dharmavijaya*, i.e., conquest through peaceful means, is to be understood and evaluated. It was a means by which the hostile and unruly tribes were sought to be brought into the fold of the expanding state power voluntarily. Any type of imperialism or expansionism needs the pretext of certain ideals for its justification. The traditional method of conquest by force appeared to Aśoka to be inconsistent with the reality of his time and hence he required an ideal, a new state theory which was likely to inspire the neighbouring peoples to transcend the narrow limits of their isolated group-life and to develop a broad and nationalistic approach albeit under the shadow of the Maurya empire. He sought to achieve this by promoting the concepts of a welfare state, the paternal ruler, religious tolerance and an ideal society run on ethical principles. To popularise these concepts he made mass contact through a well-organised publicity medium which he invented. Not only did he get numerous edicts containing his message inscribed and placed in different parts of his empire but he also appointed a class of officials called *dharma-mahāmātras* whose job was to spread the message of the Dharma to the remotest corners of his empire. An open reference to the tribes is found in his R.E. XIII: "Here in the king's dominions, among the Yavanas and Kambojas, the Nābhakas and Nābhapanthis, the Bhojas, Andhras, and Pariṃdas, everywhere they follow the teaching of the beloved of the gods in respect of Dharma." Aśoka was also eager that the neighbouring kings should also appreciate and adopt his viewpoint and course of action. He sent missions to Antiochus Theos of Syria and also to other Greek kings who ruled in Egypt, Macedonia, Cyrene and Epirus.

"All my subjects are my children," is the expression of the paternal concept of rulership on which Aśoka insisted. The administration of his welfare state was, however, planned in a bureaucratic model. In his inscription Aśoka states frankly that his policy is one of conciliation towards all. It is difficult to determine to what extent the policy of Aśoka was successful in bringing the whole of this vast subcontinent, comprising numerous communities with varying degrees of material, mental and intellectual attainments, under an organised and orderly pro-national framework without destroying their ethnic and cultural identity by force. The problem which Aśoka had to confront persists, though in a different way, in India even today, and it is impossible to conceive of means other than a non-violent and ideological approach by which it can be tackled. The problem of maintaining the cultural identity of different developed, semi-developed and undeveloped social groups was partially solved by the elaborate growth of the caste system. But, as we have seen, this system generally encouraged allegiance to the localised group or community and not to the broader entity of the state as a whole. The law-givers of India had tried to include both the aspects in a single framework. On the one hand, they insisted on the Aśokan concept of paternal rulership and, on the other, they suggested that the king should maintain *varṇāśrama* or the traditional caste system so that the cultural identity of different social groups is not shaken. The Aśokan concept of a value-oriented political system was later accepted and supported by the writers of the Dharma and Artha Śāstras, all of whom insisted on the rule of law and not of command.

3. *The Post-Mauryan Age: Kings and Feudatories* (200-30 B.C.)

The Mauryas were able to build up a vast empire, but it does not mean that they conquered every inch of land they held under their control, or that the empire was under their direct administration even though they had a few provincial governors of their own. For example, Aśoka was the governor of Taxila during his father's rule. In Candragupta's time there was a governor in Saurāṣṭra. But, it was customary, especially in the case of smaller powers, to acknowledge—willingly or unwillingly—the suzerainty of a big power and to continue on their own way by offering a token submission. The latter tradition was more effective in the subsequent political history of India.

After the fall of the Mauryas, the Śuṅga clan ruled in Magadha. The first ruler was Puṣyamitra (187-151 B.C.) whose kingdom comprised the cities of Pāṭaliputra, Ayodhyā and Vidiśā as well as the Jālandhara and Sākala regions of Punjab. While still a general of the Mauryas, Puṣyamitra resisted Greek invasions at Sāketa (Ayodhyā or Oudh) and Madhyamikā (near Chitor in Rajasthan). He had to face a second Greek invasion during his region which was resisted by his grandson Vasumitra on the lower Sindhu. Puṣyamitra is said to have performed the Aśvamedha ritual twice in order to achieve symbolic recognition of universal sovereignty.

Puṣyamitra was succeeded by his son Agnimitra but no event of his reign is known to us except the fact that during the reign of his father, when he was acting as his viceroy at Vidisā in central India, there was a dispute over the Vidarbha region between two Śuṅga feudatories which required his armed interference. The tenth and last Śunga king Devabhūti was killed by his minister Vāsudeva about 75 B.C. who founded the Kāṇva line of kings in Magadha. Four kings of this line—Vāsudeva, Bhūmimitra, Nārāyaṇa and Suśarman—ruled for a period of 45 years. According to the Purāṇas, the Kānvas were exterminated by the Andhrabhṛtyas or Andhras.

Two princes, Indrāgnimitra and Bṛhasvātimitra, are mentioned in the epigraphs belonging to the Śuṅga period. It is learnt that one Āṣāḍhasena, who was the maternal uncle of Bṛhasvātimitra, had excavated a cave at Pavosa near Allahabad during the tenth regnal year of Udaka, supposed to be the same as the Śuṅga King Bhadraka. These princes might have been relations of the Śuṅgas ruling as vassals over some small principalities. Coins with names of rulers ending in *mitra* have been found over a vast region of northern India. They might have been scions of the Śuṅga and Kāṇva clans who, after the decline of the main branches, ruled over small holdings.

4. *The Foreign Hordes: Relation between Kings and Clan Leaders*

At the beginning of the second century B.C. Demitrius, son of Euthydemus and ruler of Bactria, led an invasion within India proper and was able to occupy a few territories in the north-west. Some time after 165 B.C. the Indian territory occupied by Demitrius was conquered by one Eucratides. While Greek rule in Bactria ended in 140 B.C. it was continued in Afghanistan and northwestern India. Names of more than thirty rulers, mostly clansmen of Eucratides and Demitrius, have been found from coins, but it is impossible to understand their mutual relations and the time and place of their rule. Among those who have been identified is Menander whose coins have been found in Kabul, Sind, Gujarat and Uttar Pradesh. His name has also been found in a Kharosthi inscription from Bajaur near the confluence of the Panjkora and the Swat. He probably ruled between 115 and 90 B.C. and is often identified with king Milinda of the Buddhist text *Milindapañha*. The name of another Greek ruler—Antalcidas—is found on a column at Besnagar which was inscribed by his ambassador Heliodorus of Taxila in honour of Lord Vāsudeva. The end of Greek rule was caused by the invasions of the Scythians, Parthians and Kuṣāṇas. The Eucratedan rulers of Taxila and Puṣkalāvatī were exterminated by Saka Maues (20 B.C.-A.D. 22). Greek rule in Kabul valley was ended by the Parthian Gondophernes (A.D. 21-50).

So far as the Greek coins are concerned, which created the problem of accommodating so many kings and rulers within a short span of time, the most likely explanation is that they ruled over various small areas almost independently. One should not fail to recall in this connection that not all the Greeks lived in Greece proper. Rather, they were Asiatic Greeks. The poet Homer himself belonged to Asia minor. As in Greece proper so also in western Asia, the character of the state was not the same everywhere. The Asiatic Greeks during Alexander's campaign were still in a tribal stage. When the tribal chiefs received their share of the conquered territories of the Macedonian invader they became kings in the new set-up. The tribal kinship ties, however, were not broken. Thus when a relation of the king—the local ruler belonging to his own tribe—issued coins in his own name it was not regarded by the king as a case of transgressing or challenging his authority.

The Sakas, or Scythians of central Asia, in the course of their migration settled in Iran where they intermingled with the Pahlavas or Parthians. The Pahlava chief Mithradates (c. 171-136 B.C.) occupied Herat and Kandahar region. Later Vonones, a Pahlava chief of eastern Iran, came into prominence and occupied southern Afghanistan. After the termination of his rule in c. 20 B.C., a Saka chief called Moga or Maues (20 B.C.-A.D. 22) consolidated his power, occupied Gandhāra and advanced as far as Mathura. He was succeeded by Azes I (c. A.D. 5-28) who exterminated the Greeks from the Punjab region. Azes I was succeeded by Azilises (A.D. 28-40) and the latter by Azes II (A.D. 40-79). While the Sakas were thus gaining a foothold in India proper, there was a revival of Pahlava power under Gondophernes (c. A.D. 21-50) who had defeated Harmeus, the last Indo-Greek king of Kabul. The Takht-i-Bahi inscription testifies his Indian conquest which included the areas held by Azes II.

In the case of the Sakas and Pahlavas it is found that a number of rulers have been associated with the king. The king and the crown prince may rule at the same time and their coins may contain both names. But there are cases, as is found in the coins of Gondophernes, when the associated rulers are many, all being mentioned in the coins while none are known to have been blood-relations. Others who are associated with Gondophernes in his coins are his nephew Abdagases who was the ruler of Seistan and Kandahar, two other rulers Sapedana and Satavastra and his generals Aspavarman and Sasa. Among these persons Sapedana and Satavastra assumed the title *mahārāja-dhirāja* which shows that their allegiance to Gondophernes was purely formal. Aspavarman had also figured in the coins of Azes II. This indicates that previously he was a local ruler in some part of northwestern India under Azes II and that he subsequently changed his allegiance.

The history of the Kuṣāṇas may throw some light on the development of such features. Like the Sakas and the Pahlavas, the Yueh-chis or Kuṣāṇas were a pure tribe. About 165 B.C. when they began to migrate in different directions and settle permanently in certain regions, there was no institution of kingship among them. They were divided into five clans, each under a Yabuga or chief. One of these chiefs, Kujula Kadphises, in the course of time put an end to this clan-rule by subduing the four other groups and assumed the title of a king. Here the process of transition from tribal settlement to state took a period of less than a hundred years. Needless to say that the same process held good in the case of the Sakas and Pahlavas.

Notwithstanding such changes the tribal customs did not disappear all of a sudden. The time taken depended on the strength of tribal ties; where it was not so strong the royal line was easily established—the king, his son and grandson. But where the ties were stronger, the tribal chief, raised to the rank of the king had usually to accommodate the other 'clan-leaders' in administration and coinage. This is the only explanation for the problem of the existence of so many rulers along with the king on the coins of the Sakas and Pahlavas.

5. *The Kuṣāṇa Empire* : *Central Asian Horizon* (A.D. 15-176)

The Kuṣāṇas were one of the five branches of the Yueh-chi tribe. According to the Chinese annals Kio-sio-kio or Kujula Kadphises (A.D. 15-55) subdued the four branches of the Yueh-chi, occupied Ngan-si (a region in Parthia), Kao-fu (Kabul), Po-ta (a place near Kabul) and Ki-pin (Kafiristan and adjacent areas) and assumed the titles of sovereignty. A few of his coins on the obverse bear the name of Harmeus, the Greek ruler of Kabul and on the reverse the legend in Kharosthi meaning "of the Kuṣāṇa chief Kujula Kasa who is steadfast in Law." It appears that Kujula initially had acknowledged the sovereignty of Harmeus and took the latter's help in subduing the four other Yueh-chi clans. But Harmeus was defeated and killed by the Pahlava chief Gondophernes. After the death of Gondophernes about A.D. 50 Kujula defeated the Pahlavas and occupied the territories previously ruled by them. That Kujula was a follower of Buddhism is indicated by his epithet *saca-dharma-thita.*

Kujula was succeeded by his son Yen-Kao-Chen, also known as Vima Kadphises, whose territory comprised part of north-western India, the Tien-chou region of the Chinese annals. The reverse of his coins shows the Śiva emblem with the legend: "of Vima Kadphisa, the great king, king of kings, lord of all people, lord of the earth (or devotee of Maheśvara) the saviour." Coins of a nameless king containing the Greek legend *basileus basileuon sotar megas* (king of kings, the great saviour) have been recovered from Punjab, Kandahar and the Kabul valley. On some coins there is exact Indian rendering of this legend in Kharosthi : *maharajasa-rajadhirajasa-mahatasa-tratarasa.* This unknown king with the title 'great saviour" has been identified by some with Vima Kadphises. Others think that these coins should be ascribed to the nameless Kuṣāṇa king or kings of the Panjtar and Taxila inscriptions of A.D. 65 and 79 respectively.

Vima Kadphises must have died before A.D. 78 when the entire Kuṣāṇa territory came to the hands of Kaṇiṣka, the greatest king of the Kuṣāṇas. It is not known what was the exact relation of Kaṇiṣka with Vima Kadphises so far as dynastic lineage is concerned. From epigraphic evidence it is known that Kaṇiṣka ruled over a vast region. His empire comprised the North Western Frontier province, the Bhawalpur region to the north of Sind, the entire Punjab region and most parts of the present Uttar Pradesh. Apart from his numerous inscriptions that have been found in the Mathura region, the inscriptions of his successors, the Chinese and Tibetan sources, as well as the testimony of Al-Bīrūnī's book show that the sphere of his influence was indeed very wide. Outside India proper, the region from Balkh to the Tarim basin was under his control. Hiuen Tsang wrote that he conquered as far as the Sung-ling ranges.

Kaṇiṣka's mastery over the Tarim basin and its adjoining regions is attested by the evidence of his coins which show a variety of deities belonging to different nationalities. Some of these deities are the Iranian gods Waodo, Mao, Mihira, the Sumerian goddess Nana, the Greek god Helios, etc. In his vast kingdom different peoples followed different cults and for obvious political reason Kaṇiṣka had to recognise all of them. Personally he was a Buddhist. From an epigraph it is known that Kaṇiṣka had convened a Buddhist council in Kashmir. Some sources refer to Jālandhara or Gandhāra as its venue. This was the fourth Buddhist council in which the Sarvāstivāda school gained prominence. Kaṇiṣka must have contributed to the expansion of Sarvāstivāda form of Buddhism in central Asia. A few sites on the roads from Kashgar to China have yielded archaeological remains which include ruined cities with hundreds of sanctuaries, images, wall-paintings, manuscripts, etc., and clearly demonstrate that Indians settled in large numbers all over this region. To a great extent the spread of Indian culture and religion in central Asia was due to the Kuṣāṇa occupation of this region.

The Tarim basin, also known as Chinese Turkestan, lies immediately to the west of China, to the north of which is the Tien Shan and to the West the Pamir mountains. In the south the Kun-lun range and in the east the Nan Shan range separate it from the plateau of Tibet and China respectively. Towards the end of his life Kaṇiṣka fought a futile war to the east of the Nan Shan range against the Chinese. According to the Chinese annals he was defeated by the Chinese general Pan-chao and was obliged to pay tribute to the Chinese emperor Ho-ti.

Historians do not agree in regard to the date of Kaṇiṣka. It is generally assumed that the era introduced by Kaṇiṣka was no other than the Saka era beginning from A.D. 78. This date is supported by the Chinese evidence. Kaṇiṣka was succeeded by Vāsiska : his coins belonging to A.D. 102-106 have been recovered from Mathura and Bhopal. Vāsiska's successor Huviska (A.D. 106-138) ruled jointly for sometime with the former. From his Wardhak inscription it is evident that his control extended over the Kabul area. A variety of deities, belonging to different countries outside India, occur on his coins. The last important Kuṣāṇa king was Vāsudeva who ruled between A.D. 145 and 176.

6. *Regional Powers* (A.D. 100-200)

The lower Sindhu region, western Rajasthan, Gujarat and parts of Maharashtra were ruled by the Saka Kṣatrapas in the first century of the Christian era. For some time they acknowledged the authority of the Kuṣāṇās but later they became independent. Bhūmaka and Nahapāna of the Kṣaharāta clan of the Sakas were able to build up a powerful kingdom in western India. The latter assumed the title *mahākṣatrapa.* About A.D. 124-25 Nahapāna was defeated and killed by the Sātavāhana king Gautamīputra who annexed his southern territories. After Nahapāna another Saka clan known as the Kārdamaka became powerful in western India under Caṣṭana who later assumed the title of *mahākṣatrapa.* He ruled jointly with his grandson Rudradāman as is indicated by an inscription of A.D. 130-31 found at Andhau in Kutch. Rudradāman whose Junagarh inscription was composed about A.D. 150-51 defeated the Sātavāhanas and reconquered the lost territories held by Nahapāna. The Junagarh inscription describes him as the lord of Ākara, Avantī, Anupa, Aparānta, Saurāṣṭra and Ānarta. The capital of the Kārdamaka Śakas was Ujjayinī. There was a steady decline of Saka power after the death of Rudradāman; internal strife was mainly responsible for their downfall.

While the Kuṣāṇas and the Sakas were ruling respectively in northern and western India, a major portion of the Deccan was ruled by the Sātavāhana clan which was an offshoot of the ancient Andhra tribe. Under Simuka, Kṛṣṇa and Sātakarṇi I the Sātavāhanas rose to prominence between 30 B.C. and A.D. 30. They became masters of the Deccan and parts of western India under Gautamīputra Sātakarṇi (A.D. 106-130). Gautamīputra's outstanding achievement was the extirpation of the Kṣaharāta clan to which the Saka chief Nahapāna belonged. His inscriptions in the Nasik and Poona districts show how Nahapāna's viceroy, Ṛṣabhadatta, was ousted by him from the southern provinces of the Kṣaharāta dominions. Of the territories which were under Gautamīputra's rule according to the Nasik inscription, Aparānta (northern Konkan), Anupa (the Māndhātā or Maheswar region on the Narmada), Ākara (east Malwa), Surāṣṭra (Saurashtra), Kukura (a locality in the Gujarat region) and Avantī (west Malwa) were conquered from Nahapāna. Apart from these territories Gautamīputra held sway over Ṛṣika (the district around Ṛṣika-nagara on the

Krishna), Aśmaka (territory about Bodhan in Andhra Pradesh), Mūlaka (with Pratiṣṭhāna, modern Paithan on the Godāvarī as its capital) and Vidarbha (the Berar region). Thus Gautamīputra's claim to have been the lord of the Vindhya, Ṛksavat (portion of the Vindhyan range to the south of Malwa), Pāriyātra (western Vindhya), Sahya (Western Ghats), Malaya (Travancore hills) and Mahendra (Eastern Ghats) was not without foundation. His epithets like *tri-samudra-toya-pīta vāhana* (one whose charges drank the waters of the three seas), *śaka-yavana-pahlava nisūdana* (destroyer of the Sakas, Yavanas and Pahlavas) and *sātavāhana-kula-yasaḥ-pratiṣṭhāpana-kara* (establisher of the fame of the Sātavāhana clan) were not mere feats of boasting. Towards the close of his reign Gautamīputra lost most of the territories he had conquered from the Kṣaharāta Sakas. This is proved by the evidence of the Junagarh rock inscription of Rudradāman of the Kārdamaka Saka clan which says that most of the provinces which Gautamīputra had previously conquered from Nahapāna were reconquered by Mahākṣatrapa Rudradāman who was then acting as the collaborator of his aged grandfather. This is also indirectly supported by a Sātavāhana inscription from Kanheri which indicates that Gautamīputra tried to save a few of the conquered territories by arranging the marriage of his son with a daughter of the Mahākṣatrapa. The Sātavāhana kingdom which rose from a tribal principality to the level of a powerful state by the efforts of Gautamīputra, survived up to the middle of the third century A.D.

In the east about the end of the first century B.C., the country known after the Kaliṅgas, which comprised parts of the present Cuttack, Puri and Ganjam districts of Orissa, became powerful under Mahārāja Khāravela, the events of whose life are recorded in the Hathigumpha inscription. He led an expedition to the southwest crossing the Ṛṣika country on the Krishna, subdued the Rāṣṭrikas and Bhojakas, destroyed Gorathagiri, a fortress in the Barabar hills, attacked Rājagṛha, defeated Bhasātimitra, the king of Magadha, and a Yavana king known by the name of Dimita, destroyed the city of Pṛthuda near Masulipatam and went as far as the Pāṇḍya country in the far South. A devout Jain, Khāravela had assumed the title of Kaliṅgādhipati or Kaliṅga Cakrāvartī. After Khāravela Kaliṅga lost much of its political influence.

Though the demarcation line between the Deccan and south India varied from time to time, the ancient concept of south India as a geopolitical unit comprised the region south of the river Krishna which was known from the earliest time to have been divided into three tribal territories—Cola on the Kaveri delta and the adjoining area, Pāṇḍya to the south of it and Cera extending along the west coast. The Colas came into prominence in the first century B.C. under their chief Karikāla who brought about political unity of the entire south by defeating the joint forces of the Pāṇḍyas and Ceras in the battle of Venni near Tanjore. Early Tamil literature credits him with the conquest of the whole of India, which surely is an exaggeration. It is a fact, though, that he conquered Ceylon, he brought 12,000 Ceylonese captives and put them to work in the sea port town of Puhar. He is also credited to have controlled the river Kaveri for the purpose of irrigation. Like Cola Karikala, the Pāṇḍya chief Neduñjaḷiyan, whose exact date is not known, has been credited with exterminating a powerful hostile confederacy of the Colas and Ceras at the battle of Talaiyālaṅgām. The Ceras joined the Pāṇḍyas against the Colas and the Colas against the Pāṇḍyas as it suited them. However, none of the Cera chiefs achieved the political celebrity either of Karikāla or of Neduñjaḷiyan.

7. Tribal Principalities and Feudatories of the Pre-Gupta Period

While in the case of the Mauryas, Śuṅgas, Sakas, Pahlavas, Kuṣāṇas, Sātavāhanas and other ruling dynasties we come across a political process in which the tribal leaders having assumed effective political power introduced dynastic rule and monarchical form of state system and wrecked the existing tribal institutions from within, there were a few cases in which the tribes could maintain their identity and follow their own political and administrative system, though under heavy pressure from the expanding state powers. In north India, a few tribes came into prominence after the decline of Kuṣāṇa power. From the coins of the Ārjunāyanas it appears that their territory lay in the Bharatpur and Alwar region of Rajasthan and the western areas of Agra and Mathura. Previously they were under the Sakas and the Kuṣāṇas and after a short-lived independence, they again came under the dependency of the Guptas. The Mālavas originally lived in the Punjab region and subsequently migrated to Rajasthan. Their new centre of power was Mālavanagara in the Uniyar locality of Jaipur. In the socond century they fought against the Uttamabhadras of Ajmer and also against the Sakas. One of their branches, the Aulikaras, became powerful in the Mandasore region to which clan belonged the celebrated Yaśodharman. In the fourth century A.D. the Mālavas came under the dependency of the Guptas. The Yaudheyas had settlements in eastern Punjab, parts of Rajasthan and Uttar Pradesh. Their coins and inscriptions have also been found. From the evidence of the Junagarh inscription of Rudradāman it appears that they fought against the Sakas. Like other tribes of northern India, the Yaudheyas also came under the sway of the Guptas.

Apart from the tribes there were also a number of small states powers, with a transparent tribal background, in post-Kuṣāṇa north India which were later exterminated by the Guptas. For example, there were a number of Nāga feudatories of the Kuṣāṇas, ruling in different parts of central and northern India, whose coins have been found in abundance. Some of them changed their allegiance while the others, being defeated, had to cede their territories to the imperial Guptas. From the Gupta inscriptions it is known that there were four Nāga dynasties at Vidisa, Kantipura, Mathura and Padmavati respectively. In the list of kings of northern India routed by Samudragupta occur two Nāga kings, Gaṇapatināga and Nāgasena. From Ahicchatra, Ramnagar in the Bareily district of Uttar Pradesh, a few copper coins containing the name of a king called Acyuta have been found. He may be the same as the king Acyuta of the Allahabad pillar inscription who was defeated by Samudragupta.

Coins of local rulers with the surnames *mitra* and *datta* have been found in the Mathura region. These rulers were vassals of the Kuṣāṇas and flourished about the second century A.D. after the extirpation of the Śakas of Mathura. Coins of the Kuṣāṇa feudatories, with names of local rulers ending in *mitra*, *pāla* and *gupta*, have been found in Ahicchatra. Those from Ayodhya contain names of vassals ending in *deva, datta, mitra, varman* and *sena.* The records of the later rulers of Kausambi contain references to the Saka era introduced by Kaṇiṣka. The Māgha feudatories of the Kuṣāṇas in the Kausambi region attained some degree of prominence.

The Ābhīras were feudatories of the Sakas. After the decline of the Sakas they declared independence in northwestern Deccan. The Ābhīra chief Māṭhariputra Īśvarasena extended his sway over the Nasik region where his inscription has been found. That the Ābhīras continued to remain as an independent power even in the fourth century A.D. is proved by the Candravalli inscription which refers to their fight with the Kadamba chief Mayuraśarman. They were subjugated by Samudragupta. The Bodhis were also feudatories of the Sakas. They founded a principality in northwest Deccan in the third century A.D. Their coins refer to the names of Śivabodhi, Candrabodhi and Vīrabodhi. The Bṛhatphalāyanas were feudatories of the Sātavāhanas and later of the Ikṣvākus. In the Masulipatam region, in the Bandar subdivision of the Krishna district, they established a principality. The Kondamuni inscription refers to a chief of this tribe, named Jayavarman. The Ikṣvākus were also feudatories of the Sātavāhanas. They established a powerful kingdom in the third century A.D. in the region between the Krishna and the Godavari under Śāntamūla I, Māṭhariputra Vīrapuruṣadatta and Ehuvula Śāntamūla II. The territories of the Bṛhatphalāyanas and Ikṣvākus later came under the Pallavas of Kanchi. In northwestern Deccan and parts of Madhya Pradesh the Vākātakas became powerful under Vindhyaśakti and Pravarasena I in the third century. Previously they were also feudatories of the Sātavāhanas.

8. *The Imperial Guptas* (A.D. 320-467)

The first three kings of the Gupta dynasty were Śrīgupta Ghaṭotkachagupta and Candragupta I. The Chinese traveller I-tsing recorded that five hundred years before his arrival, one king Śrīgupta had made a religious endowment in Magadha for the sake of the Chinese pilgrims. This Śrīgupta might have been the same as the founder of the Gupta royal dynasty. I-tsing, however, was confused in regard to the date of Śrīgupta.

Nothing is known about Ghatoṭkachagupta, but it is interesting to note that he is mentioned as the founder of the Gupta royal dynasty in an inscription of Prabhāvatiguptā and also in an inscription found at Rewa.

The third king, Candragupta I, was a sovereign monarch as is proved by his epithet *mahārājādhirāja* and the gold coins issued by him, the obverse of which depicts the king and his queen Kumāradevī and the reverse the likeness of a lion-mounted goddess with the inscription Licchavi, to which tribe Kumāradevī belonged. One should recall too that Candragupta's son Samudragupta described himself as the grandson of the Licchavis. It appears that Candragupta gained Licchavi territory on his marriage with its heiress. The date of his accession was 26 February A.D. 320.

We are not sure about the extent of Candragupta's kingdom. The Purāṇas contain a verse which says that the Guptas were rulers of Sāketa, Prayāga and Magadha. Some scholars hold that Candragupta's kingdom comprised these three regions. From the accounts of Samudragupta's conquests, it appears that the Guptas originally ruled in Bihar and parts of Bengal and Uttar Pradesh.

From the Allahabad pillar inscription of Samudragupta it is learnt that Candragutpa I made him the heir to his kingdom during his lifetime. Samudragupta is said to have exterminated nine kings of northern India. Among these nine kings were Nāgasena and Gaṇapatināga belonging to the Nāga clans which ruled in Mathura, Vidisa, Kantipura and Padmavati. However it is difficult to say precisely to which region these two Nāga kings belonged. Two other kings defeated by Samudragupta, Acyuta and Candravarman, ruled in Ahicchatra and the Bankura region of West Bengal respectively. The territories of the five other kings—Rudradeva Matila, Nāgadatta, Nandī and Balavarman—are not known. Some hold that Rudradeva might have been the Saka Kṣatrapa Rudrāman II or his son Rudrasena III. Attempts have been made to locate the territory of Nāgadatta in north Bengal but such identifications have no real basis.

Although the territories of the nine rulers of northern India which were annexed by Samudragupta to his kingdom have not been properly identified, the Allahabad Praśasti refers to the border states, the rulers of which acknowledged his authority, which helps us to determine the extent of Samudragupta's empire in northern India. There were five such border states, namely, Samataṭa (south eastern Bengal), Kāmarūpa (northern Assam), Nepal, Ḍabāka (the Nowgong region of Assam) and Katṛpura (Kartaṛpur in the Jullundhar district of Punjab).

Apart from the nine rulers of northern India and five rulers of the border states, there were nine tribes which offered submission to Samudragupta. These were the Mālavas who lived in eastern Rajasthan, especially in the Mewar, Tonk and Kota region; the Ārjunāyanas who lived in Jaipur and its adjacent areas; the Yaudheyas who lived on both banks of the Sutlej but whose territory extended up to the Yamuna including the Bharatpur area; the Madrakas who lived in the region between the Ravi and the Chenab and whose capital was at Sakala or Sialkot; the Sanakānikas who lived in the region around Bhilsa; the Ābhīras who lived in the region between Bhilsa and Jhansi; the Prārjunas, Kākas and Kharapārikas who lived in different parts of present Madhya Pradesh.

The Allahabad pillar inscription also refers to the southern conquests of Samudragupta in the course of which he is said to have defeated and humbled twelve kings of the southern region. But he was satisfied with their submission and did not annex their territories to his own kingdom for political and administrative reasons. These twelve kings were Mahendra of Kosala (southern Kosala comprising the modern districts of Durg, Raipur, Bilaspur and Sambalpur); Vyāghrarāja of Mahākāntāra (the wild area of the Jaipur region of Orissa); Mahendragiri of Piṣṭapur (Pithapuram in the modern Godavari district); Hastivarman of Veṅgī (the Sālaṅkāyana chief ruling between the Godavari and the Krishna with capital at Peddavegi near modern railway station of Elluru); Ugrasena of Pālakka (modern Nellore district in Andhra Pradesh); Dāmana of Eraṇḍapalla (either on the fringe of Ganjam district, or Erguntapalle in the West Godavari district or Erandol in Khandesh, these identifications being by no means certain); Kubera of Devarāṣṭra (a part in the Vizagapatam or Satara district, often also identified with the whole of Maharashtra); Mantarāja of Kaurāla (often identfied with Cherla in the east Godavari district); Svāmidatta of Koṭṭura (often identified with Kothur in the Vizagapatam district or with Kudligi in Bellary district or with Kothru in the East Godavari district); Nīlarāja of Avamukta and Dhanañjaya of Kusthalapura (both the places have not been identified).

Although most of the southern territories overrun by Samudragupta have not been properly identified, it appears that he made a straight southward march from the eastern part of Madhya Pradesh adjoining Orissa and then occupied the entire region now represented by Andhra Pradesh and Tamil Nadu. But he did not incorporate these territories within his kingdom. The Saka Kṣatrapas of Western India already maintained a submissive political relationship with him. So did the Kuṣāṇa king of western Punjab and Afghanistan whose title was Daivaputra Sāhī-Sāhānusāhī. Acccording to Chinese sources, a Yueh-chi chief named Ki-to-lo established an independent kingdom in the frontier region. On some coins of northwestern India the name of one Kidār-Kuṣāṅ-Shāh is found. This king was probably the same as Ki-to-lo of the Chinese sources and Daivaputra Sahi-Sāhānusāhi of Allahabad pillar inscription. From Chinese sources it is learnt that Meghavarṇa (A.D. 352-79), king of Ceylon, sought his permission to establish a monastery for the Ceylonese monks at Bodhgaya. The Allahabad pillar inscription refers to Samudragupta as a poet and musician which is attested also by the evidence on his coins. He was a follower of Brahmanical religion and performed the Aśvamedha ritual in honour of which he issued a special type of coin. Samudragupta passed away in A.D. 380.

When Candragupta II succeeded his father Samudragupta, almost the whole of northern India was under the possession of the Guptas. The border states of the north, east and west acknowledged the sovereignty of Samudragupta. So did the southern states. The Saka rulers of western India and the Vākātakas of Maharashtra were independent though they maintained diplomatic relations with him. Samudragupta was not in favour of territorial expansion because of administrative difficulties.

A change of policy, however, is observed during the reign of Candragupta II. He annexed to the Gupta empire the Saka territories of western India and transgressed the borderlands of northwestern India. This he did evidently in the interest of foreign trade. He required direct control of the ports on the western coast of India and that is why he had to fight with the Sakas. For the same reason he had to go as far as Bactria or the Bāhlika country. During the reign of Candragupta II the decline of the Roman empire had already set in hampering foreign trade both by land and by sea. It should be noted in this connection that within India proper he avoided warfare. The Vākātakas were a rising power in the Deccan, but he did not fight with them. Rather he had given his daughter Prabhavatīguptā in marriage with the Vākātaka king Rudrasena II and established friendly relations with them. From an inscription of Kākutsthavarman, the Kadamba chief of Kuntala, it is known that they had also matrimonial relation with the Guptas.

Making Malwa his base, and probably with the help of the Vākātakas, Candragupta II invaded the territory of the Sakas. In this connection we have three inscriptions. The first is at Udayagiri near Bhilsa inscribed by his minister Vīrasena; the second in the same region inscribed by one of his feudatories and third at Sanchi inscribed by his general Āmrakardava. The Saka chief, Rudrasiṃha III, was defeated and his kingdom passed to the Guptas some time after A.D. 409.

The inscription of Āmrakardava and another by his minister Śāba describe him as the conquerer of the world. The Mehrauli iron pillar inscription in the suburb of Delhi refers to king Candra as one who had exterminated a combined force of the rebels in Bengal, crossed the seven mouths of the Indus and defeated the Bactrians. The description fits well with the achievements of Candragupta II.

Chandragupta II was also known as Devarāja and Devagupta and he, assumed the title of Vikramāditya. His epithet *paramabhāgavata* indicates his faith in Vaiṣṇavism. He issued silver and copper coins. On some of his coins he is depicted as slaying a lion which is perhaps indicative of his conquest of the Gujarat region.

Candragupta II was succeeded by his son Kumāragupta I in A.D. 415. He consolidated the empire inherited from his father and grandfather, performed the Aśvamedha ritual as a proclamation of sovereignty and assumed the title of Mahendrāditya.

He was a devotee of Skanda-Kārttikeya as is proved by his coins. His inscriptions refer to numerous feudatories whose descendants subsequently became powerful. Towards the close of his reign there was a tribal invasion from outside, as we learn from the Bhitari pillar inscription. The invaders were known as Puṣyamitra. This reading of the name in the inscription may not be correct but a tribe named Puṣyamitra is mentioned in the *Viṣṇupurāṇa*. This invasion was resisted by prince Skandagupta in A.D. 455-56, the year when Kumāragupta passed away.

Kumāragupta was succeeded by Skandagupta. It was customary among the earlier Gupta kings to mention the name of their chief queens and mothers in their inscriptions. But from the non-mention of the name of Skandagupta's mother some scholars have concluded that the mother of Skandagupta was not the chief queen and that his claim on the Gupta throne was not valid. It has also been suggested that when Kumāragupta died Skandagupta was in the battlefield fighting against the Puṣyamitras. In his absence Purugupta became the king. After his return Skandagupta defeated Purugupta in a straight battle and occupied the throne. These are, however, all conjectures.

The reign of Skandagupta was not peaceful. From his contemporary inscriptions it is learnt that he had to confront both internal rebellions and external invasions. The Roman empire in the fifth century was threatened by the Huṇa invasions. One of the Huṇa tribes, known as the Epthalites, established themselves in the Oxus valley and invaded India. But Skandagupta inflicted a crushing defeat on the Huṇas as a consequence of which in the next fifty years there was no Huṇa invasion.

Skandagupta's coins are not found in abundance and they all belong to a single type from which it appears that the wars of Skandagupta told heavily on the exchequer. Another important event of his reign was the repairing of the Suduarśana dam in Kathiawar which had burst. This was erected during the time of the Maurya king Candragupta and had subsequently been repaired by Mahākṣatrapa Rudradāman. Parṇadatta, the governor of the Kathiawar region, was entrusted with the work of repairing it which was done successfully as is reported in the Girnar inscription of Parṇadatta.

9. Disintegration of the Guptas (A.D. 467-570)

Skandagupta was the last powerful king of the Gupta dynasty. After his death in A.D. 467 the empire began to disintegrate slowly. The next king was his brother Purugupta and it is not known how reigned. It is interesting to note that the subsequent kings—Budhagupta and Narasiṃhagupta—belonged to the line of Purugupta and not of Skandagupta. It has not been possible to place names of a few Gupta kings correctly in the dynastic line found in inscriptions. For example, in an inscription of A.D. 474 the name of one Kumaragupta II is found. He might have been a son of Skandagupta or of Purugupta.

Budhagupta became the Gupta king about A.D. 477 and his last known date is A.D. 495. His reigning period was marked by the decentralisation of political power which became increasingly accumulated in the hands of the feudatories as we shall see later. Budhagupta was succeeded by Narasiṃhagupta Bālāditya, Kumāragupta III and Viṣṇugupta respectively. The total period of the reign of these three kings has been fixed between A.D. 500 and 570. Apart from these three kings a few other names have been found. One of them is Vainyagupta whose inscription of A.D. 507 has been found in the Tippera district of Bengal. The other was Mahārāja Bhānugupta whose inscription of A.D. 510 has been found at Eran in Madhya Pradesh. How they were related to the imperial Guptas is difficult to say. It is not impossible that they belonged to the Gupta dynasty and served as provincial governors and, taking advantage of the weakness of the central authority, they declared independence. The second possibility is that they ruled as kings for a short time before Narasiṃhagupta but had an untimely death in war against the Huṇas.

Several incidents occurred during the reign of Narasiṃhagupta which would have been disastrous for the empire had it not been for his efficiency. The first was revolt within the empire and the declaration of independence by the feudatories and provincial governors. The second was the phenomenal rise of one Yaśodharman and the assertion of his authority over a vast region of the country. The third was the Huṇa invasion. To the credit of Narasiṃhagupta it may be said that notwithstanding occasional rebellious outbursts, he was able to receive at least a formal allegiance from his feudatories, and the sudden rise of Yaśodharman, although detrimental to the Gupta prestige, was only a temporary affair. So far as the Huṇa invasion was concerned, he was able to defeat them. The Huṇa king Mihirakula was forced to acknowledge his suzerainty and pay tribute to him.

After the death of Narasiṃhagupta, his son Kumāragupta III and grandson Viṣṇugupta successively ascended the throne. During the period of their rule—between c. A.D. 535 and 570—there was complete disintegration of Gupta power. In spite of this, in an inscription of A.D. 543 found in north Bengal, the Guptas were still mentioned as the sovereign power, although in the south, east and west Bengal independent kingdoms were already in existence. The rulers of Valabhī acknowledged the sovereignty of the Guptas till A.D. 550. The rulers of Kaliṅga did the same till A.D. 569.

10. Feudatories of the Guptas

The inscriptions of the feudatories of the Guptas, especially of the Bengal and Malwa region, prove that from the time of Purugupta and Budhagupta the vassals and the provincial rulers—some of them even belonged to the Gupta lineage—were becoming more and more powerful. The Maitrakas of the Kathiawar Peninsula began to rule dynastically. The founder of this dynasty, Bhatārka, was a general of the Guptas. He and his successor Dharasena introduced themselves as *senāpati* or general, but the next ruler Droṇasiṃha assumed the title of *mahārāja* as is known from his inscription of A.D. 502. Dhruvasena, the next king, who ruled between A.D. 525 and 545 and had sixteen inscriptions, acknowledged the sovereignty of the Guptas. It was during the reign of Mahārāja Dharapatta (c. A.D. 545-556) and Mahārāja Guhasena (c. A.D. 556-570) that the Maitrakas of Valabhī declared complete independence.

Epigraphic evidence shows that the Parivrājaka dynasty of the Bundelkhand region, the dynasty of king Jayanāga of Uccakalpa, the Pāṇḍu dynasty of Banda and Baghelkhand, the dynasty of Mahārāja Laksmaṇa of the Allahabad and Rewa region, the dynasty of Mahārāja Subandhu of the Māhismatī region, etc., were originally feudatories of the Guptas though they had initially been provincial rulers. The tendeney to disregard the sovereignty of the Guptas had already begun. During the reign of Kumāragupta I the provincial governor of northern Bengal was known by the title of *uparika*. During the reign of Budhagupta it was converted to that of *mahārāja*.

Between A.D. 530 and 540 when Narasiṃhagupta was still in power, one Yaśodharman of unknown origin established his authority in the Malwa region. In his Mandasore inscription it is stated that his empire touched the Himalayas in the north, the Mahendra range in the south, the Brahmaputra in the east and the great ocean in the west. Although it was a conventional description, Yaśodharman must have defeated the Huṇa chief Mihirakula. He was a threat to the power and prestige of the imperial Guptas. But fortunately for the Guptas his success was short-lived.

The Maukharis were feudatories of the Guptas in Bihar and Uttar Pradesh. Inscriptions at Barabar and Nagarjuni hills testify the existence of a Maukhari principality in the Gaya region in the sixth century A.D. Three rulers of this line—Yajñavarman, Śārdulavarman and Anantavarman—are known and all of them were feudatories of the Guptas. Another branch of the Maukharis, which had a greater hold in Uttar Pradesh and Bihar, has come to light. This was also feudatory of the Guptas. Their inscriptions and seals reveal that the first three rulers of this dynasty—Harivarman, Ādityavarman and Īśvaravarman—bore the epithet *mahārāja*, while the next four kings, beginning with Īśānavarman, assumed the title *mahārājādhirāja*. The known date of Iśānavarman is A.D. 554 and therefore it is reasonable to conclude that since then the Maukharis became independent of the Guptas. In the Magadha region a collateral branch of the Guptas, known as the Later Guptas, ruled as vassals of the Gupta kings. The Aphsad inscription found near Gaya records names of eight kings who did not assume high-sounding imperial titles. The fourth king of this line was a contemporary of Maukhari Īśānavarman (A.D. 550-576) whom he defeated in a battle. It was during his reign that the later Guptas became a sovereign power.

During the period of Gupta decadence, i.e., in the sixth century A.D. one Haricandra of the Gurjara tribe established an independent principality in the Jodhpur region. His sons were also able to establish their own territories in different parts of Rajasthan. Another branch of the Gurjaras began to rule in the Bhṛgukaccha or the Broach region. Their territory was bordered by the river Mahī on the north, the river Kim to the south, the western border of Malwa-Khandesh on the east and the Arabian sea on the west. Their capital was at Nāndīpurī, modern Nandod.

Two independent kingdoms developed in Bengal known as Gauḍa and Vaṅga. The former comprised northern and western Bengal and the latter southern and eastern. A few copper plates mention three kings of the Vaṅga region—Gopacandra, Dharmāditya and Samācāradeva. Gopacandra was a feudatory of the Guptas who declared independence some time after A.D. 507. The total period of the reign of these three kings may be fixed between A.D. 525 and 575. All of them bore the title of *mahārājādhirāja* and Samācāradeva issued gold coins in his own name. In the Allahabad pillar inscription of Samudragupta Kāmarupa and Ḍabāka in Assam are mentioned as border states which acknowledged his authority. The Kāmarūpa king Nārāyaṇavarman repudiated the Guptas around the sixth century and rose to prominence as the sovereign king of that region.

11. *Deccan in the Gupta Age*

Deccan and south India, and also parts of central India and the Kaliṅga region lay outside the pale of the Gupta empire. Samudragupta led a southern enpedition in course of which he defeated and humbled twelve kings and was satisfied only with their token submission. Even when the might of the Guptas was at its zenith, in the northwestern Deccan and parts of Madhya Pradesh the Vākātakas had no difficulty in becoming powerful. The Vākātaka prince Rudrasena II married Prābhāvatīguptā, the daughter of the Gupta emperor

Candragupta II. This marriage was politically significant. After the death of Rudrasena at the beginning of the fifth century Prabhāvatī became the guardian-ruler on behalf of her three minor sons. In a subsequent record of Prabhāvatī she is described as the mother of *mahārāja* Damodarasena and *mahārāja* Pravarasena II. The latter reigned during the middle of the fifth century. From his inscriptions it is known that Vidarbha and its adjoining areas formed part of his kingdom; his provincial governors bore the title *senāpati*. He had built a new capital city under the name of Pravarapura which was probably in modern Powner in Wardha district. He was also a poet; he composed *Setubandha* in Maharashtrian Prakrit. His son, *mahārāja* Narendrasena, conquered Kosala (south), Mekala and Malwa when Budhagupta was the Gupta ruler. The last known important king of this line was his son, Prthivisena II.

The Vākātakas of Vatsagulma, modern Basseim in Akola district, were represented by the line of Sarvasena. Vindyaśakti II, son of Sarvasena, who ruled in the second half of the fourth century was a powerful king from whose Basseim inscription it is learnt that parts of Berar and the north portion of Hyderabad were under his rule. From an inscription found at Ajanta it is learnt that he had military success over the Kuntalas. Subsequent kings of this line were Pravarasena, Devasena and Harisena. The latter had described himself as the lord of Kuntala, Avanti, Kaliṅga, Kosala, Trikūṭa, Lāta and Andhra. Evidently this was a convention. Both branches of the Vākātakas were eclipsed in political scene of the Deccan at the beginning of the sixth century A.D.

A tribe known as the Bhojas ruled in the Goa region towards the close of the fourth century A.D. The Mirod copper plate inscription refers to a Bhoja chief named Devarāja whose administrative centre was at Candrapura, modern Chandor in Goa. Another tribe known as the Traikūṭakas controlled the Aparānta or north Konkan region. From the Chandravalli inscription it is known that the Traikūṭakas and Ābhīras fought jointly against the Kadamba king Mayuraśarman about the middle of the fourth century. From the evidence of inscriptions and coins it is known that three Traikūṭaka chiefs—Indradatta, Dahrasena and Vyāghrasena—ruled over the western coastal area from Surat to Kanheri. The Traikūṭakas were later overthrown by the Gurjaras and Kalacuris about the middle of the sixth century A.D.

In southern Mahārashtra, about the middle of the fifth century A.D., one Mānāṅka established the rule of the Rāṣṭarakūṭa dynasty with his administrative centre at Mānapura, modern Man in the Satara district. From the Pandurangapalli inscription of his grandson, Avidheya, it is known that he had conquered Vidarbha and Aśmaka. He was succeeded by his son Devarāja. This dynasty could not rule for long and the southern Maharashtra region eventually came under the Cālukyas.

Coming to the eastern side we find that in the Guntur district and its adjoining regions, a tribe known as the Ānandas rule from mid-fourth century to mid-fifth century A.D. Names of three of their ruling chiefs are known Kandara, Attivarman and Dāmodaravarman. The Ānandas were eventually annihilated by the Pallavas.

The Sālaṅkāyanas were masters of the eastern portion of the region between the Godavari and the Krishna. Their capital was at Vengi, modern Pedda-vegi near Elluru. The ruling dynasty was founded by Hastivarman I who was defeated about the middle of the fourth century A.D. by Samudragupta. His successors ruled up to the end of the fifth century A.D. till they were defeated by the Pallavas.

The original home of the Viṣṇukuṇḍins was at Vinukonda, about 60 miles to the east of Śrīśaila in the Kurnool district. The first known king of this dynasty was Vikramahendra (c. A.D. 500). He was succeeded by his son Govindavarman, and the latter by his son Mādhavavarman I (c. A.D. 535-85) from whose time the dynasty rose to prominence. Almost the whole of the present Andhra Pradesh was under his control. His Polamuru inscription records that he crossed the Godavari and conquered the regions on its northern bank. The Viṣṇukuṇḍins continued to be in an important power in the Andhra Pradesh region till the middle of the seventh century.

Among the kings defeated by Samudragupta, at least four belonged to the Kaliṅga region, i.e., the land between the Mahanadi and the Godavarī. They were Svāmidatta of Koṭṭura, Mahendragiri of Piṣṭapura Dāmana of Eraṇḍapalla and Kubera of Devarāṣṭra. Siṃhapuram (near Srikakulam) and Vardhamānapura (Badam in the Palkonda subdivision of the Vizagapatam district) were under a tribe called the Pitṛbhaktas, while Piṣṭapura (Pithapuram in the east Godavari district) was under the Māṭharas. The Vasiṣṭhas held sway in the Vizagapatam region. In the central Kaliṅga region, the Eastern Gaṅgas rose to power in the fifth century A.D. Their capital was at Kaliṅganagara, modern Mukhalingam in Ganjam district. They had another administrative centre at Dantapura, modern Dantavaktra near Śrikakulam while a branch ruled at Śvetaka, modern Chikti in the Sompeta Taluka of Ganjam district. The Raipur-Bilaspur-Sambalpur region of Madhya Pradesh and Orissa was known as southern Kosala and was ruled by king Mahendra who was also defeated by Samudragupta. Another dynasty in this region had its centre at Śarabhapura. Later on the whole of the southern Kosala region came under the Pāṇḍuvaṃśī kings.

12. Political Fragmentation after the Guptas

In the post-Gupta period there was political fragmentation. In western India, the Kathiawar region and its adjoining territories were ruled by the Maitrakas of Valabhī. The Maukharis of Kanauj became powerful under Īśānavarman (known date A.D. 554), Śarvavarman (A.D. 576-80) and Avantivarman (A.D. 580-600). Avantivarman was succeeded by his son Grahavarman who married Rājyaśrī, daughter of Prabhākaravardhana of Thaneswar after whose death Kanauj was incorporated within Harṣa's empire. A rival power of the Maukharis were the later Guptas of Magadha. Māhasenagupta of this dynasty led a victorious campaign up to the Lauhitya or Brahmaputra and defeated the Kāmarūpa king Susthitavarman. Towards the close of Mahāsenagupta's reign, Devagupta, a scion of the Later Guptas was able to establish his authority in the Malwa region. He came to a political understanding with Śaśāṅka, the Lord of Gauḍa, and established diplomatic relations with him.

The Puṣpabhūtis ruled in modern Haryana region from the sixth century A.D. Their capital was Thaneswar. They probably began as the feudatories of the imperial Guptas and later declared independence. Ādityasena of this dynasty married a Later Gupta princess, the sister of Mahāsenagupta, and his son Prabhākaravardhana began to rule from A.D. 580. From the *Harṣacarita* of Bāṇabhaṭṭa it is known that he held sway over the territories of the Huṇas, Sindhus, Lāṭas, Gurjars, Gandhāras and Mālavas though it is doubtful whether these territories were actually conquered by him. Prabhākaravardhana died when the crown prince Rājyavardhana was fighting against the Huṇas. Almost at the same time Prabhākaravardhana's son-in-law, the Maukhari king Grahavarman, was killed by Devagupta, king of Malava. Prabhākara's daughter Rājyaśrī, the widowed queen of Kanauj, was taken captive. Thereupon Rājyavardhana launched a campaign against Devagupta and killed him in a straight battle. However, he was himself slain owing to a conspiracy of Śaśāṅka, the ruler of Bengal. After Rājyavardhana's death, his illustrious brother Harṣavardhana (A.D. 606-46) changed the face of the political situation of northern India by making himself master of a vast territory including Kanauj.

Towards the end of the sixth century A.D. Śaśāṅka of Gauḍa (north and West Bengal), who was a feudatory of the Later Gupta king Mahāsenagupta, declared independence. Śaśāṅka defeated the Māna ruler Samubhūyaśas or his son and annexed the region between the districts of Midnapur and Gaya to his own kingdom. He subdued the Śailodbhavas of Koṅgoda, advanced as far as Mahendragiri in Ganjam district and declared himself as the lord of Daṇḍabhukti, Utkala and Koṅgoda. After the decline of the Later Guptas, he apprehended danger from the Maukharis, who had formed a political alliance with the powerful Puṣpabhūtis of Thaneswar through matrimony. Śaśānka came to terms politically with Devagupta of Malwa, a scion of the Later Guptas. Their joint force invaded Kanauj, and before help from Thaneswar could reach, Grahavarman, the Maukhari king, was defeated and killed and his wife Rājyaśrī was imprisoned. Śaśāṅka stayed at Kanauj to settle up affairs and Devagupta marched towards Thaneswar. There seems to have been a miscalculation and, contrary to their expectations, Rājyavardhana wasted no time in facing his enemy with the result that Devagupta was defeated and killed. It appears that at Kanauj there was some political agreement between Rājyavardhana and Śaśāṅka, obviously in favour of the former, but the cunning Śaśāṅka, taking advantage of Rājyavardhana's trust, had him killed and returned to Bengal where he consolidated his power.

In Kāmarūpa, or Assam, Nārāyaṇavarman disregarded the Gupta authority in the middle of the sixth century A.D. The next king, Bhūtivarman, annexed Ḍabāka and Surma valley to his kingdom and performed an Aśvamedha ritual. His successors were Candramukhavarman, Sthitavarman and Susthitavarman. The last-named king was defeated by Mahāsenagupta of the Later Gupta dynasty. His sons were Supratiṣṭhitavarman and Bhāskaravarman. The latter made a political alliance with Harṣavardhana to confront their common enemy, Śaśāṅka, king of Bengal.

In the post-Gupta period Orissa was divided into numerous small principalities. One Pṛthivīvigraha ruled in northern Kaliṅga. The Mānas established their authority towards the close of the sixth century A.D. in the region between Gaya and Midnapur and also in the Puri and Balasore districts. The Koṅgoda region was ruled by the Śailodbhavas. The names of a few Śailodbhava kings have been found—Raṇabhīta, Sainyabhīta-Mādhavarāja I, Ayaśobhita, and Sainyabhīta-Mādhavarāja II. The Mānas and the Śailodbhavas ruled as feudatories of Śaśāṅka.

The Nalas held sway in the Jaipur-Bastar region between Orissa and Madhya Pradesh whence they shifted towards the Vākāṭaka territories. A copper plate, composed in the first half of the sixth century A.D. and issued from Nandivardhana, the first capital of the Vākāṭakas, refers to one Nala chief named Bhavattavarman or Bhavadattavarman and a place called Kadambagiri, i.e., Kalamba in Berar. Other Nala inscriptions found at Bastar and Koraput testify to their struggle with the Vākāṭakas of Vatsagulma, the Rāṣṭrakūṭas of Mānapura and Pāṇḍuvaṃsīs of southern Kosala.

In the second half of the sixth century A.D. the Kalacuris came into prominence in parts of northern Maharashtra, Gujarat and Malwa. Śaṅkaragaṇa of this dynasty was a powerful king. From an inscription of A.D. 595 found at Ahabon in Nasik it is known that he conquered the entire region between Nasik and Malwa. From the Badner inscription of his son

Buddharāja it is known that Śaṅkaragaṇa had also conquered the eastern Malwa region. The Kalacuris had a prolonged struggle with the Cālukyas of Vātāpi and eventually they became a vassal power. The Mankani inscription of A.D. 594 refers to a branch of the Kalacuris which ruled in the Gujarat region.

In southern Kosala, that is parts of Madhya Pradesh and Orissa, more precisely the Raipur-Bilaspur-Sambalpur region, evidence of the existence of local ruling dynasties has been found. Among these local powers, a ruling dynasty of the Śarabhapura or Raipur region came into prominence in the sixth century A.D. Later the Pāṇḍavaṃśīs or Somavaṃśīs became masters of the entire southern Kosala. In order to survive they had to fight constantly against the Nalas and the Cālukyas of Vātāpi. A branch of the Pāṇḍuvaṃśīs ruled in the Mekala country, the region around the Amarakantaka range.

In the eastern part of the Deccan, the Viṣṇukuṇḍins held sway over the Andhra region. Among the powerful rulers of this clan mention may be made of Indrabhaṭṭārakavarman (c. A.D. 590-620) and his son Vikramendravarman III (A.D. 620-631). The Viṣṇukuṇḍins were eventually exterminated as a consequence of Cālukya expansionism. In the Kaliṅga region the Eastern Gaṅgas rose to prominence under Indravarman I who described himself as *trikaliṅgapati*, or lord of the three Kaliṅgas in his inscriptions. From the sixth to the eighth century A.D. this dynasty somehow maintained its independent existence.

In western Deccan the Cālukyas founded a kingdom in the beginning of the sixth century at Badami (Vātāpi) in the Bijapur district under Jayasiṃha and his son Raṇarāga. This dynasty came into prominence under Pulakeśin I (A.D. 535-66) and his son Kīrtivarman (A.D. 566-598). The latter defeated the Mauryas, Nalas and Kadambas and occupied portions of Konkan, Karnataka, southern Maharashtra and Tamil Nadu. Kīrtivarman was succeeded by his brother Maṅgaleśa (A.D. 598-611) who defeated the Kalacuris and occupied the Ratnagiri district of Maharashtra. Towards the close of his reign there was a civil war among the Cālukyas during which he was defeated and killed by his brother's son, Pulakeśin II, who was destined to play an important role in the subsequent political history of India.

The original area of the Pallavas of Kanchi was between the north Penner and the Kaveri. Sometimes their northern boundary reached up to the river Krishna. The Prakrit inscriptions of the Pallavas were composed between A.D. 250 and 350 while the Sanskrit ones between A.D. 350 and 600. The era of Pallava greatness started with Siṃhaviṣṇu who flourished towards the close of the sixth century A.D. It is said that he conquered Colamaṇḍala. The southern boundary of his kingdom extended till Kumbhakonam. The long drawn Cālukya-Pallava rivalry started when Siṃhaviṣṇu's son Mahendravarman I ascended the Pallava throne.

There were two settlements of the Colas at Uraiyur, or the Trichinopoly region, and at Renandu which comprised portions of Cuddapah, Anantapur and Kurnul districts. The two lots were still minor powers in the sixth century A.D. The Kaḷabhra tribe also had some prominence in Tamil Nadu. The Āḷupas occupied the southern Kanara region while the Bāṇas had settlements in the Kolar and North Arcot districts. The Pāṇḍya kingdom, situated in the far south across from Srilanka, became powerful during the reign of Māravarman (A.D. 620-45) and Sindun (A.D. 645-79). The Western Gaṅgas had a stronghold in the Karnataka region while the Kadambas were rulers of Kuntala.

13. Harṣa: The Lord of Uttarāpatha (A.D. 606-46)

On the ruins of the Gupta empire a political unity was brought to northern India by Harṣavardhana in the first half of the seventh century. He was acclaimed even by his opponents as *sakala-uttarāpathanātha* or the Lord of entire northern India. Originally a prince of the Puṣpabhuti dynasty of Thaneswar in modern Haryana, he became master of a vast region taking advantage of the unsettled political condition of northern India in the post-Gupta period. On behalf of his widowed sister Rājyaśrī, Harṣa took possession of Kanauj and shifted his capital there. But from a seal found at Nalanda it appears that his sister's late husband, Grahvarman of the Maukhari dynasty, might have had brothers to succeed him and that the throne of Kanauj was not really vacant, contrary to what Harṣa's biographer Bāṇabhaṭṭa had said. It is not improbable that in order to safeguard the interests of his sister, Harṣavardhana occupied Kanauj, and driving away all claimants to it declared himself as its king. This took place about A.D. 612.

The military expeditions of Harṣa were directed against four powers: the rulers of Valabhī and Gujarat; the Cālukya king, Pulakesin II; Sind; and the eastern countries, namely Magadha, Gauḍa, Oḍra and Koṅgoda.

Valabhī, as we have seen, became powerful under Śilāditya I Dharmāditya. He was succeeded by Kharagraha (A.D. 613-16), Dharasena III (A.D. 616-28), Dhrūvasena II (A.D. 628-41) and Dharasena IV (since A.D. 641) respectively. All of them were contemporaries of Harṣa and it is difficult to say against whom he fought.

From an inscription of the Gurjaras of Broach it is known that their earlier ruler Dadda II achieved celebrity by defeating the illustrious Harṣadeva having taken the side of his overlord, the king of Valabhī. From this it may be assumed that in his fight against Valabhī Harṣa was successful in the initial stages but when Dadda II came in support of the king of Valabhī the tide turned against Harṣa. No such event is recorded in Dadda II's own inscription.

It should be taken into account that in the Aihole inscription of Cālukya Pulakeśin II it is said that the Gurjaras, Mālavas and Lāṭas had become feudatories of Pulakeśin in order to save themselves from a formidable enemy. Probably the Gurjara Dadda II incurred the wrath of Harṣa for siding the king of Valabhī, and that is why Dadda, in order to protect his own territory, took shelter under the powerful Cālukyas. This might have been the reason for Harṣa's fight with Pulakeśin. Again it is also possible that Dadda II was a minor and insignificant power, but he took part in the wars against Harṣa having sided first with the king of Valabhī and then with Pulakeśin II, and that his descendants eulogised him more than his due.

The Valabhī king, Dhrūvasena II (A.D. 628-41) became the son-in-law of Harṣa. This points to two possibilities: either that Dhrūvasena when defeated could maintain his territory by marrying Harṣa's daughter or that Harṣa was defeated by

Dhrūvasena and in order to put an end to the protracted war sought peace with him through a matrimonial alliance. It is not improbable that the war began earlier during the reign of Dharasena III or Kharagraha, but it ended during the reign of Dhruvasena II. Some hold that Harṣa's war against Valabhī kingdom took place after A.D. 641, during the reign of Dharasena IV, because the imperial titles assumed by the latter appear to challenge Harṣa's honour and prestige.

The second military campaign of Harṣa was directed against the Cālukya king Pulakeśin II. This war took place on the bank of the river Narmadā. According to Hiuen Tsang, Harṣa mustered a huge army and appointed efficient generals against Pulakeśin. He was himself present on the spot but failed to achieve success. The exact date of this war is not known, but it must have taken place before A.D. 635.

It is also doubtful whether Harṣa could achieve any real success in Sind, though Bāṇa has written that Harṣa had abducted the goddess of fortune of the King of Sindhu.

So far as his eastern campaigns are concerned Hiuen Tsang says that about A.D. 643 when he was in Kāmarūpa, Harṣa was waiting at Kajaṅgala on the banks of the Gaṅgā after conquering Oḍra and Koṅgoda. Ma-twan-lin has written that in A.D. 641 Harṣa assumed the title of the king of Magadha. This is also supported by Hiuen Tsang's statement that he was in Magadha in A.D. 637-38 when Śaśāṅka, the Lord of Bengal, was already dead. It appears thus that Harṣa's conquest of Magadha was completed after A.D. 638.

If Harṣa could achieve some success in Gauḍa, evidently it was after the death of Śaśāṅka. Although the *Mañjuśrimūlakalpa* refers to Harṣa's victory over Śaśāṅka, inscriptions testify the overlordship of Śaśāṅka in Orissa in A.D. 619. Śaśāṅka died in A.D. 637-38. Hiuen Tsang says that before his death Śaśāṅka was in full possession of Magadha. It therefore appears that in the course of his campaigns in Oḍra and Koṅgoda Harṣa conquered some territories belonging to Śaśāṅka when the latter was no more on the scene.

Harṣa's empire comprised present Haryana, parts of Uttar Pradesh and Rajasthan, the northern region of Madhya Pradesh and a few districts of Bihar and Orissa. There is no evidence that Sind formed an integral part of his empire. Hiuen Tsang came across independent kingdoms in Kapiśa, Udyāna, Kaṣhmir, Punjab and Malwa. As a militarist Harṣa was not very successful. He was not even the master of entire north India. But it has to be admitted, at the same time, that the sphere of his influence was very large, evidently due to his charismatic personality in which respect he was peerless. Even in the south he was celebrated as the Lord of Uttarāpatha.

Harṣavardhana probably heard about the Chinese emperor from Hiuen Tsang. He sent an embassy to China in A.D. 641 and in A.D. 643 two Chinese envoys, Li-yi-piao and Wang-hiuen-tse, came to his court. The Chinese emperor, having heard of him from Hiuen Tsang, sent a second embassy in A.D. 646 the year before Harṣa died.

Harṣa's personal accomplishments made him celebrated all over India. He composed three dramatical works in Sanskrit—*Ratnāvalī*, *Priyadarśikā* and *Nāgānanda*. I-tsing wrote: "Śilāditya was well versed in literature. Not only did he put on paper the episode of Boddhisattva Jīmutavāhana (*Nāgānanda*), but he staged it as well with dance and miming." Harṣa's immense financial contribution to the University of Nalanda has been recorded by Hiuen Tsang. He was liberal to all religions. He was a devotee of Śiva though his father and grandfather were sun-worshippers and his elder brother a Buddhist. Harṣa was also attracted towards Buddhism. In his time a religious conference, in which the Buddhists were predominant, was held in Kanauj and he was its chairperson. It was attended by twenty kings including Bhāskaravarman of Kāmarūpa. Harṣa was also famous for his liberality. He established an era of his own, which was counted from A.D. 606 the year of his accession. Al-Biruni says that this Harṣa era was popular in the Kanauj and Mathura region. Harṣa left no heir to his kingdom.

14. Deccan and South India: Cālukya-Pallava Rivalry

The Cālukyas of Badami (Vātāpipura), as we have seen, became powerful under Pulakeśin II (A.D. 611-42) who consolidated his power by defeating the Kadambas of Vanavāsi, the Gaṅgas of southern Karnataka, the Āḷupas of the Shimoga district, and the Mauryas of Koṅkan. According to his Aihole *praśasti*, composed by his court poet Ravikīrti, the Lāṭas, Gurjaras and Mālavas were his feudatories. He earned a great reputation by defeating the illustrious Harṣa on the banks of the Narmada. He defeated the Kosalas (probably the Pāṇḍuvaṃśīs of southern Kosala) and the Kaliṅgas (probably the Eastern Gaṅgas of the Ganjam district), marched to Piṣṭapura (Pithapuram) and Kunāla lake (Kolleru near Ellore) and overthrew the Viṣṇukuṇḍin king Vikramendravarman III. The Andhra region thus came under control where he installed his brother Kubja-Viṣṇuvardhana as king. The latter's dynasty came to be known as that of the Eastern Cālukyas of Veṅgī.

The southern conquests of Pulakeśin II led him into a direct confrontation with the Pallavas of Kanchi who became masters of the entire Tamil area during the reign of Siṃhaviṣṇu (A.D. 575-600). The next king, Mahendravarman I (A.D. 600-630), apprehending danger from the Cālukyas made an alliance with the Kadambas, but in no time Pulakeśin marched into the heart of the Pallava kingdom and defeated Mahendravarman at Pallalur, fifteen miles north of Kanchi. Mahendravarman was, however, able to save Kanchi. The next Pallava king, Narasiṃhavarman I (A.D. 630-668) rebuilt the fortune of the family by subduing the Colas, Ceras, Kaḷabhras and Pāṇḍyas. He also sent two naval expeditions to Ceylon and got his protégé Māravarman crowned there. After thus having consolidated his power, he defeated the aggressive Cālukyas in three battles, including one at Manimaṅgalam. Then he took the offensive, reached the heart of Cālukya country, destroyed the capital, and assumed the title *vātāpikoṇḍa*, i.e., captor of Vātāpi. Pulakeśin II was defeated and killed (A.D. 642).

After the death of Pulakeśin II there was turmoil in the Cālukya house, and probably internecine wars for a period of no less than thirteen years took place until Vikramāditya I came to power (A.D. 655-681). With the help of his maternal relations, the Gaṅgas, he was able to liberate his capital. He renewed the struggle against the Pallavas, his adversaries being Narasiṃhavarman I, his son Mahendravarman II (A.D. 668-70) and his grandson Parameśvaravarman I (A.D. 670-695). He took the Pallava capital Kanchi and then pushed southward to Trichinopoly. But Parameśvaravarman defeated him in the battle of Peruvalanallur and compelled him to withdraw to his own country. The Cālukya and Pallava inscriptions show conflicting claims of success on either side which indicates that both the powers had limited success in the various battles against each other and neither could obtain complete victory. A brother of Vikramāditya I, Dhārāśraya Jayasiṃhavarman founded a Cālukya vassal line in the Lāṭa region of Gujrat.

After Vikramāditya I his son Vinayāditya ruled over the Cālukya kingdom from A.D. 681 to 696. There was no Cālukya-Pallava rivalry during his time while Parameśvaravarman I was still the Pallava king. The latter was succeeded in A.D. 695 by his son Narasiṃhavarman II who ruled till A.D. 733 in unbroken peace. The Cālukya-Pallava conflict was resumed towards the end of the reign of the next Pallava king, Parameśvaravarman II (A.D. 722-730), the Cālukya adversary being Vijayāditya (A.D. 696-733). From the Ulachal inscription of his reign it is known that around A.D. 730 the Cālukyas conquered Kanchi and levied tribute from the Pallavas. The next Pallava king Nandivarman II (A.D. 730-795) had his Cālukya rival in Vikramāditya II (A.D. 733-745). This was the last phase of the Cālukya-Pallava rivalry, and though the Cālukyas were victorious and advanced as far as Kanchi, there was no tangible result.

15. Struggle for Matsery over Kanauj

The political unity which was achieved in a considerable area of northern India during the reign of Harṣavardhana was shattered after his death. Heirless as he was, his kingdom passed in the hands of the Later Gupta princes—Kumāragupta and Mādhavagupta—who were related to him through their mother's line and had received shelter at his court for a long time. This dynasty had a short and uneventful career and was finally exterminated by one adventurer named Yaśovarman who became master of Kanauj in the first half of the eighth century A.D. Yaśovarman is said to have conquered a vast area and defeated the Arabs. But his untimely death ushered in the traditional resurgence of petty fragmentary kingdoms in northern India, a medley of powerless small states. In western India the Gurjara-Pratihāras came into prominence while in eastern India the Pālas became powerful. It was therefore natural both for the Pratihāras and the Pālas to aspire for the mastery of the defenceless plains of Hindustan. In the struggle that followed, the Rāṣṭrakūṭas of the south could not keep away. They were also involved. The story of the rise of these three powers in the second half of the eighth century is narrated below.

The long drawn struggle between the Cālukyas and Pallavas ruined both the powers internally; taking advantage of this the Rāṣṭrakūṭas became masters of the Deccan. From the Samangarh plates of A.D. 754 and the undated Daśāvatāra cave inscription at Ellora it is learnt that the Rāṣṭrakūṭa Dantidurga built the fortunes of his family at the cost of the Cālukyas whose feudatory he was. He defeated the Gurjaras of Nāndipurī and made his nephew Karkka ruler of that province. He invaded Malwa and occupied Ujjayinī. By about A.D. 750 he was the master of southern Gujarat and parts of central India. He defeated his own overlord, the Cālukya Kīrtivarman II, about A.D. 753 and established his authority firmly over Maharashtra. After his death in A.D. 758 his uncle Kṛṣṇa I became the Rāṣṭrakūṭa king and exterminated the Cālukyas. He defeated the Gaṅgas of Karṇāṭaka and also the eastern Cālukyas of Veṅgī. He was succeeded by his son Govinda II in A.D. 773. During the reign of his younger brother, Dhruva I, who came to power in A.D. 780 the prestige of the Rāṣṭrakūṭas reached its zenith. He annexed Gaṅgavāḍi to his own kingdom, led a successful campaign against the Pallava king Dantivarman and received submission from the Eastern Cālukya ruler of Veṅgī. Thus, being the undisputed lord of the Deccan he turned his eyes towards northern India.

In western India, the Gurjara-Pratihāras came to prominence under Nāgabhaṭa I whose forefathers had established a kingdom in parts of Malwa and eastern Rajasthan. The western boundary was extended by Nāgabhaṭa I to Broach. He resisted successfully the Arab invasions in the beginning of the eighth century by bringing under his flag the Pratihāra ruling chiefs of that region and also the Cāhamanas, Guhilaputras, Cālukyas (of Gujarat) and Paramāras, and these powers later acknowledged his suzerainty which formed the basis of Pratihāra empire. The Arab adversary of Nāgabhaṭa was either Junaid or his son Tamin. After the death of Nāgabhaṭa I in A.D.

756, his sons, Kakkuka and Devarāja ruled for some time. Devarāja was succeeded by his son Vatasarāja in A.D. 778 during whose time Malwa and Rajasthan came under the direct control of the Pratihāras.

In eastern India the Pāla kings of Bengal and Bihar consolidated their power. The forefathers of the Pālas were probably feudatories of Śaśāṅka. It is said that for many years after the death of the latter anarchy and confusion prevailed caused by the rivalry of small local chiefs. Taking advantage of these internecine struggles, an ambitious chief named Gopāla made himself the ruler of Bengal around A.D. 750 having managed to get support from the ruling local chiefs. Gopāla hailed from Varendrī or North Bengal and was succeeded in A.D. 770 by his son Dharmapāla whose valour and political shrewdness helped to make him the most powerful ruler of Bengal and Bihar.

The imperial city of Kanauj was under the influence of the Pratihāras and was ruled by their protégé Indrāyudha. Dharmapāla dislodged him from power and replaced him with his own protégé Cakrāyudha. The Pratihāra king Vatsarāja could not tolerate this; he marched against Dharmapāla and defeated him in a straight battle in the Gaṅgā-Yamunā Doab region. But before Vatsarāja could enjoy the fruits of his victory, the Rāṣṭrakūta king Dhruva appeared on the scene from the south with a huge army and defeated the Pratihāras. Vatsarāja, exhausted and humiliated, sought refuge in the desert region of Rajasthan far from the reach of Dhruva. Dharmapāla was diplomatic enough to submit to Dhruva. The latter stayed for some time by the banks of the Ganges, earned religious merit, made gifts to the Brāhmaṇas, and then returned to his own country with huge presents and immense booty. After his departure, Dharmapāla convened a *durbar* at Kaṅauj, received obedience from the ruling feudatories, put Cakrāyudha in charge of Kanauj and declared himself as the lord of northern India.

But the matter did not end here. Vatsarāja was succeeded by his son Nāgabhaṭa II. From the Gwalior inscription of his grandson it is known that Nāgabhaṭa received submission from the kings of Andhra, Saindhava, Vidarbha and Kaliṅga, defeated Cakrāyudha and the king of Vaṅga and conquered the forts of the Ānartas, Mālavas, Kirātas, Turuṣkas, Vatsas and Matsyas. Although these tributes were largely conventional, it is a fact that Nāgabhaṭa revived the fallen fortune of his family, annexed to his kingdom the lost territories and received submission from many feudatories. In the Deccan the situation also changed. After the death of Dhruva, his son Govinda III came to power in A.D. 793 after defeating his elder brother Stambha.

The Pratihāra Nāgbhaṭa II, after consolidating his power, first reoccupied Kanauj, dislodged Cakrāyudha and put Indrāyudha in his place and then marched eastwards to take revenge on Dharmapāla whom he defeated near Monghyr. But again history was repeated. The Rāṣṭrakūṭa king, Govinda III, marched through Bhopal and Jhansi and defeated Nāgabhaṭa II near Bundelkhand. This happened some time before A.D. 809. According to the Sanjan plates of the Rāṣṭrakūṭas, both Dharmapāla and his protégé Cakrāyudha submitted to Govinda III who stayed for some time on the banks of Narmada. On his way back he conquered Malwa and received submission from the the kings of Kosala, Kaliṅga, Veṅgī, Ḍāhala and Odraka.

Thus, although Kanauj came under the influence of the Pālas, they could not retain it for long. Eventually Kanauj came under the Pratihāras.

16. The Three Kingdoms: Expansion and Degeneration

Dhramapāla, notwithstanding his defeats in the hands of the Pratihāras, through his diplomacy maintained control over the vast region of northern India. He assumed the titles of *parameśvara, paramabhaṭṭāraka* and *mahārājādhirāja*. He was a devout Buddhist and erected monasteries at Vikramaśīlā and Somapurī.

After Dharmapāla, his son Devapāla (A.D. 810-50) retained the Pāla empire and extended its boundary. From the inscriptions of his time it is known that he established his sway over the Kamboja and the Vindhya regions, exterminated the Utkalas, conquered Prāgjyotiṣa, destroyed the Huṇas and humbled the Drāviḍas and the Gurjaras. There was, however, no Huṇa race during the time of Devapāla but the Kamboja region of the northwest, where Devapāla is said to have extended the sphere of his influence, was still named after the Huṇas. His Gurjara adversaries were Nāgabhaṭa II, Rāmabhadra and Bhoja against whom he was successful. His Drāviḍa rival was probably not the Rāṣṭrakūṭa king Amoghavarṣa but some Tamil power of the far south. In an inscription of the Pāṇḍya king Śrīmāra Śrīvallabha it is stated that he fought against a confederacy led by the Magadhas and Utkalas—the Magadhas might have denoted the Pālas of Bengal and Bihar. Like his father, Devapāla was also a devout Buddhist whose fame spread far and wide. Bālaputradeva, the Śailendra king of Malayasia, wanted a grant of five villages near Nalanda from Devapāla for erecting a monastery.

After the death of Devapāla, during the weak rule of Vigrahapāla and Nārāyaṇapāla, Pāla power began to disintegrate. The Rāṣṭrakūṭas had a victory over the Pālas in A.D. 860. The Pālas were even dislodged from Magadha or south Bihar. In Assam king Harjara declared independence. In Orissa the Śailodbhavas became powerful. Even north Bengal fell into the hands of the Pratihāra Mahendrapāla. However, the Pāla King Nārāyṇapāla was able to reconquer north Bengal and Magadha taking advantage of the struggle between the Rāṣṭrakūṭas and the Pratihāras though the ancient glory was not revived. From the inscriptions of the Candellas and Kalacuris it is known that they had defeated the rulers of Gauḍa, Rāḍha, Aṅga and Vaṅgāla. This implies that towards the close of the tenth century A.D. the original dominion of the Pālas was itself fragmented into smaller kingdoms the rulers of which might have acknowledged the sovereignty of the Pālas. In fact, we come across the existence of an independent Kamboja dynasty ruling in northern Bengal in the middle of the tenth century A.D. Inscriptions from Chittagong indicate the existence of an independent kingdom in Harikela in far eastern Bengal at about the same time. Inscriptions also testify the existence of an independent kingdom of the Candras in eastern Bengal in the tenth and eleventh century.

Despite such reverses the Pālas were able to recoup their fortunes under Mahīpāla I (A.D. 988-1038).

* * * *

The Pratihāra power was revived by Bhoja (A.D. 836-885), the grondson of Nāgabhaṭa II. From his Bara copper plate of A.D. 836 it is known that he had become the master of Kanauj and made it his capital but he had to devote much time to consolidating his power. The Jodhpur branch of the Pratihāras had declared independence under Kakka. We learn from the Daulatpur copper plate that about A.D. 843 he subdued the Jodhpur Pratihāras and established his full authority over Gurjaratrā, i.e., central and eastern Rajasthan. However, Bhoja suffered setbacks between A.D. 845 and 860; he was defeated by Devapāla, the Pāla king of Bengal and Bihar, by the Rāṣṭrakūṭas and by the Kalacuri king Kokkala. These defeats did not discourage him and after the death of Devapāla, when the Pāla power became weak, Bhoja defeated Nārāyaṇapāla and occupied portions of northern and western Bengal. He also defeated the Rāṣṭrakūṭa king Kṛṣṇa II. His kingdom extended up to the Punjab in the northwest. The Kalacuris of the Gorakhpur region were his feudatories. So also were the Candellas of Bundelkhand. Malwa was under his authority. Bhoja was succeeded by his son Mahendrapāla (A.D. 885-909) who was able not only to retain his ancestral kingdom out to extend its boundary as well. His inscriptions have been found in the Kathiawar Peninsula, eastern Punjab, Jhansi, Ayodhya, southern Bihar and northern Bengal.

The next powerful Pratihāra king was Mahīpāla who ruled up to A.D. 942. The Arab writer Al Masudi has referred to his prowess and prosperity. Rājaśekhara was his court poet. The fortunes of the Pratihāras began to decline after the defeat of Mahīpāla by the Rāṣṭrakūṭas. Although Mahīpāla was able to retain the territories from Saurashtra to Varanasi, under his weak successors the Pratihāra kingdom ceased to exist towards the close of the tenth century A.D. The factors responsible for the downfall of the Pratihāras were the Rāṣṭrakūṭa and Candella invasions, the independence of the feudatories and the incompetence of the Pratihāra kings. Subsequently, on the ruins of the Pratihāra kingdom three powers came to existence the Cāhamānas of Rajasthan, the Caulukyas of Gujarat and the Paramāras of Malwa.

*   *   *   *

The Rāṣṭrakūṭas of Deccan reached the zenith of their power and prosperity during the reign of Govinda III who was in fact master of entire southern India. The Gaṅgas of Karnataka, the Eastern Cālukyas of Andhra Pradesh and the small powers of the far south acknowleged his sovereignty. During the period of his absence on the northern expedition the Pallavas, Pāṇḍyas, Keralas and Gaṅgas formed a united front against him. But Govinda defeated them in A.D. 802 and occupied Kanchi. The king of Ceylon also offered his submission to Govinda.

After the death of Govinda III in 814 A.D., his minor son Amoghavarṣa ascended the throne. His guardian was his uncle Karkka, the Rāṣṭrakūṭa ruler of some regions of Gujarat, who subdued the rebellious feudatories on behalf of the minor king. Amoghavarṣa himself defeated Vijayāditya II, the Eastern Cālukya ruler of Veṅgī who disregarded Rāṣṭrakūṭa authority in A.D. 830. He waged a protracted war with the Gaṅgas of Karnataka which was utlimately brought to end through a matrimonial alliance. According to the Sirur inscription the rulers of Aṅga, Vaṅga, Magadha, Mālava and Veṅgī acknowledged the suzerainty of Amoghavarṣa. For Veṅgī and Mālava it was quite natural and Aṅga-Vaṅga-Magadha must have denoted the Pāla kingdom. The Draviḍa king defeated by Devapāla, as claimed in the Pāla inscriptions, was not Amoghavarṣa. The reference to Aṅga-Vaṅga-Kaliṅga as his subdued territory might have been a recollection of the achievements of his forefathers. Amoghavarṣa made his new capital at Mānyakheṭa or Malkhed. Towards the close of his reign there were rebellions which were suppressed by his able general Vaṅkeya. Apart from suppressing revolts Amoghavarṣa did not involve himself in any aggressive war. He was a devout Jain and also a sound scholar. His *Kavirājamārga* was the first work in Kannada on poetics.

In A.D. 878 Amoghavarṣa was succeeded by his son Kṛṣṇa II whose reign was marked by constant struggle with the Pratihāras and the Eastern Cālukyas of Veṅgī. His Pratihāra adversary was Bhoja against whom he fought till A.D. 888. In his struggle against the Pratihāras he was assisted by Kṛṣṇarāja of the Rāṣṭrakūṭa feudatory branch of Lāṭa or southern

Gujarat. His Eastern Cālukya opponent was Vijayāditya who had not only withstood Rāṣṭrakūṭa suzerainty but also invaded the territories of the Gaṅgas and the Noḷambas who were the feudatories of the Rāṣṭrakūṭas. It was with much difficulty that Kṛṣṇa was able to subdue the Eastern Cālukyas. In A.D. 914 Kṛṣṇa II was succeeded by his grandson Indra III who defeated the Pratihāra king Mahīpāla and conquered Kanauj.

The last important Rāṣṭrakūṭa king was Kṛṣṇa III (A.D. 939-967) who, with the help of his brother-in-law Bhūtuga, the ruler of Gaṅgavādi, conquered Kanchi and Tanjore in A.D. 943. The Cola king Parantaka tried to drive the Rāṣṭrakūṭas out, but he was defeated at the battle of Takkolam in A.D. 949. Kṛṣṇa marched up to Ramesvaram where he erected a pillar of victory. As a result the whole Toṇḍamaṇḍala region came under the Rāṣṭrakūṭas. Kṛṣṇa also led an invasion towards northern India and occupied Ujjayinī. He maintained the tradition of Dhruva, Govinda III and Indra III and has rightly been described as *sakala-dakṣiṇa-dig-adhipati*. Kṛṣṇa III, being sonless, was succeeded by his brother Khoṭṭiga. The latter was succeeded by his nephew Karkka II, who was defeated and ousted by his own feudatory, the Cāḷukya Taila II of Bijapur.

17. Distribution of Regional Powers in Northern India

The political importance of the Pālas, Pratihāras and Rāṣṭrakūṭas was due to a few of their powerful kings; and when these kings were no more it became apparent that these so called powerful kingdoms had feet of clay. There was geographical realignment of political powers, but the earlier structure characterised by the existence of countless small principalities and feudatories remained unchanged. The comparatively powerful kingdoms fought against one another to have mastery over the feudatories.

Kashmir was almost isolated from the rest of the country. The country passed through many vicissitudes of fortune and after a long rule of local kings it passed to the Kuṣāṇas and Hunas. The Kārkoṭaka dynasty was established in Kashmir by Durlabhavardhana in A.D. 627. Lalitāditya Muktāpīḍa (A.D. 724-760) of this dynasty defeated the Tibetans, Dards,

Kambojas, Turks (Arabs) and the Kanauj king Yaśovarman. From the middle of the ninth century Kashmir came under the Utpalas. Most of the princes of this dynasty were irresponsible and their tyrannical rule was limited only through armed popular rising, deposition or assassination by rivals. At the beginning of the eleventh century Kashmir was ruled by Saṅgrāmarāja of the Lohara dynasty whose minister Tuṅga helped the Shahi King Trilocanapāla against Sultan Mahmud. The death of Saṅgrāmarāja in A.D. 1028 ushered in a period of anarchy and confusion in Kashmir under incompetent rulers.

In western India, the Saindhavas, to whom goes the credit of resisting the Arabs, ruled in western Saurashtra which their capital at Bhumili, about 25 miles to the northeast of Porbandar. There were two ruling dynasties of the Cāpas, one at Vardhamānapura (modern Wadvan) and the other at Anahilapāṭaka. They were reduced to vassalage by the Pratihāras. The Caulukyas established a kingdom in Sarasvatī-maṇḍala, with its capital at Anahilapāṭaka in the tenth century under Mūlarāja. A branch of the Caulukyas settled in the Lāṭa region under Barappa. In Rajasthan the Cāhamānas had kingdoms at Śakambharī (Sambhar region of Jaipur), Naddula (Nadol in Jodhpur), Dhavalapurī (Dholpur) and Partabgarh. One branch of the Guhilas ruled at Madapāṭa or Mewar and the other at Dhavagarta modern Dhol in Udaipur. In the Delhi region the Tomaras were the feudatories of the Pratihāras.

In central India the Candellas founded an independent kingdom in Bundelkhand and extended their territories as far as the bank of the Yamunā on the north, Jabalpur on the south, Khajuraho on the west and Kālañjara on the east. Candella Vidyādhara fought twice against Mahmud of Ghazni in A.D. 1012 and 1022. The Kalacuris, who originally hailed from western India, founded a kingdom at Tripuri in Madhya Pradesh. Another branch of the Kalacuris had their settlement at Saryupāra on the bank of the modern Ghogra river. In the first half of the eleventh century Kalacuri Gāṅgeyadeva and his son Lakṣmīkarṇa conquered a part of southern Kosala, Aṅga or the Bhagalpur region and Vārānasī and defeated the Candellas, the Pālas of Bengal and the Turks of northern India. The Paramāras had also founded an independent kingdoms in the Malwa region. Paramāra Bhoja ascended the throne of Malwa in A.D. 1000. By contracting an alliance with the Kalacuris and Colas he defeated the Cālukyas of Kalyāṇa. He helped the Shāhī Ānandapāla against Sultan Mahmud in A.D. 1008 and gave shelter to his son Trilocanapāla. In 1043 he organised a military alliance of a few Hindu powers and seized the Lahore fort for seven months.

The Śailodbhavas ruled till the middle of the eighth century in Orissa. During the next 250 years numerous ruling dynasties are found all over Orissa. Among these, the Bhauma-Karas or Karas ruled in Balasore, Cuttack and Puri districts between A.D. 800 and 1000. References to two branches of a Bhañja dynasty, one at Khiñjali (parts of Baudh, Sonepur and Ganjam) and the other at Khijing (in Mayurbhanj) have been found in more than thirty inscriptions. The Tuṅga dynasty was probably a vassal of the Karas in the Yamagarta-maṇḍala (parts of Talcher, Pal-Lahar and Keonjhar). The Maurya dynasty ruled in the present Bonai region where their inscriptions have been found. The Śulkis ruled in parts of Dhenkanal and Talcher. The Somavaṃśīs of southern Kosala, who had their capital at Śrīpura, modern Sripur in the Raipur district of Madhya Pradesh, conquered the greater part of Orissa in the middle of the tenth century. The Kaliṅga region which was extended up to Srikakulam in Andhra Pradesh was ruled by the Eastern Gaṅgas.

After Bhāskaravarman numerous dynasties ruled successively in Kāmarūpa or the Assam region. During the reign of Harjaravarman (A.D. 828) and his son Vaṇamāla a part of north Bengal was annexed to Assam. King Ratnapāla of the dynasty founded by one Brahmapāla towards the close of the tenth century A.D. is said to have fought successfully with some kings of northern India. His grandson Indrapāla faced an invasion of Jātavarman, the Yādava king of eastern Bengal. The next important dynasty which ruled in Kamarupa from the beginning of the twelfth century was that of Vaidyadeva. Among his successors, Rāyārideva is said to have vanquished a king of Vaṅga. His grandson Vallabhadeva, one of whose known dates is A.D. 1185, suffered a defeat at the hands of Laksmaṇasena.

In A.D. 988 when Mahīpāla I ascended the throne of Bengal, the Pāla empire existed precariously only in south Bihar.

Mahīpāla reconquered northern and eastern Bengal, northern Bihar and eastern Uttar Pradesh as far as Vāraṇasī. It was during his reign that Rajendra Cola invaded Bengal. His successor Nayapāla (A.D. 1038-55) and grandson Vigrahapāla III resisted the Kalacuri invasions. During the reign of the next king Mahīpāla II there was a revolt led by one Divya belonging to the Kaivarta caste and the king was killed. Thus Varendrī or north Bengal was lost to the Pālas where Divya began to rule from A.D. 1075. During the reign of his successor Bhīma, Rāmapāla, brother of Mahīpāla II, reconquered Varendrī with the help of his fourteen feudatories. Rāmapāla defeated Harivarman, the Yādava king of eastern Bengal, and for some time he was also master of Kāmarūpa. After Rāmapāla's death in A.D. 1120, during the reign of Kumārapāla, the Pāla kingdom disintegrated once again owing to the rebellion of the feudatories. Taking advantage of the weakness of the kingdom, Anantavarman Coḍagaṅga of Orissa advanced as far as the Hooghly district of West Bengal. Kumārapāla was succeeded by his son Gopala III in 1125 and the later by Madanapāla in 1144 who was the last king of the Pāla dynasty.

The Pālas were succeeded by the Senas. The founder of this dynasty was Sāmantasena who was probably a feudatory of the Pālas in the Rāḍha region. His son Hemantasena increased his power during the Kalacuri raids in Bengal. Hemantasena was succeeded by his son Vijayasena in 1095 who made an alliance with the Kaliṅga king Anantavarman Coḍagaṅga with whom he came to the Hooghly district. He sent a naval invasion against the Gāhaḍavāla Govindacandra and on the way he defeated Nānyadeva of Mithila. He defeated the Yādava ruler of eastern Bengal, the Kāmarūpa king Rāyārideva, and Rāghava, the son of his previous ally Anantavarman Coḍagaṅga. Having taken Varendrī from the Pālas he became master of Bengal. His son Ballālasena (1158-78) retained all the territories he inherited from his father. He was succeeded in 1178 by his son Laksmaṇasena who defeated the Gāhaḍavāla king Jayacandra. He also campaigned successfully in Assam and Orissa.

18. Regional Power in the South

On the eastern coast, between the Godavari and the Pennar,

corresponding to a large part of modern Andhra Pradesh, was the kingdom of the Eastern Cāḷukyas with their capital at Veṅgī. It was a collateral dynasty of the Cāḷukyas of Badami; it maintained relations with the main branch and expanded its territories in the north, south and west and also had feudatories. From the middle of the eighth century the Eastern Cālukyas became subordinates of the Rāṣṭrakūṭas though they ruled almost independently often helping the Rāṣṭrakūṭas or fighting against them. In the tenth century there were internecine wars among rival claimants until in A.D. 999 Śaktivarman came to the throne of Veṅgī with Cola Rājarāja's help. Likewise the Western Gaṅgas of Karnataka had a protracted dynastic rule as subordinates of the Rāṣṭrakūṭas.

The Eastern Gaṅgas rose to prominence in the political scene of India under Anantavarman Coḍagaṅga. The Somavaṃśīs continued to rule in southern Kosala and Odra often extending their sphere of influence in the neighbouring territories. They later became feudatories of the Eastern Gaṅgas. The Telugu-Coḍas ruled in Cuddapah, Karnul and Anantapur districts as vassals of the Eastern Cālukyas and often changed their allegiance in conformity with the changing pattern of power. The region between the Krishna and the Godavari was subsequently ruled by the Kākatīyas with their capital at Warangal.

Among the minor powers of the south before the region came under Cola influence, mention may be made of the Bāṇas to the north of Kolar, the Noḷambas of Noḷambavāḍi or the Chitaldung district of Karnataka and the Vaidumbas of Renandu in the north Pennar valley. In Kerala there was an independent principality in the beginning of the ninth century ruled by Ceruman of the Perumal dynasty. Sthānu Ravi of Kerala was a contemporary of the Cola king Āditya I (A.D. 871-907). Bhāskara Ravivarman ruled between A.D. 978 and 1036.

Between A.D. 800 and 900, the Pallavas of Kanchi maintained their independent existence under Dantivarman, Nandivarman III, Nṛpatuṅgavarman and Aparājita. During the reign of Dantivarman the Pallava kingdom was threatened by Rāṣṭrakūta and Pāṇḍya invasions. His successors defeated the Pāṇḍyas repeatedly but when the last king of this line, Aparājita, was defeated by Āditya Cola in A.D. 893 the

Pallavas disappeared from the political scene of south India. The Pāṇḍyas of Madura became masters of big territory under Neduñjaḍaiyan (A.D. 765-815). His son Śrīmāra Śrīvallabha (A.D 815-62) was also a conquerer. However, constant struggle with the Pallavas made the Pāṇḍyas weak. During the reign of Rājasimha II (A.D. 900-920) the Cola king, Parantaka I, defeated the Pāṇḍyas and conquered Madura. There was a temporary revival of the Pāṇḍya power under Vīra Pāṇḍya in A.D. 949 when the Colas were defeated by the Rāṣṭrakūṭas in the battle of Takkolam. But eventually the Pāṇḍya kingdom passed into the hands of Colas during the reign of Rājarāja I.

The Colas were originally feudatories of the Pallavas, but taking advantage of the weakness of the latter the Cola Āditya I (A.D. 871-907) defeated his Pallava overlord Aparājita and occupied Toṇḍamaṇḍalam. He also conquered Koṅgudeśa (Salem and Coimbatore districts) from the Pāṇḍyas and received submission of the Western Gaṅgas. The next Cola king, Parantaka (A.D. 907-953), defeated the combined army of the Pāṇḍyas and the king of Ceylon in the battle of Vellur and with the help of the Western Gaṅgas he defeated the Bāṇas and the Vaidumbas and routed the Pallavas. Rāṣṭrakūṭas under Kṛṣṇa II were also defeated by him at Tiruvallam in North Arcot district. But the tables were turned in 943 when the Rāṣṭrakūṭa Kṛṣṇa III inflicted a signal defeat on him in the battle of Takkolam as a result of which he lost all the occupied territories including Toṇḍamaṇḍalam. After that the Colas were reduced to an insignificant power until their glory was revived by Rājarāja I (A.D. 985-1014).

After the fall of the Rāṣṭrakūṭas, the Western Cālukyas under Taila II became masters of the major portion of Maharashtra and Karnataka from the middle of the tenth century A.D. This dynasty became powerful under the leadership of Satyāśraya, Vikramāditya V and Jayasiṃha II. Jayasiṃha was succeeded by his son Someśvara Āhavamalla (A.D. 1043-68) whose reign witnessed the prolonged Cola-Cālukya rivalry. The Kalacuryas, originally feudatories of the Western Cālukyas, ruled in Kālyaṇa between A.D. 1156 and 1181 under four kings—Bijjala, Someśvara, Saṅkama and Āhavamalla. The northern Konkan, the southern Konkan and the south Maratha country were ruled by three branches of the Śīlāhāras. Subsequently, the major portion of western and central Deccan came under the Yādavas of Devagiri who were originally feudatories of the Rāṣṭrakūṭas and Western Cālukyas. The Yādavas declared independence under Bhillama (A.D. 1185-93) and were in constant conflict with the northern powers of Gujarat, Malwa and Rajasthan, the eastern powers of the Gaṅgas and Kākatiyas and the southern powers of the Hoysalas and Colas.

19. Colas under Rājarāja and Rājendra

The foundation of the Cola empire in the south was laid by Rājarāja I. His career of conquest began with the destruction of the Cera navy at Trivandrum. About A.D. 991 Rājarāja invaded the Western Gaṅga territories and annexed Gaṅgavāḍi Tadigaivāḍi and Noḷambavāḍi to his own kingdom. Sometime before A.D. 1007 he launched a campaign against Iraṭṭapāḍi or the Western Cālukya kingdom and plundered its cities. He put Śaktivarman on the throne of Veṅgī and strengthened Cola relations with the Eastern Cālukyas by giving his daughter in marriage with Śaktivarman's brother Vimalāditya. He then conquered Kaliṅga which was necessary from a military point of view so that the Eastern Cālukyas could be threatened from the north in case they sided with the rival power of the Colas, i.e., the Western Cālukyas. He also conquered Ceylon and the Maldives.

Rājarāja died in A.D. 1014 but long before that he had nominated his son Rājendra I as the crown prince. The imperialistic designs of Rājarāja were achieved by Rājendra. His Tirumalai rock inscription refers to his conquests of the following territories : Iḍaiturraināḍu or the Raichur Doab, Vanavāsī, Kollippakkai (Kulpak near Hyderabad), Mannaikkadakkam (Mānyakheṭa, Malkhed), Iḷam (Ceylon), the Maldives, Sandimattivu (an island in the Arabian Sea), Iraṭṭapāḍi (Western Cālukya territories), Musaṅgi (Maski), Śakkarakoṭṭam (part of Bastar district), Maduramaṇḍalam, Namanaikoṇam, and Pañcapalli (eastern Madhya Pradesh), Ādinagara (Jajnagar in Orissa), Indraratha (part of southern Kosala), Oḍḍa-Viṣaya (Orissa), Kosalai-nāḍu (regions on the Mahānadī), Taṇḍabhukti (Daṇḍabhukti in Midnapur district of West Bengal), Takkaṇalāḍam and Uttiralāḍam (southern and northern Rāḍha) and

Vaṅgāladeśa (eastern and southern Bengal). About A.D. 1018 Rājendra conquered Ceylon and in the same year some territories of the Ceras on the Malabar coast came under his sway. In 1019 he appointed one of his sons as the ruler of Madura. In 1021 he defeated the Western Cālukya king Jayasiṃha at the battle of Musaṅgi (Maski). Then he crossed the Godavari and passed through Bastar and Orissa to reach Bengal where he defeated the Pāla king Mahīpāla. He made his new capital at Gaṅgaikoṇḍacolapuram near Chidambaram. About 1025 Rājendra launched a naval campaign in Malaysia and Indonesia. He conquered Śrivijaya (Sumatra), Pannai (the eastern region of Sumatra), Malaiyur (an island near Sumatra), Māyirudiṅgam (Ligor), Ilaṅgāśoka (the region south of Ligor), Māppapāḍam (the Isthmus of Kra), Mavilimbaṅgam, Valaipandur, Talaitakkolam (Takkol), Mādamāliṅgam (Bandan region), Ilāmurideśam (Lamri in north Sumatra), Mānakkavaram (the Nicobar islands) and Kaḍāram (Keda near Penang). In fact, he made the Bay of Bengal a Cola lake. The purpose of his naval expedition was really to safeguard trade interests in the Far East.

20. Western Cālukyas: Someśvara and Vikramāditya VI

The Rāṣṭrakūṭa royal line of the central and western Deccan was supplanted by the Western Cālukyas, also known as the Cālukyas or Kalyāṇī, who steadily consolidated their political power between 997 and 1043 A.D. Having made themselves masters of the Deccan down to the banks of the river Tuṅgaḥadrā they had to confront their natural southern rival, the Colas. Both the powers had aggressive imperialistic designs. The territory of the Eastern Cālukyas of Veṅgī, which was almost a buffer state, was the bone of contention between the two powers. The rulers of Veṅgī were distant kin of the Western Cālukyas while they were related with the Colas through matrimonial alliances. Both the Western Cālukyas and the Colas simultaneously wanted to achieve overlordship of the Eastern Cālukyas of Veṅgī. This was one of the causes of the prolonged Cola-Cālukya rivalry which started during the reign of Someśvara Āhavamalla (A.D. 1043-68).

The offensive was taken by Cola Rājādhirāja in 1044 who, after smashing the Cālukya resistance at three places, sacked and burnt the capital city of Kālyaṇa. The second invasion was in 1047 when Rājādhirāja plundered the city of Pundur on the Krishna but it was resisted by Cāmuṇḍarāja, the ruler of Vanavāsī who was a feudatory of the Cālukyas. The third Cola attack was in 1051-52, and in the battle of Koppam the Cola Rājādhirāja was shot dead. His brother Rājendra II reorganised the Cola army in the battlefield and turned impending defeat into a complete victory. However, in spite of the defeat, the Cālukyas suffered no territorial loss. Thereafter Somesvara took the offensive and in 1054 he occupied Kanchi. He led a second invasion in 1058 and a third between 1059 and 1068, but in the battle of Mudakaru he was defeated. Subsequently he was defeated twice by the Cola Vīrarājendra. Despite these repeated defeats he challenged the Colas to fight once again at Kudala Saṅgamam. In response to this challenge Vīrarājendra went there with his army in 1067, but Someśvara did not turn up. Vīrarājendra erected a pillar of victory on the banks of the Tuṅgabhadrā and returned. Towards the close of his reign Someśvara had the satisfaction of success when in 1068 his son Vikramāditya sacked the Çola capital Gaṅgaikoṇḍa.

Someśvara extended his sway over the Śīlāharas of Konkan, successfully fought against the Caulukyas, Paramāras and Kalacuris and exerted some influence on the Eastern Cālukyas. He was succeeded by his son Someśvara II (A.D. 1068-76) who was ousted by his brother Vikramāditya VI (A.D. 1076-1125), the greatest king of the dynasty whose exploits have been recorded in Bilhaṇa's *Vikramāṅkadevacarita*. He subdued the rebellion of his brother Jayasiṃha who was the ruler of Vanavāsī, Santalige and Kadur. He also invaded Gujarat and defeated the Caulukya Karṇa. In 1105 he conquered Kanchi from the Colas. Between 1091 and 1093 he destroyed Veṅgī, defeated Belanāṇṭi I Gonka and wrested some portion of the Andhra country from Vīra Coḍa. One of his vassals, Paramāra Jagaddeva, subdued the Hoysalas and another Sinda Aca II of Erambarage subdued the rebellions of Kadamba Vijayāditya and the Pāṇḍya Uccaṅgī. Vikramāditya's kingdom comprised the districts of Hasan, Tumkur and Cuddapah to the south, the districts of Khammamet and Godavari on the east and southeast, and the territory up to the Narmada on the north, but the sphere of his influence was far greater. He was succeeded by his son Someśvasa III (A.D. 1126-1138) who resisted a Hoysala upsurge but lost some of his Andhra dominions to Kulottuṅga Cola. The next king Jagaddakamalla (1138-51) subdued the rebellions of the Hoysalas of Gaṅgavāḍi, Kadambas of Goa and Noḷamba-Pāṇḍyas; defeated the Paramāra Jayasiṃha and put his own nominee Ballāla on the throne of Malwa; and successfully fought Kulottuṅga Cola and Anantavarman Coḍagaṅga of Kaliṅga. But during the reign of the next king, Taila III (1151-56), the Western Cālukya kingdom was usurped by his feudatory Kalacurya Bijjala. The Kalacuryas ruled upto 1181, and then Taila's son Someśvara IV was able to regain his ancestral kingdom. However, he was defeated in 1189 by Yādava Bhillama and spent the rest of his life with Kadambas of Goa with whom he took refuge.

21. Increasing Importance of the Feudatories

Inscriptions refer to numerous feudatories who played an important part in the political turmoil of the period under review. Among the feudatories of the Gurjara Pratihāras, were minor Pratihāra dynasties at Rajorgarh, Devagarh, Siyodoni and other places, besides the well known ones like the Candellas of Jejākabhukti, the Tomaras of Delhi, the Guhilas of Mewar and so on. The dynasties which were successors of the Pratihāras like the Paramāras, Candellas, Caulukyas, Gahaḍavālas, Cāhamānas, etc., had also their feudatories. The Caulukyas of Gujarat who were originally feudatories of the Cālukyas, Rāṣṭrakūṭas and Pratihāras, very often changing their allegiance, had under them several feudatory lines like the Guhilas of Mongrol, Mahāmaṇḍaleśvara Vapanadeva of Godrahaka, the Cāhamānas of Nadol, the Cāhamānas of Brahmapāṭaka, the Paramāras of Candrāvati, the Rāṇakas of Mandali, the Vodanas of Nadol, etc. The feudatories of the Candellas included the Kacchapaghātas of Gwalior and another line represented by Mahārāṇaka Kumārapāla. At Vagada a collateral branch of the Paramāras served as feudatories of the Paramāra kings. Among other Paramāra feudatories mention may be made of

Lakṣmīvarman of Bhopal who styled himself as Mahākumāra and also as Sāmanta. In the south Kosala area we have epigraphic references to certain feudatories such as Mahārāṇaka Kīrtivarman of Kakkaredika, Bhogikapāla Nirihullaka, etc. Among the Gāhaḍavālas we have the lines of Rāṇaka Lavanapravāha, Singara Vatasarāja, Rāṣṭrakūṭas of Badaun, Rāṣṭrakūṭas of Magadha, etc. The terms Rāṇaka and Mahārāṇaka were later transformed into Rāṇā and Mahārāṇā.

In the Deccan the Yādavas were feudatories of the Western Cāḷukyas of Kalyāṇa. The Raṭṭas were probably descendants of the local barons ruling in Maharashtra. The Rāṣṭrakūṭas themselves were originally one of these families. The Raṭṭa *sāmantas* were many and their inscriptions are numerous. Two of their lines appear to have been prominent, namely, those of Saundatti and of Lattatura. The Sindā Mahāmaṇḍaleśvaras had different branches. The Kadamba Mahāmaṇḍaleśvaras were scions of the Kadambas of Vanavāsī and held power at Palasika, Hangal, Uccaśṛṅgī and Triparvata. Some of them became powerful in the Konkan region. Scions of the Pāṇḍya dynasty acted as feudatories at Konkan and Noḷambavāḍi. The Śīlāhāra princes called themselves Mahāmaṇḍaleśvaras. One Śīlāhāra Mahāsāmanta Pullaśakti and his son Kapardin II described themselves as lords of Konkan. The principal feudatories of the Cālukyas of Kalyāṇa included the Kadambas of Haṅgal, the Noḷambas, the Hoysalas, the Raṭṭas and the Yādavas. The Noḷambas were originally under the Gaṅgas and then under the Rāṣṭrakūṭas, Western Cālukyas and Colas successively. The Ganga-Pallavas were also a feudatory family with their capital at Nandigiri. The Pāṇḍyas of Ucchaṅgī claimed to have been Mahāmaṇḍaleśvaras and lords of Kanchipura. They were feudatories of the Cālukyas but were hard-pressed by the Colas and ultimately became the vassals of the Hoysalas. Other minor feudatory families of the south were the Kerala princes, the Koṅgalvas, the Chaṅgalvas, etc. Under the Western Cālukyas and the Yādavas, the feudatories often had sub-feudatories holding seigniories (*mānneyas*) under them.

It appears from the inscriptions of the feudatory princes that many of them held authority in their territories for continuous periods extending over two or three centuries. Among such lines were the Raṭṭas, the Śīlāharas, the Pāṇḍyas of Konkan, the Noḷambas, etc. who maintained themselves by transferring their allegiance to the rising power of the day. In many cases they were subject-allies or friendly-dependents, often having matrimonial relationship with the family of the overlord. Bhūtuga secured the throne with the help of the Rāṣṭrakūṭa Amoghavarṣa II, married his daughter, helped Kṛṣṇa III to gain the throne against the usurper Lalliyam, and fought for his overlord. On account of this he received the principality of Vanavāsi-12000 and Belvolā-300. In lieu of the privilege of enjoying unmolested local authority within their territories the feudatories were required to render military help to their overlords in time of need. Amoghavarṣa sent Baṅkesa to subdue the Gaṅga Racamalla. The Gaṅga Mārasiṃha fought to restore the Rāṣṭrakūṭa Indra. The Hoysalas were employed against the enemies of the Cālukyas of Kalyāṇa. The Sindā princes fought on behalf of their overlord. The Caulukya Bhīma sent his feudatory the Paramāra Dhārāvarṣa against the Ghurids.

However, there are cases of certain feudatories who did not conform to the restrictions imposed on them by their overlords. In many cases when the overlord was weak the feudatory did not hesitate to declare independence and fight against him. Many of the founders of the great dynasties were in origin feudatories. Thus Bhatārka, the founder of the Maitraka line was only a *senāpati*. His successors assumed the higher title of *mahārāja*. The earlier Cālukyas, the Rāṣṭrakūṭas, the Kalyāṇī Cālukyas, the Hoysalas, the Yādavas, the Kākatiyas—all were feudatories in the beginning. It was customary to put the name of their suzerains in their grants and inscriptions though in the case of land grants it was not compulsory. Many of them had separate crests and banners. We also have instances of private war between two feudatories under the same king. Thus the Una inscription records a fight between the Cālukya feudatory Avanivarman and the Cāpa Dharaṇivarāha. Similarly, the Terahi inscription records the fight between two feudatories of the Pratihāras, namely, Guṇarāja and Undabhaṭṭa.

The fragmentation of political power was never so pronounced as on the eve of the Turkish conquest. Numerous principalities continued to fight amongst themselves, as a result of which the rulers were so economically exhausted that in most cases it was just not possible for them to maintain a standing army and a centralised administrative structure. Thus, dependence on the feudatories became imperative. If we take into account the case of two rival powers, the Western Cālukyas and the Colas, we find that the former depended more on the feudatories while they were at war with others, but the latter relied more on their own strength. The Colas had economic power as well since the objective of their wars was mostly plunder which they did ruthlessly. Secondly, they had the advantage over the Western Cālukyas of an extensive maritime trade. The Colas controlled the Malabar region where there were actual sttlements of the western traders. The Bay of Bengal was also virtually a Cola lake and they had full advantage over the eastern sea-borne trade. The northern states which had no such avenues depended more on the feudatories which is indicated in the Paramāra, Caulukya, Candella, Eastern Gaṅga, Kalacuri and Gahaḍavāla records which refer to numerous feudatories having different grades of titles. The danger of such dependence was, especially during times of decaying state power, that feudatories with limited vision and rural vanity were tempted to usurp the royal power which they tried to do in most cases. This also accounts for the success of the Turkish hordes because the powers which should have offered resistance were themselves wrecked from within by the continuous turmoil created by the ambitious feudatories.

22. *Beginnings of the Medieval Period* (A.D.1000-1300)

While the demarcation line between the medieval and the modern periods of Indian history is more or less clear, that between the ancient and the medieval is indistinct and problematic. The period between A.D. 1000 and 1300 which witnessed the invasion and expansion of Muslim power (this term is used in a broad comprehensive way since the invaders belonged to different races and nationalities) is generally suppossed to represent the emergence of the medieval period in India. This period, however, was not qualitatively different from the preceding ones in terms of the overall socio-political situation. There was no change in the traditional political system which was characterised by the existence of numerous small feudatory states. Occasionally comparatively big powers emerged which wanted to bring the feudatory states under the sphere of their influence. The feudatories very often changed their allegiance, which sometimes caused wars. The pattern remained the same since the downfall of the imperial Guptas.

Between A.D. 1000 and 1028 the states of northern India bore the burnt of successive invasions of the Ghaznavids under Slutan Mahmud which resulted in the ruthless destruction of cities, the indiscriminate massacre of the people and the plunder of wealth to an unconceivable extent. The ruling Shahi dynasty of Udabhāṇḍapura was exterminated. Punjab was conquered and made a province of the Ghaznavid kingdom. But the appointed governors of the Ghaznavid Sultans in the Punjab who belonged to the Yamini clan, did not fare well. They were constantly harassed by the Paramāras, Kalacuris, Cāhamānas and Gāhaḍavālas. About 1186 the Ghaznavids were routed from Punjab by the Ghurids.

In order to avoid the invasion of Sultan Mahmud in 1019, Rājyapāla, the Pratihāra ruler of Kanauj, shifted his capital to a place called Bari. Kanauj came under the Yamini governors of the Ghaznavids between A.D. 1068 and 1080. The Yaminis posted one Chānd Rāya to look after Kanauj. This Chānḍ Rāya was probably Candradeva of the Gāhaḍavala dynasty who later declared independence. His inscriptions testify that Kanauj, Vārāṇasi and Ayodhya were under his authority. His grandson Govindacandra defeated the Yaminis; he ruled between 1114 and 1154 and resisted the invasions of Rāmapāla of Bengal, Anantavarman Coḍagaṅga of Kaliṅga and Nānyadeva of Mithila. During the reign of his grandson Jayacandra, Muhammad Ghuri occupied Kanauj in 1193 by defeating him at a place called Chandawar. But his victory was not final. In 1197, Jayacandra's son Hariścandra was able to reconquer Kanauj, Jaunpur and Mirzapur. Hariścandra's successor, Aḍakkamalla, lost Kanauj to Iltutmush some time before 1236.

In the beginning of the eleventh century the Caulukyas became powerful in the Gujarat region. Bhīma I after his rout at the hands of Sultan Mahmud was able to reconquer his lost territories. His descendants—Karṇa (1064-94), Jayasiṃha (1094-1145), Kumārapāla (1145-72) and Ajayapāla (1172-76)—fought against the local powers like the Paramāras, Candellas, Ābhīras and different Rajput chiefs. During the reign of Mūlarāja II Muhammad Ghuri attempted unsuccessful invasion of Gujarat in 1178. The next king, Bhīma II who ruled up to 1242, faced the attacks of the Paramāras, Yādavas and the Mameluk Qutabuddin, but he was able to protect himself owing to the help of his Vāghela feudatories. The next king, Tribhuvanapāla (1242-1250), resisted the invasions of the Yādavas, Paramāras and Guhilas. Eventually the feudatory line of the Vāghelas became rulers of Gujarat and Sāraṅgadeva (1274-96) of this line successfully resisted the Mameluk inroads. Gujarat was occupied in 1299 by Alauddin Khalji during the rule of the next king Karṇa, who became a fugitive in the Yādava court at Devagiri.

In Rajasthan and the adjoining areas numerous small dynasties ruled between the eleventh and thirteenth centuries. The Yadu dynasty ruled in Bayāna-Śrīpatha, i.e., the Bharatpur region, from A.D. 1000 to 1193. One branch of the Kacchapaghātas ruled in Gwalior, which was occupied by the Ghurids in 1196. When Aram Shah was the Sultan of Delhi king Vigraha of the Pratihāra dynasty occupied Gwalior but it was reoccupied from his successors in 1258 by Balban. The second branch of the Kacchapaghātas ruled at Dubkund while a third at Narwar. Different branches of the Paramāras ruled in Mount Abu, Bagur, Jhalor and Bhilmal respectively. The Guhilas ruled in the Mewar region till Alauddin Khalji defeated Ratan Singh and occupied Chitor in 1303 A.D. A branch dynastry of the Guhilas ruled in Sisodia. The Cāhamānas had five branches ruling in Sakambhari, Raṇthambhor, Nadol, Jalor and Sanchor respectively. The main branch was that of Sakambhari which rose to power and prominence. Prthvīrāja III of this dynasty was defeated by Muhammad Ghuri in 1192 at the second battle of Tarain.

In the Malwa region the Paramāras became powerful under Muñja and Sindhurāja. Bhoja, son of Sindhurāja, ascended the throne of Malwa in A.D. 1000. After his death in A.D. 1055 Malwa was occupied by the Caulukyas and the Kalacuris, but Bhoja's son Jayasiṃha was able to recover the lost kingdom with the help of the Cālukyas of Kalyāṇa. Subsequently, the Paramāra kings struggled for survival against a variety of forces, chief among them being the Caulukyas of Gujarat. One of the

Paramâra kings, Lakṣmadeva, resisted successfully the attack of Mahmud, the governor of Punjab in Ujjayini. Between 1170 and 1180 Vindhyavarman re-established Paramāra authority in Malwa by defeating the Caulukya Mūlaraja II. During the reign of later Paramāra kings Malwa was weakened by the repeated invasions of the Yādavas of Devagiri. In 1233, during the reign of Devapāla, there was a Turkish invasion in Malwa when Iltutmish conquered Bhilsa and plundered Ujjayini. Before the final conquest of Malwa by Alauddin Khalji in 1305 A.D., the country was successively raided by the neighbouring powers.

Between 1117 and 1202 the Candellas were weakened owing to the repeated attacks of the Paramāras, Caulukyas and Cāhamānas. In 1202 Qutabuddin attacked Kalanjar and the Candella king Paramardī made peace with him on humiliating terms. At this his minister Ajayadeva contrived to have him killed and continued the war but without any success. The next king Trailokyavarman (1205-41) routed the Turkish army and recovered all the territories lost to them. He also conquered Dāhala-maṇḍala, a part of Madhya Pradesh, from the Kalacuris. After his death Candella power declined, and the vast region ruled by them became fragmented.

In 1034 Ahmad Niyaltigin, the governor of Punjab, plundered Varanasi and in retaliation the Kalacuri Gāṅgayadeva counter-attacked in the Kangra valley. His son Lakṣmīkarṇa defeated the Turks in the same region in 1037 A.D. He also made a southern campaign and occupied a part of the Rāḍha region of Bengal, probably after defeating Raṇaśūra. In 1051 he occupied Bundelkhand by defeating the Candella king Kīrtivarman but was unable to retain it. In collaboration with Caulukya Bhīma I he defeated Paramāra Bhoja in 1055 and occupied Malwa. But Bhoja's son Jayasiṃha ousted him with the help of the Western Cālukyas. His tragedy was that notwithstanding his wide-ranging military successes he could retain only the Allahabad region under his control. Lakṣmīkarṇa was succeeded in 1073 by his son Yaśaḥkarṇa and the latter in 1151 by his son Gayākarṇa under whose successors the Kalacuri kingdom disintegrated, the greater part of it taken by the Candellas.

It was during the reign of Lakṣmaṇasena of the Sena

dynasty that some portion of West Bengal went under the Turks. Muhammad Bakhtyar occupied Nadia and north Bengal in A.D. 1202 when Lakṣmaṇasena shifted his headquarters to eastern Bengal. In 1205 Lakṣmanaseṇa was succeeded by Viśvarūpasena from whose inscription it is known that he defeated the Turks. His adversary was probably Giasuddin Aiwaz, the ruler of Lakhnauti. In Kāmarūpa the Turks failed to achieve any success. The Ahoms established themselves in eastern Assam in A.D. 1258. At about the same time the Kacharis occupied the region between Dikhu and Kaliṅga to the south of Brahmaputra.

In Orissa, the Turkish invasion under Giasuddin Aiwaz was resisted in the middle of the thirteenth century by Anaṅgabhīma III. The next king, Narasiṃha I, led an aggressive war against the Turks. In the Deccan the Yādava king Rāmacandra was defeated by Alauddin Khalji. It is said that the gold which Alauddin plundered from Devagiri helped him to consolidate his power at Delhi. Seizing the opportunity of the Yādava disaster, the Kākatīya king Pratāparudra occupied the Yādava territories of Medak and Raichur and the Hoysala Ballāla II, took Vanavāsī, Santalige and Kogali. In 1307, Malik Kafur, the general of Alauddin Khalji, defeated the Yādava Rāmacandra once again. He was imprisoned at Delhi for six months but Allauddin Khalji sent him back to Devagiri as his vassal. Rāmacandra helped Malik Kafur in conquering Telengana and Dorasamudra and was succeeded in 1113 by his son Śaṅkaradeva, who came in conflict with Delhi as a result of which he was defeated and killed by Malik Kafur. Thus Devagiri came directly under the Khalji rulers of Delhi. In 1309-10, Malik Kafur attacked and defeated the Kākatīya king Pratāparudra. But after the withdrawal of Malik Kafur, Pratāparudra again became master of his own area. In 1322 he was defeated by Ulugh Khan, the son of Giasuddin Balban. But his inscription of 1326 found in the Guntur district shows that he reigned even after this defeat.

The Hoysalas hailed originally from Karnataka and had their capital at Dorasamudra or Dvārasamudra (modern Helebid). Hoysala Viṣṇuvardhana conquered Gaṅgavādi, Noḷambavāḍi and Koṅgudeśa and proceeded as far as the river Krishna towards the north. Ballāla II of this line initiated the long-drawn Hoysala-Yādava struggle for supremacy in southern India. The next king, Narasiṃha II (1220-34), resisted a Yādava invasion. He also rescued the Cola king Rājarāja III who was imprisoned by the Pāṇḍyas by inflicting upon them a crushing defeat on the banks of the Kaveri. Ballāla III of this line had a remarkable victory in 1291 over the Yādavas. However, in 1310 he was defeated by Malik Kafur and forced to acknowledge the sovereignty of the Delhi Sulanate. Subsequently, taking advantage of the weakness of the Khaljis and Tughluqs he started a protracted war against the local Turkish powers. His resistance was an inspiration which helped in the formation of the Vijayanagara kingdom.

The Pāṇḍyas of the far south under Jatavarman Kulaśekhara (1190-1216) were almost on the verge of extinction because of civil war and repeated Cola invasions. The situation remained unchanged till the emergence of Jatavarman I Sundara Pāṇḍya (1251-68) who defeated the Ceras, Hoysalas, Telugu-Coḍas and the Kākatīyas. His greatest achievement was the extermination of the Cola power. Northern Ceylon also came under his authority. The next king, Māravarman Kulaśekhara Paṇḍya (1268-1310), selected his illegitimate son Vīra Pāṇḍya as his heir, in consequence of which he was killed in 1310 by his legitimate son Sundara Pāṇḍya who declared himself as the king. However, Vīra Pāṇḍya ousted him and Sundara sought the assistance of Alauddin Khalji's general Malik Kafur. Whether Kafur actually interfered, or whether his interference yielded any tangible result, is not known to us.

4

The Political System: Theoretical and Practical Aspects

1. Vedic Concept of the Popular Sanction of Sovereignty

We have seen that the concept of sovereign monarch was popularised by the authors of the post-Ṛgvedic texts and that some form of divinity was attributed to the institution of kingship. Gone were the days of the tribal chiefs and the popular assemblies which guided them. However, although the king's absolute power was theoretically recognised, side by side it was also held that the absolute power of the king rested on popular consent. This is amply testified by the evidence of rituals like the Aśvamedha, Rājasūya and Vājapeya which the king had to perform in order to attain the status of sovereignty. The ingredients of these rituals convincingly prove that the king had to demonstrate his symbolic identity with the people. He was, thus, the visible representative of the popular will.

In the Vedic texts it is said that all the kings who were actually consecrated with the *aindra-mahābhiṣeka* (Indra's great function consisting of five important ceremonies) were entitled to perform the Aśvamedha ritual for the attainment of the status of a paramount king (*sārvabhauma-rājā*). Originally the Aśvamedha was an agricultural rite in which the chief queen had a symbolical union with the priest, later substituted by a chosen horse, with a view to invoking the forces of natural productivity in terms of human productivity. It was necessary for the queen to conceive in order that the earth might bear fruit. The Vedic institution of divine kingship was probably derived from the belief that the well-being of the social and natural orders depended on the vitality of the king, or his ritualistic representative, the priest who, in a series of magical acts had to unite with the goddess-queen, mark out the soil or cattle for distribution among the clans, turn the first sod with his sacred hoe, cut the first ear of corn with his sacred sickle. Finally, at harvest, he was symbolically put to death by sacrificing a horse so that his prowess could be renewed by the unimpaired vitality of the slain animal. The ceremony also demanded the presence and sanction of the representatives of all classes and sections of peoples. The features of the ritual included panegyrics of the sacrifice commemorating righteous kings of yore.

Even as early as in the Brāhmaṇa literature the Aśvamedha has been regarded as a ritual of hoary antiquity which subsequently became *utsanna* or went out of vogue. It is very difficult to explain how a collective agricultural ritual became transformed into an exclusive ritual for the king and came to be looked upon as a symbol of royal greatness. In the Rājasūya ritual, however, the process is more clearly observed. In this ritual the popular sanction of sovereignty is observed in the following practices : (*i*) The king had to offer presents to his retinue or the royal officials. (*ii*) The besprinkling ceremony by which the king was consecrated was done by representatives of all the castes. (*iii*) The king had to enact a symbolic walk in the presence of his subjects towards the various quarters as an indication of universal rule. (*iv*) He had to tread upon a tiger's skin and thus gain the strength and pre-eminence of the tiger. (*v*) The enthronement ceremony required a miming of election. (*vi*) He had to take part in a mimic cow-raid against a relative, or a sham fight with a member of the ruling aristocracy; this ritual was a hangover legacy of the tribal war-leader of ancient days plundering cattle-wealth of the enemy. (*vii*) The Hotṛ priest was to narrate the story of Śunaḥśepa of the *Aitareya Brāhmaṇa* VIII. 13 ff. as a promise on the king's behalf that he would not invoke the reign of *nirṛti* (where righteousness was annihilated). (*viii*) The king had to take part in a game of dice—a legacy of the ancient custom of distribution by casting the lot.

The Vājapeya was one of the principal rituals of royal inauguration which bestowed upon the performer a superior kind of monarchy called *sāmrājya*. The ritual began with a collective drinking of wine in which the king and his kinsmen participated. Then the king had to win a chariot race. This might either have been a relic of an old national festival, or perhaps intended to acquire by magic the swiftness and strength of the victorious steeds. The race might also have had something to do with the ancient system of distribution like the game of dice in the Rājasūya if we believe the evidence furnished by the *Śatapatha Brāhmaṇa* V.1.1.2-3. The king and his wife are described as being mounted on a chariot-wheel, a symbol of the sun, as a magic device to secure exaltation. The people greet him with salt, the token of mutual faithfulness. The king is then touched as the phrase *annāya tvā*, is uttered, i.e., 'to you for the sake of food'. It refers to the responsibility of the king for *kṛṣi* or agriculture. He is invoked as specially blessed by the Maruts, the 'people among the gods': "With that strength be thou strong and wealth-winning for us, O Courser, and victorious at the gathering. Wealth means food. He thus means to say: And be thou a food-winner for us at this our sacrifice, at the gathering of the gods win thou this sacrifice, Prajāpati" *Sat.Br.*V.1.4.10.

It is not, after all, impossible to demonstrate how the simple agricultural rites, originally based upon human experiences projected on varied objects—such as the analogy of human and natural fertility—were transformed into rituals of kingship. Their original kernel was gradually thrown aside, leading to the development of the accretions which ultimately became sophisticated in tone and colour. Thus, the primitive social characteristics conducive to popular sanction of the prerogatives of the earlier tribal chiefs ultimataly became decorative features of royal ceremonies. Faith in the ideal or happiness resulting from popular cooperation is apparent from the king's prayers in the Aśvamedha and the Rājasūya: "O Brahman! Let there be born in the kingdom the Brāhmaṇa illustrious for religious knowledge; let there be born the Rājnya heroic skilled archer, piercing with shafts mighty warrior; the cow giving abundant milk; the ox good at carrying; the swift courser; the industrious women. May Parjanya send rain according to our desire. May our fruit-bearing plants ripen. May acquisition and preservation of property be secured to us." *Vāj Saṃ* XXII. 22.

In the subsequent stages the old king-electors themselves became dependent on the royal will. Instead of Rājakṛts or king-makers they came to be described as Ratnins or jewels round the throne. These Ratnins included some of the early officials in the royal entourage. The king's position was further strengthened by the alliance with the priestly functionaries. This introduced fundamental changes in the political ideals and also modified the perceptions of political concepts. The chief ideal both in society and in politics was a regulated social existence, with well-defined duties and functions. The king came to be regarded as the protector of *dharma*, the established social norm. The idea of territorial sovereignty gained prominence. A consolidated royal authority strengthened by a military aristocracy and a priesthood was established. A tendency developed towards political integration through ritual and religion and the regulation of the functions of the various elements in the body-politic. The functions of the sovereign authority were defined: the oath of the king reminded him of his pledge to govern according to the accepted rules of conduct.

2. *The Buddhist Political Ideals*

The Buddha did not believe in monarchy. He himself belonged to a republican clan which was democratically governed by the the tribal elders. He framed the constitution of his Saṅgha or monastic order on the model of tribal democracies, on those laws found among the Vṛjis, Mallas, Licchavis and other tribes. His views are contained in his address to Ānanda on the eve of Vassakāra's visit with a imperialistic mission from Ajātaśatru who wanted to exterminate the democratic tribal confederacy of the Vṛjis. The Buddha sided with the Vṛjis saying that so long as they adhered strictly to their democratic codes of conduct they would remain invincible. His illustrious contemporaries, such as Lord Mahāvīra, also shared similar ideas.

Surprisingly enough, both the Buddha and Lord Mahāvīra were able to see that state and political authority originated from the contradiction between social production and individual appropriation. He said: "I behold the rich in the world, of the goods they have acquired, in their folly they give nothing to others; they eagerly heap riches together and further and go on in their pursuit of enjoyment. The king, although he may have conquered the kingdoms of the earth, although he may be the ruler of all land this side of the sea, up to the ocean's shore, would still insatiate, covet that which is beyond the sea. . . .The princes, who rule kingdoms, rich in treasure and wealth, turn their greed against one another, pandering insatiably to their desires. If these acts thus restlessly in the stream of impermanence carried along by greed and carnal desire, who then can walk on earth in peace ?" (Oldenberg 64). The Jain *Āyāra* I.2.1 begins with the following statatement of Lord Māhavīra: "The (living) world is afflicted, miserable, difficult to instruct and without discrimination. In this world full of pain, suffering by their different acts, see the benighted ones cause great pain." The *Sūyagaḍa* I.1.2 is more categorical: "He who owns even a small property in living or lifeless things or consents to others holding it, will not be delivered from misery."

The Buddha and Lord Mahāvīra modelled their *saṅghas* or 'community of brethren' on the pattern of tribal democracies—meant to be the ideal substitute of a vanished way of life—and took great care to see that the members therein would live a perfectly detached life. They, however, had to face the dual requirement of their age, and this alone explains why a considerable number of contemporary merchants and aristocrats formed their front-rank associates, and why Buddhism and Jainism gave moral support to the interests of the trading class. It was impossible for the Buddha or Lord Mahāvīra to change the course of historical transformation but what they could do under such conditions was to make the traditional society aware of the changes and to revive certain ethical values of the past in the changed socio-economic set-up.

The Buddha's theory of the origin of state and government, as found in the *Dīgha Nikāya* III.27 resembles that of a social contract. According to him, in hoary antiquity, conditions similar to that of the 'state of nature' or 'primitive communism' existed when men used natural resources according to their daily need. But in the course of time, a few individuals became greedy and misappropriated in their personal interest things which were meant for all. This was illustrated by the Buddha with reference to the produce of a particular field which was very often stolen by a few persons. They were caught and punished, but the misappropriation of common property by greedy individuals could not be stopped. So the people elected a Kṣetrapāla or protector of the field who had the power of inflicting *daṇḍa* or punishment on offenders and offered him one-sixth of the produce as remuneration for protection. According to the Buddha, this Kṣetrapāla was the potential king and the remuneration he received was the potential-tax.

The Buddhist concept of the ruler as the protector was not fundamentally different from the Brahmanical concept. The Jātaka preambles repeatedly speak of the Buddha as Dharma-Cakravartin and his lieutenants as Senāpati, Saciva and Bhāṇḍāgārika which were the traditional designations of the royal officials. It is also interesting to note that although the Buddha was personally in favour of republicanism, later Buddhist writers insisted on monarchy. The closing verses of the first canto of Aśvaghoṣa's *Saundarnānanda* show that the poet believed in the evils of anarchy and go on to narrate the election of a king at Kapilavāstu. The king-elect accepted royalty for the sake of maintaining *dharma*. Aśvaghoṣa went further and made Śuddhadana a crowned-king instead of an elected president. The king received a sixth part of the produce as his share. Aśvaghoṣa deviates from the Brahmanical ideology only in his denunciation of the spirit of caste and recommendation for the recognition of the position of men through merit and not because of social status or birth.

The paternal concept of kingship which was introduced by Aśoka is reflected in Āryaśūra's *Jātakamālā* in which the Śibi king is projected as the father of his subjects. He is distinguished not only by his charity, but also builds alms-houses, relieves the distress of all and calls upon his subjects to inform him of their grievances. Āryadeva pleads for the reign of righteousness. He condemns the acts of kings of the 'Iron Age' who substituted violence for paternal care and rationalised tyranny in the name of the Dharma Śāstras. He castigates the displays of arrogance on the part of such despots and reminds the kings that they are but servants of the multitude who subsist on the wages given by the people they rule: *ganadāsasya te darpah sadbhāgena bhṛtasya kaḥ.*

3. *The Mauryan Policy of Centralisation and its Limitations*

The first phase of the process of transition from tribal settlements to smaller kingdoms and from the latter to some sort of political unity was completed when the Mauryas were able to occupy the greater portion of the Indian subcontinent. Candragupta, the founder of the Maurya line, followed the traditional method of conquest by force, but his grandson Aśoka, having understood the futility of armed aggression in such a vast country where regional and local political ambitions and aspirations were so varied and heterogeneous in nature, resorted to the policy of *dharmavijaya* or moral persuasion which offered the neighbouring kingdoms and tribal settlements the scope to come within the ambit of Mauryan authority without giving up their socio-political and cultural identities.

However different the outlook of Candragupta and that of Aśoka, the fact remains that both of them were in favour of a centralised administration run by the bureaucrats. For information on the administration of Candragupta we have to depend solely on the fragmented account of Megasthenes. According to him, the king was the supreme head of the state having all military, executive and judicial functions vested in him. The empire was divided into a number of provinces ruled over by viceroys and governors who were sometime princes of royal blood. A centralised army was maintained—a standing army comprising more than 600,000 men—controlled by a war office constituted by a total of thirty members who formed six boards of five members each. There was a well-planned espionage system as well. The town officials were called *astynomoi* also constituted of thirty members divided into six bodies of five each. The district officials, known as *agronomoi*, were in charge of various departments such as agriculture, forestry, timber works, metal foundries, mines, roads, etc. The inscriptions of Aśoka also speak of a centralised system led by provincial governors and various types of government officers.

The question is how far were the Maurya emperors successful in establishing a centralised form of administration.

Certainly, to an extent they were, as we can see from the fact that Aśoka's edicts were inscribed in various parts of India and abroad—a feat impossible but for a centralised government having complete authority over provincial administration. It is not likely that Aśoka was present at the sites where the edicts were inscribed or pillars set up. But we find that the task was accomplished with great care which implies that the provincial governors faithfully followed all the instructions coming from the centre. From the Junagarh inscription of Rudradāman it is known that in the time of Candragupta Puṣyagupta was the *rāṣṭrīya* or governor of western India and that in the time of Aśoka Rājā Tuṣāspha, a Greek by birth, held the same office. Aśoka himself was the governor of Taxila when he was a prince. According to *Divyāvadāna* his son Kuṇāla was also the viceroy at Taxila. Aśoka's inscriptions mention four such viceroys—in Taxila, Ujjain, Tosalī and Suvarṇagiri.

Notwithstanding all this, complete centralisation was impossible in this vast subcontinent and there is reason to believe that even in the Mauryan period the provincial rulers acted as feudatories offering only a token submission to the emperor. Initially, the allotments of the provinces were done on a kinship basis. Subsequently, the charge of some provinces was handed over to persons not belonging to the royal clan, as a mark of recognition of services they offered to the emperor. For all practical purposes, a political-cum-administrative sub-infeudation—though not a proper feudal system as a whole—was required despite the fact that in the history of ancient India it was only the Maurya kings who were able to post viceroys or governors to the four quarters of this subcontinent. The provincial governors had to be given freedom and the right to appoint local rulers with almost the same extent of freedom and right as they themselves enjoyed. The reality was that only the capital and central zone was directly administered by the royal bureaucracy and the statement of Megasthenes that Candragupta maintained a standing army consisting of 600,000 persons should not be taken seriously. Resources in the fourth century B.C. must surely have been insufficient to fund the maintenance of such a vast army, which is difficult even in modern times.

4. The Kauṭilyan State

The *Arthaśāstra* of Kauṭilya is a comprehensive work on the science of Indian polity. There is disagreement among scholars with regard to its date. Some hold that it was composed in the Mauryan period and its author was none other than the minister of Candragupta. Others maintain that it is a later work which was composed about A.D. 300. The exact date is of little consequence since it was customary among the ancient Indian writers to depend more on the existing traditions rather than on existing realities. That is why there is not much difference between the views of Kauṭilya and those of the authors of the Dharmaśāstras and the *Mahābhārata* in regard to the political questions and the social norms.

Regarding the question of the origin of the state Kauṭilya says: "People suffering from anarchy first elected Manu to be their king and allotted one-sixth of the grains grown and one-tenth of the merchandise as sovereign dues. Fed by this payment, kings took upon themselves the responsibility of maintaining the safety and security of their subjects." He holds that state and kingship evolved out of the necessity to mitigate the evils of anarchy. But the former is an organic whole and the latter is one of its limbs. Kauṭilya, unlike Manu and other authorities, expressly says that, apart from giving protection, the king should have a wide range of activities pertaining to the material and spiritual welfare of the subjects. In this respect he might have been inspired by the system introduced by Aśoka. The Kauṭilyan state is undoubtedly totalitarian. According to him all professions and trades are to be controlled by the state. The state should regulate all the economic life in order to promote prosperity.

Kauṭilya holds that a benevolent monarchy carrying out its function through an efficient bureaucracy is the ideal form of government. He believes in the need for quick detribalisation and as such he is very much hostile to the republican or democratic system by which the tribes are governed. He urges upon the kings to destroy the tribes by exploiting their weakness, chiefly by sowing dissension among the members of the tribal council. In regard to the ministers and other officials Kauṭilya says that sovereignty is possible only with assistance because a single wheel cannot move. That is why the king should employ ministers (*mantri*) and also have a council (*mantrī-pariṣad*). He mentions different state departments like Audit and Accounts, Records, Stores, Treasury, Forest, Weaving, Agriculture, Pasture Lands, Cows, Slaughter-houses, Weights and Measures, Goldsmithy, Mines, Ocean-mines, Metals, Mint, Salt, Wastelands, Commerce, Tolls, Excise, Passports, Ships, etc., and holds that these departments should be run under superintendents assisted by accountants, scribes, coin-examiners, stock-takers and observers.

Kauṭilya recommends land-tax in various forms, duties on the sale of goods in the market, taxes on imports and exports, road-cess, canal-dues, ferry-dues, tax on loads, fee on passports, tax levy on artisans, fishermen, prostitutes, gambling houses, wine houses, slaughter houses, income derived from royal properties such as forests, mines and manufactories, the monopoly of salt and other commodities, forced labour, fines from law courts, and incomes from excheats, lost articles and treasure-troves. Like all ancient law-givers Kauṭilya holds that the primary function of the king is to exercise *daṇḍa* or punishment judiciously. He says that each important city or locality shall have a court of justice, consisting of three members acquainted with sacred law and three ministers of the king. Although Kauṭilya recommends capital punishment for serious offences he is against cruel punishments like mutilation and the like. He is also against torture to elicit confession of guilt. "If witnesses differ judgement may be given in accordance with the statements of a majority of pure and respectable witnesses; or the mean of their statements may be followed or the amount under dispute may be taken by the king." Also, in the case of the application of laws, he does not make any distinction among the castes.

As has been stated above, Kauṭilya prescribes considerable state control in both trade and industry, state monopoly of mines, oilfields and important industries and state supervision of prices, weights and measures. The state's absolute right to raise tax from export and import, octroi and excise has been recognised. He describes the taxes on agriculture as comprising *bhāga* or the state's share of produce, *bali* or an extra cess above *bhāga*, *kara* or tax on property levied periodically, *vivita* or a levy on pastures, *rajju* or the cess payable for survey and settlement and *cora-rajju* or police cess.

The Kauṭilyan model of state system did not, however, develop in India. A centralised state power controlling all the walks of public life through a well-knit bureaucracy was probably the ideal visualised by the Maurya kings when they tried, with considerable success, to bring some sort of political unity in India. Whether Kauṭilya was a contemporary of the Mauryas is not the main question. But it appears that Kauṭilya was inspired by the policies of Candragupta and Aśoka to formulate the concept of a fatherly king as the fountainhead of a variety of ever-expanding state activities. An incipient form of a nation-state was inherent in Kauṭilya's vision; he thought it could be achieved by the efforts of a *vijīgisu rājā*, a king intending to bring political unity through conquest and expansion. In the subsequent history of India there were a few isolated attempts in this direction, but such attempts could not yield any permanent result under the diverse historical conditions.

5. *The Post-Maurya State System*

The post-Maurya period witnessed the emergence of powerful kingdoms in different parts of India. The Kuṣāṇas were able to build up virtually an empire in north and northwestern India which even transgressed the natural frontier of India proper. In western India the Śakas had founded a powerful kingdom, while in the Deccan the Sātavāhanas held sway. In Kaliṅga a powerful kingdom was created by Khāravela.

A striking observation in this connection is that the political unity in the different regions of the country was brought about in most cases by enthusiastic tribes. The Kuṣānas were a branch of the Yueh-chi tribe and, as we have seen above, the founder of the Kuṣāṇa kingdom was originally known as a *yabuga* or tribal chief who later assumed the title of a king. The Śaka kingdom was established by the Kṣaharāta and Kārdamaka clans. The Sātavāhanas were also a clan of the Andhras. The tribal settlements were transformed into powerful kingdoms in two or three generations, and their chiefs assumed high-sounding royal titles like 'king of kings', *cakravartin*, *adhirāja*, *rājātirāja*, etc. The Kuṣāṇa kings of the line of Kaṇiṣka had the title *devaputra* which was probably an expression of the theory of the divine origin of kingship. One of the Kuṣāṇa kings, Kaniṣka of the Ara inscription, assumed the title of *kaisara* or *caesar*.

Notwithstanding the high-sounding royal titles and the continuous glorification of the king's power and authority in contemporary literature, the tribal character of the state system continued to thrive. The tribal chiefs, when they became king, had to accommodate the other clan leaders and relations in the administrative system either by offering them direct executive posts or by admitting them as vassals or feudatories, very often giving them the right to use royal titles and to issue coins in their own names. We have already had occasion to note how relations and collaborators of the Indo-Greek, Parthian and Scythian kings held the position of subordinate colleagues. The Sātavāhanas had many feudatories, some of whom at least enjoyed the right to issue their own coins.

We also come across names of different officials in coins and inscriptions, but it is difficult to say whether these incumbents belonged to the king's clan or were selected freely on the basis of merit. The Sātavāhana records reveal a number of high officers styled Mahārathīs, Mahābhojas, Mahāsenāpatis, Amātyas, Mahāmātras, Bhāṇḍāgārikas and Lekhakas. The Śaka kings styled themselves as Kṣatrapas and Mahākṣatrapas, which were in themselves suggestive of vassalage, probably in recognition of some supposed overlord of their original homeland with which they had no connection in reality, just as it was a practice among the Muslim kings of India to hold the crown in the name of Caliph. The Śaka inscriptions refer to two kinds of higher officials, the *mati-saciva* or ministers and *karma-saciva* or executives. The Junagarh inscription of Rudradāman mentions, in addition to the traditional Indian terms of office-bearers, such foreign designations as *satrap* (provincial governor), *maridarch* (district officer), *strategos* (military governors), etc. The Manikala inscription of the Kuṣāṇas refers to *daṇḍanāyago*, *navakarmigo*, etc.

Notwithstanding the existence of a number of officials, it was not possible for the king to run the administration of the entire kingdom directly. The functions of the royal officials were confined only to a limited area—in and around the capital city. Other parts of the kingdom were ruled by the vassals or feudatories, who were in most cases men of the king's clan, his collaborators in conquest and in the consolidation of power. They were supposed to be loyal to the king in the name of tribal-bond and in many cases they were granted the power of ruling almost independently in their respective provinces against a token submission. This explains why within the territorial jurisdiction of a particular sovereign king, inscriptions and coins of other kings belonging to the same period and the same clan or dynasty are so frequently found. In the later period of ancient Indian history we have references to numerous feudatories or vassals whose kinship relation with the sovereign monarch has been stated in clearer terms.

6. *Jaimini on King's Land-Right: Some Questions Relating to the Hypothesis of a Feudal Structure*

In view of what has been stated above it appears that in the post-Maurya period there was a system of extensive vassalage without the help of which it might not have been possible for the king to rule over the vast territory of which he was the overlord. If this be the case, there must have existed some relation of obligation between the king and his feudatories. Now the question is whether or not this relation can be explained in terms of a feudal system.

Earlier historians of ancient India, who were all well versed in European history as well, had used the term feudalism indiscriminately in the Indian context to denote the agrarian conditions by which Indian economy was characterised through the ages without taking into account the wide difference between European and Indian conditions. In Europe, feudalism was a system sanctioned and encouraged by Christian theology; it stressed a spiritual hierarchy in ecclesiastical services, from Pope to the lower clergy. The temporal reflection of this culminated in the formation of a parallel worldly hierarchy ranging from the king to the land-labourer, through various steps of intermediaries, in all of which there was a bond of direct obligation between the master and his man. In theory, the Pope was the master of the earth, being the sole vessel of Christ, but he preferred to remain content with his spiritual kingdom by relegating his temporal authority to the king. The king would distribute the land, of which he was the absolute owner, to his tenants-in-chief on certain terms and conditions, the latter would redistribute their portions to the sub-tenants in the same way and the process would be multiplied and continued to the lowest step of the social ladder represented by the landless peasants. The individual in this system was the subject of his immediate overlord, who was his master and protector, both the parties having mutual obligations to each other, ratified by feudal oath in the church.

Needless to say that such a system never existed in India which had always been characterised by a caste society which had nothing in common with the principles of feudalism. The extensive use of the term feudalism in the Indian context by historians naturally became the subject of scrutiny and controversy. The concept again had come into prominence with the development of Marxian historiography, because in the Marxian interpretation of history feudalism was regarded as an inevitable and universal stage which preceded the growth of capitalism. So the need was felt, almost worldwide, because conditions were different in every place, to have a broad definition of feudalism. Marc Block was able to do this in the European context but nothing of that sort has yet been done in the Indian context. D.D. Kosambi's theory of feudalism from above and below, no doubt thought-provoking, suffered from the fallacy of misplaced concreteness. R.S. Sharma dealt with this problem merely by changing the definition of feudalism as a socio-economic formation in which a landlord class emerged due to alienation of tax-rights by the rulers.

These points will duly arise in the course of our discussion, but what we are suggesting here is that the relation, which must have been obligatory, between the king and his feudatories in the post-Maurya period was in most cases due to ties of the clan. The overlordship of the king or the subordinate position of the vassal does not imply any feudal relation unless there is an hierarchy of subordinates of various ranks having mutual obligatory relations to each other from the top to the bottom. Such is not the case so far as the early period of ancient Indian history is concerned. In the case of the classical feudalism of Europe the king was theoretically the owner of all land and he distributed it to the feudal lords on certain conditions. In India, however, the situation was somewhat different as we can see from Jaimini's *Pūrvamīmāṃsāsūtra* which was composed about 200 B.C.

Jaimini (VI.7.3) says that in the Viśvajit sacrifice the king can donate everything but not land since earth is common to all. Śabara in his commentary on this statement says that others have as much right over the earth as the king and that the latter is entitled to a share of the crops produced from the earth since he protects the people to whom the earth belongs. On the authority of Jaimini and Śabara the author of the *Vyavahārapramukha* categorically states that the ownership lies with the holders of land alone while the kings are entitled to collect taxes. Therefore, when kings make what are technically called gifts of fields, no gift of land is effected thereby, but only that a provision is made for the maintenance of the donee from the taxes which are alienated by the king. This suggests clearly that the king was not the owner of all lands but was merely entitled to levy taxes from the holders of the land.

Some scholars insist that according to Manu and other law-givers, the king was the owner of lands and the subjects were only occupants. But P.V. Kane says that "from Manu and other Smṛtikāras it appears that so far as lands already brought under cultivation are concerned, they appear to hold that the ownership of the land is in the cultivators and the king is only entitled to levy taxes for the protection he affords. . . ." Manu IX.44 states that a field belongs to him who uproots the stems of trees and shrubs from waste or uncultivated land. Manu VIII.39 provides that any ancient treasure-trove found underneath the ground and in mines the king is entitled to a share because he affords protection and because he is lord of the earth. This militates against the view that the king is owner of all lands, since, if that were so, Manu would have declared that the king took all the mines and treasure found in a cultivated field. . . . That is further supported by the conduct and practice of powerful but good kings who purchased lands from their holders when they wanted to donate lands already cultivated." (*HD.*, II. 867-68.)

7. *Socio-Political Ideas as Reflected in the Manusmṛti*

Among the Dharmaśāstras or Smṛtis, is the *Mānava Dharmaśāstra* or *Manusmṛti,* which was put in its present form in the Gupta age. It is a most comprehensive work on Hindu law and social customs. It reflects the complete social philosophy of the Gupta age in all its aspects and has been the model for the writers of all subsequent legal treatises. It is still regarded as the most authentic manual of what is known as Hindu way of life and is held in greatest esteem even today all over India.

The State, according to Manu, has seven constituents, called *aṅga* or limbs. These are the king, the minister, the country, the fort, the treasury, the army and the friend. Each limb is particularly qualified for the fulfilment of a distinct purpose (IX. 295). Kingship is of divine origin, created by the Lord for the protection of the whole creation (VII.3). For protecting his subjects the power of inflicting punishment or chastisement (*daṇḍa*) is vested in the king. The *daṇḍa* alone governs all created beings, protects them, watches them over while they sleep (VII.18). If the king does not inflict punishment on the wicked the stronger will roast the weaker, like fish on a spit (VII.20). But at the same time Manu says that while a just king prospers, one who is a voluptuary, partial and deceitful will be destroyed (VII.26). Protection of the people is equal to the performance of the greatest ritual (*yajña*) and is conducive to bliss and prosperity (VII.84). If the king should do wrong, where a common man is to be fined one *kārṣāpaṇa* the king shall be fined one thousand (VIII.336). The king should have good education and he must be well versed in *vārtā* or the science of economic pursuits (VII.43). He must actively encourage agriculture, improve the highways, exploit the mines, clear the forests, colonise barren lands, tame elephants, build forts and bridges (VII.154).

According to Manu, land belongs to him who clears the timber, and a forest animal to him who owns the arrow. Manu believes in the sanctity of private property. The enjoyment of a property for ten years gives a prescriptive right to it, but "a pledge, a boundary, the property of infants, an (open) deposit, a sealed deposit, women, the property of the king and the wealth of a *śrotriya*" are exempt from the operation of this rule (VIII, 145-49). As regards inheritance, the division of property should take place only after the death of the father. The eldest son should receive the greatest share. Maiden daughters should have also a share. The land-tax should be one-sixth, one-eighth or one-fourth of the crops, i.e., of the gross produce which is to be levied on the basis of the fertility of the soil. A fiftieth of cattle and gold may be taken by the king. Manu awards the king a sixth part of trees, meat, honey, clarified butter, perfumes, herbs, substances used for flavouring food, flowers, roots, fruits, pot herbs, grass and cave objects, skins, vessels and articles made of stone. Traders should pay one-twentieth of the value of each saleable commodity as calculated by experts. Artisans and manual labourers should pay tax by working for the king for a day in each month (VII.127-139). The king is entitled to one-sixth, one-tenth or one-twentieth of the property lost and found afterwards. Manu exhorts the king to appoint experts to look after the mines and inspectors to attend to concerns which yield revenue to the state (VII.62; VII.81).

Manu has given a regular classification of the law under eighteen heads or titles which are: (1) non-payment of debts; (2) deposit and pledge; (3) sale without ownership; (4) concerns among partners; (5) resumption of gifts; (6) non-payment of wages; (7) non-performance of agreements; (8) rescession of sale and purchase; (9) disputes regarding boundaries; (10) dispute between the owner and his servants; (11) assault; (12) defamation; (13) theft; (14) robbery and violence; (15) adultery; (16) duties of man and wife; (17) partition of inheritance; and (18) gambling and betting (VIII.3-7). The king should normally preside over the law courts. In addition, he has to appoint learned judges (VIII. 12-15). If the defendant denies the charge, the complainant must call witnesses or adduce other evidence. The witnesses are strongly exhorted to speak the truth and seven penalties are laid down for giving false evidence (VIII.60-100).

Caste privileges and disabilities are reflected in the criminal law of Manu. The Brāhmaṇas are to be exempt from capital punishment. At the worst, a Brāhmaṇa can only be banished and even then he must be allowed to take away all his properties with him. For defaming a Brāhmaṇa, a Kṣatriya is to be fined one hundred *paṇas*; a Vaiśya from one hundred and fifty to two hundred, while a Śūdra is to suffer corporal punishment. If a Śūdra insults a twice-born man his tongue shall be cut off. If he is arrogant enough to teach the Brāhmaṇas their duties, the king shall cause hot oil to be poured into his mouth and ears. With whatever limb a man of a lower caste injures a man of the three higher castes, that limb shall be cut off. Manu prescribes capital punishment for the murder of the Brāhmaṇas, women and children, tampering with the loyalty of the ministers, treason and false proclamations. Multilation, banishment, imprisonment and fines have been recommended according to the extent and degree of the offences. Manu allows that the law may be taken into one's own hand on certain occasions, as in self-defence (VII.319, VIII. 48-50, 279, IX.225, 232-242, 270-293).

8. *The Gupta and Post-Gupta Polity*

The Allahabad pillar inscription refers to Samudragupta quite in accordance with Manu's concept of kingship—as a god dwelling on earth. We shall later see that although theoretically the idea of a centralised state-power under a sovereign ruler with supreme authority exercised through a well-knit bureaucracy was popularised by the Dharma and Arthaśāstras, and that the Gupta kings, like their predecessors, the Kuśāṇas and Mauryas, tried to put this idea into practice, it was possible only on a limited scale, in areas which lay within a manageable distance from the capital. The rest of the empire and the occupied territories were put in charge of local rulers who were in most cases the former masters of the land, acting almost independently as feudatories or vassals who paid only a token submission to the imperial authority.

Among the officials mentioned in the Gupta inscriptions, besides the *mantris* or ministers, we have references to *mahabalādhikṛta* or commander-in-chief, the *mahādaṇḍanāyaka* or the chief executive general, and *mahāpratihāra* or chief of the palace guards. A high imperial officer, heard of for the first time in the Gupta records, was the *sāndhivigrahika* or minister of peace and war looking after the external affairs. A link between the central and provincial administration was maintained by a class of officials called *kumārāmātyas* and *āyuktakas*. *Amātyas* stand for a general body of officials, but the prefix *kumāra* is suggestive of the fact that princes of the royal line were put in charge of the supervision of provincial administration as agents of the centre. The provinces—called *bhuktis*—were usually governed by officers called *uparikas*. The district, or *viṣayas*, were under officers known as *viṣayapatis*. Villages were administered in the traditional way by village elders called *mahattaras*, while in the case of the towns there was some kind of a council formed by *nagaraśreṣṭhī* or the guild-president, *sārthavāha* or chief merchant controlling inland trade, *prathamakulika* or the chief artisan corresponding to the modern executive engineer and *prathamakāyastha* or chief scribe.

Notwithstanding this apparent centralised structure, direct administration was not possible for practical reasons. In cases where the existing rulers were violently exterminated, as we find in those of the nine kings of Āryāvarta who were completely annihilated by Samudragupta, two types of provincial governors might have been posted. The first type comprised junior members of the royal family including the younger brothers and sons of the king and sometimes uncles, sons-in-law and relatives of the king by marriage, while the second type comprised eminent officials or trusted ministers or generals. In most cases, however, the conquered and distant territories were under feudatories or vassals who acknowledged the paramount authority of the king, obeyed his commands, paid him tribute and fought for him. In some cases the feudatories were bestowed with official designations. At least three categories of feudatories may be detected: (i) feudatory lines existing from before the rise of the suzerain power but reduced to vassalage ; (ii) feudatory lines established by junior branches of the imperial dynasty; and (iii) feudatories by creation. The first category was the most common. In the history of ancient India there are numerous examples of small feudatory dynasties coming repeatedly to prominence and then falling into oblivion.

Whether the chief feudatories themselves had small feudatories, who stood with them in more or less in the same relation in which they stood towards their suzerain, or whether there were third, fourth and even further layers in the political hierarchy in the Gupta period is difficult to say. But in the subsequent history of India it has been observed that the greater feudatories had vassal princes under them and that the latter in their turn ruled by hereditary right. The terms on which they maintained themselves were similar to those enforced on their own overlords. This gradation of ruling authority eventually appeared to have been an important principle in the administrative and political history of these feudatories. From the inscriptions we find various titles assumed by them. Some called themselves *mahāsāmantas* or *maṇḍaleśvaras*; others assumed the title of *rājā* or *mahārājā*. Feudatories of the earlier periods who were mostly the king's clansmen enjoyed the right of issuing coins. The Valabhī princes too issued coins with the names of the Gupta kings but with their own trident symbol replacing the peacock of the Guptas. Later this system was discontinued. The status of the feudatories probably varied according to their relative strength in comparison with that of the paramount power. The Parivràjaka *mahārājās* ruling in the Baghelkhand region habitually issued their land grants "during the enjoyment of the sovereignty by the Gupta emperors" but were completely silent in their records about the name of the reigning emperor. King Jayanātha of Uccakalpa issued land grants with the mention of the Gupta era but these grants do not contain any reference to Gupta sovereignty. The same holds good in the case of the land grants of *mahārāja* Lakṣmana and *mahārāja* Subandhu of Central India. A land grant from Indore of A.D. 397 records the consent of one *mahārāja* Svāmīdāsa, probably a Gupta feudatory, to the grant of a field by a merchant. In this case we find that the feudatory was empowered to endorse the religious grant made by an individual without the need for imperial consent.

Under the Guptas the big provinces were designated as Rāṣṭras or Deśas, though the term Deśa was sometimes also used in a different sense. In the eastern regions provinces were called Bhukti. Districts and subdivisions were known as Viṣayas and Maṇdalas while a landlord's area was known as Bhoga.

Smaller subdivisions were known by such terms as Patta, Pattika, Patha and Sandika, especially in Central India. The Deo-Baranak inscription of the later Guptas mentions the following administrative divisions: Bhukti, Maṇḍala, Viṣaya, Grāma and Agrahāra. The territory of the Valabhī princes was subdivided into Rāṣṭra, Viṣaya and Āhāra. Under the the Pālas, the highest division was Bhukti, subdivided into Maṇḍalas and Viṣayas. The same held good in the case of Orissa. Under the Pratihāras and their central Indian feudatories, in addition to the major subdivisions mentioned above, we have Paṭhaka, Pattana and Paṭṭalā. Under the Cālukyas and the Rāṣṭrakūṭas of the Daccan, the main division was Rāṣṭra, subdivided into Viṣaya and then into Grāma. Under the Pallavas, at the bottom of the system was the village or Grāma. A number of villages constituted a Kottaṃ or Deśa and a number of Kottams made up a Rāṣṭra which was more often synonymous with Maṇḍala. Under the Pāṇḍyas the smallest administrative divisions were villages or Grāmas. The higher unit was Nadu or Nāḍ or the Kurram.

The Gupta administrative structure and posts were retained by Harṣa and the Later Guptas. The Valabhī princes had in addition Cāṭa, Bhāṭa, Viniyuktaka, Rājakula and Pratiṣaraka. Among the extra officials of the Pālas we have Mahāsāmanta (chief of the feudatories, though *sāmanta* originally meant neighbour), Mahākaṛtakṛtika (meaning unknown) Mahādauḥsādhanika (chief of the spies), Pramatṛ (official for assessment), Sarabhaṅga (meaning unknown), Daśagrāmika (official in charge of a group of ten villages), Daśaparādhika (meaning not clear), Daṇḍapāśika (jail superintendent), Kṣetrapa (official in charge of *kṣetra* or fields), Prāntapāla (in charge of borders), Koṭṭapāla (in charge of *Koṭṭas* which meant either block houses or places of garrison), Ṣaṣṭādhikṛta (in charge of the royal sixth, i.e., revenue collector), etc. In Orissa an inscription of Mahābhavagupta refers to Samāhartṛ, Sannidhātṛ, Piśuna (spies), Vitrika (holder of rods), Rājavallabha, Cāṭa and Bhāṭa. In other inscriptions we find Sthānāntarika, Antaraṅga, Aṅgīkaraṇika, Ekasaraka, Khola, Mahākaṭuka, etc. In the Deccan, in addition to the known officials of the Gupta type we have Rāṣṭrapati, Viṣayapati and Grāmakūṭa.

In southern India, under the Pallavas, the provinces (*rāṣṭra*) and subdivisions were under the charge of Deśādhikṛta. Minor officials were known as Vipittas (*vyāpṛtas*) who looked after the royal interests in the villages. Amātyas supervised administration. War leaders were known as Nāyikas (Nāyakas) and customs officials were known as Mandapi. Other important officials were the Tīrthikas who took charge of bathing places and ferries, Gulmikas who were in charge of forests, Sañcarantaka or roaming spies, etc. Among the higher officials we have the Amātyas, Rahasyādhikṛtas (Privy Councillors enjoying royal trust) and Senāpatis (military officers). Villages and towns were administered by local assemblies, i.e., Sabhās and the Nagarattaras. The elaborate development later of local self government under the Colas was an original feature of the southern polity.

9. *The Nītīsāra of Kāmandakī*

The *Nītīsāra* of Kāmandakī, composed about A.D. 700, is a treatise on Hindu polity. Divided into 20 *sargas* and 36 *prakaraṇas* and modelled after the *Arthaśāstra* of Kauṭilya, it deals with the theories of social order, authority and the obligation of the imperial ruler; theories of state-structure and organs of government; principles and policies of government; interstate relations; functions of envoys, ambassadors and spies; application of different political expedients; varieties of battle arrays; attitude towards morality; etc. Of the author of the work very little seems to be known. According to a commentary on this work, its author was a disciple of Cāṇakya or Kauṭilya. This cannot be true historically but the form and contents are based on the Kauṭilyan model. The work has not any of the antiquated grammatical forms which are so frequently met with in Manu and other Smṛtis. Judged by the metres used it may be said that it is post-Kālidāsa. The first chapter is devoted to the inculcation, in princes, of the necessity of study and of controlling their passions. The second deals with the division of learning, the duties of different castes and the importance of criminal jurisprudence. In the third occurs an exposition of the duty of princes to their subjects, of the necessity for impartial justice and the impropriety of tyrannising over the people. The fourth affords a description of the essential constituents of good government. The duties of ministers and servants take up the whole of the fifth chapter, and the mode of removing difficulties or rather of punishing the wicked, forms the subject of the sixth. The seventh is devoted to the duty of guarding the persons of the kings and crown princes; it includes a variety of expedients against surprise, poisoning, the infidelity of servants, wives and relatives and the dishonesty of the medical attendants. The mode of consolidating a kingdom by providing it with necessary officers of state, and including within it a number of dependencies and subordinate chiefs, form the subject of the eighth chapter. The ninth to the twelfth chapters are a series of rules regarding negotiations and disputes with foreign powers, conferences, embassies and spies. The thirteenth opens with an exhortation in favour of constant activity and attention to business and the evils which attend illness and vicious propensities. Other chapters are devoted to the seven limbs of state, military expeditions, fortification and other aspects of warfare. As a text dealing with the norms of administration it has the same merit as the other works belonging to the Dharmaśāstra and Arthaśāstra schools. Like all other authorities on polity the author of the *Nītīsāra* is in favour of centralisation of state power and the bureaucratic form of administration. The work lacks an awareness of objective conditions—it says nothing about the role of the state in regard to economic policies, the subject on which his illustrious predecessor Kauṭilya had laid so much emphasis.

10. The Economic Perspective

The main trends of ancient Indian political history up to the end of the eighth century A.D. emphasise the role of small kingdoms, feudatories and dynasties. The writers of the Dharma and Arthaśāstras had always thought of a political system under a strong and powerful imperial authority controlling a vast region down to the grassroot level directly through the imperial officials and also of an economic system directly under the crown, administered by trained bureaucrats. In spite of some efforts in this direction and the occasional rise of big powers like the Guptas, statepower could not be all-embracing. The big powers enjoyed some sort of sovereignty over the smaller powers, but failed to carry this through mainly due to the lack of social mobility and productive dynamism which may otherwise have imposed state supervision in every sphere of life.

There was no change in the traditional mode of production which was entirely caste-oriented, having little or no scope for innovation or change in the technique of production. The base was undoubtedly agrarian. Industries and crafts were also village oriented. The cities, unlike their modern counterparts, could not subsist by themselves, being solely dependent on village surplus, and once the source of this surplus was blocked owing to natural calamity, famine, pestilence or failure of production, they dwindled into nothingness. There was little scope of changing the caste-professions; whatever changes had taken place were not caused by the urge to reach a better standard in the field of production but by the inadequacy of certain trades to feed their followers. Unable to earn a livelihood in the approved caste-professions, many persons had to take up agriculture which only created pressure on land and multiplied agricultural subcastes. Again, there were sub-specialisations in different trades and crafts owing to the influx of the tribals into the caste-hierarchy. This also caused multiplication of subcastes, but no betterment in the field of production.

The occasional prosperity which was sometimes enjoyed in different regions of India was due mainly to the personality and initiative of certain aspiring monarchs whose policies stirred up the stagnant pool of a sluggish economy, or perhaps a favourable trade balance with foreign countries. But such phenomena were few. In an all-Indian context the role of foreign trade was marginal, though in a local or regional context it had a greater economic and political significance. The trade with Rome continued to flourish till it was disrupted by the Huna invasion and the disintegration of the Roman empire. There was, however, trade with the Eastern Roman or Byzantine empire through Iran. This explains why the Cālukya king Pulakeśin II sent a special embassy to the Iranian Shah Khusruv. After the fall of the Roman empire, the southern states of India developed trade relations with China and Indonesia on the east and with Iran, Arabia and Ethiopia on the west. Since the land routes were not safe, sea routes were preferred which gave the southern states a greater advantage. One should not fail to notice that ever since the seventh century the southern states with sea ports on both the coasts achieved greater political prominence. In fact two power blocs developed in the south with the river Tungabhadra as the dividing line. There was constant rivalry between these two regions which began with the Cālukyas and the Pallavas and continued up to the age of the Vijayanagara empire. On the west the ports of the Saurāṣṭra-Gujarat region were still active and so was Tāmralipti in Bengal. It is interesting to note that both the regions became powerful in the seventh century A.D. and Harṣavardhana, the mighty Lord of Uttarāpatha, failed to achieve any military success there just as he also failed in subduing his Cālukya adversary in the Deccan.

The source of royal income was traditional, comprising taxation in various forms but enterprising kings often undertook military campaigns for the sake of the acquisition of wealth. Just as the gold of Devagari put Alauddin Khalji on the Delhi Sultanate so also, for instance, did the southern conquests of Samudragupta give him resources which were utilised for consolidating the Gupta empire. However, waging warfare also involved some difficulties. The overall requirements for waging war did give a favourable and encouraging impetus to the field of production, but if the military adventure failed to achieve the desired result, it also meant a drain on the royal treasury and at the end of it economic depression followed. Aspiring and calculating kings like Samudragupta were few and far between. Even the big kingdoms, except for a manageable area around the capital, were ruled by vassals and feudatories. While there were feudatories, there was no proper feudal system or feudal hierarchy linking the bigger units to the smaller.

The feudatories had the right to grant land with or without the consent of imperial authority. Land was granted mainly to the Brāhmaṇas in order to acquire religious merit and did not entail any bond of obligation between the donor and the donee. Very often the grantee would have exclusive right, without any intervention from the grantor, to receive the entire revenue from the tenants. The donor not only abandoned his revenues but also the right to govern the inhabitants of the villages that were given in grant. It was a form of landlordism without any feudal obligation or responsibility. In the Gupta period there is no direct epigraphic evidence of grants made to officers for their military and administrative services. Even in post-Gupta inscriptions there is no direct reference to the mode of payment to officials by grants of land. Notwithstanding the fact that Manu and Kauṭilya refer to such a custom and Hiuen Tsang's comment that the governors, ministers, magistrates and officials had each a portion of land assigned to them for personal support, there is no epigraphic evidence in favour of this view. Indirect epigraphic evidence to such titles as *bhogika*, *bhogapatika*, *mahāsāmanta*, etc., may be suggestive of a landed nobility having administrative power but none of these prove the existence of a functioning feudal system.

The only conclusion which may be drawn after examining all the available land grants of the Gupta and post-Gupta period is that land was granted predominantly, if not exclusively, to the Brāhmaṇas and religious establishments with all the rights of collecting revenue and even with the rights of administration in the granted area. It does not, however, mean that there were no secular grants, but such grants were rare. The mere handing over the ownership of land, along with rights associated with it, to another by the king or the feudatory, as we find in the Indian context, does not reflect an ordered system in the political, social and economic spheres. In the European context subinfeudation of land under different categories of feudal lords was meant to secure and maintain a socio-political order in which the grantee was interlinked with the grantor, his immediate overlord, at all levels by a chain of obligation and responsibility, sanctified by feudal oaths on both sides. In the Indian context the grant of land was meant chiefly for the purpose of securing religious merit and when it was secular, it was for personal gratitude or benevolence or, at best, for services received by the donor from the donee. This basic difference in viewpoint is important and should not be overlooked.

11. Feudalistic Formations: Extent and Degree

We have already had occasion to refer to the fact that in spite of the existence of a large number of feudatories in all regions of India, and at all times of the known periods of ancient and early-medieval Indian history, the feudal system in the European sense did not have favourable ground for its growth. In support of this view we have stated that according to the Indian tradition land did not belong to the king. When the epithet 'lord of the earth' was attributed to the king it implied his right to receive tax as the protector of the land: there are instances of kings purchasing land from their subjects. Secondly, the existence of feudatories and of a lord-vassal complex does not always imply the existence of feudalism unless other conditions implicit in the latter are fulfilled. As Hallam pointed out long ago:

> It is easy to find partial resemblance to the feudal system. The relation of patron and client in the republic of Rome has been deemed to resemble it, as well as the Barbarians and Veterans who held frontier lands on the tenure of defending them and the frontier; but they were bound not to an individual, but to the State. Such a resemblance of fiefs may be found in the Zamindars of Hindustan and the Timariots of Turkey. The clans of the Highlanders and Irish followed their chieftain into the field; but their tie was that of imagined kindred and birth, not the spontaneous compact of vassalage. (*Middle Ages* I, 200).

Thirdly, as has already been pointed, European feudalism had ecclesiastical sanction and was connected with some theological intricacies of Christianity—a point which has been overlooked by most scholars. Indian society is a caste society which has been sanctioned by the Dharmaśāstras or legal texts and it was demanded of the kings to maintain *varṇāṣrama* or caste-society in which the allegiance of an individual is not to another individual but to the caste-group to which he or she belongs. Every caste, high or low, has its own profession, unencroachable by other castes, having well-defined rights, duties and privileges. Very naturally this system, which governs the country even today, has nothing to do with the canons of feudalism. Fourthly, so far as the land grants are concerned, in most cases villages were granted to the Brāhmaṇas or religious establishments. Secular grants were few and these were given in recognition of services rendered previously to the king by the grantee. Lastly, there was no obligation on the part of the donee to the donor. Lands or villages given to the Brāhmaṇas were solely for the purpose of earning religious merit.

Notwithstanding these special conditions, going against the concept of pure feudalism, there are certain trends—in form rather than content—which may be regarded as feudalistic. One point which should be taken into consideration is that in most cases villages were granted with the transfer of all sources of revenue and the surrender of administrative functions. In central and western India some royal donors conferred on the grantee the exclusive right of trying cases in the donated villages. R.S. Sharma has laid special emphasis on this alienation of tax-rights and surrender of administrative functions by the rulers and viewed the situation as a socio-economic formation along feudalistic lines which fostered the emergence of a landed class. According to him, this socio-economic formation was characterised by two conditions. The first was the exploitation of the peasantry by increasing the burden of taxation on the villagers, imposition of forced labour and the right of subinfeudation. What adversely affected the peasants in the donated area was the transfer of communal rights, presumably from the villagers to the donee. The second was the existence of self-sufficient economic units. This was indicated by the absence of coins, the prevalence of local weights and measures and the transfer by the kings and the chiefs of income in cash and kind from trade and industries to the religious establishment. Monasteries and temples formed large economic units, some of them comprising more than a hundred villages. According to Sharma, the land grants served as an important means of bringing virgin soil under cultivation, of providing the administrative mechanism for maintaining law and order in the donated areas and of introducing Brahmanisation and acculturation of the tribals. The grant of villages to the priests may be compared to the practice of benefices given to the Church in medieval Europe with the difference that the Brāhmaṇas and temples were not an organised group in India. According to Sharma, if by feudalism is meant merely a political disintegration and administrative decentralisation brought about by chiefs and vassals we shall have to admit that it occurred again and again in the history of India, but if by it is meant a form of social order in which the possessing class appropriated the surplus produce of the peasants by exercising superior rights over their land and persons we shall have to admit that such phenomena were occasional and that in the present state of our knowledge we have no conprehensive view of the situation. He holds that from the age of the Guptas India saw the beginnings of land grants to temples and Brāhamaṇas, and that the number of such grants increased steadily and their nature changed basically in the kingdoms of the Pālas, Pratihāras and Rāṣṭrakutas. In the earlier period only usufructuary rights were generally given, but from the eighth century onwards proprietory rights were transferred to the donees.

Whether we call it feudalism or not, this peculiar socio-economic formation, as has been outlined from different sources, cannot be ignored and requires explanation. B.N.S. Yadava (*SCNITC*, 139ff) holds that "those who identify feudalism only with vassalage and political disunity may find it at any time and also many times in the history of a country. But these features in their emphasised form are to be counted among the essential features of feudalism as a wider concept." Seen from this viewpoint, he says that some sort of lord-vassal complex existed in the post-Maurya polity, that the Gupta empire had some fedual elements and that from the post-Gupta times "there were protracted periods of political confusion and chaos leading to economic decline, which must have naturally created fit circumstances for the growth of feudal tendencies." Referring to the extreme paucity, crudeness and debasement of the coins belonging to c. A.D. 600-1000 he concludes: It is obvious that trade, commerce and urban life suffered a decline, and society tended to become increasingly agrarian. The circumstances were bound to lead to the emergence of localism and a comparatively closed economy giving rise to a number of more or less self-sufficient local economic units." His final conclusion is that "as in medieval Europe, here also under the conditions characterised by the weakness of trade and monetray circulation, which is clearly indicated by the poor state of coinage, there was no option for the rulers but to grant lands and estates in return for the services of officials, armed followers, etc."

D.C. Sircar, however, has a different set of arguments. He holds that Sharma and Yadava have misinterpreted landlordism in terms of feudalism. Neither of these historians claimed that their task was to prove the existence of feudalism in the Indian context (in fact they tried to understand or explain certain socio-economic phenomena against the backdrop of the existing political structure). Sircar was probably misled by title of Sharma's work. His criticism of Sharma and Yadava has two aspects. The first is related to the question of the feudatories and the second to the economic conditions. In regard to the feudatories and the land grants, Sircar stresses the anomalies of various kinds pertaining to the emergence of the feudatories and those which exist in the lord-vassal relationship. He holds that the concept of vassal kings in the Indian polity occurred much earlier than the post-Maurya period. In fact, subordinate rulers under more important kings can be traced even to the later Vedic period when there was no question of the existence of any form of feudalism. Inscriptions reveal the fact that under independent and semi-independent kings at different levels there were feudatories or subordinate chiefs and that they are not mentioned in royal charters as people responsible for the creation of the rent-free holdings. Often a person is found to enjoy both a feudatory title and an official designation and it becomes difficult to determine whether he was a feudatory employed in a certain office or an officer of the king on whom feudatory status or title was conferred, which suggests the absence of any great difference between the two categories of the king's subordinates. Another problem arises with the large number of official designations mentioned in the records as being enjoyed by a single person. There is epigraphic evidence to prove that absolute ownership of landed property could be purchased by people from the king, so that a wealthy man was in a position to purchase the ownership of villages not only from the landlords but also from the kings. But Sircar has failed to note that in a vast country such as India, with different customs everywhere, there will always be a scope for anomalies. Moreover, it is not clear what he really wants to suggest with reference to the points he has raised.

Sircar's criticism of Sharma and Yadava in regard to the economic aspects seems to be justified. Architectural activity from the seventh to the twelfth century bears testimony to a large amount of surplus which was accumulated in the hands of the kings and nobles. Also, contemporary evidence of the Arab merchants about the prosperity of the Rāṣṭrakūṭas, Pratihāras and Pālas goes against the conjecture regarding the poverty of the kings and kingdoms of India. Rabbi Benjamin of Tudela Idrisi, Maṣudi, Sulaiman and others spoke of extensive foreign trade. While describing Sultan Mahmud's conquest of the fort of Nagarkot, Al Utbi says: "The treasures were taken on the back of as many camels as they could procure, and the officers carried away the rest. The stamped coins amounted to seventy thousand thousand (i.e., seven crore) royal *dirhams*." The Shahi king Jayapāla paid to Sabuktigin by way of ransom 1000 packets of 1000 *dinar* sterling, i.e., ten lakh gold coins. Ibn Haukal says: "The reason why Multan is designated the boundary of the House of Gold is that the Muhammadans, though poor at the time they conquered the place, enriched themselves by the gold they found in it." According to the Muslim writers, the Pāṇḍya kings used to purchase an exceptionally large number of horses from the Arab traders, each of them costing 200 *dinars* of red gold. So the theory of the paucity of coins does not stand valid. Sircar has also pointed out that the idea that the lack of coins was a major factor underlying the rise of feudalism in England has now proved to be wrong. There is thus no longer any necessity to emphasise the paucity of coins in early medieval India as the factor giving rise to feudalism.

In the history of the later Vijayanagara kingdom among the Amaranāyakas we have some glimpses of a lord-vassal relation which recalls certain prominent feudalistic features. This was due to the fact that Vijayanagara was the only state based on the idea of absolute militarism, and that is why Amaranāyakas were legally bound to provide men and money for the king in lieu of their land-privileges and they in turn made subinfeudation on similar terms. In the history of Kashmir we come across the existence of a social class called the Ḍāmaras which often functioned as king-makers, having enormous influence on the administrative machinery. But the Ḍāmaras were not feudal chiefs, nor were they landed aristocracy. They were wealthy peasants, with the exception that, unlike other peasant communities, they were highly organised and could go to any lengths for money.

Again, in the case of the Rajputs, we come across a system which had apparently some points of similarity with feudalism. Colonel Todd pointed out that each Rajput king had under him a number of chiefs, each bound by ties of fidelity and service and commanding a specified number of soldiers in the field supplied by him; that the chiefs holding grants from the king had their distinctive badges, crests and banners and in some cases the right of coining silver; that the chiefs were obliged to attend the court of their master; that they were subject to the laws of relief and forfeiture; that they could not alienate land without the consent of the king; that wardship of minors was claimed by the king and his permission was required for the marriage of the vassals; and the vassals were required to render aid like contributions at the time of marriage of the lord's daughter. But this analysis was not wholly correct because the rules were not inflexible. Todd had found a system of land-holding with some sort of obligations, which were formal rather than legal. He also overlooked the clan-element as the binding force between the overlord and his vassal. If the term feudalism is to be used at all to denote the system, it may be described as a sort of clan-feudalism in which the vassals enjoyed their rights on kinship considerations.

5

State Within the State

1. The Caste System: An Introduction

The caste system which has characterised the social fabric of India through the ages may be described as a cluster of autonomous and functionally interrelated self-contained units grouped in a hierarchy of varying status. We have already had the occasion to refer to this peculiar structure of well-integrated social groupings commanding absolute obedience from their members, describe its principal features and deal with some aspects of its genesis and development in terms of incomplete detribalisation. There has been no dearth of scholarly works on the caste system. Earlier writers on this subject—such as Senart, Risley, Nesfield, Ibbetson and others—who were influenced on the one hand by the values of the Western civilisation and on the other by the evolutionist approach of the nineteenth century tried to explain this multiple-cum-crystallized system on the basis of a single standard or principle, as a result of which their conclusions became mostly subjective. While modern writers like Louis Dumont have criticised the earlier approaches as one-sided and based on preconceived notions, they in their turn have introduced a kind of complex and highly sophisticated sociological terminology in the name of objective analysis. The concepts popularised by them must have some relevance in a limited scale or local extent; but they are not sufficiently capable of comprehending and explaining such a vast and complicated social phenomenon. Moreover, since the caste system is still a living institution with a profound influence on public life, scholars working in this field sometimes, owing to secret machinations, knowingly or unknowingly, become victims of abstruse political purposes. In fact, since the British period the caste system has been efficiently utilised for political interests. Hutton himself has admitted that many researches on the caste system were politically motivated, that in the background of every census political considerations had the leading role and that numerous subcastes were arbitrarily created by the British rulers with the professed aim of dissociating them from the main current of Hindu society.

In many cases studies on the caste system have been influenced by the personal views and prejudices of the scholars. Sherring, Maine and Fick describe it as an artificial invention due to the contrivances of the crafty Brāhmaṇas which is the most disastrous and blighting of all human institutions, the most baneful, hard-hearted and cruel social system that could possibly be invented for damning the human race. On the other hand Dubois, Low, Townsend, Hutton and Farnival hold that this system provides everyman with place, career, occupation, companionship, club, trade-union, benefit society and a sense of community with others; it is a form of socialism which through ages protected the Hindu society from anarchy and from the worst evils of industrial and competitive life. Various such views may be quoted, but eulogy or condemnation is not the right way of approach. The existence of the caste system is not dependent on how one views it. So long as the diverse historical processes under which this system has come into existence and the various social, economic, political and cultural forces by which it has been sustained—in other words, the objective conditions on which it survives—do not become defunct or inefficacious, it will continue to exist. There are certain features of which one should take note. The system has never remained standstill; every now and then new castes and subcastes have come into existence; their mutual relations have been readjusted. The most interesting feature is that internally the system is essentially flexible, always subject to change; but externally it is rigid; the changes can not transgress the given limit. The designs change, but the frame does not.

The following observation of N.K. Bose may provide us

with some basic clues to the understanding of the caste phenomenon as a whole:

> At the outset it is observed that the Indian society is constituted by a synthesis of many races. This also happens elsewhere, and owing to the influence of the conquering race, the conquered race in many cases loses its political and economic independence. One creates a new production and distribution system by exploiting the other. With the passing of time when a new technique of production is devised, change of relation among persons takes place. This has also happened in India, but here the Indian talent had found a new expression in consequence of which, amidst various political upsets and disasters, she could save her cultural traits from annihilation. That art we come across in the caste system. According to the ancient Indian sociologists, the caste system is applicable to all forms of society. Where numerous races meet and mingle, it is possible to synthesise them in a greater society by placing them in four basic castes. For the need of society if different groups of persons work according to their capacity and skill in diverse walks of life, and if the society guarantees that the persons concerned and their descendants following their traditional occupations will not die of starvation, the society thus formed by mutual cooperation of each social group naturally becomes more powerful. Apart from this cooperation another assurance was given to the village masses. It was absoulte cultural freedom. Every group was allowed to follow their traditional social practices, cults and rituals, laws and customs (abridged rendering from the Bengali original).

According to Bose, it was because of the fact that the caste system could offer economic security and cultural freedom to the masses there was no revolt of the conquered races against their victors. But while the ideal of a plural society was thus achieved through these two well calculated means by the caste system, it was unable to treat all its constituents in terms of equality. Owing to this inequality of status and position of different castes in the social body, the Indians failed to offer united resistance against foreign invaders. It was not also possible to make the entire production system solely caste oriented. That is why transformation from one caste to another and emergence of new castes and subcastes were not infrequent. But despite such limitations the caste system survives in India even today. It is due to the fact that notwithstanding industrialisation and modernisation the peoples of India are mostly attached to their hereditary occupations. They have not as yet found any alternative to repudiate the caste system. Some writers, probably under the influence of certain political theories, try to show that with the introduction of modern technology in the field of production persons from different castes change their hereditary occupations and thus having lost their caste-identity transform into various economic classes. Such a theory lacks credibility and goes against the existing reality. In a country of seventy millions where more than eighty per cent live in villages and are still engaged in agriculture and other traditional hereditary occupations, having no scope of professional change in near or distant future, such a rapid transformation of social structure is hardly possible.

2. *Caste System in the Dharmasūtras and Dharmaśāstras*

While dealing with the Vedic society we have referred to the growth of various occupational groups in the age of the *Ṛgveda*. The *puruṣa-sukta* (X.90) of the *Ṛgveda* indirectly refers to a four-fold social division. This division has been more clearly outlined in the later Saṃhitās and Brāhmaṇas in which although the position, status and privileges of the priestly and warrior castes have been precisely defined, there is an anomaly on the question of the inclusion of other professional groups and the tribals in the four-fold hierarchy. In the Dharmasūtras and the Dharmaśāstras we come across a structural completeness of this system. Since the Dharmasūtras were composed in the later Vedic period we are in a position to suggest that the concept of the caste society was theoretically accepted by the Indians as early as the sixth century B.C., although a functional acceptance was there even from the age of the *Ṛgveda*.

In the Dharmasūtras, and later in the Dharmaśāstras, the duties and privileges of the four castes have been explained in categorical terms. Six pure professions have been attributed to the Brāhmaṇas among which teaching of the Vedas and performance of religious rituals are important. A moderate standard of living has also been prescribed for the Brāhmaṇas. It is also clearly stated that if a Brāhmaṇa is not sufficiently competent to follow the pure occupations prescribed for him by the Śāstras, he can, for the sake of his livelihood, take up the professions of a Kṣatriya, Vaiśya or a Sūdra, but in such cases his social status will be lowered in accordance with the status of the occupation he takes up. Some special privileges have also been granted to the Brāhmaṇas. The king is the master of all, but not of the Brāhmaṇas. They are exempt from taxation and certain forms of punishment. These privileges are, however, applicable only to those who follow the pure professions. It should be noted that a very high ideal of Brahmanism has been upheld in the Dharmasūtras and Dharmaśāstras. Although it is said that the Brāhmaṇa belongs to the highest caste, that he is to be respected by all, that he may take up any occupation, and that he has some social and legal privileges, it is also clearly stated that a Brāhmaṇa who does not follow the pure Brahmanical occupations and the code of conduct prescribed for him, must be socially treated as a Śūdra.

Regarding the Kṣatriyas and the Vaiśyas the Dharmasūtras and the Dharmaśāstras have not many words to say. While the six pure occupations of the Brāhmaṇas are teaching, study, worship, officiating at worship, making gifts and accepting gifts, those of the Kṣatriyas are study, worship, making gifts, profession of arms and offering protection to others. The occupations of the Vaiśyas are study, worship, making gifts, agriculture, cattle-rearing and trade. Like the Brāhmaṇas, if the Kṣatriyas are not sufficiently qualified, they can also adopt the occupations of the Vaiśyas and the Śūdras. While occupational devolution is allowed to roll down in the case of the Brāhmaṇas and the Kṣatriyas, in no case the Vaiśyas and the Śūdras are allowed to take up the prescribed occupations of the Brāhmaṇas and the Kṣatriyas. The Śūdras have four occupations—service, production of wealth, arts and crafts. They have no right to recite the Vedas and to perform Vedic rituals. Instead of reading the Vedas they can read Itihāsa and Purāṇa. They are entitled to have the results of Vedic rituals by performing *pūrtadharma*, i.e., excavations of wells and tanks, construction of temples and other works of public welfare. There is no restriction on the part of the Śūdra to acquire wealth. Except *upanayana* (initiation ritual of the twice-born, i.e., Brāhmaṇa, Kṣatriya and Vaiśya), they can perform all the sacraments without uttering the Vedic *mantras*.

While the rights and duties of the four *varṇas* have been defined in the Dharmasūtras and Dharmaśāstras, the real position of the castes was different. The idea of a four-fold social division was purely theoretical. In reality there were innumerable castes of varying importance and status. The Brāhmaṇas were never a homogeneous caste. There were hundreds of Brāhmaṇa caste-groups each functioning as a distinct caste. This holds good in the case of other three *varṇas*. The position of the Kṣatriya caste was always anomalous. The Indianised foreign tribes who happened to rule in some parts of India claimed the status of Kṣatriya. The Śūdra kings (kings of ancient India were mostly Śūdras) often wanted to be known as Kṣatriyas. We shall later see that many Kṣatriyas had taken up the occupations of agriculture, cattle-rearing and trade as a result of which they lost their original caste identity and came to be regarded as the Vaiśyas or the Śūdras. Likewise, the Vaiśyas were divided into numerous sub-castes. But most occupational castes, almost seventy-five per cent of the known castes, fall in the category of the Śūdras.

The problem of the writers of the Dharmasūtras and the Dharmaśāstras was to incorporate these innumerable castes into the idealised scheme of four-fold social division. In order to achieve this end they devised an imaginary and unrealistic, but effective, theory which was known as the theory of *varṇasaṅkara* or mixed castes. They tried to explain the origin of different occupational castes by describing them as descendants of persons born of hypergamic (*anuloma*) and hypogamic (*pratiloma*) matrimonial unions among the four idealised castes. Thus, the offspring of a Brāhmaṇa male and a Kṣatriya female is Murdhābhiṣikta, that of a Kṣatriya male and Vaiśya female is Māhiṣya, that of a Vaiśya male and Śūdra female is Karaṇa, that of a Brāhmaṇa male and Vaiśya female is Ambaṣṭha, that of a Brāhmaṇa male and Śūdra female is Niṣāda or Pārasava, that of a Kṣatriya male and Śūdra female is Ugra and so on. The hybrid castes thus emerged from morganatic and reverse forms of marriages produce many other hybrid castes of the second rank and they in their turn produce mixed castes of the third rank. Following this system innumerable functional social groups can be accommodated as mixed castes or subcastes within the structure of the four-fold system. But since the formation of such subcastes through intercaste marriages was not practically possible what the writers of the Dharmaśāstras really did was to classify the existing numerous castes, mostly belonging to the Śūdra category, on the basis of the nature of their occupations and place them in the scheme of the mixed castes.

Those who belong to the lowest rank of the caste hierarchy are known as Antya, Antyaja or Antyavasāyi. They are regarded in the Dharmaśāstras as descendants of persons born of the union of the lower caste males and higher caste females. Their occupations are also of low type. There is, however, no unanimity in the Dharmaśāstras among the specific caste-names belonging to this category. The specific caste-names frequently found in this connection are Rajaka (washerman), Carmakāra (leather worker), Naṭa (public entertainer), Buruḍa (bamboo-worker), Kaivarta (agriculturists and fishermen), Meda (hunters), Bhilla, Caṇḍāla, Kṣatri (scavenger), Suta (charioteer), Vaidehika, Māgadha Āyogava (weavers and metal workers), Pulkasa (hunters) and a few others. Though these castes theoretically belong to the lowest order, their status is not same everywhere. Many caste-names such as Bhilla, Vaidehika or Māgadha have tribal affiliations. Foreign tribes such as the Yavanas, Pahlavas, Pāradas, Cīnas, Ābhiras, etc., have been regarded as degraded Kṣatriyas, born of union between Śūdra males and Kṣatriya females. In such castes of hybrid categories the well known Indian tribes like the Ambaṣṭhas, Āvantyas, Oḍras, Kambojas, Daradas, Kirātas, Mekalas, Ḍrāviḍas, Lāṭas, Pauṇḍras, Madgus, Andhras, Niṣādas, Licchavis, Pulindas, Bhojas, Mahiṣakas, etc., have been accommodated.

Among the castes subsisting on hunting or fishing the Dharmaśāstras refer to the Andhras, Kirātas, Caṇḍālas, Cuñcus, Medas, Madgus, Pulindas, Mataṅgas, Śabaras, Svapacas, Lubdhakas, Mārgavas, Kaivartas, Dhīvaras, Mallas, etc. These castes are mentioned as hybrids of the lowest category (*adhama-saṅkara*) being born mostly of the union between females of good ranked hybid castes (*uttama-saṅkara*) and males of middle-ranked hybrid castes (*madhyama-saṅkara*). Among other occupational castes belonging to the hybrids of the three categories mentioned above the Dharmaśāstras refer to the Ābhira, Gopa, Gopālaka, Golaka (dependent on cattle rearing), Ambaṣṭha (mostly physicians but of varying occupations in different parts of India), Ayaskāra, Takṣaṇa, Upakruṣṭa, Kāṃsakāra, Vardhakī, Suvarṇakāra, Sauvarṇika, Hemakāra, Tāmropajīvī (blacksmiths, carpenters, goldsmiths, coppersmiths etc.), Kumbhakāra, Kaulāla (potter). Tantuvāya (weaver), Rajaka, Udbandhaka, Cailanirṇejika (washerman), Aiśvika (horse-dealer), Tailika, Cakrī, Cākrika (oil-presser), Nartaka (dancer), Tāmbulika (dealer in betel leaves), Paṇḍusopāka (bamboo-worker), Mālākara, Mālika (flower-dealer), Kuntalaka (barber), and many others, besides the agricultural castes. Certain hybrid castes are mentioned without any specific occupations attributed to them.

3. Inconsistencies in the Varṇasaṅkara Theory

The emphasis of the Dharmaśāstras on the theory of *varṇasaṅkara* or mixed-castes by which the origin of various subcastes has been traced to inter-caste marriages may suggest that such marriages were very common in ancient India. But it was far from the real situation. Since endogamy was one of the basic features of the caste system, its denial through inter-caste marriages in a greater scale was expected to tell upon the system itself. When the castes functioned as well-integrated social groups, each preserving its distinct cultural and social entities, inter-caste marriages were almost impossible, as it is difficult even today. Every caste entails upon its members to follow strictly its own laws and customs. Most of the occupational groups, regarded as hybrid castes of various order in the Dharmaśāstras, belonged to the Śūdra category; the situation and social environment did not permit their members to transgress the limit of their community norms. Even in the case of the so called higher castes the question of the purity of blood and lineage was vital. Though Manu and other writers of the Dharmaśāstras hold that a Brāhmaṇa can keep a non-Brāhmaṇa wife, they do not encourage it. The wife in such cases is regarded almost as a mistress; the children born of her are not entitled to have a share of the family property, though it is said that the father ought to give them something because, after all, he is their begetter. Under these circumstances inter-caste marriages were bound to be infrequent.

Secondly, regarding the fixation of the rank and status of these so called mixed castes in the hierarchy, the writers of the Dharmśāstras did not follow any reasonable standard. For example, the Caṇḍālas have been assigned the lowest rank in the hierarchy by Manu and other law-givers who emphasise that they should be excluded from all contacts with others. They are to live as untouchables outside the village with marks of identification; their very presence makes other impure. That the Caṇḍālas were regarded as the most despised caste is also supported by the evidence of Buddhist literature and foreign accounts. But it is difficult to understand what could have been the reason for treating them so contemptuously. If we accept the interpretation of the Dharmaśāstras we are to admit that the Caṇḍālas are descendants of persons born of the union of Śūdra male and Brāhmaṇa female. Side by side we find that the Carmakāras or leather workers are a similar hybrid caste born of the union of Śūdra male and Vaiśya female. In such case the Caṇḍālas should have to be given a higher rank than the Carmakāras, because a Caṇḍāla is a Śūdra-Brāhmaṇa combine and a Carmakāra is a Śūdra-Vaiśya combine. But in the caste hierarchy the Carmakāras have been given a better position than the Caṇḍālas. Probably the reason behind this deeply rooted apathy towards the Caṇḍālas is the belief in the sanctity of a Brāhmaṇa female. The law-givers wanted to popularise the idea that a Brāhmaṇa female is always a taboo to men of other castes; to have sexual relation with her is a crime.

Thirdly, the writers of the Dharmaśāstras failed to make an exhaustive list of all the castes and subcastes or specify their actual occupations, status and role in society. This was due to the fact that they had no direct touch with the functional castes which were far more numerous than those known to them only conventionally. Their difficulty was that they had only to give a religious and moral sanction to a system under which they were themselves born and brought up. Commenting on the list of mixed subcastes found in the *Yājñavalkya-smṛti*

Vijñāneśvara says that this list is only exemplary; in reality mixed castes are endless. Sixty-four castes have been mentioned in the *Vaijayantī* among which 4 have been described as principal castes, 12 as originating from morganatic marriages and 48 as their offshoots. In the *Bṛhaddharma Purāṇa* 41 sub-castes are mentioned among which 20 have been regarded as good hybrid, 12 as middle hybrid and 9 as low hybrid. In some Smṛtis and Purāṇas the hybrid sub-castes are usually divided into two broad categories—clean and unclean Śūdras. In such classifications no unanimously accepted standard was followed.

Historically speaking, the origin of most subcastes was due to the growth of occupational divisions and specialisations as well as adoption of new occupations by groups of detribalised peoples who came into the bigger fold of the Hindu society. It had very little to do with morganatic marriages on which the writers of the Dharmaśāstras laid so much emphasis for devising the strange *varṇasaṅkara* theory. The function of the king, as the Dharmaśāstras state, is to maintain Varṇāśrama so that the hereditary occupations of different castes are not disturbed. But instances of the change of hereditary occupations are not rare. Examples are not infrequent of various castes having one single occupation or of castes adopting new occupations having repudiated the hereditary ones. Again in many cases it has been observed that subcastes of a particular caste have come into existence owing to economic division of labour or various specialisations in a single occupation. It has also been observed that while the major section of a particular caste retains its hereditary occupation, another section has responded to new callings. This has happened especially in the case of the persons belonging to the higher castes. In the case of the Brāhmaṇas and the Kṣatriyas such changes are given the recognition of validity by the law-givers who have thus allowed some form of occupational mobility in the upper levels of society. But this was not encouraged in the lower levels.

4. Caste and the Reformistic Religious Systems

It is generally believed that the anti-Vedic religious systems like Buddhism or Jainism repudiated the caste system. But this is not true. The Buddha and Lord Mahavīra believed in the social efficacy of the caste system. They were only opposed to its inequality factor and therefore tried to popularise the idea that if a man is pious and virtuous he should be regarded as superior to the Brāhamaṇas, thus offering a new interpretation of the caste theory. The same attitude was shared by the medieval saints. Śrī Caitanya, for example, said that if a Caṇḍāla is a devotee of Hari he is far superior to a Brāhmaṇa; he should be respected or even worshipped by persons belonging to the higher castes including the Brāhmaṇas. But this elevation in individual status only means that he is superior to a Brāhmaṇa, but not a Brāhmaṇa socially.

A high ideal of Brahmanism has been maintained in the Buddhist texts. "No one becomes a Brāhamaṇa or a lower caste only on the basis of his birth; it is by his deeds alone that a man becomes a Brāhmaṇa or otherwise." "By growing matted locks or being born in a Brāhmaṇa family no one becomes a Brāhmaṇa; only the just, truthful and virtuous can be a Brāhmaṇa." "Birth and caste are causes of human vanity; merit alone is to be counted." The Buddhist texts are burdened with such passages. Notwithstanding such statements, the question of birth which determines to which caste one should belong, could not be avoided. Thus in the Ambaṭṭha Sutta of the *Dīgha Nikāya* the Buddha categorically says that the offspring of a Kṣatriya male and a Brāhmaṇa female cannot be regarded as a Kṣatriya owing to the fault of the mother and that of a Brāhmaṇa male and Kṣatriya female cannot be regarded as a Kṣatriya owing to the fault of the father. This strange logic purports to hold that the Kṣatriyas were superior to the Brāhmaṇas.

In most Buddhist texts the Kṣatriyas are really regarded as superior to the Brāhmaṇas. It was probably due to the fact that the Buddha himself was regarded as a Kṣatriya, though basically he was a tribal like his illustrious contemporary Lord Mahāvīra. In the *Lalitavistara* it is said that the Bodhisattvas (to which spiritual category the Buddha belonged) are never born in lower castes; they are born either in a Brāhmaṇa or in a Kṣatriya family. We shall later see that although the Brāhmaṇas formed the first caste, they did not represent the dominant caste. For some time in ancient India the Kṣatriyas were really the dominant caste, just as in modern India the economically and politically powerful middle-ranked castes are dominant. So the Buddha had to be born in a Kṣatriya family. According to the Jain legends, Lord Mahāvīra was originally conceived into the womb of a Brāhmaṇa lady called Devanandā, who was the wife of one Ṛṣabhadatta, but the god Indra, thinking that the would-be Tīrthaṃkara should belong to a powerful and wealthy family, got his embryo transferred from the womb of Devanandā to that of the Kṣatriya lady, Triśalā, through his agent Hariṇegamisī.

Apart from the Brāhmaṇas and the Kṣatriyas, the Vaiśyas (Vessa) and the Śūdars (Suddas) are mentioned in the Buddhist texts. The Vaiśyas were commonly known as Gahapatis and Kutumbikas. Numerous occupational castes belonging to the Śūdra category are mentioned in the Buddhist texts as Hīnajātis. Since nothing is known about the social life of the Buddhists in ancient India it is not possible to say how the caste system worked in the Buddhist societies. But so far as the Jains are concerned, it may be said that the Jain society, notwithstanding its theoretical opposition to the caste system, was caste oriented. Traditionally there are 84 castes among the Jains. The Jain castes are endogamous and a few of them are common to both the Śvetāmbaras and the Digambaras. No prominent position is assigned to any of them, not even to the Jain Brāhmaṇas. But in practice we find some castes claiming superiority over others and this feeling is obviously due to differences in economic position, moral standards, social practices, customs and manners. Thus castes following lower occupations are generally regarded as low. Those who do not allow widow remarriage look down upon to those who allow, and in this way restrictions have grown as regards inter-dining, inter-marriage and other social practices. Of the important Jain castes of modern times reference may be made to the Agravāla Osavāla, Śrīmālī, Porāvāḍa, Khaṇḍelvālā, Paravāra, Humbaḍa (Hummaḍa), Śetavāla (Saitavāla), Caturtha, Bogāra, Upādhyāya and others.

The leaders of the reformistic religious movements of the early medieval and medieval period did not make any distinction between man and man on the basis of caste. But they did not ignore the importance of the caste system. It is frequently said that they tried to abolish this system. In favour of this argument it is said that a good number of the medieval saints belonged to the lower ranks of the caste hierarchy and that many Brāhmaṇas were their disciples. Tulasīdāsa, who was a champion of Brahmanical supremacy, while dealing with the customs of the Kali age, says in *Rāmacaritamānsa* that it is really deplorable that the Śūdras have adopted the role of religious teachers and the Brāhmaṇas have become their disciples. The Telis, Kumārs (potters), Caṇḍālas, Kirātas, Dombs, Kalwars have all shaved their heads and become preceptors and the Brāhmaṇas are kissing their feet. His attack was evidently directed against such religious teachers as Ravidās, Dharnā, Senā and others who belonged to the lower castes. Most of the 84 Siddhas belonging to the Tantric Buddhist tradition were of lower occupations. Though a Śūdra Tukārām was the *guru* of the Brāhmaṇas. Many non-Brāhmaṇa followers of Śrī Caitanya, such as Narahari Sarkār, Narottama Ṭhākur, etc., acted as preceptors of the Brāhmaṇas. Śaṅkaradeva of Assam was a Kāyastha. But the point which is forgotten is that in the so-called orthodox Brahmanical tradition the right of the Śūdras to earn religious merit or to act as religious preachers has always been allowed. So Tulasīdāsa had no reason to lament. It has also been observed that the sects or religious communities introduced by many of these religious teachers became in no time caste oriented or began to function as distinct castes.

The most revolutionary religious community which seriously repudiated the caste system was the Vīraśaiva or the Liṅgāyata founded by Vasava. The Vīraśaivas laid much emphasis on social reform. This sect was also against child-marriage and favoured widow-remarriage. Their mission was to serve the cause of the downtrodden with greatest stress on economic upliftment. Owing to the teachings of Vasava and their mutual unity and cooperation the Liṅgāyatas became a prosperous and powerful community within a very short time. But what happened to them afterwards? A community which made its appearance by denouncing the caste system and incorporating within its body members of various castes of lower order was later transformed into a well organised dominant caste. It is indeed difficult to explain the cause of this transformation. It appears that the unchangeability of the Indian system of economic production was partly responsible for this. In the field of the early medieval and medieval religious systems there was undoubtedly a growth of liberal ideas. But in conformity of the growth of such ideas there was no qualitative change in the system of production. As a result no such condition was created in which the liberal religious ideals could find the real ground of their natural expression.

In many cases the founders of the neo-religious movements were Brāhmaṇas or members of the higher castes. Although they tried to denounce the caste system from the viewpoint that all men are equal—the principle for which they stood—their successors attempted to revert the trend in order to re-establish Brahmanical supremacy, as a result of which the sect concerned was split into a number of subsects which in their turn were transformed into various castes within the framework of the existing caste system. Some religious reform movements like Sikhism went outside the fold of Hindu society and religion. Even in such cases the caste factor did not cease to function. For example, among the Sikhs the Jats are the dominant caste. Then there are Rajputs, Gujars, Arora, Kṣatri and others. The Chuhras belong to the lowest rank of the caste hierarchy in the Punjab region. Among them, those who have been converted into Sikhism are known as Majhvi and those into Islam as Musalli. Despite conversion their caste status has not been enhanced.

Because the caste system is a special form of social structure which is interwoven with the totality of society by diverse cause-effect relations, its influence could not be avoided even by the egalitarian socio-religious systems such as Islam or Christianity which came to India from outside. Though the Muslim societies of India cannot be called 'caste societies' in the Hindu sense, yet the basic features of the caste system—such as endogamy, occupational distinction, hierarchy and restrictions—are present in them. A Momin's son becomes a Momin by birth and he should marry a Momin's daughter—it is the rule in practice, though not in theory. The Muslim social groups functioning as castes are broadly divided into two categories—Ashraf belonging to the higher and Ajlaf belonging to the lower ranks. While the development of certain features of the caste system took place in the Muslim societies automatically under the influence of the existing traditional socio-economic conditions without any encouragement from the priestly or ruling class, the case was somewhat different so far as the earlier Christian communities were concerned. The Christian missionaries like De Nobili or Zeigenbalg believed that the caste system was a social institution of India totally unconnected with the basic principles of Hinduism, and as such there was no reason why a converted Christian should give up his caste identity, social position and traditional norms and customs. Hence for the propagation of Christianity not only did they make compromise with the caste system, but actively encouraged caste distinction even within the church, as a result of which caste feeling was more pronounced among the Christians of India, especially those of South India, than any other non-Hindu religious community.

5. *Hierarchy and Social Position*

In order to determine the relative status and position of various castes in the social hierarchy scholars have insisted chiefly on four aspects—physical or ethnic characteristics, numerical strength, economic standard and purity-impurity factor—none of which seems to be satisfactory. It is really doubtful whether the castes or the subcastes can at all be identified with various ethnic groups. In Uttar Pradesh and Bihar and also in some regions of Bengal some difference in physical characters is observed between persons of the higher and lower castes. But this difference is mainly found in the fringe areas in which the transformation from tribes into castes is a recent phenomenon. Again, the Namah Sūdras who belong to a lower rank of the caste hierarchy have no difference with the Brāhmaṇas so far as the bodily appearance is concerned. The same holds good in the case of the Suvarṇa Vaṇiks who excel the Brāhmaṇas in the fairness of skin. The Maratha Brāhmaṇas belong to the same ethnic category as other Maratha castes. D.N. Majumdar and K. Kishen have informed that the peoples of the Gujarat region do not show much difference in physical appearance. G.S. Ghurye's conclusion is the same in regard to South India and Orissa. No caste traces its origin to any ethnic tradition.

All castes have mythology or folklore; they trace their origin to different gods, sages or heroes. For example, the Barhis (carpenter) of Uttar Pradesh claim themselves to be the descendants of the god Viśvakarman. Castes belonging to the lower ranks hold that their low position was due to some misdeed of a remote ancestor or to the wrath of Śiva.

The idea that a particular caste in a particular area becomes a dominant caste owing to its numerical strength is also fallacious. The surveys made in the district levels show that in most castes the dominant castes do not form the majority of the populace. When one speaks of the influential or dominant caste, the special area of its power and influence should also be located. It has also been observed that a caste which is powerful in the village level may not be powerful in the district or state level. The economic power of a particular caste is expected to have something to do with its position in the hierarchy; but the fact is that the economically powerful agricultural or commercial castes like the Jats or Banias have not that exalted position in the society. Srinivasa has shown that the commercial castes of Karnataka want to designate themselves as Vaiśyas, but other castes are unwilling to give them this status. The same holds good in the case of the commercial castes of Bengal. Still, it has to be admitted that the middle ranked agricultural and commercial castes owing to their economic and political strength attain a special position which cannot be easily ignored.

There is obviously a difference between what the Dharmaśāstras say about the position of various castes in the hierarchy and what exists in practical life. It is fact that some castes are powerful owing to their political and economic strength. But what one should observe is that in most cases the area of their influence is essentially local. One caste which is dominant in a particular village or district may not have the same position in a different village or district. Secondly, the time factor also cannot be ignored. A caste which is dominant today may not remain the same tomorrow; the emergence of competitive and challenging castes is very likely. Thirdly, the dominant castes have conflicts among themselves, both within and without, as a result of which disintegration and split very often take place yielding a number of smaller castes with varying status.

The cause of the rise of the dominant castes is mainly political and economic. These are constituted mostly by land-holders, warriors and traders. The land-holding dominant castes of northern India prefer to call themselves Rajputs and claim a Kṣatriya origin. The Nayars of the Malabar region, a caste of warriors and landholders, also like to introduce themselves as Kṣatriyas, but the Brāhmaṇas treat them as Śūdras. The Maratha castes comprising various occupational subcastes are also claimants of Kṣatriyahood, their upliftment in the hierarchy being due to the political power they assumed in the Mughal period. In eastern Uttar Pradesh the Brāhmaṇas, Rajputs and Banias and in western the Jats are the dominant castes while in some places the Gujars and Ahirs are more powerful. In Rajasthan it has been observed that in most villages the caste of the village chief becomes the dominant caste. In the Karnatak region the Brāhmaṇas, Liṅgāyatas and Vokkaligas (equivalent to the Jats of the north) and in Andhra the Kammas and the Kapus or Reddis (Kapu means village-head) are powerful. In the Coorg region, in the village levels the Kannada-speaking Okkaligas and the Tulu-speaking Gauḍas are prominent but in the higher levels the Amma Kurgis are more powerful since they are agriculturists and warriors at the same time and follow strictly the Brahmanical customs.

In the case of these so called dominant castes there is no social or cultural uniformity which is found among the Brāhmaṇas. For example, the Nayars have matrilineal inheritance and matrilocal marriage; the Kurgis have the system of divorce and widow remarriage; but such social practices are absent among the Rajputs. Although the political and economic power of these middle-ranked dominant castes is able to dislodge the Brāhmaṇas from their social supremacy this has not happened in practice. It is due to the fact that the Brāhmaṇas are regarded as intermediaries between men and the gods. The idea that the Brāhmaṇas possess special spiritual power is also deeply rooted in the mind of the Indian masses. Secondly, the Brāhmaṇas are regarded as representatives and symbols of all the noble aspects of Indian life and of all the beliefs and rituals on which the Hindu society subsists even today. That is why there has always been a tendency among the non-Brāhmaṇa castes to follow strictly the Brahmanical way of life and the

Brahmanical concept of purity. For example, the Banias of Madhya Pradesh, Uttar Pradesh and western India do not drink wine or eat fish and flesh. Referring to the Banias of Deoli in Rajasthan Carstairs says that they are more critical than the Brāhmaṇas in regard to the question of purity and impurity. Amma Kurgis of the Kaveri river region call themselves Kāverī Brāhmaṇas having given up the habit of meat-eating. Gough has noticed the increasing influence of the Brahmanical way of life among the Nayars. She has described this tendency as Sanskritisation. Russell says that the Rajputs of Madhya Pradesh were previously fond of wine and meat; but such habits were given up for embracing the Brahmanical way of life.

On the other hand whatever the Brāhmaṇas may think about the middle ranked powerful castes, they do not ignore them publicly. Srinivasa has shown that in the villages of Karnataka the relation between the village chiefs and the Brāhmaṇas is outwardly that of reciprocal obedience and toleration. This holds good also in other parts of India. The Brāhmaṇas know that the village chiefs or men belonging to the dominant castes, despite their lower occupations like agriculture, are quite capable of doing good or bad to them; on the other hand persons belonging to the dominant castes, because of their poor intellectual standard and traditional preoccupations, believe that the Brāhmaṇas should not be lightly approached. In the relation between the Brāhmaṇas and the dominant castes local elements also have a significant role.

6. The Brahmanical Exploitation: Anatomy of an Exaggeration

The Brāhmaṇas have been represented by many historians as a class of exploiters. It is generally said that taking advantage of their social and religious position and also of the political influence which they could wield upon the ruling class, the Brāhmaṇas have unjustly exploited the Indian masses for their own profit and advantage through the ages. Even such theories have been popularised by responsible historians that the Vedic rituals were invented by the greedy Brāhmaṇas to befool the common people. Without going into the details of the arguments of the historians who like to see Brāhmaṇas as social villains a few questions may pertinently be raised. The first question is whether the structure of the caste system in itself can afford the scope of exploiting one caste by another. The answer is bound to be negative, since every caste, whatever its position in the hierarchy may be, is independent and autonomous with its own society and occupation; one caste cannot be master of another. The second question is more important. Unless the Brāhmaṇas are treated as a single homogeneous social class, like the bourgeoisie of the present day, how is it possible for them to assume the role of the exploiter of the masses?

It is interesting to note that, unlike all other castes, the Brāhmaṇas are not a homogeneous social group. It is due to the fact that the ancient law-givers allowed maximum occupational mobility to the Brāhmaṇas. As we have seen above, the Vedic, Buddhist and Jain texts refer to numerous callings of the Brāhmaṇas. It is approved by the Dharmaśāstras though it is stated there that the Brāhmaṇas following the occupations of the Vaiśyas and Śūdras should have inferior social status. While among the non-Brāhmaṇa castes occupational rigidity contributed to the growth of caste solidarity, the laxity granted to the Brāhmaṇas yielded the opposite result. The term Brāhmaṇa is really no more than a generic name attributed to a number of social groups functioning as subcastes of various rank and status.

The social status of the agriculturist Brāhmaṇas is not high. For example, the Taga Gauḍa Brāhmaṇas of the Haryana region are regarded as Śūdras. Men of other castes do not touch their feet. The Mahāsthānī Brāhmaṇas of Orissa are known as Haliyā Brāhmaṇas for their agricultural occupations and they are regarded as Brāhmaṇas of inferior type. The same holds good in the case of the Trigula Brāhmaṇas of south Maratha country, the Sopara Brāhmaṇas of the Bassein region, the Sajhodra and Bhatela Brāhmaṇas of Gujarat, Devrukera, Kirvant and Kasta Brāhmaṇas of Maharashtra, Haiga and Hale Brāhmaṇas of Karnataka, etc. The Brāhmaṇas living on trade and commerce are also regarded as lower class Brāhmaṇas. The Sanādhyas of Uttar Pradesh, who are a branch of the Kanaujiās, are regarded as of inferior status owing to their association with trade and commerce. The Kanaujiās do not make any matrimonial alliance with them. The Jabala Brāhmaṇas of the Konkan region, the Sacora Brāhmaṇas of Gujarat, the Jaipura Brāhmaṇas of Orissa, etc., are also regarded as no better than the Śūdras because they are professional cooks.

Even many of those who are associated with religious functions are regarded as Brāhmaṇas of the inferior rank. Those who accept gifts from the non-Brāhmaṇas, or officiate in the religious functions of the lower castes as priests are regarded as degraded Brāhmaṇas. Among such Brāhmaṇas mention may be made of the Mahābrāhmaṇas of North India (the prefix *mahā* meaning 'great' is applied in contemptuous sense), the Agradānī Brāhmaṇas of Bengal, the Agrabhikṣus of Orissa, the Ācārya Brāhmaṇas of western India, etc. They are regarded as belonging to the lower rank because they accept gifts for expiation of the sins of the dead. The Sawalakhis are regarded as degraded Brāhmaṇas because they accept gift from the pilgrims. The Bhaṭṭa Brāhmaṇas of Uttar Pradesh are low grade Brāhmaṇas because they perform rituals to remove the sins of their clients. The Brāhmaṇas who utter *mantras* before the cremation of the dead are regarded as worse than the Śūdras. The Dakot and Śanicar Brāhmaṇas also belong to the lower class because they officiate in the worship of Śani. Even those who are associated with the famous temples—such as Gayālīs of Gaya, the Chaubes of Mathura, Puṣkara-sevakas of Pushkar, Prayāgwalās of Prayaga, Gaṅgāputras of Kasi, Pandarams and Moylars of south India, Diwas of western India, Ambalavasis of the Malabar region, Numbis of Karnataka, etc.,—are regarded as inferior Brāhmaṇas and have no social status.

The Brāhmaṇas who officiate in the religious rituals of the Śūdras and the lower castes are known as Varṇa Brāhmaṇas. Their status is also very low. In Bengal the caste names of their clients are prefixed to designate them, e.g., Rajaka-Brāhmaṇas, meaning Brāhmaṇa of the washerman. In Mithila such Brāhmaṇas are known as Tatoyā-Brāhmaṇa, Telī-Brāhmaṇa, Kāmār-Brāhmaṇa, Sonār-Brāhmaṇa and so on. In Gujarat and Rajasthan the Varṇa Brāhmaṇas are known as Ābhira-Brāhmaṇa, Kunbi-Gaur, Gujar-Gaur, Muchi-Gaur, Gandharpa-Gaur, Garudya, etc. Gaur or Gauḍa is a term for priesthood. Among the Varṇa Brāhmaṇas of South India mention may be made of Gond-Draviḍa, Nambi-Vorlu, Eledu, etc. Brāhmaṇas following astrological callings and known by the general name Grahavipra are also regarded as belonging to the inferior category.

In fact, after the decline of the Vedic rituals the position of the Yājñika or priestly Brāhmaṇas began to be lowered, though a class of the Brāhmaṇas who acted as preceptors or *gurus* of the kings and powerful persons began to prosper. The Brāhmaṇas who were in the profession of teaching were also honoured and rewarded. A good number of Brāhmaṇas acted as ministers and councillors and also as government officials. Such Brāhmaṇas were granted lands and villages. But the condition of the priestly class was dwindling. The early followers of Buddhism and Jainism did not require any priestly assistance for earning spiritual merit. The development and popularity of the monotheistic religious systems like Vaiṣṇavism or Śaivism made direct contact of the individuals with God easier through *bhakti* or personal devotion. The utility of priesthood was thus reduced to a considerable extent. They survived somehow on undignified occupations. On the other hand the descendants of many of those who were granted lands or villages failed to retain a uniform standard of social status. Those who got their land cultivated by others belonged to a higher social rank than those who cultivated their land themselves.

Ten classes of Brānmaṇas are described in the Dharmaśāstras: Deva Brāhmaṇas (those who follow the Brahmanical way of life strictly), Muni Brāhmaṇas (those who live in forest avoiding the company of worldly-minded peoples), Dvija Brāhmaṇas (those who live by imparting spiritual and philosophical knowledge), Kṣatra Brāhmaṇas (those subsisting on the profession of arms), Vaiśya Brāhmaṇas (those who follow the occupations of the Vaiśyas), Śūdra Brāhmaṇas (those who follow the occupations of the Śūdras), Niṣāda Brāhmaṇas (those who follow the occupations of the Niṣādas like hunting), Paśu Brāhmaṇas (those who wear the sacred thread only), Mleccha Brāhmaṇas (those who are devoid of any sacrament) and Caṇḍāla Brāhmaṇas (those who care for nothing). The Buddhist texts also mention ten kinds of the Brāhmaṇas who are not associated with pure Brahmanical occupations: physicians, messengers, tax collectors, wood-cutters, traders, peasants, pastorals, butchers, guards and hunters. While dealing with the professional Brāhmaṇas the writers of the Dharmaśāstras have not lost their sense of humour. "Those who have not any knowledge in the Vedas earn their livelihood by reciting the Purāṇas; those who are even unable to read the Purāṇas earn their livelihood by agriculture and other occupations; and those who are unable to take up any calling become a Bhāgavata (i.e. Vaiṣṇava or Śaiva monk)". Thus a homogeneous Brāhmaṇa caste was in fact non-existent even in earlier times; instead we have rather a hierarchy of social groups known by the genetic name 'Brāhmaṇa'. The fate of those belonging to the lower ranks of this hiérarchy was not at all envious. A theory insisting on the exploitation of the masses by the Brāhmaṇas therefore lacks credibility, although in all periods of our known history there were the exploiter and the exploited classes. It must be admitted that some politically and economically powerful Brāhmaṇa individuals obviously belonged to the former class along with their counterparts from other dominant castes. But to stigmatise the Brāhmaṇas as villains is unjust and unhistorical. It cannot also be said that the Brāhmaṇas exploited the masses in the name of religion. We have seen that the institution of priesthood began to be treated with diminishing importance since the decline of the Vedic rituals and that the priests of the so called lower castes were treated with comtempt.

But, side by side, it should also be admitted that there is an ambivalence in the attitude of the Indian masses towards the Brāhmaṇas. The deep-rooted feeling of reverence for the *brāmaṇya* in the Indian mind is not owing to any caste consideration. It is the kind and not the functional phyla that commands universal respect. According to the Indian tradition the Brāhmaṇas are superior to others for four reasons—*brāmaṇya* (purity of birth as Brāhmaṇa), *pratirūpacaryā* (boldness of character), *yaśaḥ* (fame) and *lokapakti* (upholder of moral values in public life). Being taught by the Brāhmaṇas men find fulfilment in life and that is why the Brāhmaṇas are to be honoured. The commitment is to this ideal of Brāhmaṇahood and not to any specific social group. When an individual or a community of Brāhmaṇa is looked down upon, it is owing to the failure of the individual or the community to maintain the idealised Brahmanical standard. This idealised Brahmanical standard may be an illusion and not a reality; still the illusion dominates the mind of the masses.

7. The Practice of Untouchability

It is generally believed that one of the consequences of the caste system is the development of the practice of untouchability, because certain castes are regarded as untouchable. There is, however, no invariable concomitance between untouchability and the caste system. According to the Dharmaśāstras no one can be untouchable; all hybrid castes, including the lowest ones, have come into existence owing to morganatic marriages among male and female members of the four traditional *varṇas* either in the ascending or in the descending order; since they all emanate directly or indirectly within the frame of the divinely approved four-fold division, none of them can be regarded as untouchable or impure. In order to trace the origin of the practice of untouchability some scholars, however, insist on certain injunctions found in the Dharmaśāstras. Manu (IX.235-39) says that persons guilty of serious moral lapses should be regarded as outcasts; no one should act as their teacher or assist in the rituals they perform or establish matrimonial relation with them. Secondly, members of certain anti-Vedie creeds—such as the followers of the Buddhist, Jain, Lokāyata, Kāpila, Pāsupata, Śaiva and Nāstika systems—are regarded as dangerous and people are warned to avoid them. Thirdly, persons belonging to alien cultures are regarded as *mlecchas* with whom the establishment of social relation is discouraged. Such injunctions might have contributed to the growth of some forms of social differences. But with these the practice of untouchability had nothing to do.

The question of untouchability may be approached from different viewpoints. In some form or other untouchability or similar practices are found everywhere. The policy of apartheid pursued by many European nations is an example of this. In British India the European clubs contained signboards with the label: Dogs and Indians are not allowed to enter. Such attitudes were owing to racial hatred. The Indian concept of untouchability has, however, a different background; it is only connected with the question of purity and impurity. The Indian psychology of purity and impurity is rather strange and its expressions are also varied. There is a tendency to regard certain castes as unclean because of the unclean nature of their caste professions. The professions which require killing of life or handling of filth—such as those of the hunters, butchers, scavengers, etc.,—are regarded as unclean. Birds or beasts like fowls or hogs subsist on dirty things. So their flesh is not clean and should not be consumed. To touch a dog is sometimes a contaminating factor. The idea of the sacred and the profane pertains not only to the social life but to the individual way of life as well. Close relations like mother, wife, sister or daughter become unclean and hence untouchable during the period of their menstruation. If death occurs in a family its members remain impure for a certain period of time within which they should not be touched by others. In the time of eating one should not even touch one's own son. Such ideas of impurity and contamination may have something to do with hygienic notions, but have nothing to do with the caste hierarchy.

The ideas of impurity were current in other countries also. The Brahmanical law books hold that a menstruating woman must be dreaded and regarded as impure. Among the European peasants it was believed that flowers and fruit trees were withered by contact with a menstruating woman. Pliny's account of the effects produced by a menstruating woman expresses substiantially the beliefs which were current even in the nineteenth century among most of the rural population of Europe. Menstrual blood is also dreaded in the *Quran* (II.122,II.228) as well as in the Mosaic Law Book of the Holy Bible (*Leviticus*, XV.19-28, 33; XX.18). But in India, a unique situation was created in which, apart from the well known taboos, avoidance of all external contamination was regarded as a means to achieve spiritual salvation. For various reasons a class of Brāhmaṇas laid supreme emphasis on the purity of body. Geographical, linguistic and other differenes prevented the formation of their all round integration. To the Brāhmaṇas of Uttar Pradesh it was difficult to maintain contacts with their counterparts of

Bengal. In both the regions they were susceptible to get mixed with other castes owing to linguistic, cultural, economic and other considerations. So in both the regions this class of Brāhmaṇas tried to maintain their exalted position and difference with others under the armour of a rigid form of purity.

It was not the caste or racial hatred but a fear of contamination with the unclean which was responsible for regarding certain castes as impure. The company of the impure castes subsisting on impure professions was generally avoided by members of other castes. This accounts for the growth of the practice of untouchability. The process may be described as follows. In the first stage, the earlier writers of the Dharmaśāstras associated the notions regarding purity, pollution and kindred features with religious practices. In the second stage these notions were attributed to certain occupations as a result of which such occupations began to be regarded as impure. In in the third stage, castes following such impure occupations became separated from other castes. The nature of their professions on the one hand and the fear of contamination on the other were mainly responsible for this separation. In the fourth stage, when untouchable castes became a social reality the later law-givers and their commentators had to devise certain ways and means to rationalise the process which led to the emergence of the so called untouchable castes. On this point their attitude was confused, imaginary and contradictory. According to the logic of the Dharmaśāstras no caste can be branded as untouchable; even the lowest castes are associated with the four-fold *varṇa* system, and as such they are pure. The Dharmaśāstras elaborately describe the social and religious rights of the *antyaja* category—the category in which most of the untouchable castes belong—even allowing them to erect temples. But there was a wide gulf of difference between theory and practice. In the Brahmanical, Buddhist and Jain texts and also in the foreign accounts we find that untouchability was widely practised in different parts of India.

A specimen of the strange logic of the commentators on the Dharmaśāstras may be cited in this connection. Manu (IV.30) says that no one should consciously tread the shadow of an idol, a king, a preceptor, a *snātaka*, a teacher, a brown cow and a person having Vedic initiation. It has no reference to any so called untouchable castes. But, commenting on this verse, Kulluka says that the letter *ca* meaning *and* which occurs at the end of the verse must be the first letter of the word Caṇḍāla. Now, as we have already noted, among the castes of the *antyaja* category, the law-givers were very unkind towards the Caṇḍālas. Although, according to the logic of the hierarchy of the hybrid castes the position of the Caṇḍālas should be in the higher rank, as they are supposed to have originated from the union of Brāhmaṇa female and Śūdra male, the law-givers, rather ignoring the norms set up by themselves, placed them in the lowest rank and treated them almost as untouchables, probably for making it a point that the Brāhmaṇa woman is a taboo; anyone attempting to seduce her will meet the fate of a Caṇḍāla. Kulluka had probably taken it for granted that the Caṇḍālas were untouchables and was thus eager to bring them in connection with the verse of Manu mentioned above. But the verse in question has nothing to do with untouchability. Even if we say that the interpretation of Kulluka is correct—the shadow of the Caṇḍālas should not be treaded upon—it does not imply that the Caṇḍālas were untouchables. It is also interesting to note that although in theory they belonged to the lowest rank in the hierarchy in actual social life they enjoyed a middle ranked status. This holds good also in the case of some other castes belonged to the *antyaja* category.

8. The Subcastes

According to the Dharmaśāstras, the hybrid castes which come into existence owing to morganatic marriages in ascending or descending order among the four original *varṇas* or the principal castes are known as *upavarṇas* or subcastes belong to three categories—good hybrid (*uttama-saṅkara*), medium hybrid (*madhyama-saṅkara*) and low hybrid (*adhama-saṅkara*). But in the real life, the demarcation line between a caste and a subcaste is not at all clear. For example, the Ābhiras, or Ahirs, who are said to have been born of the union of Brāhmaṇa male and Ambaṣṭha female are a subcaste or *upavarṇa* of a good-hybrid category. But ordinarily they are treated as a caste and their various branches as subcastes. There are certain problems regarding the subcastes and their ramifications. The subcastes are generally regarded as branches of some important castes. But side by side there are copious examples that very often small regional castes like to introduce themselves as branches of some bigger caste. There may or may not be any invariable link between a caste and the subcastes claiming as its offshoots. Again, owing to regional or linguistic differences the relation between the castes and their supposed subcastes may vary.

According to Ketkar, there are more than three thousand castes among the Hindus most of which are, in fact, subcastes. Only in the case of the Brāhmaṇas there are more than eight hundred subcastes. The terms 'caste', 'subcaste' 'and sub-sub-caste' are relative and thus contain no fixed sense. When we say Maratha Brāhmaṇa and Konkana Brāhmaṇa, by the former is meant a caste and by the latter a subcaste. But when the generic term Drāviḍa or Southern Brāhmaṇa is used, the Maratha Brāhmaṇa becomes a subcaste and Konkana Brāhmaṇa a sub-subcaste. Referring to the subcastes and sub-subcastes of northern India, E.A. Blunt says that the numerous ramifications of the Jats, Ahirs and Kurmis contain specific names and these names are variously geographical, occupational, commercial, communal, totemistic, customary, religious and legendary. According to Risley, the subcastes are really offshoots of the major castes and their origins are due to migration and change of customs. Members of a particular caste, having settled elsewhere make their own society and gradually become localised. But they retain their original caste name but it is prefixed by the name of the region in which they settle, e.g., Avadhiya Kurmi and Kanaujiya Kurmi. Risley says that the subdivision from kind to phyla is an eternal characteristic of Indian society. J.H. Hutton and A.M.T. Jackson also subscribe to this view. The latter has shown that most subcastes of Maharashtra contain the names of the regions in which they have settled. A.C. Mayer and E.K. Gough insist on kinship and localisation. A subcaste is generally a near or distant kin of a more well known caste and its provenance comprises only a limited area.

Iravati Karve on the other hand has a different view. She says that the subcastes are not at all subdivisions of some particular caste. In reality, they are castes. What actually exists may be described as a cluster of castes which functions under a generic caste name. According to Karve, three types of social groupings are found among the Hindus—caste, cluster of castes and *varṇa* (the traditional four-fold division). G.S. Ghurye also admits that subcastes are really castes, but he has some differences with Karve in regard to the structural and functional aspects of the subcastes. According to him certain characteristics pertain to the caste system as a whole. The status of a subcaste in the caste hierarchy depends on the status of the parent caste. But the subcastes retain exclusively their own way of group life, social relations and customs as well as specific names. The subcastes function quite independently in their own way, but when the question of status or social position arises they insist on their identity with the bigger castes. According to Ghurye, a formal relation always exists between the subcastes and the bigger castes, but the basis of this relation may be genuine or false. A subcaste may be a branch of a bigger caste; if not it can claim to be so.

In most cases, however, the subcastes are branches or ramifications of the more widely known castes. Under diverse circumstances they have become separated from the main stream. The Sarwaria (Sarayupāriyā) Brāhmaṇas of Uttar Pradesh hold that their forefathers accepted gifts from Rāma for performing rituals to save him from the sin of killing a Brāhmaṇa (in fact Rāvaṇa was a Brāhmaṇa). For this they were deserted by the Kanaujiyā Brāhmaṇas. Thereafter they made a separate settlement on the bank of the Sarayu and came to be known as Sarayupāriyā. In this case, the cause of separation from the original caste has been attributed to a hearsay. Again among the Brāhmaṇa subcastes of Maharashtra and Konkan we have such names as Bardeskar, Bhalwalikar, Kudaldeskar, Lotlikar, Pednekar, Sastikar, etc. The suffix *kar* means 'from some place'. The formations of these subcastes were due to geographical reasons. In many cases it has been observed that change of customs or adoption of new customs often led to the growth of subcastes. For example, for having a better place in the caste hierarchy certain sections of the Kurmis, Kalwars, Lohars, Telis and other castes of northern India adopted stricter Brahmanical practices and became subcastes of a better type. By abolishing the custom of widow-remarriage or by giving up certain practices which are not approved in the Brahmanical codes some members belonging to a particular caste could form a purer subcaste. The reverse also happened which would result in the emergence of subcastes of a lower category. But in most cases the growth of the subcastes was due to occupational specialisations. In the first stage the producers and the dealers became two different subcastes, e.g., the Bārujībī (producers of the betel plants) and the Tāmbulika (dealers of the betel plants). In course of time with the requirement of more and multifarious specialisations in different trades various subcastes were formed, each handling a single aspect.

9. *A Note on Slavery in Ancient India*

Slavery was once in vogue in different parts of the ancient world. In ancient Egypt, Babylon, Greece and Rome slavery was an important feature of the socio-political system. In the 'democratic' system of ancient Greece nearly seventy per cent of the total population were slaves without any human right. It was so extensive in Europe and Western Asia that some historians and sociologists want to characterise a particular period of ancient history as 'the age of slavery'. The European nations who made colonies in America imported slaves from Africa for the purpose of cultivation. As a result of this slave trade became a lucrative profession among the European nations. Westermarck writes : "The system of slavery, which at least in the British Colonies and slave states surpassed in cruelty the slavery of any pagan country ancient and modern, was not only recognised by Christian governments but was supported by the large bulk of the clergy, Catholic and Protestants alike" (*ODMI*, I, 711). The heritage of West Asian slavery influenced the Muslim societies as a result of which this system became popular in the Muslim states.

Slavery was not unknown in ancient India. But it was limited both in extent and in degree. In the *Ṛgveda* there are not many passages where the word *dāsa* can be said to have been used in the sense of slave. The word has been used especially to denote the vanquished enemy. There are references to *dāsa* kings. Etymologically *dāsa* means 'a man who serves' and *dāsī* means 'a woman who serves'. These terms might have been applicable to free persons as well. In the Vedic literature there are references to the gifts of *dāsīs*; the epics and the Purāṇas mention *dāsīs* as companions of the queens and princesses; in many cases they bore children for the kings. In the *Taittirīya Saṃhitā* (VII.5.10.1) dancing *dāsīs* with pitchers on their heads' around the sacrificial fire are mentioned. These *dāsīs* might have been serving girls and not slave-girls. In the *Bṛhadāraṇyaka Upaniṣad* (IV.4.23) after receiving the knowledge of *brahman* from Yājñavalkya king Janaka said: "I make a gift to your honour of the Vedehas together with myself for being your slave." This does not mean that the king and his subjects really became slaves; it was an expression of the king's sense of gratitude for his teacher.

But the sale and purchase of human beings were not unknown. According to a legend found in the *Aitareya Brāhmaṇa* a Brāhmaṇa named Ajīgarta sold his son Śunaḥśepa to the prince Rohita for one hundred cows. According to the Puranic accounts king Hariścandra sold himself to the sage Viśvāmitra and became his slave. The Buddhist and Jain texts also mention the existence of slavery. Though, some forms of slavery was thus known, it had not that much of social importance as it had in countries outside India. Since the Indian society was a caste society and every caste or subcaste had its own occupation, the system of slavery was inconsistent with the general pattern of Indian life. Even the lowest occupations were caste oriented. Thus the slaves could only be employed as servants in household works. There were other problems as well. It was forbidden to use men belonging to the Dvijāti category (Brāhmaṇa, Kṣatriya and Vaiśya) as slaves. So far as the Śūdras were concerned, Jaimini (VI.7.6) categorically states that when a man makes a gift in the Viśvajit sacrifice of everything belonging to himself he can not make a gift of the Śūdra who waits upon him as his duty. Commenting on this statement Śabara says that the Śūdra is not bound to serve the man to whom he is handed over. According to Manu (I.91; VIII. 413-14), the principal duty of a Śūdra is to wait upon the three higher castes, but he has not been created as a slave.

But there was a difference between the theory and the practice. Though Megasthenes said that there was no slavery in India (because in the Greek sense it was really absent), the ninth Rock Edict of Aśoka enjoins that the Law of Piety consists in the kind and proper treatment of slaves and hired servants, which shows that slavery was current in Mauryan age. Manu (VIII.299-300) says that when a slave requires to be punished the dose of punishment should not exceed that is generally done in the case of an unruly son by his father. It means that a slave should be treated as a family member. Elsewhere Manu (VIII.415) has spoken of seven kinds of slaves: one captured in battle; one who becomes so for food, i.e., in scarcity or in a famine; one born in the house of a female slave; one bought; one given by parents, relatives or friends; one inherited; and one who becomes so for paying off fine or judicial decree. Kautilya (III.13) says that the *mlecchas* (Śaka, Yavana, etc.) are not punishable if they sell or pledge their children but the *āryas* (those belonging to the traditional four-fold system) can not be reduced to slavery. He refers to several kinds of slaves, viz., *dhvajāhṛta* (captured in battle), *ātmavikrayī* (who sells himself), *udaradāsa* (one who is born of a slave woman from a slave), *āhitika* (one who is a slave owing to debt), etc. But Kauṭilya makes easy provisions for freedom from slavery. Kātyāyana refers to fifteen kinds of slaves: one born in the house, one acquired, one inherited, one saved in the time of famine, one pledged by the master, one discharged from a large debt, one captured in a battle, one vanquished in a bet, one who accepts slavery, one who is a runway monk of an order, one who stipulates to be a slave for a certain time, one who is a slave for food, one who accepts slavery for loving a slave girl and one who sells oneself.

But the law-givers were more willing to liberate the slaves rather than to encourage an elaborate growth of the institution of slavery in social life. This is amply testified by restrictions which the law-givers have prescribed for the slave holders. As a rule, members of the twice-born castes cannot be made slaves. Even a slave of the Śūdra category of the social division can not be given any work which is not the occupation of the subcaste to which he belongs. Yājñavalkya (II.182 ff) says that if a slave saves his master from an imminent danger becomes a free man; one saved in a femine becomes free by giving a pair of cows; one who is a slave for a debt becomes free after the repayment of the debt or after a stipulated period of service. Kauṭilya (III. 13) says that if a master has sexual intercourse with a female slave and she is delivered of a child, both the slave and the child becomes automatically freed. Kauṭilya also says that a slave can earn and retain wealth of his own and that the heirs to the wealth of a slave are his relations and not his master. No master has the right to inflict corporal punishment upon a slave (Medhātithi on Manu VIII.299). Of course, there is no reason to believe that the masters always behaved towards their slaves quite in accordance with the Dharmaśāstra rules. The fate of the slaves Sthāvaraka and Madanikā, as has been described in the *Mṛcchakaṭika*, shows how the treatment of slaves depended upon the temperament of the individual owners. While the former had been brutally treated by his master, the latter was regarded by her mistress as a friend and confidante. In the character of the gambler, who offers himself for sale in payment of a debt due to a gambling master, we have an illustration of the class of selfsold slaves mentioned in the Dharmaśāstras.

In his *Laws* Plato says: "We have now made excellent arrangement to free our citizens from the necessity of manual work; the business of arts and crafts has been passed on to others; agriculture has been handed over to slaves on condition of their granting us a sufficient return to live in a fit and seemly fashion." While the law-givers of Greece wanted to organise the society on the basis of slavery, their counterparts in ancient India wanted to do the same on the basis of the *varṇa* or caste system. Both the systems had independent growth. The existence of slavery in different countries outside India was not unknown to the ancient Indians. In the Buddhist *Assalāyana Sutta* it is categorically stated that in the country of the Yavanas there are only two *varṇas*, Ārya and Dāsa. Slavery in ancient India, notwithstanding its existence, could not be a regular feature of Indian social life because, as we have stated above, a slave-oriented social system was inconsistent with a social system based on caste division. This explains why the law-givers maintained a lenient attitude towards the slaves. Whether or not they were ill-treated is a different question but, unlike other countries, in ancient India slaves had the right to enjoy an undisturbed family life and the right to have exclusive ownership of their earnings. The medieval legal texts and the commentaries on the older ones maintain the liberal stand taken by the early writers of the Dharmasastras.

Inscriptions, however testify that in the Cola period many persons, men and women, unable to earn a suitable livelihood, offered themselves voluntarily in the temple services and they were purchased as lifelong slaves by the authorities. Often the parents use to sell their children for temple services. A considerable section of the Devadāsīs was constituted by slave girls. Since all the occupations were caste oriented, only some unspecified occupations could be given to the slaves, service in temple being one of them. In a text entitled *Upamitibhavaprapañcakathā* we come across an interesting fact that the Bhils were efficient slave traders. The degree and extent of slavery of course varied from region to region; there was also a difference between the Dharmaśāstra injunctions and what was actually practised in social life.

6

Cities and Villages

1. Uneven Development of Urbanism

As in modern India, where the urban population is the fourth largest in the world and where urbanism has not grown consistently with the changing demands of time, so in the past, notwithstanding various developments in different walks of city life, no real urbanism could take place. The process of urbanisation, according to V. Gordon Childe, depends on certain factors like population, extension of territories, formation of ruling classes, role of the sovereigns, trade and commerce, guilds, existence of a non-producing surplus population, professionalism, religion, education, knowledge of technology, and so on. These preconditions must have existed in ancient India from time to time and in different parts of the country. They contributed to the growth of cities, references to which are found in literature and the remains of which have been unearthed by archaeological excavations. But urbanisation or growth of cities does not necessarily mean urbanism; the latter involves a qualitative change in the ideas, attitudes and ways of life of the people.

The distinctive characteristic of the 'urban mind' is a broad perspective, which encompasses a horizon wider far beyond the 'narrow domestic walls' of the village or group life. Owing to the lack of a proper 'urban consciousness' there was, in ancient India, a total indifference towards what was happening outside at large. As a necessary consequence of this indifference there was no real political consciousness among the people. State power could not be strong or prolonged enough to maintain the safety and permanence of the cities. Constant changes of rulers and territorial boundaries and the destruction of the cities by repeated invasions from outside neither created among the citizens a spirit of resistance nor a better political wisdom for survival. They did not sever their village roots and when a situation became adverse they returned to their villages.

The caste system was also a strong factor which arrested the growth of urban consciousness. This 'state within a state', as we have called it, had directed all human endeavour into certain rigid channels. The basic allegiance, and it is even so today, was to the caste or subcaste to which an individual belonged. The limits of group life have been with us for centuries. Even in modern times, say in a city like Calcutta, the original localities were formed on the basis of caste. In the industrial towns around Calcutta we come across a strange growth of villages and of village cultures within the urban set-up. Outwardly and inwardly these villages are the same as those of Bihar and Uttar Pradesh from where the factory-workers came, and each of these villages has its own caste orientation. The inhabitants do not bother about the facilities of urban life; their vision is strictly rural. They are lulled by the dream of having some more plots of land and some more cattle in their ancestral village with which they have been maintaining contact for no less than four generations.

In rare cases the cities had natural growth in ancient and medieval India though they were never thought of as the nerve-centres of the state. They could hardly subsist by themselves and when the source of their subsistence from outside was disturbed or arrested, the cities used to decline and get ruralised.

A good number of cities were created by kings and rulers with the sole purpose of perpetuating themselves. These were rather administrative colonies with royal palaces and buildings for the officials and nobles. Such cities could not last long. When new rulers started new cities the older ones lost their importance and became deserted or depopulated. Some cities were developed as military strongholds. However, their strategic importance and defensive utility could not be permanent, barring some exceptional cases. The same is true in the case of market towns, the existence of which depended on various external factors. The cities which were developed as sites of pilgrimage had a better fate. Most of them survive even today because a place of pilgrimage subsist by itself.

2. *The Nature of Urbanisation*

The evidence of the Harappan cities indicates an urban system which was capable of appropriating the agricultural surplus from the non-urban regions to support its own population. In view of the extent of the Harappa civilization, its stability for several centuries, the wide-reaching trade network and the elaborate growth of professionalism, it may be suggested that the Harappan cities sheltered a mixed population under the active supervision of a state power. The civilization was to a certain extent representative in character. Eventually the Harappan cities failed to subsist by themselves under the diverse economic, political and other conditions, and became ruralised and deserted. The Harappan professionals and craftsmen, however, migrated to other parts of the country and contributed to the development of technology and commerce.

The Vedic civilisation was rural in character. Notwithstanding a few references to cities, strongholds and administrative centres in the Vedic literature, it may be said that the Vedic way of life in general was inimical to urbanisation. The Vedic texts refer to numerous professionals, but the centres of production were in the villages. This tradition persisted through the ages. The Buddhist texts refer to a good number of cities like Rājagṛha, Śrāvastī, Pratiṣṭhāna, Sāketa, Vārāṇasī, Pāṭaliputra, etc., but these were mainly market towns though a few of them served as royal capitals also. The *Miliñdapañha* gives an idealised description of an ancient city: "Fine and regular, measured out into quarters, with excavated moats and ramparts about it, with stout gatehouses and towers, with market places, croass-roads, street-corners and public squares, with cleanly and even main roads, with regular lines of open shops, well provided with parks, gardens, lakes, lotus ponds and wells, adorned with many kinds of temples of the gods, free from every fault and standing in all its glory." A few of these features have been noticed in the excavations at Ahicchatra. The reliefs of Bharhut, Sanchi,

Amaravati and Mathura also depict the same outer view of some ancient cities.

Referring to the Mauryan capital city of Pāṭaliputra Megasthenes observed that it had the shape of an oblong with a length of 80 stades and a breadth of 15 stades. It was surrounded by a moat 60 feet deep and 200 yards wide and was protected by a massive timber palisade running along the moat. The city wall had 64 gates and was adorned with 570 towers. Referring to Aśoka's palace Fa-hien observed that it was the work not of men but of spirits. Fragments of the huge wooden palisade of the city have been unearthed at Bulandi Bagh near Patna ; the size of which proves that the account of Megasthenes was by no means exaggerated. The excavations at Kumrahar have unearthed the remains of a palace with an immense pillared hall.

That the Mauryan emperors were keen on urbanisation is attested by Megasthenes who had referred to the municipal officials called Astynomoi who were divided into six bodies of five each, supervising respectively the industrial arts, entertainment of foreigners, recording of births and deaths, trade and commerce, sale and manufacture, and collection of taxes and fees. But in the subsequent history of India the process of urbanisation was inadequate. Under the Kuṣāṇas Mathura attained celebrity, but from the Gupta age onwards we do not come across any celebrated city of a cosmopolitan character. In texts like the *Periplus* we come across the names of ports and coastal market towns. These appear to have been big *bazars* rather than cities in the real sense of the term. Hiuen Tsang described almost all the Indian states of his time and their capitals giving the measurements of their area and the places of interest. But from his description it appears that these cities were simply administrative headquarters. There are many instances of kings establishing cities after their own names, but most such cities became ruralised within two or three generations.

Undoubtedly there were many factors which hindered the growth of urbanisation proper. One of the main reasons was caste-orientation and essentially a localised productive system. Constant internecine warfare among the states and inroads from outside were also responsible for obstructing the natural growth of the cities as was the existing political system. No empire or kingdom could have lasted for more than three or four generations. There was subdivision of the states, because the law of primogeniture could not always be followed. Struggles for succession created political fragmentation and with the emergence of the new dynasties the administrative centres were constantly shifted.

3. *Economic Life in Cities and Villages: Evidence of Early Buddhist Literature*

The rise of urbanisation from the sixth century B.C. onwards is attested by archaeology. We also find support of this in the Buddhist texts. Even before the Mauryan period cities like Śrāvastī, Campā, Rājagṛha, Sāketa, Kausāmbī, Vārāṇasī and Kuśīnagara rose to prominence. To this list Pāṭaliputra was added subsequently. The Pali texts (cf. *Suttanipāta* 101ff.) speak of the caravan of the merchant prince Anāthapiṇḍika going southeast from Śrāvastī to Rājagṛha via Kuśīnagara. Another route led from Śrāvastī southwest to Paithan with six intermediate halts and frequent crossings of rivers. A third led westward to Sindhu and Sauvīra. The longest route was that which went from Rājagṛha through Vārāṇasī, Sāketa and Śrāvastī towards Taxila and the frontier (*Vinaya*, II. 176, III.382, 401ff.).

These cities and trade routes presuppose the existence of flourishing trade. The existence of a money economy is mentioned in the Pali canon. This is supported by the discovery of the ingots of silver marked with three dots or bent bars of silver with some symbols, going back probably to the sixth century B.C.—which were replaced by rectangular or circular flat pieces cut from a hammered sheet of metal and clipped to the proper weight. These are widely known as punch-marked coin because the symbols were marked by punches. Some cast coins with devices are also known. Buddhist texts use the terms *kahāpana*, *nikkha*, *suvanna*, *kāṃsa*, *pāda*, *māsaka*, *kākanikā*, etc., for coins. The title Seṭṭhi (Śreṣṭhī) possibly implied headship over some class of industry or trading. The term also denoted treasurer and chairperson of the merchant guild (Senī, Śreṇī) and there might be a chief (*mahā*) *seṭṭhi* and an *anu-seṭṭhi* or subordinate officer. References to the insignia of *seṭṭhi-chatta*, that is a working group under a *seṭṭhi*, are found. In the arts and crafts a considerable proficiency and specialisation of industry had been reached (cf. *Milinda* 201, 330ff). Among the trade names one comes across *kammāra* (smith), *vaddhaki* (carpenter), *thapati* (mason), *tacchaka* (planer), *bhamakāra* (turner), etc.

Eighteen guilds (*śreṇī*) of craftsmen are recorded though details of only four are given, namely, of the wood-workers, the smiths, the leather-dressers and the painters. At the head of each guild was a president (*pramukha*) or elderman (*jeṭṭhaka*) and there was also a treasurer (*bhāṇḍāgārika*). Other instances of trade under such leadership are seamen (*niyyāmaka*), garland makers, caravan traders and guards, and often robbers and brigands. Localisation of industry can be observed in the case of craft villages of woodwrights, ironsmiths and potters. We hear of the street (*vīthi*) of the ivory workers in Benaras, the dyers' street, the weavers' place (*thāna*,) the Vessas' (Vaiśya, merchant) street, etc. (cf. *Jātaka* I.356, VI.81, IV.485). Partnerships in commerce, either permanent or on specified occasions only, are frequently mentioned in the Jātakas. The learners and apprentices were known as *antevāsīkas*.

Naval trade was known as is indicated in the *Milinda* 359. According to the Jātakas, sea-going trade was done from Campā, Vārāṇasī, Tāmralipti and other centres. Traders coasted around India from Bhārukaccha to Suvaṇṇabhūmi. The vessels, according to the Jātaka tales, seem to have been constructed on a fairly large scale for we read of 'hundreds' embarking on them. Among the trade objects there are references to silk, muslin, the finer sort of cloth, cutlery and armour, embroideries and rugs, ivory and ivory-work, jewellery and gold. So far as inland trade was concerned, textile fabrics, groceries and oil, greengroceries, grain, perfumes and flowers, articles of gold and jewellery were among the items sold. The *Vinaya* III.343 refers to the sale of strong liquors and the existence of taverns. Instances of price-haggling are not rare. References to capital wealth secured by loan (*ina*, *ṛṇa*) through bonds (*paṇṇā*) in terms of paying interest (*viddhi*, *vṛddhi*) are frequently found.

Notwithstanding the rise of urbanisation and commercialism, which had been fully supported by the Buddhists and Jains, the basic economic structure was agrarian. The rural economy of India was based chiefly on a system of village communities of landowners to which the Buddhist texts bear very clear testimony. The king had a right to a tithe on raw produce measured out either by the village syndic or headman (*gāmabhojaka*) or by any official (*mahāmātta*) and only to this extent could he be considered as the *de jure* owner of the land. The village professions were caste-oriented but there are cases of violation of the caste-rules, especially by the higher castes. This violation was legally justified when men of the Brāhamaṇa and Kṣatriya castes were not competent enough to follow their prescribed caste professions. Here and there in the Jātakas and Suttas, the Brāhmaṇas who engage in agriculture, trade, and other callings are declared to have fallen from their Brāhmaṇahood. The same holds good in the case of the Kṣatriyas. Notwithstanding the economic importance of agriculture, it was not a respectable profession. Even the ownership of a large holding was not considered as a mark of nobility.

A great many arts and crafts are mentioned as *hīna-sippas* and the followers of these trades were held in lower social esteem than others. Among them mention may be made of the hunters, trappers, fishermen, butchers, tanners, snake-charmers, actors, dancers, musicians, rush-weavers and chariot-makers. To this list may also be added the trades of ivory-working, weaving, confectionary, bow and arrow-making, pottery, garland-making and hair-dressing. The hirelings, wage-earners, day labourers, etc., were no man's chattel, yet their life was probably harder than that of the slaves. They were employed largely on the bigger land-holdings. They were paid either in board and lodging or in money wages. The Buddhist texts refer to slaves mainly employed in household or domestic services. A runaway slave could not take shelter in the Buddhist and Jain Saṅghas.

4. Glimpses of Village Life in the Gāthā-Saptaśatī

The Epics, Purāṇas and Dharmaśāstras throw some light on the norms of social life, but it is not possible to know from these texts how people actually lived. That is why, instead of depending on the traditional sources, we have selected a particular anthology, the *Gāthā-saptaśatī*, the stanzas of which reflect the social realities of the post-Maurya period and a keen perception of the life-style of the unsophisticated people at large. The *Gāthā-saptaśatī* is a collection of seven hundred stanzas in Mahārāṣṭri Prākrit which passes under the name of Hāla Sātavāhana who flourished in the first or second century of the Christian era in the Kuntala branch of the Sātavāhana family.

The *Gāthā-saptaśatī* gives interesting information on the village life, particularly of the Deccan region. The characters, so well depicted, all come from a rural background—the farmer and his wife, the village headmen and his daughter, the householder, his wife, and children and so on. The villages, their areas, the cultivable lands, hilly tracts, trees, the shrines and deities installed therein, the religious sentiments of the villagers, the house-holders, their ways and the variety of their kinsmen and relatives, the unchaste women, wild tribes and a host of other things come into focus through this collection.

The villagers were mostly agriculturists. They were divided into two classes, *pāmaras* and *hālikas*, and they produced rice, especially of *śāli* brand, and also oilseeds, cotton and hemp (I.8-9, II.34-37, VI.49, 67-68, VII.89-92, etc.). Their houses, made of straw were surrounded by walls (III.20, 21, 57, IV.15). The villages contained banyan trees, a variety of flowering trees, plants, and tanks (I.94, II.10, III.94-95, VII.26) in which water lilies grew. Of the domestic birds we have references to *kīra* or *śuka* (I.75, VII.66); peacock (IV.94, VII.36); parrot (I.64); swan (VII.76); duck (II.10); hen (VII.98); crow (II.2, III.5); etc. Shells and crabs are mentioned (I.4.18), and also spiders (I.63) and bees (I.37, II.28) as well as different types of deer (I.25, III.87, VIII.29); cows and buffaloes (I.65, II.38); elephants (II.73, III.58, VII.30); monkeys (II.71); cats (III.83); dogs (VII.62) and lions (II.75). There is reference to wide and narrow routes (II.19, III.41) which became muddy and slippery during the monsoons (IV.92), wells for drinking water (III.94) and small factories for producing sweetmeats (VI.54). Wooden utensils were used (II.53).

The village administration rested on the *grāmaṇī* (VII.28. 32) while the bigger administrative divisions were in charge of the *gaṇādhipatis* and *maṇḍalādhipatis* (V.3). The function of maintaining law and order in the villages rested on the *grāmabhojakas* and *tittillas* (V.3, VI.56). Among the higher classes the sense of aristocracy was keen (I.24, I.38). There were village doctors (IV.63, VI.100) who used to cure various types of diseases (I.50-51, IV.17, etc.). The game of dice was known (II. 28). Begging was a recognised profession (II.62). Wealth and riches were sometimes stored under the ground for safety (II.25, IV.18,V.23,VI.76). Theft and robbery were also prevalent (I.54, VI.27, VII.85). Seditious talk was discouraged (IV.96).

Of the musical instruments we have references to drums and lyres and also to flutes made of bamboo (III.53,VI.26, etc.). The art of painting with various colours was known (III.17, V.85, VIII.12). The *Gāthā-saptaśatī* mentions the existence of shrines dedicated to different gods (I.64 etc.) like Sūrya (IV. 32, VII.53); Madana (IV.25-17); Agni; Varuṇa (III.13); and others. The love legends of Kṛṣṇa and Rādhā are mentioned (I.89, II.12, II.18, IV.47, VII.55) and Buddhism was known (IV.8). The Kāpālikas are also mentioned (V.8) Astrology had an important place in social life (IV.19,V.35).

Polygamy was prevalent among men of the higher classes (I.79, II.6, etc.). We have references to mutual conflicts and jealousy among cowives (IV.62 etc.). Ordinary housewives had to spend most of their time in the kitchen (I.13-14). Poverty often disturbed their peace of mind (I.18). In some cases they had to support their poor relatives which was an additional burden for them (V.72, VII.6). Wives did not talk with their husbands in the presence of elders (IV.25). For garments they used two pieces of cloth, one for covering the breasts and the other for the lower torso; the dress for festivals was known as *navaraṅga* (III.41,V.61). Married women used to wear bangles and other ornaments made of gold (II.91,VII.27), pearls and gems (I.4, II.73, IV.94). Songs were sung during the marriage festivals (IV.42, VII.43). Pre-nuptial love was not unknown (III.98). The custom of *sati* was prevalent (V.7,VII. 33). There were unchaste wives also who in many cases selected their consorts from among the brothers of their husbands (I. 28, II.59, IV.13) and also from healthy youths belonging to the lower rank of society (IV.60). It was forbidden to cohabit during the time of menstruation (VI.26) but this taboo was sometimes broken (I.22, VI.28). During the menstrual period women used to smear their bodies with yellow powder (I.22, III.89,VI.19).

The wife and daughters of the village headman were subjects of public gossip and stories about their secret love with others were manufactured (I.30.31, V.10, V.69, VI.70, VII.3, etc.). The daughters of agriculturists were very expert in love-making (I.84, etc). Unchaste wives used to make their commerce with youthful persons in selected solitary places (IV.50 etc.). They kept trained dogs whose barking would alert them to the arrival of their husbands or paramours (VII.62). Prostitution was also prevalent (V.74). Women used to take part in popular festivals on which occasions they used a variety of cosmetics (I.39). We have references to *madhūtsava* or the spring festival which was celebrated by musical performances and drum-beatings (VI.35). Young women, dressed in *kuñcukikā*, flocked there and drank wine (VI.44-45). In the *phalgutsava* men and women would engage in erotic sports (IV.69). There were public bars (III.27) and old wine was appreciated (II.97).

5. *Ports and Market Towns: The Periplus*

The Maurya emperors had links with the Greek kingdoms of the west; there were trade contacts through land and sea routes. The more important route was by sea to the Persian Gulf and then up the Tigris to Seleucia which was connected with the Western countries by land and river routes. Egypt was directly accessible by sea but the sea voyage was a long and tedious one as the sailors had to keep close to the coast. The situation, however, changed about A.D. 45 after the discovery by Hippalus of the monsoon winds blowing regularly across the Indian ocean and this enabled the ships to sail across the Indian ocean. There was a large volume of trade between India and Rome during the first century A.D. Pliny states that nearly fifty million *sesterces* flowed every year from Rome to India to pay for the balance of trade. This is proved by the discovery of a very large number of Roman coins in India. Sewell concluded, from the discovery of a large number of Roman coins in different parts of Madura, that the Roman merchants also used to reside in different parts of India, either temporarily or permanently. Hultzsch also thought that there was a Roman settlement and mint at Madura. Tamil works also atteest that

Kaveripattanam at the mouth of the Kaveri was frequented by western merchants.

The active part taken by Indians in trading with the Western countries and by foreigners in trading with India in the first century A.D. is proved by certain statements in the *Periplus of the Erythraean Sea* in which the island of Dioscorida, or Socotra, is said to have been peopled by Indian, Arab and Greek traders and the city of Barygaza, or Broach, is described as a great sea port from which large vessels were regularly sent to the Western countries. In fact the anonymous author of the *Periplus* was himself actively engaged in trade with India in the course of which he made the voyage from the head of the Red Sea. Strabo, during his stay at Egypt, noticed that many Greek merchants used to make direct voyages to India. The author of the *Periplus* belonged to such a class of merchants. According to him the Indus (Sinthus) had seven mouths; the middle one was navigable on which was situated the emporium of Barbaricum wherefrom merchants carried their commodities up the river to the metropolis of Scythia called Minnagara. Beyond the mouth of the Indus was a deep bay called Eirion (Rann of Kutch) divided into a lesser and greater gulf of that name. Next was the gulf of Baraca, or Dvārakā, followed by another called Barygaza, i.e., Bhṛgukaccha or modern Broach on the mouth of the Narmadā. Merchandise from Ujjayinī and other remote places of the north, as far afield as Kashmir and the Hindukush mountains, was brought here for export to foreign countries.

The commodities of export and import were cloth, linen, perfume, medicinal herbs, glass vessels, silver, gold, tin, lead, iron, copper, pigment, precious stones such as pearls, diamonds, sapphires, turquoise, lapis lazuli, coral, spices, sandalwood, skin, muslin, indigo, ivory, porcelain, tortoise-shell, etc. The author of the *Periplus* sailed along the western coast from Barygaza to Cape Comorin, and passing round Cape Comorin he came across many harbours in the eastern coast among which Masalia near Masulipatam and Gange at the mouth of the Ganges were important. He states that Indians loaded ships with merchandise from these harbours and sent them to the African and Arabian ports. The author of the *Periplus* not only mentions the ports and market towns of the western coast and the nature of trade articles shipped and unshipped from these ports but also gives information about the inland cities and market towns, and how and whence the trade articles were deposited there. Coastal India, according to the author of the *Periplus*, was comprised of two major political units: the Dachinabades or Dakṣiṇāpatha, i.e., Deccan proper, and Damirica or Tamilaka, the Tamil land or the Draviḍa country. To the former belonged the ports and market towns such as Calliena, or Kalyāṇa, a suburb of Bombay, Sopara or ancient Śurpāraka, now in the Thana region of Maharashtra, Tagara or Ter and Paithana or Pratiṣṭhāna, the city of the Sātavahanaṣ which attained much celebrity in the post-Maurya age being a town where all roads met. To the latter belonged the ports and market towns such as Naura, Tyndis, Muziris, Nelcynda, etc. These were all on the Malabar coast between Cannanore and Cochin. The last two were the Greek renderings of Muchiripattanam and Nīlakaṇṭha. Muziris, we are told, abounded "with ships sent there with cargoes from Arabia and by the Greeks."

6. *Life of the Urban Elites: The Kāmasūtra Evidence*

The *Kāmasūtra* of Mallanāga Vātsyāyana, which was composed in the Gupta age, is the first complete work dealing with the science of erotics. Its celebrated writer had a profound knowledge of the society of his patrons, the Nāgarakas or city dwellers, who lived a life of luxury and pleasure and had their source of wealth in the surplus provided by the villages where they had property and also in the favourable trade balance which India enjoyed in the Kuṣāṇa and Gupta periods. There are graphic descriptions of the gilded life of the Nāgaraka, his house luxuriously furnished, his friends and assistants in *l'affaires d'amour*, his taste and accomplishments in poetry, music and various arts, his elaborate toilet and personal adornment, his round of pleasures, his interest in various sports and amusements, etc.

The house of a Nāgaraka was divided into two blocks, the inner one beloning to the ladies. There were a number of rooms, each set apart for a special purpose, and attached to the house was a garden with flowering plants and fruit trees. The outer facade was colonnaded, and the walls were beautifully coloured. The floor was sometimes of polished mosaic work. In the garden there was *samudra-gṛha* or summer house surrounded by water. In the bedroom there were usually two beds, soft and comfortable, with two pillows on either side. At the head of the bed was a niche and an elevated shelf on which were placed articles necessary for the morning toilet. On the floor stood a spitoon, and on the walls, on brackets, were ranged the *vīṇā*, a casket containing materials for paintings and sketching, a book and garlands. On the floor was spread a carpet with cushions, and there were boards for playing chess and dice. Outside the room was an aviary in which were hung cages of birds (I.4.4-13).

The Nāgaraka used to get up early in the morning and attend to his morning duties. He applied on his body a fragrant ointment made of sandalwood paste and then dressed himself properly. Admiring his own person in a looking glass and chewing spiced betel-leaves he attended to his daily work. After attending to his business he had his bath. His limbs were to be massaged on alternate days; on every third day *phenaka* or soap was to be applied to the thighs; on every fourth day the face was to be shaved while on every tenth day other parts of his body were shaved. He took two meals everyday, in the forenoon and afternoon, which comprised hard or soft food and drink (I.4.16-20). Of stronger drinks the Nāgaraka used various kinds of wine like *surā*, *madhu*, *maireya* and *āsava* which he drank from *caṣaka*, a vessel of wood or metal, often accompanied by various kinds of sweets (I.4.38, II.10,15,17). After the forenoon meal he indulged himself by teaching and listening to domesticated birds, watched fights between quails, cocks or rams, and diverted himself by pleasant talk with his friends—the *Pīṭhamarda*, the *Vīṭa* and the *Vidusaka*. Having entertained himself with repartees and witticisms he finally enjoyed a siesta (I.4.21).

Those who earned their living through service at clubs and pleasure houses were called Vītas; those by their skill in arts they displayed as itinerant professors at the clubs and the abodes of the courtesans were called Pīṭhamardas; and those by professional jesting were called Viduṣakas (I.4.14-46).

In the afternoon the Nāgaraka went out to attend a *goṣṭhī* or social gathering where he engaged himself in pleasant diversions with his friends and in tests of skill in various arts. Social parties were organised in the house of every Nāgaraka by turn. At these parties, *gaṇikās* or courtesans would ply the Nāgarakas with the fare provided and also themselves share the various delicacies of salt, fruits, green vegetables, pungent, bitter and acid flavoured dishes. Sometimes the parties were held at the house of the *gaṇikās*, or they would assemble in the *sabhā* or in the *gaṇa* or group to which they belonged. At the *goṣṭhīs* the sixty-four *kāmakalās* or erotic arts were discussed and a person possessing knowledge of these arts would naturally become the principal speaker. Literary competitions were also held. A Nāgaraka was expected to be liberal in spending on *goṣṭhīs* and his success in courtship and love depended in no small measure on his ability to shine in the sports and festivities held there. Besides the *goṣṭhī*, at the temple of Sarasvatī, on a fixed day every fortnight or every month, a *samāja* or assemblage of the Nāgarakas was held regularly at which performances by musicians, dancers and other artistes became essential features (I.4.21-36, 50-52; II.10.50-51, VI.1.12).

On some of these occasions there were joint processions of males and females (*yātrā*) which afforded opportunities for meeting one's lady-love (V.4.41). The Nāgarakas also met at each other's homes (*āpaṇaka*) to hold drinking parties (II.10. 15-17; VI.1.12). *Udyāna-yātrā* or picnics in a garden were also held on different occasions. They would go out of town, followed by their lady companions and attendants, and having enjoyed themselves there immensely, they would return, preserving some mementos of the pleasant excursions. Similar parties were held in connection with water sports which took place in artificial lakes or tanks (I.4.49-41). There were also occasional social diversions like spending the night playing dice, celebrating the full-moon night of Āśvina (October-November) and spring festivities. Vātsyāyana has given a few names of such festivals some of which are well known up to the present day such as the Kaumudī-jāgara, Holaka or Holi, Alokacaturthī or Hindolotsava, Hallisaka, Suvasantaka, Aṣṭamī-candraka, etc., (I.4.42).

At nightfall, the Nāgaraka enjoyed music, vocal and instrumental, occasionally to the accompaniment of dances.

Afterwards he and his friends would wait for the arrival of the ladies. After their arrival he and his friends would welcome them with agreeable ancedotes (I.4.23-25). The post-reception part of his activities at night has been dealt with by Vātsyāyana in the second chapter of his work in which he has described in ten sub-chapters and seventeen sections all the acts of love and union. The bedfellows of the Nāgarakas were courtesans (VI.1-6) or other people's wives cleverly seduced (V.1-6). Three classes of courtesans were broadly recognised: those who lived as one man's concubine (*eka-parigrahā*); those that resorted to more than one man (*aneka-parigrahā*); and those that carried on a miscellaneous trade and attached themselves to none (*aparigrahā*). Among other classes of prostitutes were included the bawd (*kumbhadāsī*), female attendant (*paricārikā*), the secretly and openly unchaste women (*kulatā* and *svairiṇī*), the female artisan (*silpakārikā*), the woman who had openly left her family (*vinaṣṭā*), and the regular courtesan (*gaṇikā*).

7. *Villages and Towns in Post-Gupta Period*

We have seen that the provinces were divided into smaller units, namely small districts, towns and villages. The districts or Viṣayas, were composed of a number of villages and they were ruled by Viṣayapatis. Smaller districts had their governors like the rulers of Maṇḍalas or Viṣayas or village groups. In western India the smaller subdivisions like Maṇḍalas, often called Pathakas, subdivided into Pattalās and groups of villages were ruled likewise by local officials. In the Deccan, the units were the subdivision of the Rāṣṭras called Viṣayas which were composed of village groups while individual villages were the smallest units. In Tamil India a number of villages (Urus) and townships (Parus) constituted the smallest subdivision of the Nāḍus or Nāḍs (Tāluks). Koṭṭams and Pallas were separated. The Kanarese districts had a peculiar organisation of their own, similar in some respects to that of the Tamil country.

Regarding the types of villages, the following may be noted. Some villages were managed by their owners to whom they had been given as *agrahāras* by the king. Villages were sometimes granted to the temples of local gods and were managed by the local people. In some cases villages came to be granted to military officers in lieu of their past services. Last of all there were ordinary villages ruled by the officials or representatives of the feudatories most of whom were local persons. In the case of the granted villages the grantee and his successors had the privilege of fiscal or revenue immunities, namely, the non-payment of ordinary taxes to the king, right to requisitions and acquisitions of everything by accession, etc., and the exemption of the entry of royal officials, menials and soldiers (Cāṭa, Bhāṭa, etc.). In addition they were endowed with lower criminal and civil jurisdiction. Such grants were made for all times in the future, and in some inscriptions it was laid down that the gift was made for a period "as long as the sun and moon endure".

In the case of non-granted villages—which were far more numerous—the smallest units were in practice managed by the local inhabitants, though minor officials represented royal authority and exacted royal dues. The village community existed throughout the whole of India though its character differed according to the environmental, economic, linguistic and ethnic peculiarities. In North India and parts of the Deccan the village community was more of an administrative and social unit than an almost perfect socio-economic communal institution as we find in Tamil India. The village chiefs were known as Grāmapati or Grāmika in northern India, Paṭṭkila in central and western India and Grāmakūṭa in the Deccan. From Paṭṭakila the present word Patel has been derived, from Grāmakūṭa Gamot and from Mahattara Mhatre. In Karnataka each village group had officials known as Māne-vergadde (household master) and Nād-pergadde or some sort of district officer. They were assisted by two Tantrapālas (councillors), a Pradhāna or coordinator and an Aliya or secretary of the village council. In Tamil country the village elders not only exercised administrative functions but also managed the economic resources of the locality. South Indian inscriptions give us details about the constitution of village assemblies, the qualification for membership, the work entrusted to the members and the grounds for exclusion from these bodies. In some southern localities we have evidence of communal ownership of land or periodic distribution of land among villagers. In Tanjore district land was *samudayam* or communally owned, *pallabhogyam* or belonging to the entire village, and *ekabhogam* or owned in perpetuity by individuals.

The inscriptions of the Kalaçuris refer to donated villages in a group of twelve. This reminds us of the system of the estates of the chiefs in the Rajput territories. Such an estate should comprise eighty-four villages, and twelve is an exact fraction of this standard size. The reference to Paṭṭakila or Patel points to the continuation of the traditional type of village administration under a headman. The Candella records speak of villages being grouped into Viṣayas or Pathakas, but there is no reference to the titles of officers placed in charge of them. Some light is thrown upon village administration by the fact that the Adhikṛtamahattamas are sometimes mentioned in the list of persons to whom the king's grant of land is announced. The villages in the Paramāra kingdom were grouped into larger units. In ascending order they were called Pratijagāraṇaka, Pathaka (or Bhoga or Viṣaya) and Maṇḍalas. They were also grouped into units bearing the name of the chief village with various numeral endings. The villages were in the charge of the usual Paṭṭakila or headman. The donated villages in the Gahrawal records are located as a rule in the Paṭṭalās which may refer to fiscal rather than administrative divisions.

Villages belonging to the South Maratha country under the Western Cālukyas were grouped into districts containing small numerical endings, which again were united into divisions with higher numerical endings. In the Kannada tract we hear of administrative divisions with numerical endings varying from 32000, 12000, etc., through 3000, 2000, 1000 etc., to 500, 300, etc. The Cola empire was divided into a number of provinces called Maṇḍalam, which were subdivided into divisions called Koṭṭam. These were further subdivided into districts called Nāḍu. Each Nāḍu consisted of a number of village unions called Kuṛṛam. The Colas encouraged local self government enabling the villages to be administered by the village assemblies. The Ūr was the assembly of the tax-paying villagers while the Sabhā was the assembly of the Brāhmaṇas. The village assemblies were elected bodies which also had the power to frame laws on local issues. The Cola model was also followed by the Hoysālas and Pāṇḍyas. In Hoysala records we have instances of a village Mahāsabhā (assembly) receiving gifts of money to provide worship in a temple from the interest generated, and of village *mahājanas* receiving another village tax-free. The village assembly enjoyed its own revenues and owned its own lands. We have an interesting reference to a judicial trial by a collective body of villages. In the Pāṇḍya kingdom justice was administered in the first instance by village assemblies and other local authorities.

Important cities were administered by royal officials. However, notwithstanding their status, the greater part of the city administration was entrusted to popular bodies. Organisations and associations of the Pauras and Jānapadas in civic and rural areas are known from the earliest times. In Nigamas or market-towns, associations and guilds came into existence and various types of guilds devoted their attention to commercial and industrial pursuits. These guilds often took upon themselves many of the local duties. They managed the affairs of temples, organised poor relief, established endowments for various purposes and did everything in their power to ensure local peace and prosperity. Sometimes a guild or corporate body strengthened its position by obtaining legal sanction from the king of the locality and came to be vested with important civic privileges and functions. The legal texts mention two kinds of corporations : one established by the king known as Rājakṛtasaṃvit and the other by the people known as Samūhakṛtasaṃvit. The duties entrusted to the former type included the protection of the grazing grounds and water-course, repair of the temple and places of public worship, feeding the poor and the helpless, control over exports, and provision of the other amenities of public life. The lands and quarters entrusted to these corporations were not liable to taxation. The duties entrusted to the latter type included maintenance and repair of public halls, tanks, gardens, temples and places of public gathering, excavation and stoppage of water courses and making of arrangements for local protection in times of apprehended danger. The executive business of controlling these corporations was entrusted to the Kāryacintakas who numbered generally from four to five. These corporations seemed to have been entrusted with the right of collecting taxes and had a common fund of their own. They could raise loans and there was a common liability to repay these. The king generally did not interfere in their affairs but he could intervene if there were factions fighting amongst themselves or when there was a quarrel between the Kāryacintakas or Mukhyas and the ordinary members.

The study of urbanism has now been taken up by the social historians but it is handicapped by the paucity of materials since inscriptions are mostly concerned with the tales of conquest and land grants. They have little so say regarding city life. In literature there are references to and descriptions of certain cities, but the descriptions are imaginative and romantic. It is interesting to note that the Arab writers were surprised at the paucity of towns in India. One of the earliest references of some aspects of urban life is found in the Nasik cave inscription which mentions that the endowment made therein was registered in the Town Hall or Nagarasabhā. During the Gupta period we hear of a guild of weavers exercising authority in Dasapura city which also had a fighting force of its own. The Lakṣmeśvara grant of the time of the Badami Cālukyas refers to a municipal charter granted to the Mahājanas and the eighteen Prākṛitis. The king's officers were to protect constitutional decrees and local customs while the householders were to pay a fixed tax in the month of Vaiśākha. Another inscription at Managauli of Vijjala mentions the Prabhus and Mahājanas under the Daṇḍanāyaka. It also mentions names of the Mahāprabhus (a sort of mayor) of four towns. The Gadag inscription refers to thousand Mahājanas of the Lakshmigundi area headed by the Sheriff. The Huli plates refer to the town- mayor (Ur-Udaya). Two inscriptions from Kolhapur refer to a corporation of five hundred of the city of Aiyavole. The Parunayial inscription refers to four assemblies and temple administration by the Yagam or corporation. But such sporadic epigraphical references do not really help us to have a complete view either of the nature of urbanism or of city administration.

8. Ports and Maritime Trade in Early Medieval India

The naval expedition of Rājendra Cola in the Malaya region was intended to secure south Indian trade with China which the Śailendra kings wanted to distrub. Likewise, his father Rājarāja's attempt to establish absolute authority over the Malabar region was motivated by the desire to break the Arab monopoly on western trade. There were good trade relations with the Roman empire in the time of the Sātavāhanas and the Kuṣāṇas and with the Byzantine empire in Gupta times. Then there was a marked decline so far as North India was concerned, but maritime trade with the western and eastern countries, mainly through intermediaries, was continued through the ports of Gujarat, Konkan and Malabar coast, Coromandel coast and Bengal, though on a lesser scale. There was a revival of foreign trade during the two centuries preceding the Turkish conquest in India. Whether any external factor was responsible for this is difficult to say. Perhaps the disruption of Arab trade with Europe on account of the Crusades diverted their attention towards India.

It appears from the Arab accounts that Ma'bar was a sort of clearing-house for the goods of the east and the west. Wassaf tells that the products of China, North India and Sind constantly arrived at Ma'bar. Idrisi mentions Fandarina as a port of call for ships from India and Sind. According to Abu Dulaf (quoted by Yakut) Quilon was a port of embarkation for Arabia. The importance of Quilon has also been attested by the Chinese sources. From Chou-K'u-fei we learn that Quilon was a port of transhipment of traders. Chau-ju-kua observes that Quilon was a port of call for ships coming from San-fo-tsi (Palembang in Sumatra) and its dependencies.

The Gujarat coast was also important for international trade. Idrisi tells that Barus (Broach) was a port of call for vessels coming from China and from Sind. There are references to other ports like Bullin, (present Shirur in the South Canara district), Subara (Supārā on the Konkan coast), Tana (Thana), Jurbatan (Srikandapuram), Sandan (Sindhu-durga in the Ratnagiri district), Sindabur (Sadasibgarh near Karwar), etc. Inscriptions in Upper Burma and Sumatra still commemorate the operations of the Indian trading corporation of this period.

From Benjamin of Tudela, a Spanish Jew, who started his travels in 1159 we learn that Indian merchants brought their commodities for sale to the island of Kish in the Persian Gulf. They carried great quantities of spices to exchange for the goods brought by the merchants of Mesopotamia, Yemen and Persia. We learn from Chau-ju-kua that Gujarat produced indigo, myrobolans and coloured cotton stuffs in such abundance that they were exported to the lands of the Arabs. In the early centuries of the Christian era India's exports consisted mainly of luxury articles: spices, silk, and fine muslins. In the twelfth century its trade was extended to tanned leather, leather-goods, buckram and other textiles and according to the Chinese and Arab accounts sugarcane and ginger were exported from Malwa and Gujarat.

As regards India's imports, horses were the most important. This trade appears to have attained phenomenal proportions in the twelfth and thirteenth centuries. Wassaf refers to an agreement made by a Pāṇḍya king with an Arab merchant to the effect that he would embark as many horses as he could procure from the islands of the Persian Gulf and land them in Ma'bar. The price of each horse was fixed at 220 *dinārs* of 'red-gold'. The number of horses exported from the Arabian and Persian ports to India reached the huge figure of 14,000 valued at 2,20,00,000 *dinārs*. The Indian princes had a craze for horses because they realised the great importance of better-bred trained horses in warfare; they had observed that one of the main reasons for the Turkish success in war was the efficient handling of war horses. Horses, ponies and mules were available in India but they were not very good in war. It should not be forgotten, if the account of the Turkish conquest of Bengal as given by Minhajuddin is at all to be trusted, that Muhammad Bakhtyar could gain access to the capital city of Nadia only in the disguise of a horse-dealer! Though horses were imported in abundance, Wassaf says that the Indians were so ignorant of training horses that under their management even the best animals were soon disabled for active work. The Indians had no farriers and the foreign merchants prevented any farrier from going to India for fear of losing their profitable trade. Secondly, in their ignorance of the treatment of horses the Indians fed them with such food as did not suit them.

7

India in Some Foreign and Indigenous Accounts

1. Preliminary Remarks

Epigraphic and literary evidences undoubtedly throw light on the social and economic history of ancient and early medieval India, but they do not convey a complete picture. It is only in the history of religion and art that we have continuity but information on other spheres of human activities is much too meagre and sporadic. Therefore, instead of trying to reconstruct the outlines of a socio-economic history on the basis of available materials, we will present here summaries of some selected indigenous and foreign accounts which relate to different aspects of the life and activities of the Indian people in general. Some of the foreign sources are well known like the accounts of Megasthenes, Hiuen Tsang. Al-Bīrūnī and Marco Polo and they are indeed valuable for the information they provide. So far as the indigenous sources are concerned we will quote from a few texts which have not hitherto been used sufficiently. Among these we have taken into account Medhātithi's commentary on Manu. The law book of Manu is the source of Indian jurisprudence and all other works on this subject are either its imitations or modifications. Manu's text is normative; but how the principles outlined by him could work within an established socio-political set-up cannot be understood unless it is known how the said principles were interpreted under diverse conditions of time and space. That is why we have insisted on Medhātithi's commentary. We will also give brief extracts of the works of Dāmodaragupta and Kṣemendra which deal with the activities of the underworld, of those who went against the established social norms. The practical aspects of life are presented from a text called *Mānasollāsa* which is of the nature of an encyclopaedia. This text has been previously used by scholars only for the study of images and sculptures but the scope of this work is much wider and embraces almost all the aspects of human activities.

2. *The Account of Megasthenes*

Megasthenes, the Greek ambassador of Seleucus at the Maurya court at Pāṭaliputra, worte a book called *Indica*. Although it is lost, extracts from it are preserved in quotations by later classical writers who regarded it as the standard authority on India of the time of Candragupta Maurya. The account begins with a statement in regard to the dimensions of India. The extent from north to south is measured as 22,300 *stades*, though the real distance is not more than 16,000 *stades*. The distance from west to east is mentioned as 16,000 *stades* (1838 miles). This distance was apparently calculated by combining the 10,000 *stades* measured along the royal road from the Indus to the Maurya capital Pāṭaliputra and the estimated distance from Pātaliputra by way of the Ganges to the sea, that is, 6000 *stades*. The monsoons of India attracted the curiosity of Megasthenes. This was, according to him, the cause of the astonishing fertility of the Indian soil. Among the plants, the sugarcane and those yielding cotton interested him. As to minerals, gold and gems attracted his notice, and he believed in the traditional story of gold-digging ants. Among the animals, it was elephants, the monkeys and the snakes which especially drew his attention. As to the human specimens, they were tall and slender, more lightly built than any other people. A noble simplicity was their predominant characteristic. They indulged a love of richness and bright colours, wearing ornaments of gem and gold. Their staple food was pulpy rice. They drank rice-beer only in religious ceremonies. Among the deities of the

Indian pantheon, he could recognise the prototypes of Dionysus and Heracles in Śiva and Viṣṇu respectively.

"All their towns which are down beside the river or the sea are made of wood; for towns built of brick would never hold out for any length of time with the rains on the one hand, and, on the other, the rivers which rise above their banks and spread a sheet of water over the plains. But the towns which are built on elevated places out of reach, these are made of brick or clay." The capital city of Pāṭaliputra was built at the confluence of the Ganges and the Son. It formed an oblong, 80 *stades* by 15 *stades*, surrounded by a wooden palisade, with loopholes for the archers to shoot through, and outside the palisade a ditch 30 cubits deep and 6 plethora wide which served both for defence and as a public sewer. Along the palisade were towers at intervals, 570 in all, and 64 gates.

So far as the political structure was concerned, Megasthenes refers to the highly elevated position of the king in whose hands political power was consolidated. The officials were of three kinds: Agronomoi or district officials, Astynomoi or town officials, and members of the War office. The older tribal custom of consultation among administrative members for coordination in different walks of governmental service was very much in vogue. The duties of the Agronomoi were to supervise irrigation and land-measurement, hunting and pastoral professions, the various industries connected with agriculture, forestry, work in timber, metal foundries and mines and maintenance of roads which also required erection of milestones at distance of every ten *stadia*. The Astynomoi or town officials were divided into six Boards of five, their respective functions being supervision of factories, care of strangers, registration of births and deaths, control of the market (which also included inspection of weights and measures), inspection of manufactured goods and collection of tax charged on sales. Jointly they exercised a general superintendence over public works, prices, harbours and temples. The war office was likewise constituted by six Boards of five, each presiding over admiralty, transport and commissariat, infantry, cavalry, chariots and elephants respectively.

Megasthenes has viewed the existing caste system of India in terms of its functional and professional appearance. Certain features of the caste system were known to him since he tells that no one is allowed to marry out of his own caste, or to exchange one profession or trade for another, or to follow more than one business. He has enumerated seven castes: Philosophers, Husbandmen, Herdsmen, Artisan, Military, Overseers or Spies, and Councillors and Assessors. The Philosophers have been divided into two categories—Brachmanes (Brāhmaṇas) and Sarmanes (Śramaṇas). It appears that the Śramaṇas of the non-Brahmanical tradition were viewed by people of his time as belonging to the same status of the Brāhmaṇas. It is interesting to note that Megasthenes did not find here the existence of any institution called slavery. According to him "all the Indians are free and not one of them is a slave. The Indians do not even use aliens as slaves and much less a countryman of their own." Although the legal texts of India refer to slaves, they were simply purchased persons, or rather persons appointed permanently on the basis of one-time payment and were meant exclusively for minor domestic work. "We hear nothing of such later (Western) developments of slavery as rendered the Greek mines, the Roman latifundia or the plantations of Christian slave-owners, scenes of misery and oppression. For the most part the slaves (in India) were household servants, and not badly treated, and their numbers seem to have been insignificant" (Rhys Davids, 55). Whether they were treated badly or decently depended on the nature of the masters, but there was no 'age of slavery' in Indian history. This was due to the fact that in the Indian system all possible types of works and services were entrusted to different castes or occupational endogamous and autonomous social groups. Even the scavenger's work belonged to the exclusive domain of certain castes and it also could not be encroached upon by others. Under these circumstances the institution of salvery was inconsistent with the Indian system.

3. Hiuen Tsang's Description of India

The period of the travels of the Chinese pilgrim, Hiuen Tsang, extended from A.D. 629 to 645. He entered Kabul from the northwest via Bamian about the end of May 630 and crossed the Indus at Ohind in April 631. He studied Buddhism for several months at Taxila and then he proceeded to Kashmir where he stayed for two years. On his journey eastward he visited the ruins of Sangala, and after a stay of fourteen months in Chināpati and of four months in Jālandhara, for further study of Buddhism, he crossed the Sutlej in the autumn of A.D. 635. Then he took a circuitous course; he came to Mathura and returned to the northwest to Thaneswar whence he resumed his easterly route via Śrughna on the Yamuna and Gangādvāra on the Ganges to Ahicchatra. He then crossed the Ganges and visited the cities of Sāṇkāsya, Kanauj and Kausāmbī and then turning northward reached Śrāvastī. Thereafter he resumed his easterly route, visited Kapilavāstu and Kuśīnagara, and then once more turned to the west to visit Benaras. Then he came to the city of Vaiśālī, made an excursion to Nepal, returned to Vaiśālī, crossed the Ganges and reached Pāṭaliputra. From Pāṭaliputra he came to Bodhgayā, visited Kuśāgarapura and Rājagṛha, and stayed at Nālandā for a period of fifteen months for study.

Towards the end of A.D. 638 Hiuen Tsang resumed his easterly route, following the course of the Ganges to Modāgiri and Campā and crossing the river to the north, visited Puṇḍravardhana and went as far as Kāmarūpa. Then he turned south and passing through Samataṭa and Tāmralipti he reached Oḍra in A.D. 639. Continuing his southern route he went to Kaliṇga and then turning to the northwest he reached South Kosala. He then took a southeastern route and reached Dhanakaṭaka in Andhra Pradesh and proceeded as far as Kanchi. Thereafter, passing through Koṅkana and Maharashtra, he arrived at Broach and after visiting Ujjayinī and Valabhī he reached Sindhu and Multan towards the end of A.D. 641. He then suddenly returned to Nālandā and remained there for two months to resolve some religious questions. He next paid a second visit to Kāmarūpa. Early in A.D. 643 he was once more at Pāṭaliputra in the company of Harṣavardhana with whom he returned to Kanauj through Prayāga and Kosambi. From Kanauj he went to Jalandhara and after staying there for some time recrossed the Indus at Ohind. He reached Lamghan in March and Kapisa in July A.D. 644. Towards the end of the year he passed through Kashgar, Yarkand and Khotan and in the spirng of A.D. 645 he returned safely to China.

Hiuen Tsang was a keen observer. Although the main purpose of his visit was religious, he had a very wide range of interests. Moreover, he was well acquainted with Indian myths and legends, religion and philosophy, customs and traditions. According to him the people of India, In-tu in Chinese, called their country by different names which varied from region to region. The countries, under the name In-tu, were generally spoken of as the five Indies consisting of north, south, east, west and central region. It was 90,000 *li* in circuit, bordered on three sides by the great sea and on the north by the snowy mountains. It was divided into eighty kingdoms, each of which had its separate ruler although most of them were tributaries to a few greater states. Thus in northwestern India Kabul, Jalalabad, Peshawar, Ghazni and Bannu were all subject to the ruler of Kapisa. In the Punjab proper Taxila, Siṃhapura, Urasa, Punach and Rajaori were subject to the Rājā of Kashmir, while the whole of the plains, including Multan, Shorkot and Jālandhara, was dependent on the ruler of Taki or Śaṅgala near Lahore who in his turn was dependent on the Kanauj king Harṣavardhana whose realm extended from Thaneswar to the mouth of the Ganges. In western India, the provinces were divided between the kings of Sind, Valabhī and Gurjara. Bengal and Assam had different rulers. The dominion of southern India was nearly equally divided between the nine rulers of the states of Mahārāṣtra and Kosala in the north, Kaliṅga, Andhra, Koṅkana and Dhanakaṭaka in the centre, and Jorya, Drāviḍa and Mahākūṭa in the south.

According to Hiuen Tsang the seasons of India were rather hot; the land was well watered and humid. The north was a continuation of hills and mountains, the ground being dry. On the east there were valleys and plains, which being well watered and cultivated, were fruitful and productive. The southern districts were wooded and herbaceous. The western parts were stony and barren. The climate and the quality of the soil being different, the produce of the land also varied. The flowers and plants, the fruits and trees, were of different kinds and had distinct names. Different kinds of corns were cultivated according to the season and nature of the soil. Among the products of the ground rice and wheat were most plentiful. Ginger and mustard, melons and pumpkins were also produced. Onions and garlics were little grown.

The peoples of India were divided into castes. The Brāhmaṇas were particularly noted for purity and nobility, and tradition had hallowed them so much that people generally spoke of India as the country of the Brāhmaṇas (Pu-lo-men). The Kṣatriyas (T'sa-ti-li) had for ages been the ruling class. The Vaiśyas (Fei-she-li) were the merchant class engaged in commercial pursuits, making profit at home and abroad. The Śūdras (She-t'o-lo) were the agricultural class engaged in ploughing and tillage. The social difference among these four castes lay on the question of the degree of purity. When there were hypergamic or hypogamic marriages, the status of the persons concerned varied according to their new relationships. The Indians did not allow promiscuous marriages between relations. A woman once married could never take another husband. Besides these, there were other castes of many kinds having different callings. The mixed castes and the base-born differed in no way as to food and drink from the rest, except in respect of the vessels they used, which were different both as to value and material. There was no lack of suitable things for household use. Vessels made of dried clay were very much in use while those made of metal were used only occasionally.

The usual food was made of butter, milk, cream, soft-sugar, sugar candy, and the oil of mustard seed. All sorts of cakes made of corn were used as food. Fish, mutton, gazelle and deer were generally eaten. It was forbidden to eat the flesh of certain animals and those who did were despised and scorned. Different kinds of wine and liquor were in use. Strong fermented drinks were taken by most castes, but the Brāhmaṇas and the Śramaṇas drank a sort of syrup made from the grape or sugar-cane which was not of the nature of fermented wine. The clothing was not cut or fashioned. Men wound their garments round the middle and then gathered them under the armpits and let them fall down across the body, hanging to the right. The robes of women completely covered their shoulders and reached down to the ground. The garments were made of cotton, jute, silk, wool and skin. People mostly roamed barefooted. Few wore sandals. They stained their teeth in red or black. They were very particular about their personal cleanliness. All washed themselves before eating.

The towns and villages had inner gates. The walls were wide and high. The thoroughfares were dirty. Stalls were arranged on both sides of the road with appropriate signs. Butchers, fishers, dancers, executioners and scavengers had their abodes outside the city. The earth being soft and muddy, the walls of the towns were mostly built of bricks and tiles. The towers on the walls were constructed of wood or bamboo. The houses had balconies made of wood, with a coating of lime or mortar, and were covered with tiles. The walls were plastered with lime and mud, mixed with cowdung for purity. The monasteries were constructed with extraordinary skill. A high tower was erected at each of the four angles. The beams and the projecting heads were carved with great skill in different shapes. The doors, windows and the low walls were painted profusely. In the middle of the building was the hall, high and wide. There were various storeyed chambers and turrets of different heights and shapes.

Gold, silver, copper, white jade and fine pearls were objects of merchandise. Besides these there was an abundance of rare gems and various kinds of precious stones of different names which were collected from the islands of the sea. The merchants used to exchange these objects for other goods generally using the barter system. The administration of the government was founded on benign principles. The families were not entered on registers and the people were not subject to forced labour. The special duties of the crown were divided into four principal parts. The first was for carrying out the matters of state and providing ritualistic offerings. The second was for providing subsidies for the ministers and chief officers of the state. The third was for rewarding men of distinguished ability. The fourth was for charity to religious bodies. The taxes on the people were light, and the personal service required of them moderate. Those who cultivated the royal estates paid a sixth part of their produce as tribute. The merchants were also moderately charged. The river-passages and the road-barriers were open on payment of a small toll. When public works required it, labour was exacted but paid for. The payment was in strict proportion to the work done.

The military guarded the frontiers. The cities were guarded at night. The soldiers were levied according to the requirement of the service. They were promised certain payments and were publicly enrolled. The governors, ministers, magistrates and officials had each a portion of land assigned to them for their personal sustenance. The soldiers were mostly hereditary professionals. There were four divisions of the army: infantry, cavalry, chariots and elephants. During war the General remained in the chariot and was surrounded by a file of guards who kept close to his chariot wheels. The cavalry spread themselves in front to resist an attack, while the infantry by their quick movements contributed to the defence. They carried a long spear and a great shield. Sometimes they held a sword and advanced to the front with impetuosity. All their weapons of war were sharp and pointed.

Hiuen Tsang had the rare privilege to become acquainted with several kings of India. Foremost among them was the emperor Harṣavardhana, his patron. Apart from dealing in detail with the events of his reign, his personal magnanimity and accomplishments, Hiuen Tsang also focussed on Bhāskaravarman, the king of Kāmarūpa, whom he knew to be an enlightened monarch. Regarding Śaśāṅka, the king of Gauḍa, he states that when he came to Kuśīnagara he was distressed to hear of Śaśāṅka's oppression of the Buddhists. He also heard that in Bodhgaya Śaśāṅka had cut down the *bodhi* tree and destroyed its roots. He visited Maharashtra during Pulakeśin II's reign and referred to his power, beneficent activities and command over the people who were stern, vindictive and warlike in nature, though honest, simple and fond of learning. He visited the Pallava capital at Kanchi during the reign of Narasiṃhavarman I and said that the city was about six miles in cirumference and abounded in Buddhist monasteries.

According to Hiuen Tsang, the countries beyond the northern borders of India, as also those in the farthest north of India, e.g., Tenki, Kuchi, Poh-lu-ka, Balkh, Ka-chi, Bamian, Kashmir, Tamasāvana as well as Thaneswar, Śrughna, Prayāga and Kosāmbī continued to be the exclusive centres of the Hīnayānists, particularly the Sarvāstivādins, except Bamian where the Lokottaravādins dominated. He noticed adherents of both Hīnayāna and Mahāyāna in Kapisa, Jālandhara, Mathura,

Sāketa, Nepal, Puṇḍravardhana, Ceylon, Koṅkana and Maharashtra. The countries where he came across only the followers of Mahāyāna were Lampa, Taxila, Kulu, Magadha, Orissa and Vidarbha. The Sāmmityas had centres in Visoka, Ahicchatra, Sāṅkāśya, Śrāvastī, Kapilavāstu, Vārāṇasī, Vaiśālī, Karṇasuvarṇa, Malwa, Valabhī, Sind and Kutch. In Samataṭa and Drāviḍa he found 30 and 100 monasteries respectively with 2000 and 10,000 monks of the Sthavira school.

The pre-eminence of Nālandā University and the accomplishments of its scholars had been recorded by Hiuen Tsang. Names of successive royal donors of monasteries at Nālandā, according to him, were Śakrāditya, his son Buddhagupta, his successor Tathāgatagupta, his succcessor Bālāditya, his son Vajra and an unnamed king of mid-India. The buildings consisted of eight halls, besides the great college, with numerous apartments. The revenues of about 100 villages were endowed by the local kings for the upkeep of Nālandā. Names of distinguished teachers are also given in his account. He noted the unique fact that since the establishment of the monastery there was not a single case of breach of its discipline. The young learners, after finishing a work called 'the twelve chapters' were introduced in their seventh year to a group of five sciences—the science of sound or grammar, the science of arts and crafts, the science of medicine, the science of reasoning and the science of the internal. There were aslo specialised courses in addition to all these.

4. *Early Arab Accounts on Society and Economy*

An Arab account of India, composed in A.D. 851 and attributed to Sulaiman, refers to the great power and resources of the Gurjara Pratīhāras (Guzr) and their king Bhoja. It states that "this king maintains numerous forces and no other Indian king has so fine a cavalry. He is unfriendly to the Arabs, still he acknowledges that the king of the Arabs is the greatest of kings. Among the princes of India, there is no greater foe of the Muhammedan faith than he is. His territories form a tongue of land. He has got riches, and his camels and horses are numerous. Exchanges are carried on in his states with silver (and gold) in dust, and there are said to be mines (of these metals) in the country. There is no country in India more safe from robbers." Sulaiman has referred to the Pāla kingdom as Ruhmi Rahma, a name which cannot be satisfactorily explained. According to him the Pāla ruler was at war with his neighbours, the Gurjaras and the Rāṣṭrakūṭas, but his troops were more numerous than those of his adversaries. The Pāla king took 500,000 elephants in his military campaigns, and ten to fifteen thousand men in the army were employed in supplying and washing clothes.

The early Arab geographers belonging to the ninth and tenth centuries noticed the paucity of towns. Ibn al-Fakih observes that in India there are no towns unlike China. Sulaiman says that the greater part of the country is without towns while in China fortified and large towns are found in every part of the country. Speaking of the tract from Cambay to Saimur (Chaol), Ibn Haukal says that because of the extreme heat the men used fine muslin garments. According to Abu Zaid, Indian kings wore necklaces of precious red and green stones mounted on gold and they held pearls in the greatest esteem. Ibn al-Fakih says that the Indians used to wear ear-rings, and both males and females adorned themselves with golden bracelets. According to Sulaiman, Indians, both male and female, decorated themselves with golden bracelets and precious stones. The Indian concept of purity and purification of body did not escape their notice. According to Sulaiman and Ibn al-Fakih, the Indians, unlike the Chinese, cleansed their teeth with tooth-picks and bathed daily before taking meals. Belief in omens and portents has also been recorded. Abu Zaid refers to the 'most astonishing feats' of the diviners and those who drew omens from the flight of crows. According to Abu Zaid and Masudi a body of king's companions who had shared in taking rice with him at his coronation would burn themselves to the last man after his death. Again it appears from Abu Zaid and Ibn Khordadbah that on getting old persons would often commit suicide by drowning or by burning themselves. Abu Zaid says that in the case of adultery both the man and the woman were put to death, while the man alone was punished if the woman was found to have been forced against her will. The custom of dedicating maidens for service in temples has also been mentioned by him. According to Sulaiman, wives of kings sometimes burnt themselves on the funeral pyres of their husbands, but it was for them to exercise their option in the matter. As regards the custom of *purdah*, Abu Zaid furnishes the information that most Indian princes, while holding court, allowed their women to be seen unveiled by men present, whether natives or foreigners. The Arab writers of the ninth and tenth centuries refer to the fertility of the soil and the rich cultivation, both of grain and fruits, specially in western India with which area they were particularly acquainted. Some cities of Gujarat grew mangoes, coconuts, lemons and rice in great quantity and also produced honey. One such city also grew canes and teak trees, while Malabar produced pepper and bamboo. According to Masudi, ships from India along with those from Basra, Siraj and Oman, from Djawaga and Champa, ascended the Khanfu river to reach Canton. On the coast of Sind, near the mouths of the Sindhu, lay Debal, "a large mart and the port not only of this but also of the neighbouring regions." On the Gujarat coast were Cambay, Thana and Sopara, and further south of Sindan, modern Sanjan, from which was exported pepper. On the Malabar coast lay the important port of Kaulam Malaya, modern Quilon, where the ships sailing from Muscat took in fresh water before crossing the sea of Harkand (Bay of Bengal) for the journey to Kalah-bar. As regards the export trade, so far as agricultural products were concerned, Ibn Khordadbah mentions Indian exports to be diverse species of aloewood, sandalwood, camphor and camphor-water, nutmeg, clovepink, cubele, coconut, vegetable stuffs and textures of velvity cotton. Costus, rattan, indigo and bamboo were exported from Sind. According to Ibn Rosteh, teak was exported from the Rāṣṭrakūṭa kingdom of western India. The pepper which was exported from Sindan, and the sandals for which Cambay was famous, according to Arab writers, were sent from South India. Again Kāmarūpa, according to Abu Zaid, produced a variety of aloewood called *kamarubi* which was very valuable. It was brought all the way from Kāmarūpa to the temple of the Sun-god at Multan, where the merchants bought it from the priests of the deity. The textiles of Rahma (the Pāla kingdom), according to Ibn Khordadbah, were of velvity cotton, while Sulaiman declared them to be so light and fine that a robe made of that cloth could be passed through a signet ring. Sulaiman and Masudi also tell that the horns of rhinoceros were exported from the kindom of Rahma to China for being made into fashionable girdles. They heard reports of the existence of gold and silver mines in the Pratīhāra kingdom of Kanauj. Sulaiman and Ibn al-Fakih refer to the paucity of horses in India. Ibn Said mentions the import of dates from Basra into Daibal. We learn from several Arab works written between the tenth and the thirteenth century A.D. that a number of standard Hindu treatises on medicine, materia medica and therapeutics were translated into Arabic by order of the caliph Harun Al Rashid (A.D. 786-809). These included, among others, such famous works as the *Caraka*, the *Suṣruta* the *Nidāna* and the *Aṣṭāṅga* of Vāgbhaṭa. The names of a number of Indian scholars who visited Baghdad are preserved in Arabic works, but unfortunately it is hardly possible to restore the original Indian form of their names form the Arabic transliteration. "The Hindus", says Masudi, "were distinct from all other black people in point of intellect, government, strength of constitution and purity of colour."

5. *Medhātithi: Interpreter of Hindu Jurisprudence*

The period from A.D. 750 to 1000 was associated with the works of the great Smṛti commentators and makers of Digests. Their works marked the advent of a new stage in the history of Hindu jurisprudence. Foremost among them was Medhatithi (c. A.D. 825-900), the celebrated commentator on the *Manusmṛti*. The critical and constructive views on the contemporary aspects of Indian life furnished in this commentary should be viewed with historical interest.

Medhātithi equated *rājadharma* to the whole duty of the king and regarded it as synonymous with the entirety of politics. The traditional theory that kingship should be the profession of the Kṣatriya alone did not find favour with him since non-Kṣatriya royal dynasties existed in reality. He therefore did not hesitate to fix the stamp of legitimacy upon rulers who were not Kṣatriyas. The laws laid down by the king for peoples' observance, according to him, should only refer to the executive arrangement (*kāryavyavāsthā*) but not to the canon laid down by the legal texts. In other words, the king had no power of law-making by himself. He could only issue some directive principles of administrative policy. He had a two-fold obligation of protection, compulsory or *nitya* and optional or *kāmya*. The former was contractual protection on which the very concept of kingship rested. The latter was general protection comprising different welfare activities. As regards the civil rights of the individuals, Medhātithi holds that people are entitled to carry and use weapons for self-defence because, although it is the duty of the king to protect his subjects, the king cannot stretch his arms so as to reach every man within his kingdom. The slayer of a desperado is liable neither to punishment by the king, nor to penance, and he can kill the latter by any means, either publicly or secretly. The individual's right of self-defence extends to the protection of his family and property and to the protection of others as well.

Regarding the administration of justice, it is interesting to note that Medhātithi was conscious about the class-orientation of the judicial members of the law courts which he thought as detrimental to the proper administration of justice. According to him, the *kula* or body of relatives, *śreṇī* or body of traders and others following the same profession, and *gaṇas* or persons who always move about in groups have vested interests and hence may be prejudiced. That is why an authorised person is needed who should be a Brāhmaṇa learned in the Vedas and have the quality of impartiality. While other courts are entitled to pronounce judgements, the king alone has the right to inflict punishment. Medhātithi makes a difference between the spirit of the king's executive and judicial administration. "When he is seated upon his royal throne, the king regards wealth (*artha*) as the most important matter even in preference to morality. But when he is engaged in deciding suits, he regards morality as the most important thing." Medhātithi insists on the essential difference between civil and criminal cases. In civil matters there may be negotiation between the parties by themselves. "If the parties settle it themselves, it is no business of the king to interfere." But crimes are essentially offences against the state. Discrimination on the basis of castes is not favoured by him. The order of investigation based upon castes is to be observed only when the troubles of all the suitors are of the same degree. When, on the other hand, the business of the lower caste is very urgent or very important, then it should be taken up first.

Medhātithi says that the people of one village, afflicted by constant encroachment on the grazing grounds and water-reserves by the people of another village, would form a compact for defence of the ancient privileges of the village and any one breaking the compact and joining the other party would be liable to the penalty of banishment or fine. He includes *saṅghas* or associations of the same or different castes among those whose members are liable to a fine for breach of contract. He defines the guild or *śreṇī* as consisting of people following a common profession, such as tradesmen, artisans, money-lenders, coach-drivers and so forth. From Medhātithi's illustration of the laws of guilds we find that they sometimes compounded with the government for payment of a fixed sum in place of the usual share of their profits. The same holds good in the case of *saṅghas* which is defined by Medhātithi as a community of persons following the same pursuit though belonging to different castes and regions. He lays down the rule that among architects, masons, carpenters, and the like wages shall be distributed on the principle that he who does the most difficult part of the job shall receive more and he who does the easier part shall get less. Regarding interest and wages Medhātithi has simplified Manu's rules insisting on the relative status of occupations.

Medhātithi's attitude to the Śūdras is liberal. He says that a Śūdra does nothing wrong if, being in possession of wealth, he lives without dependence upon a Brāhmaṇa. This clearly shows that Medhātithi recognises the Śūdra's absolute right to personal freedom. He explains Manu's term *śūdraśiṣya*, or pupil of a Śūdra, to mean that Śūdras were sometimes teachers of grammar and other sciences. Regarding their religious rights, he says that while Śrauta rites are not open to a Śūdra, because of his ineligibility for initiation, there is no prohibition against their performing those non-Śrauta rites which are laid down in the Smṛtis. He allows the higher castes to take up the occupations of the Vaiśyas and Śūdras in times of distress or when there is no other alternative. For a Brāhmaṇa the occupation of agriculture is the worst, then comes trade and next the tending of cattle, handicrafts and so forth. According to him slavery for the Śūdra is not innate but voluntary for he acquiesces in it only with a view to acquiring merit and, even then he cannot be given away or pledged. As regards inter-caste marriages Medhātithi makes marriages of Brāhmaṇas with Kṣatriya and Vaiśya women altogether exceptional while forbidding the marriage of a Brāhmaṇa with a Śūdra woman. He says that in the case of *anuloma* or inter-caste marriage in hypergamical order the son takes the caste of the mother and in the case of *pratiloma* or inter-caste marriage in hypogamical order the son takes the caste of the father.

Regarding the position of women the views of Medhātithi are characterised by a more rational and liberal attitude than other contemporary law-givers. Insofar as the unmarried sister is concerned, Medhātithi rejects the view which objects to her being given a share in the family property on the ground that the girl is entitled by custom only to the benefit of her marriage being performed. All property, whether movable or unmovable, obtained by a woman, either as a maiden, or at marriage, or after marriage, from her parents or from husband and his family is included within the category of *strīdhana* or 'women's property'. The wife, according to him, must not be forsaken unless she becomes an outcast, and 'forsaking' in this case means not that she is to be deprived of food and clothing but that she is to be cut off from all intercourse and forbidden to do household work. The husband has no dominion (*prabhūtva*) over his wife. They differ only in their bodies but are entirely united in their functions. A wife persecuted by the husband, just as a husband troubled by the wife, can appeal to the king for a decision to settle their disputes. The virtuous wife must be maintained even by committing a hundred bad acts. Again, on the question of the alternatives open to a wife after she has waited for the prescribed period for her husband's return from abroad, Medhātithi urges that while she must live by unobjectionable occupations before the expiry of her waiting term, she may live by objectionable pursuits thereafter.

Judged by modern standards the outlook of Medhātithi appears to be rather conservative, but in the context of his contemporary age he was undoubtedly liberal and progressive. His interpretations of the laws of Manu were characterised by a spirit of awareness of the requirements of his age. The deep insight he displayed in his observation and analysis ensured that his views continued to remain relevant even in the subsequent periods of Indian social history.

6. *Dāmodaragupta and Kṣemendra*

Dāmodaragupta was a Kashmiri poet and a minister of king Jayāpīḍa (A.D. 779-813) whose *Kuṭṭanīmata* is rich in information regarding the life, social customs, the state of society, religion, literature, etc., of Kashmir of his times. It is a sort of manual for the guidance of the *hetareae* in which a prostitute is instructed by a procuress as to how she should feign true love for a rich young man and employ the arts of erotic love without giving him the least hint that all these are done for extracting wealth from him. The various cunning arts for ruining feeble-minded and innocent young men are described in a realistic way. The demand for accomplished courtesans was in vogue even as late as the ninth century A.D. as revealed by the testimony of Dāmodara. The accomplished courtesan should not only have physical beauty but she was also required to possess good knowledge of the erotic texts and dramatic manuals, of the science of medicine and trees and of the arts of painting, sewing, drawing, modelling, cooking, playing musical instruments, dancing and singing. The ideal lover also had to be sweet in speech, entertaining in his tales and anecdotes, endowed with sufficient means and have a beautiful complexion. From the *Kuṭṭanīmata* it appears that the connection of a Brāhmaṇa with a courtesan came to be regarded at that time as a disgraceful act, but it was not so in the times of Bhāsa and Śūdraka. This work lacks any special reference to the type of city-bred man of fashion (*nāgaraka*) so well described by Vātsyāyana. On the other hand we have a remarkably full and vivid picture of a country squire, who is the object of a courtesan's attention, undoubtedly drawn from real life. The hero has not the refinement and artistic taste of Vātsyāyana's *nāgaraka*. His dress and manners are showy and he likes to be surrounded by flatterers and to enjoy extravagant praises showered on him by them for his demonstration of poor knowledge of everything. He wears colourful dresses and sits and gossips with his flatterers in a huge dancing hall crowded with guild-masters, merchants, parasites and gamblers.

Kṣemendra's *Samayamātṛkā* (meaning procuress, literally 'teaching mother'), composed about A.D. 1050, relates the story of a would-be-prostitute who is introduced by a barber to Kalāvatī, an expert in her arts. As a young girl she was a thief and a harlot, married several persons one after another, and occasionally lived as a rich widow. Her fortune varied and in the course of her life she had many careers: thief, nun, procuress, swindler, public housekeeper, food-vendor, beggar, flower-dealer, sorceress, landlady, Brāhmaṇa lady, and lastly again a procuress. The *Kalāvilāsa* of Kṣemendra has a greater value than the *Samayamātṛkā* from the view point of social history. In this work various of the follies of men are described; the author's sense of social consciousness makes him dwell upon cheats. A salesman brings his son to Mūladeva, an expert in all wicked arts, trickery and cunning who initiates him in this line. The teachings of Mūladeva, consisting all sorts of cheating, forms the subject-matter of this work. It helps us immensely to know how the prostitutes, physicians, goldsmiths and Kāyasthas satisfied their wicked ambitions, and the state of the society in which they worked. The religious hypocrites have been particularly subjected to description and the modes of their cheating are exposed. Men of various professions like the officials, ascetics, astrologers, physicians, servants, traders, goldsmiths, actors, soldiers, singers, bards, wizards, etc., have been taken into account and their misdeeds recounted.

7. *Al-Bīrūnī's India: Kitab-ul-Hind*

Among the earliest Arab writers on India the works of Sulaiman Ibn Khurdadba, Abu Zaid, Al-Itkhari, Masudi and others are undoubtedly valuable sources of information. The difficulty is that these writers depended mostly on second hand information collected from half-literate sailors and merchants whose observations were devoid of insight. However, there were some Arab scholars who came across fragments of Indian wisdom through the Arabic translations of certain Indian texts and wanted to know more about India in terms of her rich cultural heritage. Foremost among them was Al-Bīrūnī (A.D. 973-1048).

As a scholar, Al-Bīrūnī's position was unique and unparalled. He was the first to view the development of Indian civilisation and the Indian way of life in a historical perspective. The Chinese pilgrims who visited this country came with a feeling of reverence because to them India was the land of Buddha; they learnt Sanskrit in order to study the Buddhist texts. But India was not the land of Buddha only. There were in this country numerous religious systems, variety of manners and customs, different types of society and social norms, various schools of philosophy and science and widely divergent views on different walks of life. It was Al-Bīrūnī alone who tried to view and present these manifold streams in their totality. His style of presenting is analytical and at the same time critical. Apart from Sanskrit, he knew Greek and Hebrew as well, and that is why while he dealt with Indian philosophy, science, mathematics, astronomy and allied subjects he cited Greek and Hebrew parallels.

Before he began to write his account of India, he had translated a few Sanskrit works into Arabic like the *Sāṅkhyasūtra* (not the present version, but an earlier one), *Yogasūtra*, Brahmagupta's *Khaṇḍakhādyaka*, *Brahmasphūṭasiddhānta*, Varāhamihira's *Bṛhatsaṃhitā*, *Pulisasiddhānta*, *Laghujātaka*, etc. He did not read the Vedas directly but had some idea about their contents. He knew about the existence of the eighteen Purāṇas, and had read the *Matsya*, *Āditya*, *Vāyu* and *Viṣṇudharmottara*. The *Mahābhārata* was well known to him and so was the *Bhagavadgītā*. In fact, Al-Bīrūnī was the first to introduce the *Gītā* to the Muslim world. He quoted many verses of the *Gītā* in his works. The legal treatises of Manu and others were all known to him. He had a thorough comprehension of the philosophical works of Gauḍapāda, the Sāṅkhya texts, especially the *Sāṅkhyakārikā* of Iśvarakṛṣṇa, the *Yogasūtra* of Patañjali (a different version which has not as yet been discovered), the *Nyāyasūtra* and *Nyāyābhāṣya*, the *Mīmāṃsāsūtra* of Jaimini, the *Agastyamata*, etc. In the field of astronomy and mathematics he had studied the works of Varāhamihira, Āryabhaṭa, Balabhadra, Bhānuyaśas, Bhaṭṭila, Brahmagupta, Durlabha, Kalyāṇavarman, Lāta, Mahādeva, Māṇḍavya,

Parāśara, Utpala, Vijaya Nandin, Viṣṇucandra, Citteśvara, etc. Moreover, he read the *Carakasaṃhitā* and the works of the alchemist Nāgārjuna. How thoroughly he grasped the contents of these works is proved by his brilliant and painstaking analyses of Indian mathematics and astronomy. A considerable portion of his account of India is devoted to mathematics and astronomy.

Al-Bīrūnī's account of India is commonly known as *Kitab-ul-Hind* though the English rendering of the long title of his book would be "Exact Description of all Forms of Hindu Thought-processess considered in terms of what should be Accepted or Rejected of them from the Viewpoint of Reason." The entire work comprises seventy-six chapters grouped in eight parts each dealing respectively with Hindu Philosophy; Literature; Laws, Customs and Social patterns; Topography; Practical Sciences; Physical Sciences; Mathematics and Astronomy; Religion, Modes of worship and Deities; and Miscellany. In the beginning there is a general description of the Hindus. Then the book goes on to describe the philosophical systems of India which were current during his time. It deals especially with the concepts relating to God, the problems of cognition, sensory and extra-sensory matters, causality, epistemology, ontology, cosmology, transmigration, liberation, classification of beings and other related topics of philosophical interest. The chapters on literature present a general introduction of Hindu scriptures, some notes on the Vedas, Purāṇas and other texts, and a discussion on grammar and prosody. Al-Bīrūnī's topographical studies were based on the *Bṛhatsaṃhitā* and the *Bhuvanakoṣa* section of the Purāṇas. In this connection he has dealt with the Hindu geographical concepts of the world consisting of seven concentric islands; Meru as the central zone, the continent of Jambudvīpa, the Varṣas or subcontinents, the Varṣaparvatas or continental mountain ranges, the rivers, the shape of the world, etc. While dealing with the laws, customs and social patterns Al-Bīrūnī has acquainted his readers with the views of Manu, Yājñavalkya and other law-givers. In addition, from his own experience he has thrown light on the social norms and behaviours of the Hindus, the caste system, rituals and superstitions and tried to offer reasons for their origin and development. He has described the religious systems of the Hindus, concepts of the Hindu deities and various episodes of the

Purāṇas. In connection with religion he has also thrown significant light on Hindu iconography on the basis of the *Viṣṇudharmottara*. The rest of his account of India is devoted to the practical sciences of the Hindus, especially to those relating to medicine, alchemy, metallurgy, natural sciences, mathematics and astronomy. These were subjects of his specialisation.

The credit goes to Al-Bīrūnī not for the knowledge he gained but for the insight his learning showed. Since his approach was analytical and rational, his comments on various aspects of Indian life are revealing and thought-provoking. Some of them are valid even today. In Hindu character he observed a lack of transparence and a dichotomy which allowed the peaceful co-existence of science and superstition. He was not happy with the vain pride of the Indian people in isolationism and insularity. "The Hindus", he said, "believe that there is no country but theirs, no king like theirs, no science like theirs. . . . If they travelled and mixed with other nations they would soon change their mind." Al-Bīrūnī also remarked that "their ancestors were not so narrow-minded as the present generation."

Al-Bīrūnī had the candour to admit that "the repugnance of the Hindus against foreigners increased more and more when the Muslims began to make inroads into their country . . . . Mahmud utterly ruined the prosperity of the country and . . . the Hindus became like atoms of dust scattered in all directions. . . Their scattered remains cherish, of course, the most inveterate aversion towards all Muslims. . . . Hindu sciences have retired far away from those parts of the country that have been conquered by us, and have fled to places which our hand cannot yet reach, to Kashmir, Banaras and other places." Regarding the Shahis who bravely resisted Mahmud of Ghazni for more than twenty-five years, Al-Bīrūnī remarks with a note of pathos: "The Hindu Sahiya dynasty is now extinct, and of the whole house there is no longer the slightest remnant in existence. We must say that, in all their grandeur, they never slackened in the ardent desire of doing that which is good and right, that they were men of noble sentiment and noble bearing."

Al-Bīrūnī clearly perceived the great gulf that normally

separated the Hindus from the Muslims. According to him, the first difference was in regard to language. "Secondly, they totally differ from us in religion, as we believe in nothing in which they believe, and *vice versa*. . . . In the third place, in all manners and usages, they differ from us to such a degree as to frighten their children with us, with our dress, and our ways and customs, and as to declare us to be devil's breed, and our doings as the very opposite of all that is good and proper. . . . All their fanaticism is directed against those who do not belong to them, against all foreigners. They call them *mleccha*, i.e., impure, and forbid having any connection with them, be it by intermarriage or any other kind of relationship, or by sitting, eating and drinking with them because thereby they think they would be polluted. They consider as impure anything which touches the fire and the water of a foreigner. . . . They are not allowed to receive anybody who does not belong to them, even if he wished it, or was inclined to their religion. This, too, renders any connection with them quite impossible and constitutes the widest gulf between us and them."

8. The Mānasollāsa: A Sourcebook of Contemporary Information

While the account of Marco Polo deals especially with the far south and that of Al-Bīrūnī with northern India, the *Mānasollāsa* or *Abhilasitārthacintāmaṇi*, an encyclopaedic work composed by the Western Cālukya king Someśvara III (A.D. 1226-1238) throws light on certain aspects of life in the Deccan region. Divided in five *prakaraṇas* of twenty chapters each, it deals with one hundred topics pertaining to different aspects of political, social, economic and religious life. The work is specially important since it reflects the attitude of an enlightened monarch and the fields of his interest. The first *prakaraṇa* deals with general and religious ethics, social service, manufacture of idols and deseases and their remedies; the second with polity under seven heads and private and inter-state laws; the third with architecture, picture-drawing, painting, iconography and pleasures of domestic life; the fourth and fifth with various forms of amusements and recreations, arithmetic, preparation of calendars, astrology, augury, omens, palmistry, training and treatment of horses and elephants. There are also particulars about such diverse topics as mining, alchemy, gems and precious stones, marriage and child-bearing, cookery, liquor, beverage, music, conveyances and scents.

The contents of the *Mānasollāsa* can broadly be divided into three categories: those pertaining to the exclusive sphere of the king and the ruling authorities; those pertaining to social life in general; and those pertaining to science and technology as well as arts and crafts. So far as the first category is concerned, in regard to the theories relating to the origin of the state, the functions of the king, his ministers and officials, and the principles of state policy the author of the *Mānasollāsa* has followed the line previously set forth by Manu and Kauṭilya. But the realities of the contemporary age have also to be accommodated in which connection comes the question of the rights, obligations and ranks of the feudatories on whom the Cālukyan kings depended immensely. It is stated that the king should deal with his feudatories through the Sāndhivigrahaka, the minister for war and peace, who should be expert in summoning, dismissing and installing the Sāmantas, Maṇḍaleśas and Mānyakas. The *Mānasollāsa* advises the king to make various kinds of gifts, including those of territories, to leading feudatories (*sāmantamānyakas*) and various grades of ministers (*mantrins*, *amātyas* and *sacivas*). Gifts should also be made to servants, kinsman and others who render military help to the king. Since inscriptional evidences of secular land grants are rare, the open insistence on secular grants in the *Mānasollāsa* has a great significance particularly as it comes from the pen of a celebrated king who was master of a considerable part of the Deccan peninsula and belonged to a ruling family which had many feudatories. Sixteen kinds of secular gifts are listed; they include not only distribution of villages, towns, mines and marks of honour but also that of virgin girls and prostitutes. The various kinds of territorial and administrative divisions, big or small, with or without taxes, which were assigned to the grantees were known as *deśyam*, *karajam*, *grāmajam*, etc. The gradation of the feudatories has been marked in terms of the right of having been greeted and by the number of musical instruments played in their honour.

The *Mānasollāsa* describes in detail the methods and principles of the education of princes and also their marriage. While dealing with these the author has depended solely on the tradition instituted by the *Artha* and *Kāmaśāstras*. The author says that princes should be instructed in the Vedaś as well as in military science. When the princes have completed the training and have become skilled in mounting horses and elephants and in managing chariots, the king shall test them one after another. The test applies to their skill in various branches of literature, in the fine arts, in wielding the bow and other weapons and in exhibiting their strength as well as steadiness of body and mind. The training period over, the prince should marry. He should select as his queen a girl of Kṣatriya lineage, young and beautiful, having good manners, bearing auspicious marks on her person and belonging to one or other of the best groups after the classification given in the *Kāmasūtra*. The prince might also select young and beautiful women of Vaiśya and Śūdra castes as secondary wives (*avarodha-vadhū*) for purpose of enjoyment. He might further engage wanton women (*vilāsini*) having the same physical charms and gratify them with various gifts and personal attention.

The *Mānasollāsa* makes interesting references to agrarian and industrial productions and also to exports and imports. Rice from the Kaliṅga country is included in the list of the varieties suitable for the king's diet. It refers to eight varieties of rice distinguished by their colour, odour, size and period of growth and seven different kinds of beans. It refers to the Maharashtrian women with heavy hips who were in the habit of singing *ovi* songs while husking the rice. It refers to the yellow sandals produced in Kashmir which was used as unguent in the rainy season. It gives a long list of fabrics after their places of origin, like Nāgapattana (Negapatam), the Cola country, Anilavāḍa (Anahillapataka in Gujarat), Mūlasthāna (Multan), Kaliṅga and Vaṅga. The import of Chinese silk and metal is mentioned. It also refers to maritime trade and states that Indian ships should pay one-tenth of the price of their goods as duty in the harbours of the king. It also tells that buffaloes, camels and bullocks were used for inland commercial transport and also in military expeditions.

The *Mānasollāsa* refers to both vegetarian and non-vegetarian dishes as also to the use of wine. It deals with the method of removing the pig's hair preparatory to cooking the meat as well as the process of cooking the meat of deer, sheep, birds, fish, tortoise, crab and even rats living in the fields near the bank of the river. References to the distinctive toilette of the court ladies of Kuntala, Drāvida, Mahārāṣṭra, Andhra and Gurjara are found in the descriptions of the royal court. The art of making ornaments of gold and silver is also explained. It deals with the plans of construction of houses, royal houses in particular. The methods of temple and image-making and those of casting metal for making images have been described in detail. There is a list of diseases along with prescriptions for their treatment. These were collected and summarised from the existing texts on the respective subjects. The *Mānasollāsa* devotes 2,500 verses to music and musical instruments and touches on new phases of music, especially *prabandhas*. So far as the popular and royal amusements are concerned, it refers to mock-wars, literary exercises, elephant-sports, Indian polo, combatant's duels, wrestlers' contests, fights of birds and beasts, pigeon fights, hunting, hawking and angling. Popular beliefs in omens and portents, auspicious and inauspicious times as well as charms and spells for witchcraft have been demonstrated. Speaking of the king's advance against his enemy the *Mānasollāsa* gives elaborate descriptions of the auspicious and inauspicious times for its start as well as favourable and unfavourable omens indicated by the behaviour of dogs, jackals, lizards and crows.

9. Marco Polo on India

Among the European travellers, the visit of Marco Polo to South India brought about a new epoch in direct contact between Europe and the East. Marco Polo reached the court of Kublai Khan after a hazardous journey of three-and-a-half years across Asia. He spent seventeen years in the Mongol court where he became a great favourite of the Khan. He was chosen to escort a princess of the Khan's family on her bridal journey to the ruler of Persia. He left China in 1292 and his voyage to Persia lasted about a year-and-a-half. Considering that he was only passing through some parts of South India the amount of information he was able to collect is surprising. He has much to tell about the manners, beliefs and practices of the people of South India and their maritime trade. The commerce of India he found stretching, like an immense chain, from the territories of Kublai Khan to the shores of the Persian Gulf and of the Red Sea. He found the shores and the islands of the Indian Sea luxuriantly covered with nature's choicest products. He tells us of the topaz, the amethyst, and the emerald, of the sapphires of Ceylon and the diamonds of Golconda. He held that Bengala (Bengal) produced spikenard and other spices, ginger, sugar and other articles including cotton. Incense of a brown variety was found at Tana (Thana) which city had also a great export trade in leather of various excellent kinds. An immense quantity of hide was tanned in Gujarat which produced many beautiful mats in red and blue leather. Cotton trees of very great height and of a longevity of twenty years grew in Gujarat. Malabar produced large quantities of pepper. Beautiful and delicate buckrams were also manufactured in Malabar.

Marco Polo knew that the Andhra country was ruled by a queen (Rudrāmbā), a lady of much discretion. He describes the different methods by which diamonds were gathered from the mines in her kingdom. Finest cotton fabrics were produced in Andhra region (kingdom of Mutfili, i.e., Warangal). "In this kingdom are also made the best and most delicate buckrams and those of the highest price; in short, they look like tissue of spider's web. There is no king nor queen in the world but might be glad to wear them. The people have also the largest sheep in the world, and great abundance of all the necessaries of life." Marco Polo heard the legends of St. Thomas, the Apostle, and the manner of his death in the neighbourhood of Mylapore. He noticed the presence of Jews and Christians in the kingdom of Quilon, the king of which was tributary to none. Pepper and indigo were abundant in the country which was visited regularly by merchants from China, Arabia and the Levant. "Corn they have none but rice. So also their wine they made from (palm) sugar; capital drink it is, and very speedily it makes a man drunk. All other necessaries of a man's life they have in great plenty and cheapness." Piracy was rampant throughout the Malabar coast, a fact which was not overlooked by him. "The ships that come from the East bring copper in ballast. They also bring higher clothes of silk and golds and sandals; also gold and silver, cloves and spikenard, and other fine spices for which there is a demand here and exchange them for products of these countries."

Regarding the Pāṇḍya country Marco Polo observed : "The great province of Ma'bar . . . is styled India the Greater; it is best of all the Indies . . . the finest and noblest in the world. At the end of the province reigns one of those five royal brothers, who is crowned king, and his name is Sonder Bandi Davar (Sundara Pāṇḍya). In his kingdom they find very fine and great pearls. . . . Ceil (Kayal at the mouth of the Tampraparni) is a great and noble city, and belongs to Ashar, the eldest of the five brother kings. It is at this city that all the ships touch that come from the West, as from Hormos and from Kis and from Aden, and all Arabia, laden with horses and things for sale. And this brings a great concourse of people from the country round about, and so there is great business done in this city of Cail. The king possesses vast treasures and wears upon his person great store of rich jewels. He maintains great state and administers his kingdom with great equity and extends great favour to merchants and foreigners so that they are very glad to visit his city." From the earliest times, the Pāṇḍya country has been famous for its pearls, and Marco Polo has given a substantially correct account of the fisheries, adding that the king derived great revenue from them. "Moreover, nobody is permitted to take out of the kingdom a pearl weighing more than half a saggio unless he manages to do it secretly." He describes at some length the institution of the king's Trustly Lieges, the band of bodyguards sworn to defend the king with their lives.

Marco Polo was critical about the poor equipment of the warriors whom he described as the "most wretched soldiers". He also noticed the speedy death of the imported horses owing to the unfavourable climate and the ignorance of Indian horse-keepers. The scanty dress of the South Indian peasants—a loin cloth they tie around the waist even today owing to excessive summer heat which forces them to keep the upper part of the body bare—did not escape his notice. He mentions the custom of *sati* and refers to the practice of allowing a condemned criminal who was sentenced to death to sacrifice himself to some god or other of his choice. He says that the people of this country have the custom of polishing houses with cow dung. "All of them, great and small, king and barons included, do sit upon the ground only. It is their practice that everyone, male and female, do wash the body twice everyday; and those who do not wash are looked on much as we look on the Patarins. You must know that in eating, they use the right hand only. . . . So also they drink only from drinking vessels, and every man hath his own; nor will anyone drink from another's vessel. And when they drink they do not put the vessel to the lips but hold it aloft and let the drink spout into the mouth."

Marco Polo did not fail to notice the prevalence of widespread belief in omens and astrology and popular superstitions. He mentions the presence of experts in the arts of physiognomy, astrology and sorcery, and the readiness of the people to consult them. The Brāhmaṇas of the Lāṭa (Lar) region living in the Kannada tract were the best and most truthful merchants in the world. They lived a life of chastity and temperence but, at the same time, were more prone to superstitious beliefs in omens and portents than any other people. Among the people of Ma'bar there were experts who discerned a man's character by his looks. The people recorded the date and hour of a child's birth, and they did all their acts with reference to astrology and with the advice of diviners. The merchants of Gujarat made their purchases when their shadow was of required length, and undertook their journeys when the direction of the swallow's flight was favourable. The people of Ma'bar "are very strict in executing justice upon criminals and in abstaining from wine, but did not look upon lechery as a sin. Indeed they have made a rule that wine-drinkers and sea-faring men are never to be accepted as sureties." He mentions the custom by which a creditor drew a circle round a defaulting debtor and "the latter must not pass out of this circle until he shall have satisfied the claim or given security for its discharge." He notices the widespread use of betel leaves with camphor and other aromatic spices mixed with quicklime. He says that "the nobles and great folks slept on beds made of very light cane work, hanging from ceiling by cords for fear of tarantulas and other vermin; while the common folk slept on streets." The dancing girls attached to the temples were also noticed by him. He refers to temples as "certain abbeys in which are gods and goddesses to whom many young girls are consecrated." The people of the Pāṇḍya country would not eat beef on any account, though they took meat of other animals that were killed for them by Arab and other butchers. In the Kākatīya kingdom the people lived on meat, rice and milk. The people of Quilon lived on rice and drank wine made from palm-sugar. In contrast the merchants from Gujarat living in the Kannada tract ate no flesh and drank no wine.

Marco Polo observed that ships with their goods came to Malabar both from South China and the West, the former prepondering over the latter in the proportion of ten to one. Cambay, according to him, was visited by merchants with many ships and cargoes. The products of Gujarat were loaded in ships every year for trade with Arabia and other lands. The merchants of India visited Hormuz in ships loaded with products of their land. Ships from Ma'bar visited the islands of Madagascar and Zanzibar, arriving there in twenty days, while taking more than three months for the return voyage because of the strong southern current. In the east Zayton (Chwan-chau in Fu-kien) was visited by the ships of India with spices and costly wares. Ships from the east brought to India clothes of silk and gold as well as *sendals* or a kind of silk-texture. The very practical method of training tradesmen's apprentices, especially in Ma'bar or the Pandyan kingdom, did not escape Marco Polo's notice. When the boys reach the age of thirteen the parents dismissed them from their homes with small pocket allowances for earning their living by trade. They were found running about all day from pillar to post, buying and selling. During the season of pearl-fishing they ran to the beach and purchased five or six pearls according to their ability and sold them to the merchants. In the same way they dealt in many other articles and gradually became very dexterous and keen traders.

8

The Ideological Aspects

1. Materialism versus Idealism

According to the Pythagorean definition, philosophy is 'contemplation, study and knowledge of nature'. It is the science of the general laws of being (i.e., nature and society), human thinking and the process of knowledge. In the earlier stages of human history philosophy was a science embracing the sum total of man's knowledge of the objective world. Later, as individual sciences branched out from philosophy with the gradual development of human knowledge in different directions, philosophy was singled out as an independent science for elaborating a general view of the world and to study its elements and laws. This ultimately resulted in the polarisation of philosophy into two diametrically opposed trends, materialism and idealism; and the struggle between the two has characterised the entire history of philosophy. The elaboration of specific problems of philosophy led to the various aspects being treated as more or less independent and at times sharply delineated divisions. These are ontology, epistemology, logic, ethics, psychology, aesthetics, and so on.

This historical process holds good also in the case of the development of the Indian thought. In each of the Indian systems there was an inherent conflict in the ideological sphere and the dominant forces of the conflict determined the ultimate nature of the system—whether it would remain materialistic or plunge into idealism. As a result, on the one hand we find in the Indian philosophical arena the development of absolute materialism—represented by the Cārvāka system, and on the other, that of absolute idealism—represented by the Advaita Vedānta, Mādhyamika and Yogācāra schools. In between these two extremes there are a number of systems which are basically materialistic but which eventually developed idealistic tendencies under different historical conditions. Of these systems the Nyāya-Vaiśeṣika, Vaibhāṣika and Sautrāntika became over-powered by the spirit of idealism. The Sāṅkhya and the Mīmāṃsā, despite their idealistic accretions, were able to maintain their original materialistic character. This holds good also in the case of Jain philosophy which, notwithstanding its later idealistic tone and colour, has been able to maintain its basic materialistic core.

Pandit Sukhlalji Sanghvi (*ASILM*, 1-2) writes: "Indian philosophical systems fall under two main classes: some of them are realistic (*vāstavavādin*) and others idealistic (*avāstavavādin*). Those who view the gross (*sthūla*) world, i.e., the world apprehended by empirical (*laukika*) organs of knowledge (*pramāṇa*), to be as real as the subtle (*sukṣma*) world, i.e., the world apprehended by the transcendental (*lokottara*) organs of knowledge, that is to say, those which maintain that there is no real difference between the empirical (*vyavahārika*) and the absolute (*paramārthika*) truth, that all truth is of same kind though differing in degree, that all objects revealed (*bhāṣita*) through whatever organ of knowledge are equally real even if the revelation (*bhāṇa*) be relatively full or meagre, clear or vague, and that even real objects are capable of being expressed in words (*vāṇī-partyakṣa*) are realistic systems. They may also be called positivistic (*vidhimukha*) systems or systems talking in terms of 'it is thus' and 'it is so' (*idamitthamvādin*, *evamvādin*). They include the Cārvāka, Nyāya-Vaiśeṣika, Pūrva Mīmāṃsā, and Sāṅkhya-Yoga systems, the Vaibhāṣika and Sautrāntika systems of Buddhism, and the Madhvite school of Vedānta, etc. Those which view the external (*bāhya*) perceptible (*dṛśya*) world to be unreal (*mithyā*) and the internal (*āntarika* one alone to be ultimately real (*parama-satya*)—that is to say, those which, having classified truth into the empirical and the absolute, the apparent (*sāmvṛtika*) and the real (*vāstavika*), treat as unreal everything that is apprehended by the empirical organs of knowledge and is expressed in words—are idealistic systems. They may be called negativistic (*nisedhatmaka*) systems or systems which speak in terms of 'it is not so' (*anevamvadin*). The Śūnyavāda and Vijñānavāda schools of Buddhism, the Śaṅkarite school of Vedānta, etc. are systems of this type "

In India we come across a conflict within each system of thought between the empirical and *a priori* ideas. Finally, it is the latter which triumphed. To empirical perception was added transcendental perception and this opened the door for idealism. There developed an elaborate form of logic which was able to channelise successfully the human spirit into the ideal of releasing individual souls from the bondage of physical existence. The cause of this change in approach and outlook was dependent on many conditions. One of these may be that such ideas were inherent in the Upaniṣadic idealism and that they had a very easy revival in the Brahmanical systems. In the case of the non-Brahmanical systems like Buddhism or Jainism it was probably due to the Brāhmaṇa converts who came with certain predetermined thought-structures which were not discarded but further developed within the framework of the systems to which they were converted. Moreover, within the general thought structure, there exists the distinct possibility of ideas developing according to their own peculiar qualities. This process of change may culminate in a final qualitative transformation of the original ideas.

2. *Attitude towards Science: The Conceptual Aspects*

Indian contribution to the growth of physical, chemical, astronomical and biological science was by no means insignificant. But, just as in Greece, after Aristotle the term metaphysics lost its original meaning and its subject-matter came to be identified with speculative philosophy as against the pre-Socratic naturalism of the Ionian physicists, so also most of the Indian systems, when they became sufficiently sophisticated, set to the task of prying into the transcendental concepts and relations above and beyond the physical universe. The earlier empirical basis of philosophy is clearly found in the expression *darśana* which literally means the act of perception, derived from the root *dṛś*, 'to see'. But its meaning and significance was changed, and it was argued that perception should not be physical. It should be intuitional for the realisation of the Self which is conducive to liberation or *moksa*. The Sankhyas, Mimaṃsakas, Nyaya-Vaiseṣikas, Jains, etc , bring us more or less near a quasi-materialistic conception of nature. But even these systems have failed to liberate themselves from this new fangled definition of philosophy in which the spirit of scientific enquiry was fettered.

The development of physical science presupposes the conception of a materalist cosmology, glimpses of which are found in the Sāṅkhya. But the gross elements or *mahābhūtas* characterised by earth, water, fire, air and space have not been assigned any independent entity. They have been regarded as evolutes of certain super-sensual categories. The world as an object of perception has the five *tanmātras* or subtle elements, the essence of sound, touch, colour, taste and smell conceived as physical principles corresponding to the five sense organs. The gross elements arise from the compounding of the subtle elements through the process of accumulation. The Vaiśeṣika school understands all the objects of experience by the term *padārtha* classified into substance (*dravya*), quality (*guṇa*), activity (*karma*), generality (*sāmānya*), particularity (*viśeṣa*) and inherence (*samavāya*). Earth, water, light, air, ether, time, space, soul and mind intended to comprise all corporeal and incorporeal things. The earth possesses the four qualities of smell, taste, colour and tangibility; water the three qualities of taste, colour and tangibility; light the two qualities of colour and tangibility; air the single quality of tangibility; and space the single quality of sound. The ultimate constituents of earth, air, light and water are called atoms or *paramānus*.

According to the Nyāya Vaiśeṣikas, the atoms are eternal, without origin or decay. The individual atoms combine with others and continue in that cooperative existence for some time and again disintegrate into their original solitary being to form new combinations. There thus ensues a successive disruption and reabsorption of the ultimate material substances—earth, water, fire and air. The atoms are eternal while the compounds made of them are non-eternal. The Buddhist Vaibhāṣikas also accept the atomic theory and maintain that the atom has six sides and can be perceived in a mass though we cannot see them singly. According to Vasubandhu, it is the smallest particle of *rūpa*, indivisible, unanalysable, inaudible and intangible. The atoms are the same in all the elements possessing the qualities of earth, water, fire and air. The Jains too believe in the atomic theory and hold that homogeneous atoms produce different elements by varying combinations.

Notwithstanding the existence of such conceptions conducive to the growth of physical science, it did not grow independently because of the fact that all scientific disciplines were under the direct influence of a process of reasoning in which super-empirical concepts were given precedence over empirical data. Thus, the Nyāya-Vaiśeṣikas eventually came to the conclusion that since all composite objects of the world like earth, water, etc., were effects of some cause, and since they were made up of parts and possessed a limited magnitude, the cause must be an intelligent agent without whose guidance the material factors of the composite substances namely, the atoms, could not have just that order or coordination which enabled them to produce the composite objects, the definite effects. And this intelligent agent or cause could not be other than God.

The Tantric maxim that the body is the epitome of the universe is the basis of Indian medical science; it rests on the assumption that the elements forming the body cannot be dissociated from environmental elements and that by applying the laws which govern the latter the former may be brought to order. The medical tradition of India which is manifested in works like the *Carakasaṃhitā* and *Suṣrutasaṃhitā* and also in later works like the *Aṣṭāṅgasaṃgraha* and the *Aṣṭāṅgahṛdayasaṃhitā* lays the greatest emphasis on the cause-effect relation. It is interesting to note that the Buddha himself based his doctrine of suffering on the medical tradition. The Four Noble Truths proclaimed by the Buddha remind us of similar maxims concerning diseases found in the *Carakasaṃhitā*. Although in its present form it belongs to the beginning of the Christian era, it contains much of the earlier medical tradition. The followers of the Nyāya school of logic wanted to base their arguments on the authority of the science of Āyurveda which means that they wanted to follow the same method of reasoning as was followed by the men of the medical profession. Knowledge about the humam body is presented under the categories of *śarīrotpattikramaḥ* (the process by which the body is formed), *śarīrasthānādinirṇayaḥ* (location of nerves etc., within the body) *bhūtagunāḥ* (qualities of matter by which the body is formed), *śaīrasthavāyunirṇayah* (identification of the element of air in the body) and *śarīrakoṣavarṇanam* (description of the muscles of the body).

The physicians who depended mostly on chemical drugs were known as Rasavaidyas and formed a sect of their own. They used mainly drugs produced from mercury, sulphur, iron, mica, gold and silver. In the field of mercurial drugs especially the Rasa sect made wonderful progress. On the one hand they devised a philosophy of body in terms of its chemical reactions, known as Raseśvara Darśana, and, on the other, made numerous preparations out of mercury. In the *Kubjikātantra*, a manuscript of which exists in Gupta characters, we come across a passage in which Śiva himself speaks of *pārada* or mercury as his generative principle and eulogises its efficacy when 'killed' six times. In this work we also find allusions to the transmutation of copper into gold with the aid of mercury, as also to other chemical processes. The *Rasaratnākara* of Nāgārjuna (eighth century A.D.) contains methods for the purification of important minerals—crude copper by means of 'poling', extractions of the essence of minerals, liquefaction of mica, fixation of mercury, a recipe for Aethiops mineral, killing of mercury, and also descriptions of the nature of the apparatuses.

It should also be stated in this connection that scientific principles in ancient India were inextricably blended with theological and metaphysical principles. Secularisation of scientific disciplines was a preposterous idea though there were attempts in this direction, especially in the field of medical science and mathematics. Āryabhaṭa (fifth century A.D.) was the first to treat mathematics as a distinct subject. His unique system of notation was based on the decimal place-value system. He was also the first to hold that the earth was a sphere and rotated on its axis. In his *Āryabhaṭiya* he dealt with evolution and involution, area and volume, progressions and algebric identities, and indeterminate equations of the first degree. The next mathematician was Brahmagupta (seventh century A.D.), the well known writer of the *Brahmasiddhānta* and *Khaṇḍakhādya*, who dealt with ordinary arithmetical operations, square and cube roots, rule of three, progressions, geometry, including treatment of the rational right-angled triangle and the elements of the circle, elementary mensuration of solids, cyclic quadrilaterals, shadow-problems, negative and positive quantities, cipher, surds, simple algebric identities, indeterminate equations of the first and second degrees, etc. However, it is disappointing that after some formulations were made there was no further progress. There was no following up; no innovations were made, nor any enrichment of the principles that were set up earlier. This held good in the case of most branches of science. The principles were in a sense canonised and thus held sacred. In the history of the development of European sciences, there was organised interference on free thinking from the Church authorities. Scientists were persecuted when it was found that their views did not correspond with those upheld in the *Bible*. In India there was no Pope or Church, no branded ecclesiastical authority to detect heretical ideas and punish their formulators. But still Indian scientific ideas were fettered, for reasons quite unknown, and their further growth was retarded.

3. *The Concept of God in Indian Philosophical Systems*

It is generally held that Indian philosophy is essentially spiritual, moving round the idea of God as the basic fact of life. But this is not true. It is only in the Yoga and the Vedānta, besides the Nyāya-Vaiśeṣika, that God is formally acknowledged. All other systems of Indian philosophy are basically atheistic. The ancient materialists of India whose views are found in the Cārvāka and allied systems, held that the world is a spontaneous growth promoted by the chance-combination of material elements, and no intervention by God is needed for creation. The early Mīmāṃsakas are silent about God and the later ones reject proofs of God. According to the Mīmāṃsakas, perception, inference and scriptures do not prove the existence of God. God cannot act as the supervisor of *dharma* and *adharma* since he cannot have any knowledge of them. The universe having neither any beginning nor end does not require any creator. According to the Sankhya, the assumption of God is ontologically irrelevant and logically repulsive. The Buddha's antitheistic arguments are thus summarised by Aśvaghoṣa: If all the world has been made by Isvara, there should be no change or destruction, no such things as sorrow and calamity, right or wrong; if he be perfect the world should be perfect; if he is the maker, the world should obey him if he acts with a purpose he should not be called perfect; and if he acts without a purpose, he should be called either a lunatic or a baby.

According to the Vaibhasikas, God is unreal. If things were his creation they would come into being at once. But in reality the effect comes into being following an evolutionary process. From the seed grows the sprout, from the sprout the leaves; after the leaves grow the stem and branches; then appears the flower and then fruit. Again God cannot be described as creator, since the effect is conditioned by space and time. In the Mahāyāna we find that Nagarjuna denies the possibility of the world being created by God. Santideva in his *Bodhicaryavatara* refuses to admit any omniscient and omnipotent God as creator, and his polemics are directed against the theism of the Nyāya-Vaisesikas. The same holds good in the case of Santarakṣita in whose *Tattvasamgraha* we come across pointed answers to the logical grounds on which the theists, evidently the Nyāya-Vaiśeṣikas, wanted to prove the existence of God. The Jains also launched a vigorous logical campaign against theism and the most sophisticated arguments and hair-splitting analyses are met with in the polemic of Gunaratna which was directed against the Nyaya-Vaisesika probans for the inference of God.

The original purpose of the Nyāya-Vaiśeṣikas was to discover the basis of substance which is the substratum of qualities and actions and the material cause of composite things. In order to understand the basis of substance they developed the atomic theory. The inference by which they sought to prove the existence of atoms is like this: Whatever is produced must be made up of parts. Therefore if the parts of a composite thing be separated, we shall pass from larger to smaller, from smaller to still smaller, and from there to the smallest parts which cannot be further divided in any way. These indivisible and minutest parts are called *paramānus* or atoms. An atom cannot be produced, because it has no parts, and to produce means to combine parts. Nor can it be destroyed for to destroy a thing is to break it up into its parts, whereas the atom has no parts. Thus being neither produced nor destructible the atoms of a thing are eternal.

But how could the atoms, being by definition partless and unintelligent, combine with each other? The Nyāya-Vaiśeṣikas had to face this question from the Buddhists, Vedāntists and Mīmāṃsakas. What we know from the achievements of modern science and technology was beyond the scope of the knowledge of the ancients. The Nyāya-Vaiśeṣikas depended on the technology known to them, namely, the potter's wheel or the weaver's loom, in order to explain how the unintelligent and partless atoms were combined. In the case of making a pot, the clay is the material cause and the potter is the efficient cause. According to the Nyāya-Vaiśeṣikas, just as the potter as an efficient cause or intelligent agent makes the pot from the unintelligent material cause, namely, clay, so also God, as the macrocosmic potter, makes the world by combining the partless and unintelligent material cause, namely, the atoms. Thus was the idea of God as an intelligent agent was smuggled in by the Nyāya-Vaiśeṣikas to explain what was basically a scientific problem.

The Mīmāṃsakas and others challenged this viewpoint on the ground that God in this case is an agent under bondage and not a free agent. Like the potter, God then requires a body and also the will and capacity to create. God does not create the world out of nothing, but out of eternal atoms. He is helplessly obliged to work with the materials already existing. Who then was the creator of the materials of creation prior to creation and whence did these materials come into existence? According to Kumārila, if it be said the God created the materials of creation from his own body, he must be a material entity, and assuredly his body would not have been created by himself. For this one has to postulate another creator, and another, and so on *ad infinitum*, but the problem remains the same.

The Nyāya-Vaiśeṣikas, in order to defend the existence of God put forward the following argument: All composite objects of the world, formed by the combination of atoms, must have a cause because they are of the nature of effects like a pot, being made up of parts and possessed of limited dimensions. Hence there must be an intelligent cause or agent (*kartā*) without whose guidance these objects cannot be what they are, cannot attain just that order, direction and coordination which enables them to be produced as definite effects. This intelligent cause must have a *direct knowledge* of the material causes, i.e., the atoms, the *desire* to combine and reproduce them in different forms and also *power* to accomplish the task. So he requires to be omniscient (*sarvajña*), because only an omniscient (*sarvajña*) being can have direct knowledge of all these.

Against these arguments the Mīmāṃsakas hold that an ordinary agent like a potter can produce something since he possesses a *body*, has the *will* to produce it, and further he puts forth the specific *effort* required for the production. None of these, however, is possible in the case of God. The production of things does not immediately follow the desire of the intelligent agent. The pot, for example, is not produced immediately after the potter desires to produce it. When it is said that the atoms perform the work of creation, being guided by the will of God, the inference is invalid because the atoms are devoid of intelligence and it is impossible on their part to follow, or even to understand, the will of God.

According to the Nyāya-Vaiśeṣika exponent Aviddhakaraṇa, things perceptible through the senses—like the earth, water or fire, and also the imperceptible substances, like air, must have been produced by an intelligent cause in the form of God *because they are characterised by a peculiar arrangement of their own parts*. As regards this argument the Buddhist logician Śāntarakṣita says that the probans of the inference that "because these are characterised by a peculiar arrangement of their own parts" consists in using a probans which takes for granted something that is yet to be proved. The expression "being characterised etc." means that there exists a form of conjunction (*saṃyoga*) among their different parts and that as a result of this conjunction they become a "sum total of component parts" a "whole" (*avayavī*). Thus the probans takes *for granted* the validity of the concepts of *conjunction* and the *whole*. But both these concepts, on which rests the probans, are basically unproved; and with the help of this *unproved* probans the existence of God is sought to be proved, which is logically fallacious. Śāntarakṣita has also refuted the argument of Uddyotakara that *the causes of the world like the atoms etc., need a controller with superior intelligence because their activity is intermittent.* He has also refuted that of Praśastamati that *at the beginning of creation the behaviour of men must have been due to the teaching only af God.* His final conclusion is that things that are born consecutively cannot have God for their cause.

According to the Jain logician Guṇaratna, when God is conceived as the cause of the world, the latter is viewed as the effect The world does not satisfy this condition of being an effect because it is ever existing. If it is not an effect, it is idle to conjecture that it has a cause in the form of God. Even God and the atoms are then to be viewed as effects and such will require an ancestry of intelligent causes. If for the sake of absurd argument the world is viewed as an effect, it may presuppose a cause. But this need not specifically be an intelligent cause or God, because there is no universal concomitance between "being a bare effect" and "having an intelligent cause". According to Guṇaratna, the logic of the Nyāya-Vaiśeṣikas invariably leads us to the fact that the knowledge, will, capacity, etc., of God are also to be considered as effects. Are they prepared to admit that these qualities of God, being effects, presuppose an intelligent cause in the sense in which a pot does? What about such things as wild trees, plants, etc., which inspite of being effects are devoid of any intelligent cause as is proved by perception? If it is argued that God is intrinsically imperceptible, the same inference which seeks to establish the existence of God cannot also prove his imperceptibility.

According to Guṇaratna, any probans that may be cited to prove God as the cause of the world must necessarily be contradictory and suffer from the fallacy of the 'counteracted', i.e., the fallacy of allowing scope for a counter-inference to prove the opposite of the desired thesis. God cannot be eternal, because only by virtue of some transformation of his own nature can God be conceived of as the cause of the world. His knowledge also cannot be eternal, for this is contradicted by both perception and inference. God cannot be omniscient because there is no concomitance between the varieties of worldly objects and omiscience.

4. The Doctrine of Karma

In view of what has been said above, it is sufficiently clear that in most of the Brahmanical systems and also in Buddhism and Jainism the idea of God as the creator and controller of the world has no place. All these systems argue that if God is regarded as a free agent he cannot have the desire to create and if he is regarded as an agent under bondage he cannot have the capacity to create. Every real entity is a cause and also an effect, but the first cause as an effect has no cause and as such it is no effect.

One of the reasons for this flat denial of God is the insistence on the traditional doctrine of *karma* and rebirth to which all the schools of thought, barring the Cārvākas, subscribe. The basis of the *karma* doctrine was the simple agricultural maxim: As you sow, so you reap. The law of *karma* means that all actions, good or bad, produce their proper consequences in the life of the individuals. A man's present life is the consequence of the actions committed in his past life and the actions of his present life will determine the course of his future life. Thus the doctrine of *karma* is inextricably blended with the concepts of rebirth and transmigration of soul. Every event that happens in a man's life can be explained in terms of the doctrine of *karma*. The anomalies and variations of human life, individual differences, happiness and suffering, in short everything, is due to the actions of his or her previous wordly existence.

Needless to say that in such a scheme God has no place. God cannot change the consequences of *karma* which an individual suffers or enjoys. He cannot liberate human beings from the fetters of *karma*. It is only the Nyāya-Vaiśeṣika school which holds that the law of *karma* is under the guidance and control of God. The *adṛṣṭa*, or the stock of merits and demerits accumulated by *karma*, cannot by itself lead to its porper effects because it is an unintelligent and unconscious principle. It is God who controls human *adṛṣṭa* and dispenses all the joys and sorrows in human life in accordance with the law of *karma*. But this view of the Nyāya-Vaiśeṣikas is rejected by other schools of thought. They hold that if the will of God is responsible for the world, then there cannot be any room for the doctrine of *karma* and if God creates the world under the guidance of the *adṛṣṭa* of the individual souls, he loses his independence. All other systems regard the law of *karma* as autonomous, a law which works independently of the will of God.

In the Vedas *karma* and its fruits are meant to be ritual acts and their results are not so much for moral elevation as for the achievement of objects of practical welfare. In the Vedas the doctrine of *karma* is not taken in its widest and most universal sense. It is on this point that Jainism and Buddhism depart significantly from the Vedic line. In the Upaniṣads the doctrine of *karma* is presented in two forms—simple and sophisticated. The simple form of this doctrine is that just as good seeds bring a good harvest and bad seeds bad, so also a man becomes good by good deeds and bad by bad deeds. Its ethics is that every deed must produce its natural effect in the world, and as such also leave an impression on the mind. It is this impression or *saṃskāra* that inclines one to repeat a deed. A man cannot escape the deeds but he can control them, and by self-discipline can strengthen the good impulses and weaken the bad ones. In the sophisticated level, however, *karma* is regarded as a blind unconscious principle governing the whole universe. It is not subject to the control of God.

The Buddhist and Jain doctrines of *karma* derived their main impulses from the Upaniṣadic tradition. The Buddhists divide *karma* into *kusala* (good) and *akusala* (bad) and hold that the merits and demerits a man earns through his actions cause him to take birth again and again in this world. This process works repeatedly until one achieves final salvation. The Buddhist concept of *karma* is the same as the Brahmanical one with the exception that instead of the idea of the transmigration of soul it insists on that of the transmigration of impressions. The deeds of one life leave certain impressions which become the causative factor of rebirth. *Karma* is conceived in Jainism, unlike other systems, as being material and permeating the *jīvas* (individuals) and weighing them down to the mundane level. Through the actions of body, speech and mind, *karma* is formed as a subtle matter. The passions of a man act like a viscous substance that attracts the *karma* matter, which thus pours into the soul and sticking to it gradually ripens and exhausts itself in accordance with the suffering and enjoyment of the individual. While some *karma* matter is being expanded in this way, other *karma* matter is accumulated at the same time. If through proper self-discipline all *karma* is worked out, the individual becomes free.

In the Ṛgvedic eschatology there is no direct reference to the soul's transmigration or to the doctrine of rebirth in any form. In the Brāhmaṇa literature, however, we come across the idea of repeated births and deaths, but this idea has not been established in a theoretical framework. It is only in the Upaniṣads that we come across a clear development of the theory of the transmigration of soul in three distinct stages. In the first stage the earlier Vedic idea of heaven has been replaced by the concept of *yāna* or (way) of the fathers (*pitṛ*) or of the gods (*deva*). In the second stage the doctrine of transmigration is presented without any reference to the idea of *karma* or reaping the fruits of ones deeds. In the final stage, however, we have a complete presentation of the transmigration of soul strictly in terms of the doctrine of *karma*. In subsequent philosophical traditions the law of *karma* became independent of the authority of God; it came to be conceived as a blind force guiding the formation of objects. The soul survives deaths to be able to reap the consequences of its *karma*.

5. *Growth of the Theistic Concepts*

The major Brahmanical schools of thought and also Buddhism and Jainism rejected the concept of God as the creator and controller of the universe and insisted on the doctrine of *karma* as the guiding principle of all aspects of human life. But this elitism based upon fashionable logical dispute could not satisfy the mass spirit for obvious reasons.

Ever since the rise of state power on the ruins of ancient tribal equality, tyranny, oppression and inequality became a regular feature of life—a process by which the human history has been characterised throughout the ages. However, there was awareness of the situation, and there was no dearth of individuals and schools of thought that spoke in terms of humanism to put an end to *nirṛti* (the traditional Indian term for the rule of evil) by restoring the moral values which were being trampled and undermined in reality. All the schools of Indian thought insisted on the doctrine of suffering. Not only Buddhism and Jainism, but the so-called Brahmanical systems as well had conceived of worldly existence in terms of suffering—material, mental and also intellectual. The fetters of worldly existence tormented them. Existence did not appear to them meaningful. They insisted that ignorance, i.e., lack of objective consciousness of the real causes of misery and the illusory belief in the wonder-working power of some divine or unknown forces, aggravated and perpetuated suffering. Some of them went so far as to state that worldly existence itself was nothing but an illusion.

Side by side also developed a different line of thinking—the concept of a supernatural being, a superhuman entity, an omniscient and omnipotent God controlling and preserving the world, modelled in the image of the king. By the complete surrender of the individual self to this divine will, by prayer and propitiation, the devotee is expected to have all his wishes fulfilled and all his problems solved. This is known as the *bhakti* movement which was channelised by the growth of various monotheistic religions like Vaiṣṇavism, Śaivism, etc. The first systematic exposition of this doctrine is found in the *Bhagavadgītā*.

It should be remembered that although the names of such gods, conceived of as the supreme being of different established creeds, are found in the Vedic texts, they have nothing in common with the nature-gods of the past who were invoked and controlled by rituals to ensure human welfare. Nor do these supreme beings have anything in common with the Buddhist and Jain deities who were conceived of as idealised human beings. Historically it is not impossible that such monotheistic concepts had something to do with the pre-Vedic and non-Vedic cults. But one has to admit that the concept of *bhakti* that is devotion to a personal god thought of as the creator of the world and controller of human destiny and the surrender of the individual self to God's grace as the way out of all human problems, became so popular among the masses that even systems like Buddhism and Jainism, which insisted more on the moral and mental aspects, felt it necessary to give their systems a theistic turn.

The *Mahābhārata* upholds the idea of political unification of India under a *cakravartin*, the human prototype of the divine Viṣṇu who has mastery over the universe. The *Bhagavadgītā*, composed about the second century B.C., equates the king with God and demands total submission of the individual to the divine will. Such views must have strengthened the cause of absolute monarchy, but it is not right to hold that the concept of an omniscient and omnipotent all-powerful god ruling over the universe with supreme authority was just a simple reflection of the political concept of absolute monarchy. In reality, belief in one personal all-powerful god, capable of bestowing grace (*prasāda*) and who could be approached through reverence, awe and simple devotion, is a feature of human psychology. This sentiment was not encouraged in the Vedic, Buddhist and Jain religion, all of which insisted solely on the doctrine of endless cycles of *karma* and rebirth, in which there was no room of any personal god bestowing grace on the worshippers or helping them to get rid of the fetters of *karma*.

6. *Appearance and Reality: Two Aspects of Vedānta*

The *Vedānta Sūtra* of Bādarāyana is an exposition of the Upaniṣadic doctrine of *brahman*. Bādarāyana says that the power of creation belongs to the pure, stainless *brahman*, the material and efficient cause, which for its own sport develops itself into the world without undergoing the least change. *Brahman* is pure consciousness but the world is material. *Brahman* is changeless and eternal while the world is changing and impermanent. Both are contradictory concepts. The world cannot be the *pariṇāma*, or transformation of *brahman*, since an absolutely perfect entity cannot transform itself into multiple imperfections. It cannot also be the *vivarta*, or transfiguration of *brahman*, in which case the world should have been a conscious principle like *brahman* itself devoid of any imperfection. As a way out, a number of subsequent philosophers and commentators put forward the theory that there could be no such thing as the real existence of the world. According to Śaṅkara (eighth century A.D.) the world exists only for those who are under the influence of false knowledge.

The view that the world is only an appearance and not a reality was basically inspired by Mahāyāna Buddhist ideas. The Yogācāra school of Mahāyāna Buddhism contends that consciousness is self-creative and all-producing, the ultimate principle and the ultimate type and form of reality. This school denies the real existence of everything except *vijñāna* or consciousness. This school of thought is also called Vijñānavāda. According to it external objects are unreal, since one cannot say whether they arise from existence or not, whether they are simple atoms or complex bodies. While the Yogācāra reduces all appearances to a series of ideas the Śūnyavada or Mādhyamika school goes a step further saying that even consciousness or *vijñāna* is unreal. Nāgārjuna says that the whole world of experience is an appearance, a mere network of unintelligible relations. The composite substances which come into existence, continue and cease to exist are not real since origination, continuance and extinction cannot remain jointly and simultaneously in one. Neither existence nor non-existence can be proved to be the essential property of substance. A thing is known through its qualities, but qualities cannot exist by themselves. Substance and quality are correlative, and neither can be singly applied to reality as a whole. In fact, there is no cause or effect, no production or cessation. The world has no real existence, and things are neither transient nor eternal. What is produced by concurrent causes (the Buddhist doctrine of *paṭicca samuppāda*) in not produced in itself and hence does not exist in itself.

Gauḍapāda, the ideological ancestor of Śaṅkara and the author of the *Māṇḍyukyakārikā*, was openly influenced by the Mādhyamika ideas. His work is an attempt to combine the Mādhyamika doctrine of vacuity or Śūnyavāda with the Upaniṣadic doctrine of *brahman*. In common with Nāgrājuna he denies the validity of causation and the possibility of change. However, it was Śaṅkara who raised the doctrine of illusion to a greater speculative daring and logical subtlety. Like Gauḍapāda, Śaṅkara was tremendously influenced by Buddhism—in fact he was described by his opponents as crypto-Buddhist.

Although Śaṅkara has criticised Buddhist subjective idealism (Vijñānavāda of Yogācāra) and absolute nihilism (Śūnyavāda or Mādhyamika), his own view is not very different from that of the Yogācāra school which insists on the existence of pure consciousness as the only reality. This pure consciousness of the Yogācāra school is the same as the *brahman* of Śaṅkara. He also says that the world is an appearance and not a reality, but the *appearance* of the world is taken as *real* by the ignorant and for that the ignorant cannot be blamed because the existence of external objects cannot be denied because they are *perceived to exist.*

According to Śaṅkara, this perception of the world as an existing entity is bound to be false because *brahman* is the only real entity which is without a second, and since it is not subject to transformation it cannot be the cause of the world. The world is an illusion like the cognition of snake in a rope. When a magician makes one coin appear as many, it is an illusion for the perceivers but not for the conjurer. Thus illusion is the product of ignorance which prevents the lookers from seeing the real nature of the thing and which makes them see something else in its place. *Brahman*, the great magician conjures up the world-show with magical power known as *māyā*. *Māyā* is not independent of *brahman*; the associate of the two becomes *saguṇa-brahman* or Īśvara (God). *Māyā* is thus regarded as the energy of the creator which becomes transformed into *upādhi* or limitation, the unmanifested matter from which all existence issues and by which the potential world is transformed into the actual world. Thus in order to explain the creation of the world, the *saguṇa* or changing *brahman* is conceived who, as Īśvara or God, combines within itself the nature of both the unattached *brahman* and the unconscious *māyā*. But this *saguṇa-brahman* or Īśvara or God cannot be real, like the world, because of its finite existence.

The world is also called *māyā* by Śaṅkara because of its unreality. This became a problem for the later Advaitavādins. If the world is *māyā*, and therefore unreal, how could it then be produced at all? So a need was felt to make the points clearer, and as a result of such attempts new theories came into light. Padmapāda and his followers hold that *brahman* and *māyā* may together be regarded as the cause of the world: the former as the *existence* appears to undergo change and the latter as the *non-intelligent* is subject to change. Sarvajña, the disciple of Sureśvara, holds that *brahman* is the material cause of universe working through the intervention of *māyā* which is essentially the operating condition. *Māyā* is the product of *brahman* and a process of its activity; it is not a substance and so cannot be regarded as the material cause. On the other hand the followers of Maṇḍana hold that the cause of the evolution of the world is *māyā* and not *brahman*. Prakāśānanda objects to subjecting *brahman* to any kind of relation and so holds that *māyā* alone is the cause of the world. Vidyāraṇya holds that the cause which changes into the world is *māyā* while that which is the basis of the world is *brahman* limited by *māyā*. Vācaspati holds that while *brahmam* is the cause, *māyā* is auxiliary. Since *māyā* is thus deceptive in character, it has become the target of attack from all corners. Challenging the concept of *māyā*, Vyāsatīrtha, a disciple of Madhva, puts forth the following dilemma: If the unreality of the world is unreal, the world becomes real: and if the unreality of the world is not unreal then there must exist something real other than *brahman*. Both alternatives go against the non-duality of *brahman*. In reply Madhusudana says: Taken the first alternative as granted, the reality of the world cannot be proved; the unreality of the world, and the unreality of that unreality, both belong to the same category since both of them are different from *brahman*.

But there is the other side of the coin as well. Rāmānuja has protested vigorously against the doctrine of *māyā*. He asks where *māyā* really exists? It cannot be said to exist in an individual self. Because individuality is itself produced by *māyā*, the cause cannot depend on its effect. Nor can *māyā* be in *brahman*. If it conceals *brahman* then the all-revealing nature of the latter becomes meaningless. The Śaṅkarites say that *māyā* is indescribable, neither real nor unreal. This is absurd because experience shows that things are either real or unreal. To deny the reality of the world is a falsification of immediate experience. In that case even the reality of mental states cannot be believed in. According to Rāmānuja every effect is a pre-existent material cause and the world of effect implies pre-existing souls and unevolved matter. The world is composed of conscious and non-conscious substances both emanating from *brahman* . Madhva, who stands for unqualified dualism, holds that the perceptible world is real which is the work of *brahman*. Nimbārka says that creation means the manifestation of *brahman's* conscious and unconscious power in their subtle forms. The universe cannot be dismissed as a mere illusion since it is a manifestation of what is contained as subtle in the nature of *brahman*. Such theistic interpretations of Vedānta, as we shall see in the next chapter, eventually became predominant in Indian thought and became the forerunners of a new type of *bhakti* movement under various religious systems which had a dynamic role to play in the history of medieval India.

9

Religious Gleanings

1. *Towards Theistic Transformation*

The lists of the existing religious sects and cults, as found in the *Aṅguttara Nikāya* and in the *Mahāniddesa* and *Cullaniddesa*, demonstrate the existence, side by side with the well-known sects, of a bewildering variety of primitive faiths and cults—Ājīvika, Nirgrantha, Jaṭilaka, Parivrājaka, Aviruddhaka, Muṇḍa-Śrāvaka, Māgandika, Traidaṇḍika, Gautamaka and Devadharmika, along with the worshippers of the elephant, horse, cow, dog, crow, Vāsudeva, Baladeva, Purṇabhadra, Maṇibhadra, the Yakṣas, the Nāgas, the Asuras, the Gandharvas, the Mahārājas, Agni, Candra, Sūrya, Indra, Brahman, Deva and Dik. The Yakṣas and Yakṣinīs were malevolent deities of primitive tribal conception and were worshipped in every village. Later they held a very important place in Buddhist, Jain and Brahmanical myths and legends. They were conceived of as having a physical form of large proportions and huge bulk. Since they owed their existence to primitive tribal imagination, they had a heavy earthy character of form as is found in their sculptural representations. Buddhism and Jainism, and also Vaiṣṇavism and Śaivism, incorporated a large portion of the tribal cults, all of which were cleverly woven into the texture of intellectual and rational scheme of doctrines. As a result, the old religious systems made their appearance in new and sophisticated garments, a fact which may easily be demonstrated with reference to Buddhism.

Soon after the Buddha's death, his scattered sayings relating to Sutta and Vinaya were put together in the first council. About a century thereafter, in the second council held at Vaiśālī, the Buddhist church split into two groups—the Sthaviras and the Mahāsaṅghikas. The former gradually became divided into eleven sects and the latter into seven. All the eighteen sects were fundamentally Hīnayānists. keeping the religion confined exclusively among the monks, the common people were only allowed to take the *triśaraṇa*, put candles around the *stūpas* and offer gifts to the *saṃgha*. There was no provision for organised worship or ritual. However, a few subsects of the Mahāsaṅgika group introduced new doctrines paving the way for Mahāyānism which probably blossomed in its full form from about the first century in the Andhra country. It became a recognised form of Buddhism in the time of Kaniṣka and then it spread all over northern India in the first and the second century A.D. Mahāyānism was characterised by the deification of the Buddha, the concept of the Bodhisattvas and the doctrine of the void or Śūnyatā. The Buddha was conceived of not only as *lokottara* or super-human but also as the highest god pervading and controlling the universe. The idea of the three bodies of Buddha—the *dharma* body representing the cosmic principle, the *sambhoga* body the divine principle, and the *rūpa* body the human incarnation—became popular. The early Buddhist monuments of Sanchi, Bharhut, Bodhgaya, Amaravati and other places were mostly *stūpas* or funerary structures, encircled by railings and gateways containing carvings associated with episodes of the Buddha's life. In the earlier reliefs the person of the Buddha was indicated by symbols and not by icons. But very soon image worship became popular among the Buddhists. The iconographic types—*sthānaka* (standing), *āsana* (seated), and *śayana* (recumbent)—of the Buddha made their appearance apparently simultaneously in the Hellenistic school of Gandhara and the Indian school of Mathura, both belonging to the post-Mauryan period.

Jainism, on the other hand, theoretically maintained its earlier tradition but the ever-increasing influence of the idea of devotion to a personal god eventually attributed the characteristics of a Supreme Being to the Jinas. Epigraphic evidence suggests that the practice of image worship was current among the Jains even in pre-Mauryan times. There is a reference in the

Hathigumpha inscription to the removal of Jina image from Kaliṅga by a Nanda king and its subsequent recovery by Khāravela. The torso of a nude figure unearthed at Lohanipur near Patna seems to belong to the Maurya period. The Jina images, now preserved in the Mathura and Lucknow museums belong mostly to the Kuṣāṇa period as is proved by the pedestal inscriptions. Almost all the seated Jina figures in the Mathura museum show a wheel of law below the seat which is placed in the centre on a pillar and flanked on either side by a number of devotees. This depiction is suggestive of the development of a widespread *bhakti* cult among the Jains.

Besides the Stūpas, the Caitya halls and monasteries formed important monuments of the Buddhists and Jains. The Bhakti cult gave a great impetus to the construction of images and temples. It was the custom to erect, in front of the religious buildings *dhvajastambhas*, or columns, bearing the emblem of the deity. Such columns are specifically found in association with the Vaiṣṇavite cults. The facts obtained from the *Aṅguttara Nikāya* and the *Niddesa* commentary may be supplemented by those found in the *Mahābhārata* and the *Rāmāyaṇa* in both of which we notice Vaiṣṇavism and Saivism becoming more prominent and widespread than other cults. Between them they shared the allegiance of great masses of men. To the Vaiṣṇavas the *arcā* or *śrīvigraha* or the image was the god himself (*pratyakṣa-devatā*).

Religion of this period thus shows a qualitative transformation both in form and in content. To a certain extent this change was due to the patronage of the kings and the nobles without whose munificence it would have been difficult to excavate mountains to construct Caitya halls or erect religious buildings which came to be regarded as architectural wonders. But this patronage had important side-effects. With the massive extension of the patronage of the kings, nobles, bankers and merchants, these systems became highly institutionalised. They assumed the form of universal religions, with the doctrinal changes and sophistications required for this purpose just as had happened in the history of Christianity which became a universal religion after it was adopted and patronised by the Roman kings. Since the Kuṣāṇa kings especially favoured Buddhism and they had extra-Indian territories, it was easy for Buddhism to travel beyond the Indian borders to Central Asia, China and Tibet. At a later period, Vaiṣṇavism and Śaivism reached South East Asia. At the same time, a reverse process—from universalisation to localisation—could also be observed in the history of the religious systems. The existence of protracted imperial authority in a particular region being the exception rather than the rule in ancient India ensured that the centres of political power were subject to continuous shift from one region to another, and to a varying degree, as a consequence of which the flow of patronage in regard to a particular religion was very often arrested.

2. *Hinduism in the Making*

The spiritual quests which began under the shadow of the earlier Vedic and non-Vedic traditions eventually culminated in the formation of numerous theistic and antitheistic sects. Prominent among the former were the cults of Viṣṇu, Śiva, Śakti, Gaṇapati, Sūrya, Skanda-Kārtikeya and other deities, each of whom was regarded as the Supreme Being by the distinctive sectarian devotees and thought of as capable of bestowing grace when approached with reverence and devotion. The latter was represented by Buddhism, Jainism, Ājīvikism and a few other systems which approached the problems of life and the universe from a non-theistic point of view and insisted on a moral renaissance. The influence of all these systems in general on the masses varied both in extent and in degree. Despite functional differences, all these systems had many points in common.. All accepted the same basic concepts and their representative terms, the same logical system and the same fixed points of metaphysical speculation. The goal also was the same—*mokṣa* or liberation.

To a follower of Viṣṇu or Śiva, the Buddhist or Jain monks and their monasteries were objects of respect and veneration, while lay followers of Buddhism and Jainism were attracted by the doctrine of *bhakti*, which was an easier way to get rid of worldly suffering, and the worship of image. The Jains, strict though they were in regard to the ethical codes prescribed in their texts and did not allow any form of deviation, did not hesitate to allow image worship of the Tīrthaṃkaras and also of gods of the existing systems as idealised human beings. They erected temples as well, and appointed priests who were mostly Brāhmaṇas. In Buddhism, the elaborate growth of Mahāyānism was a triumph of the *bhakti* cult. Besides the deified Dhyānī Buddhas and the Bodhisattvas, innumerable other gods and goddesses also made an appearance. The Buddhist and Jain deities were also worshipped by the non-Buddhists and non-Jains, despite obligations to their own sectarian cults. On a higher plane, the Buddhist and Jain logicians and philosophers were held in high esteem by their non-Buddhist and non-Jain counterparts. Their works were studied with great care. In fact, Hindu logical literature was thoroughly influenced by the Jain logicians. Without the Mādhyamika and Yogācāra schools of Buddhism, there could not have been such an elaborate growth of the Vedānta in the subsequent history of Indian thought.

Both Buddhism and Jainism had a glorious career in the Gupta age. So far as the Hīnayāṇa is concerned, Sarvāstivāda was the most popular form. Vasubandhu's *Abhidharmakoṣa* composed about the fifth century A.D. is a classic in the scriptural history of the Buddhists. Although it belonged basically to the Vaibhāṣika school of the Sarvāstivādins, it is studied even today by the monks of both Hīnayāna and Mahāyāna. The other branch of the Sarvāstivādins was represented by the Sautrantikas. The Mādhyamikas or Śūnyavādins of the Mahāyāna were enriched by the ideas of Nāgārjuna, Āryadeva, Mātṛceṭa, Rāhulabhadra, Kumārajīva, and others while the Yogācāras or Vijñānavādins were influenced by Maitreyanātha, Asaṅga, Guṇamati, Sthiramati, Diṅnāga and others. The Buddhist cave architecture of the Gupta age consisted of two conventional types, namely the Caitya hall or the shrine proper and the *saṅghārāma* or *vihāra, i.e.*, the monastery. The most notable groups are found in Ajanta, Ellora, Aurangabad and Bagh. The images of Buddha and Buddhist deities, numerous specimens of which have been discovered, fall into four groups of workmanship. These are represented respectively by the schools of Mathura, Sarnath, Eastern India and Deccan. The progress of Jainism also continued apace in the Gupta age. Two councils were held at Valabhī between the fourth and the sixth century A.D. in which the Śvetāmbara canon took its present shape. The great Jain logician Siddhasena Divākara flourished in the sixth century A.D. In the south the Digambara tradition was enriched by Kundakunda and his followers.

It is against this background that one has to understand the historical processes through which the development of Hinduism in the modern sense took place from the Gupta period and onwards. In the shaping of the mass-adaptability of heterogeneous religious elements the importance of the Purāṇas is most significant. In fact, the Purāṇas as well as the two great epics, "afford us far greater insight into all aspects and phases of Hinduism—its mythology, its idol worship, its theism and pantheism, its love of God, its philosophy and its superstitions, its festivals and ceremonies and its ethics, than any other works" (Winternitz, *HIL*, I. 529). The Puranic legends pertaining to different cults and sects, which were by nature very interesting and instructive, had a great appeal for the masses. Various ideals thus preached through the Purāṇas, wonderfully blended with entertaining episodes, prepared the substratum of what is known as popular Hinduism. The basic ground on which most of the Indian religious systems met comprised the concept of suffering and liberation, worldly fetters, the doctrine of *Karma* and rebirth, recognition of all accepted cults belonging to the people at various cultural levels, insistence on *bhakti* or devotion to the personal god (*iṣṭadevatā*), efficacy of temple and image worship and the way of life upheld by the Smṛti texts. Since most of the religious systems subscribed to all these points—Buddhism and Jainism being no exception—there was no difficulty in the development of that catholicity and spirit of tolerance by which Hinduism still stands unique. Buddhism was basically a religion of the monks and, unlike Islam or Christianity, it could offer no social code to its lay devotees who were free to follow the traditional social rules later regularised by the Smṛtis. Although theoretically it was opposed to the caste system, Buddhism could not change it because it was nobody's creation. The writers of the Smṛti texts did not invent it; they only legitimatised it. So the lay worshipper of Avalokiteśvara or Tārā, the personal deities that bestow grace like Viṣṇu or Śiva, was otherwise a Hindu following the Smārta-puranic way of life. And this was one of the reasons for the metamorphosis of Buddhism in India.

Jainism, on the other hand, was able, though to a limited extent, to withstand the tremendous influence of popular Hinduism because it was able to present a social code and various norms of individual and social behaviour to its lay devotees. The Jain social code, however, does not differ very much from that upheld by the Smṛti texts. The Jains are theoretically opposed to the caste system, but eighty-four Jain castes have been recorded. Jain personal laws are very similar to those prescribed by the Smṛtis.

Another important element which made its way into all the major and minor religious systems of India was the concept of the Female Principle. Evolving out of the prehistoric Mother Goddess cult symbolising the facts of primitive agricultural life, it had a manifold development—not through any particular channel but like a lot of streams, some big some small, issuing from a single source. It brought about a qualitative change in the traditional structure of theism which was admitted by all the religious systems, and resulted in the expansion of the horizon of Hindu catholicity. Here the Supreme Being manifests Itself in creation through *Sakti* or energy, viewed in terms of an eternally existing Female Principle, which is inseparable from It, just as heat from fire, yet having different functions. Symbolically, the act of creation was due to the union of the Female and Male Principle, the former being the more important functionary. In Mahāyāna Buddhism these two Principles are known as Prajñā and Upāya, or as Śūṇyatā and Karuṇā respectively. In Vaisnavism they are Lakṣmī and Viṣṇu and in Śáivism Śakti and Śiva.

3. *Neo-Bhakti Movements from South: The Nāyanārs and the Āḷvars*

While the Gupta and post-Gupta ages were characterised by an apparently sophisticated approach towards religious beliefs and practices, as was manifested by a process of institutionalism in the way of establishing organisations, monastic or otherwise, erecting temples and buildings of gigantic structures, constructing of a bewildering variety of images and receiving generous endowments from the princes and the nobility, the concept of a non-formal and personal approach towards the divine was gaining ground among the masses. The supreme being, whether approached in the first instance as Viṣṇu or Śiva, was a beloved to be wooed with love and devotion. The concept was not new; it lay at the root of all theistic religions. However, this non-formal approach had been replaced by an elaborate growth of institutionalism, organised priesthood, rigid codification and sectarianism. But such overgrowths did not bother the people at large. To them a visit to the temple, performance of rites, offering a fee for worship, pilgrimage, and other allied religious duties were routine acts which thus believed would earn for them some spiritual dividend. All these they learnt from the recitals of the Epics and the Purāṇas which had imprinted in their minds the utility and sanctity of the personal and social codes prescribed by the Dharmaśāstras on the one hand, and the efficacy of the doctrine of *bhakti* on the other. But in the latter case there had always been an inconsistency, because pure *bhakti* implied sharp ciriticism and rejection of all external formalities in regard to religious practices and spiritual quests.

The concept of pure *bhakti* in the form of the experience of the Supreme Being, of any sect or cult was revived by the Śaiva Nāyanārs and the Vaiṣṇava Aḷvārs of South India. These god-intoxicated people projected the experience as one of inexpressible happiness and ineffable radiance, waveless equipoise, absolute peace and tranquillity, and of absolute non-duality or complete unity. They transmitted their divine infatuation to millions of their contemporaries through their devotional songs. The collection and preservation of this priceless legacy of devotional poetry was possible because of the labour of the Śaiva saint Nāmbi-Āṇaḍr-Nāmbi and the Vaiṣṇava saint Śrī Nāthamuni. The former arranged the available Śaiva hymns into eleven *Tirumurais* while the latter the extant Vaiṣṇava poems into a colossal collection called *Nālāyira Prabandham*

Among the Śaiva saints, Tirumular flourished in the sixth century A.D. His work, known as *Tirumandiram*, is made up of 3000 verses and is regarded as the tenth *Tirumurai* according to Nāmbi's arrangement of the collection. Appār, Sambandar, and Māṇikkavacagar belonged to the seventh century while Sundarar to the first quarter of the eighth century. Māṇikkavacagar was born of Brāhmaṇa parents and became the prime minister of a Pandyan king. The story of his life and renunciation is found in two Tamil Purāṇas named *Tiruvilaiyadal* and *Vadavurar*.

The collection of his fifty-one songs is known as *Tiruvācakam*. It forms the eighth volume of Nambi's *Tirumurai*. It is said that *Tiruvācakam* is the quintessence of Tamil Saivism. The verses of Appar, Sambandar and Sundarar have been incorporated in the first seven *Tīrumurais*, collectively known as *Tevaram*. Appar was Vellala by çaste; his ancestral calling was agriculture. His contribution to the *Tevaram* consists of 313 poems characterised by down to earth similies and images bespeaking a ripe wisdom and experience. Sambandar and Sundarar died young; 384 poems of the former and nearly 100 of the latter survive. The mellifluous sweetness of Sambandar's poems and Sundarar's hunting lullabies of love are on every devout Tamil *bhakta's* lips even to this day and are sung by musicians.

The Vaiṣṇava Āḷvārs flourished in the period between 500 and A.D. 850 They hailed from different parts of the Tamil country and belonged to a variety of castes. The first three Āḷvars, Poykai, Bhūtattār and Periāḷvār have contributed one hundred stanzas each in *venba* in praise of Tirumal. The fourth was Tirumalisai who sang of single-minded devotion and firm faith, his chosen deity being Nārāyaṇa. Of the five Āḷvārs in the second group, Nammāḷvār and Madhurakavi were great mystics. Nammāḷvār's contribution to the *Nālāyira Prabandham* consists of the whole of the fourth part called *Tiruvāymoli*. His disciple Madhurakavi wrote that Nammāḷvār poured the cream of the Vedas into his songs. Periyāḷvār contributed about five hundred hymns remarkable for their earnestness, learning, descriptive power and metric versatility. His most famous song is Tiruppalladu. He lived in the Ramnad district. He also composed the *Tirumoli*, a splendid imaginative recreation of Lord Kṛṣṇa's life. His daughter was Āṇḍāl who in her poems saw herself as a Gopī of Kṛṣṇa. Of her two works, *Nācchiyār Tirumoḷi* and *Tiruppāvai*, the latter is more famous. Kulaśekhara, the remaining member of the second group was a king of Travancore. His *Perumāḷ Tirumoḷi* consists of 103 stanzas. Of the three Āḷvārs in the third group, Tiruppan was a member of the so-called untouchable caste. His work is known as *Amalanādippirān*. Toṇḍaraḍippodi wrote two celebrated hymns known as *Tirumāḷai* and *Tiruppaḷi Yeḷucci*. The last Aḷvār was Tirumangai who composed no less than 1,351 stanzas. It is apparent that because of the Āḷvars, their successors, the celebrated Vaiṣṇava Ācāryas of the South, were able to add new dimensions to later Vaiṣṇavism.

4. Jainism: Religion of the Merchants

We have already had occasion to refer to the fact that from the earliest period Jainism was favoured by the trading communities. One should not fail to notice that in the five vows meant for householders, which have been specified in texts like the *Uvāsagadasāo*, restrictions are mainly taken from agricultural and commercial activities. Thus gross offence against living beings is committed by fettering, beating, wounding, overloading and cruelty, especially with reference to animals used in agriculture and trade. Likewise, gross untruthfulness is understood to be falsely accusing a person, passing wrong judgements, forgery, etc. Gross appropriation consists in receiving, or dealing in, stolen goods, in theft and other illegal economic transactions, in using false weights and measures, in adulteration of goods, etc. Gross sensuality consists in offences against matrimonial faith: adultery, harlotism, incest, etc. Gross greed is understood in terms of attachment to gold, cattle, estate, carriage, jewellery, etc. All these restrictions openly suggest the ideological association of Jainism with the commercial classes.

The localisation of Jainism in those regions which were characterised by commercial enterprises also suggests the same. From epigraphic evidence it appears that the Gaṅga kings of Karṇāṭaka were patrons of Jainism. There is a tradition that the Jain saint Siṃhanandī gave a kingdom to Koṅgunivarma, the founder of the Gaṅga line, and this is supported by a few inscriptions. The commercial city of Perur was a base of Jain activity. Some of the Kadamba rulers of the Konkan coast were also patrons of Jainism as is proved by their inscriptions. A stone inscription dated at A.D. 1129 connects the Rāṣṭrakūta king Dantidurga with the Jain scholar Akalaṅkadeva. King Amoghavarṣa was a devout Jain and a disciple of Jinasena. Kṛṣṇa II made a great endowment to a Jain settlement at Mulkund, while Indra IV died by the Jain method of *sellekhanā* at Sravana Belgola. The Western Cālukyas showed the same liberal attitude towards Jainism which the Gaṅgas, the

Kadambas and the Rāṣṭrakutas had shown as is proved by the inscriptions of the Western Cālukya kings. Some of the Eastern Cālukya kings were patrons of Jainism. Three records of Ammarāja II speak of Jainism as a very popular religion in the tenth century. Later, the torch of Jainism was carried by the Hoysalas. Epigraphic as well as literary evidence suggests that from the eighth century onwards, Jainism was patronised by the Cāpas, Pratīhāras, and Caulukyas in the north. From about this period to the end of the thirteenth century, attempts were made even by the feudatories of the Karṇāṭaka monarchs to popularise Jainism as numerous inscriptions testify. Here we may refer to the Gaṅga feudatories of the Pasindi family, of the Rāṣṭrakūṭa feudatory Cākirāja, the Cellapataka noble Lokāditya, the Santara lords, the Koṅgalvas, the Cāṅgalvas, the Śīlāhāras of Karhad, the Raṭṭas of Saundatti, the nobles of Nagarakhaṇḍa, the Yādava noble Kucirāja, etc. Similarly individuals of wealth and fame contributed immensely to the cause of Jainism; in this connection we may especially refer to the celebrated Cāmuṇḍa Rāya.

In the south the chief centre of Jainism was Sravana Belgola where numerous Jain shrines were constructed in medieval and later times. Ordinary temples which contain only the image of a Jina are known as Basti, while the specially arranged kind—consisting of cloisters around an open courtyard with a colossal statue—is called Betta. A remarkable example of this is found on the summit of a hill at Sravana Belgola where the topmost section of the granite hill is fashioned into a gigantic statue of Gommaṭeśvara. Some of the Jain temples at Deogarh fort, Jhansi district, contain well known figures of Jain mythology besides the images of the Jinas. Most famous of all are the temples of Mount Abu. The Delwara group consists of four temples displaying some of the finest examples of Jain sculptures, noted chiefly for their exquisite delicacy of carving. Of other interesting Jain temples mention may be made of the shrines of Kumbharia in north Gujarat, belonging to twelfth and thirteenth centuries; the Kumarapāla temples on the Taranga hill; the temple at Sarotra in north Gujarat; and above all, the temple city of Śatruñjaya in Saurastra. The hill in Girnar, not far from Junagarh, contains a group of Jain temples, some sixteen in number.

The eleventh, twelfth and thirteenth centuries saw Jain prosperity at its zenith and it found expression in the building of the cities of temples. Although the Jains did not develop any distinct style of their own in the field of architecture, yet it must be said to their credit that they produced numerous fine specimens in different parts of the country. The marble temples at Mount Abu, the Ranapur temple in Mewar, the Pārśvanātha temple at Khajuraho, the Lakkundi temple in Karṇāṭaka etc. are some outstanding examples. Mercantile affluence undoubtedly contributed great impetus in the construction of these temples.

The contribution of the Jains to the growth and development of literature in regional languages was also immense. Only the Jains utilised different regional languages for their religious propaganda as well as for the preservation of knowledge. The result was that regional languages like the Hindi, Gujarati, Kannada, Tamil, Telugu and others became enriched. In addition, the Jain establishments undertook social work and charity, thanks to the munificence of their patrons, in an organised way. The concept of organised welfare activities was lacking among other religious systems which advocated individual kindness in order to earn spiritual merit. The Jain *maṭhas*, as a rule, offered food (*āhāra*), protection (*abhaya*), medicine (*auṣadha*) and learning (*śāstra*) to the distressed irrespective of religion, caste or creed. In fact, in order to curb the influence of Jains, the southern Śaiva schools later adopted this four-fold system of social welfare.

The history of Jainism is a history of long struggle. It made its way into the religious life of India after overcoming the tremendous pressure of its rival creed Buddhism. Theoretical opposition came from Brahmanism, as is attested by the long history of philosophical controversies. The Jains had to undergo strenuous ideological struggles against opponents of Śankarācārya's stature and in the process they produced a galaxy of logicians. In south India they had to fight against the Vīraśaivas. In the north they were persecuted by the Turks who destroyed their temples and converted them into mosques. Despite all these obstacles the Jains were able to maintain their existence as a distinct and influential community. Of the many reasons attributed to the survival of the Jain community, the following may be taken into account. The royal patronage which Jainism received, from some non-Jain rulers, during the ancient and medieval period, in different parts of the country, especially in Karṇāṭaka, Gujarat and Rajasthan, undoubtedly helped the Jain community in its struggle for survival. Secondly, since the Jains mostly belonged to the commercial class, their economic influence upon society could not be ignored even by rulers belonging to hostile creeds. Thirdly, after the Muslim conquest, the Jains earned the goodwill of the Hindus, and *vice versa*, and this evidently added new strength to the community. And lastly, thanks to their rigid conservatism, their important religious doctrines have remained unaltered up to this day. The excellent organisation of the community, the strict disciplinary measures like excommunication for the breach of the rules of conduct, etc., are the strongest safeguards of the Jains.

5. *New Theoretical Orientation of the Hindu Sects*

From approximately the tenth century onwards, the Hindu religious sects, especially those of the Vaiṣṇavas and Śaivas, acquired a new theoretical orientation. There was an increasing dependence on the theistic interpretation of the Vedānta according to which the entire creative process was the self-expression of *brahman*. This *brahman* was invested with a distinct personality, and was called Īśvara, who appeared under different names and with whom the great gods of the sectarian religions were identified. Secondly, there was a vigorous attempt to associate the concept of *śakti* with the creative process emanating from *brahman*. This concept of *śakti* as the energy of *brahman* must have received a fillip from the earlier Vedantic notion of *māyā*, the illusory material principle projected to explain the emergence of the unreal world. Also pre-existing influence of Śākta-Tāntric ideas and that of Mahāyāna Buddhism in which the doctrine of *śakti* had made its way cannot be ignored.

Rāmānuja (A.D. 1016-1137), the greatest exponent of the Śrīvaiṣṇava sect interpreted the main tenets of Vaiṣṇavism along Vedāntic lines. According to Śankara, since *brahman* is one and without a second, there can be no reality apart from *brahman*, and hence the material world is a misconception which has developed out of a false sense of duality. A dualistic approach, on the other hand, has been put forward by Bhāskara; this emphasises the transformation (*pariṇāma*) of *brahman* and holds that the material world has real existence though it is essentially of the same nature as *brahman*. Rāmānuja's interpretation falls in between these two lines and that is why it is known as Visiṣṭādvaita. According to him, *brahman* is without a second, but becomes the manifold of the sentient and non-sentient beings, the purpose of which is to give an opportunity to finite beings to realise their divine destiny. He assumes three forms: *bhoktā* or the enjoyer manifested in *cit* or individual souls, *bhogya* or the enjoyable manifested in *acit* or the material world, and *prerita* manifested in Īśvara or Paramātman, the cause of creation, preservation and destruction. This *brahman* is none other than Viṣṇu and his *śakti* is Lakṣmī. The relation between Viṣṇu and his energy or *śakti* is one of inseparable connection like that of substance and quality. The Śrīvaiṣṇavas were divided into two groups—Vaḍakalai and Ṭenkalai. The former depended on the Brahmanical tradition, Brahmanical social and legal system and Sanskrit language, and the latter on non-Brahmanical and non-Sanskritic traditions. The Ṭenkalai group was more liberal in social outlook and did not believe in the external formalities in regard to spiritual quest. The Vaḍakalai group believed in the *markata-mārga* (the devotee should cling to God just as a monkey-child clings to its mother) while the Ṭenkalai group believed in *mārjāra-mārga* (the devotee should remain effortless and surrender to God's will just as a kitten remains quite passive in its mother's mouth when she carries it from one place to another).

Nimbārka (twelfth century) was another great exponent of Southern Vaiṣṇavism though his disciples were mostly north Indians. His philosophy was known as Davitādvaita and the sect which he founded was called Sanaka Sampradāya. According to him *brahman* is both the material (*upādāna*) and instrumental (*nimitta*) cause of the world. *Brahman* is not the impersonal absolute, but a personal god. At the beginning of creation he manifests his *cit-śakti* (power of sentience) and *acit-śakti* (power of non-sentience) in the forms of soul (*jīva*) and matter (*prakṛti*), and from the latter there is a gradual evolution of the material world. Since there is always a difference between the cause and the effect, there must be some difference between *brahman* and the world. Again the non-difference between them is no less true since the essence of the effect is the cause itself. The cause-effect relation between *brahman* and the world is that of identity-in-difference. Creation is due not to any need felt by God but merely for his sport. This God is Kṛṣṇa and his *śakti* is Rādhā.

Madhva, the expounder of the Dvaita or the dualistic school and the founder of the Brahma sect, flourished in Karṇāṭaka about the beginning of the thirteenth century. According to him, *brahman* is *alaukika* (transcendent) and hence empirical knowledge will not help in determining his position. The world of *cetana* (sentient) and *acetana* (non-sentient) is real, essentially *paratantra* or dependent having derived its reality from *brahman* who is none other than Viṣṇu whose *śakti* is Lakṣmī. The sect founded by Madhva was subdivided into two groups Vyāsakūṭa and Dāsakūṭa. The former was conservative like the Vaḍakalai of the Śrīvaiṣṇavas while the latter was liberal.

Saivism in South India received much inspiration from the Nāyanār saints. The devotional tradition created by them was later developed into a religio-philosophical system called Śaiva Siddhānta through the efforts of Myekaṇḍadeva and his followers. According to the Śaiva Siddhānta, Prakṛti, the material cause of the universe, is unconscious like clay and so it cannot organise itself into the world. As a jar has the potter for its efficient cause, the staff and wheel for its instrumental cause, and clay for material cause, so also the world has *brahman* or Śiva for its efficient cause, *śakti* for its instrumental cause and *māyā* for its material cause. The Śaiva Siddhānta explains the evolution of the world in terms of thirty-six principles. In the practical aspects of religion the followers of the Śaiva Siddhānta school believe in absolute devotion. In the first stage the devotee should feel like a servant of God, in the second stage as his son, in the third stage as his associate and in the fourth as identical with him. These stages are known as *sālokya*, *sāmīpya*, *sārūpya* and *sāyujya*. The Vaiṣṇavas also believe in these four stages of devotion.

The Āgamānta Śaivas were very much influenced by Tantric ideas. This sect flourished from about the eleventh century and had its original centre at Mantrakali on the Godavari. The

Cola kings were patrons of Āgamānta Śaivism. This sect did not attach any importance to the Vedas. They did not believe in the caste system and the Brahmanical tradition. That is why their opponents called them Apamārgīs, Nāstikas, Śūdras, etc. A follower of this creed required the guidance of a teacher and had to undergo various forms of initiation or *dīkṣā*. In their opinion *brahman* or Śiva proceeds to the way of creation being influenced by the *karma* of individual souls. They hold that God and individual souls are different entities and that material cause of the world is *māyā*. The individuals are bonded with numerous fetters and by the grace of Śiva alone can they get rid of them.

Liṅgāyata or Vīraśaiva is a militant form of Śaivism which flourished in the Karṇāṭaka region about the twelfth century A.D. under the leadership of Vasava, a Kannadam Brāhmaṇa whose purpose was to establish an ideal society. The Vīraśaivas, irrespective of sex, carry with them a small *śivaliṅga*. Their attitude towards the Vedas is that of indifference. They have a special tendency towards social reforms. They do not believe in caste and are opposed to smoking and drinking. They believe in the equality of men and women. They support female education and widow remarriage and actively attend to the poor and oppressed peoples. It is the compulsory duty of Vīraśaiva to help the poor with food, water, medicine and education. According to the Vīraśaivas, the source and support of all phenomenal existence is *sthala*. *Stha* denotes *sthiti* or existence, and *la* denotes *laya* or dissolution. The Vīraśaiva philosophers start with the notion that this *sthala* represents the absolute and eternal self-consciousness, but they deny that in this condition the distinction of matter and form is abolished. The potential and material movement of the absolute is called Śiva while its actual and formal movement is called Śakti. Śiva as *brahman* is both the material and efficient cause of the world; through his *śakti* he is material cause and in his own nature the efficient cause. The relation is relative and not indicative of a real difference for there is identity between *śakti* and *śaktimat*, as between attribute and substance. Here greater emphasis is laid upon the concept of *śakti* in its *vimarśa* or vibrating form. The real nature of *brahman* is like the luminescence of a gem which the gem itself cannot realise. This realisation is possible only by *śakti*. That is why the relation between Śiva and Śakti is that of identity, *tādātmya* or *sāmarasya*, as that between heat and fire, light and sun, and so on.

A special form of Śaivism flourished in the Kashmir region from about the ninth century A.D. This was known as Kashmir Śaivism. Its exponents, such as Vasugupta, Somananda, Abhinavagupta, Kṣemarāja, etc., are reputed names also in the Tantric tradition. Kashmir Saivism does not believe in the caste system or in the authority of the Vedas. There are three principles of Kashmir Saivism—Trika, Spanda and Pratyabhijñā. Trika is the theory of Pati (God), Pāśa (worldly fetters) and Paśu (the individual soul) which is the infrastructure of all forms of Śaivism. Spanda is that process through which Śiva is manifested in the form of the individual souls and the world. Pratyabhijñā is the means of realising the experience of Śiva's identity with the individual souls. Śiva or *brahman* is the self of all beings, immutable and ever perfect. He is both immanent and transcendent, the material as well as the efficient cause of the world. Diverse conditions are all of Śiva just as diverse products of the sugarcane belong to the sugarcane itself. The creation theory is known as *ābhāsavāda*, a view which holds that the universe consists of appearances, but these are all real in the sense that they are aspects of the ultimate reality. The manifestation of the universe is effected through the *śakti* of Śiva which is not different from him. With the opening out of *śakti*, the world appears, and with her closing, it disappears. The static energy is known as *prakāśa* and the vibrating energy is *vimarśa*. The former is the store of energy while the latter is its awareness. According to Kashmir Saivism, the realisation of identity with Śiva is the way to become free from worldly fetters. No importance is attached to ceremonial worship, disciplinary practices and rituals.

The main contention of what we call the Śākta standpoint is that the ultimate reality is the *prakāśa* aspect of the supreme being; it is beyond time and space and is of the nature of pure consciousness. What is known as *vimarśa* is the independence of this *prakāśa* in relation to action, but in reality the *vimarśa-śakti* is the self of *prakāśa*, standing in inseparable and completely identical relation. When Śakti becomes active the supreme being becomes conscious. Its self-knowledge then manifests itself as *aham*. The whole universe is reflected in this *aham* like objects reflected in a mirror. The supreme being, whose *prakāśa* is Śiva and *vimarśa* is Śakti, is at the same time transcendent and immanent. According to the Śrīkula school, *brahman* or Śiva is the material and efficient cause of the world. Its approach towards the relation between *brahman* and the world is almost the same as that of Viśiṣṭādvaita. On the other hand, according to the Kālikula school, Śakti is the same as *brahman* in its three aspects of *sat* (real), *cit* (consciousness) and *ānanda* (bliss) but not its *māyā-vivarta* or transformatory aspect.

The five major cults of Hinduism—Vaiṣṇava, Śaiva, Śakti, Gāṇapatya and Saura—came to some sort of an understanding among themselves in the course of time as a result of which a composite religious system came into existence known as *pañcopāsanā*. It was settled that each sect should basically worship its own deity as the supreme being without disregarding the deities of others. One of the causes for the emergence of this united front was the Islamic onslaught. Secondly, whatever might have been the basic cause of the rise of these major sects, at a certain stage of their development they were all influenced by the theistic interpretation of the Vedānta. Their methods and arguments followed the same line. Philosophical and doctrinal terminologies were common to all of them. As a result a syncretistic outlook came into existence. Syncretistic icons, like those of Hari-Hara, Śiva-Śakti, Śiva-Sūrya, Viṣṇu-Sūrya, etc., were made and worshipped.

6. Metamorphosis of Buddhism

Referring to the fate of Buddhism and the causes of the survival of Jainism in India, H. Jacobi made an important comment: "It is evident that the lay part of the community was not regarded as outsiders, or only as friends and patrons of the order, as seems to have been the case in early Buddhism; their position was from the beginning well defined by religious duties and privileges; the bond which united them to the order of monks was an effective one—it cannot be doubted that this close union between laymen and monks brought about by the similarity of their religious duties, differing not in kind but in degree, had enabled Jainism to avoid fundamental changes within and to resist dangers from without for more than two thousand years, while Buddhism, being less exacting as regards to the laymen, underwent the most extraordinary evolutions and finally disappeared from the country of its origin." (*ERE*, VII, 470).

Buddhism may have undergone "the most extraordinary evolutions" but we cannot agree that it "disappeared from the country of its origin." In reality, the history of Buddhism is nothing but the history of metamorphoses of ideas, each stage of its transformation being marked by a qualitative change. Primitive Buddhism must have been negated to a certain extent by the Hīnayāna, and the latter by the Mahāyāna, although both these systems had preferred to work under the guise of a tradition set up by the Buddha containing some of the residues of the earlier forms. Likewise Vajrayāna negated Mahāyāna but allowed some of the elements of the latter to function. Subsequently, Vajrayāna was also negated by other forms of religious beliefs and practices in which the guise of Buddhism became redundant.

Vajrayāna represented the latest phases of Buddhism in India. The Mahāyānic principles of Śūnyatā and Karuṇā became Prajñā and Upāya in Vajrayāna, suggestive respectively of the Female and Male principles, the union of which, impersonated by the aspirant and his female partner, would provide maximum pleasure, right knowledge and experience of non-duality. The human body is the abode of all truth and therefore all the mysteries of the world should be explained in terms of those of the human body. This was the reasoning for the use of *kāya-sādhana* or disciplining of the body and sexo-yogic practices. The cultic position of Vajrayāna rested on the deified concept of Mahayanic Śūnyatā or vacuity, the real nature of things in the form of Ādi Buddha or Vajradhara and its emanations. An offshoot of this Vajrayāna was Kālacakrayāna according to which the universe with all its localities and objects is situated in the human body accelerated by Kāla or time, the controlling of which is possible by disciplining the vital winds in the nerves through *yogic* processes. By Kāla is denoted the ultimate immutable and unchanging reality of three kinds of existence, and as such the Kālacarkra is the same as the unity of Prajñā and Upāya.

Vajrayāna could not, however, avoid certain basic contradictions which were also inherent in the parent form of Mahāyāna. In order to give a popular character to Buddhism the Mahāyānists borrowed numerous popular elements, but they failed to synthesise the elements with the basic principles of Buddhism. On the one hand we have absolute idealism, the doctrine of illusion or vacuity and on the other numerous gods and goddesses—wild, rural and urban—and also a variety of rituals. The mixture was like that of oil and water. The followers of this creed justified their religious approach in the name of Buddha and utilised some of the earlier Buddhist terms and concepts to explain their standpoint. The five Dhyānī Buddhas, supposed to have been emanated from the Ādi-Buddha, represented the five *skandhas* or aggregates of existence of early Buddhism, and maintained their Śakits as consorts, Bodhisattvas and a number of their mental born male and female deities. Countless images of the Vajrāyāna deities have been discovered. Among these deities, those belonging to the abstract category eventually disapppeared from the religious panorama after the metamorphosis of Vajrayāna. But others that had popular or tribal base continued to survive in their original character though under changed names in a few cases. Certain deities made their way in from the existing non-Buddhist religious systems.

Śaivism absorbed many of the popular cults and rituals which were previously under the guardianship of Mahāyāna-Vajrayāna Buddhism. The Mahāyānic concept of Avalokiteśvara contributed greatly to the revived form of Śiva, especially in eastern India. This all-merciful Buddhist deity, who presided over almost all aspects of human life and activities, exerted a profound influence on the personality of Śiva. As in the case of Buddhism where male deities were regarded as forms of Lokeśvara and the female ones as those of Tārā, so also Śiva, officially or non-officially, was made to preside over numerous popular cults and rituals and was identified with all forms of local village male deities while the female ones came to be identified with his spouse Śakti or Devī. Enventually Śakti became the predominating partner.

The Vaiṣṇavas also did not lag behind in absorbing a few significant Buddhist elements. From the evidence of the *Gītagovinda* of Jayadeva it is clear that the followers of the Viṣṇu cult in the twelfth century did not hesitate to declare the Buddha as an incarnation of Viṣṇu and to introduce Buddhist Sahajayāna ideas into the creed. From the twelfth century onwards until the advent of Śri-Caitanya, Vaiṣṇavism was full of sexo-yogic practices which had their roots in the concept of the union of male and female principles symbolised by Kṛṣṇa and Rādhā, obviously inspired by the Buddhist concepts of Śūnyatā and Karuṇā, or Prajñā and Upāya. The Vaiṣṇava theory and practice of unconventional love (*parakīyā*) is a direct adaptation of the Sahajiyā Buddhist way of life.

Mahāyāna Buddhism in its later phase became a composite religious system of heterogeneous faiths and practices saturated with elements of esoterism, sex-rites, gods, demi-gods, demons, ghosts, magic, charms, sorcery, and what not. Sahajāyāna or Sahajiyā Buddhism was an offshoot of this composite system. There was an obvious link between Sahajayāna and various forms of Tantric Buddhism, but while the latter maintained more or less a technical character, confined among esoteric circles and secret societies, the former had wide acceptance among the masses. The followers of Sahajayāna did not believe in external formalities, rituals, scriptural authority, celibacy, penances, austerities and the like. Sahaja etymologically means *saha-jāta*, that which is the same as human instinct itself. They believed in the recognition of the experience of the ultimate reality as one of infinite happiness. The union of Female and Male principles, Prajñā and Upāya, is a significant feature of Sahajayāna. The consideration of the human body and mind as the seat of all human experience including that of *sahaja-mahāsukha*, the greatest bliss is the easiest method. The Buddhist Sahajayāna concept of the male-female union in impersonation of Prajñā and Upāya was adopted by the Sahajiyā Vaiṣṇavas whose texts like *Dīpakojjvala*, *Ratavilāsapaddhati*, etc. refer to the union of men and women in two forms, *prākṛta* (natural) and *aprākṛta* (supernatural). The body is conceived as Vṛndāvana where resides *sahaja* in the nature of pure love which flows between Rādhā and Kṛṣṇa.

Apart from the Śaivas and Vaiṣṇavas there were other sects and religious communities which absorbed many ingredients of Buddhism. Tantric texts which have a Buddhist affiliation mention eighty-four Siddhas and the sects to which they belong. Most of these sects banked on the Sahajayāna tradition. Among the Nātha Siddhas, whose spiritual exercises contained a great deal of Buddhist rituals, Mīnanatha or Matsyendranātha was identified in the Nepalese and Tibetan traditions with Avalokiteśvara. The Buddhist influence in the cult of Dharma in Bengal has long been recognised. The ideological connection of the Bauls of Bengal with the Sahajiyā Buddhists cannot be ignored. There is also reason to hold that the cult of Pīrs and tombs which is so much popular among the Muslims of Bengal was due to the influence of the Buddhist converts to Islam. Leaving aside the question whether the five celebrated Pīrs were adaptations from the Pañcatathāgatas or five Dhyanī Buddhas, it may be said that the Buddhists, despite their conversion into Islam, did not give up their old religious practices like the cult of the dead saints in the *stūpa* worship and others. "A good many Buddhists appear to have been at least nominally converted into Islam after the establishment of the Turki-Muslim rule in Bengal. . . . But Bengali Buddhists (and Hindus) who adopted Islam did not and could not adapt their mental make-up to the atmosphere of Arabic or Irani or Turki Islam. Saint-worship through which their tombs (contemptuously described as *Pīr-pirāsti* or *Gor-pirāsti*, 'worship of saints', 'worship of tombs'), an Islamised version of the Buddhist worship of *stūpas* or *caityas* built over the ashes or relics of great teachers and saints forms an important cult in the Islam of Bengal and India: and it can legitimately be looked upon as an inheritance, Islamised no doubt, from Buddhist ritual and practice." (S.K. Chatterji, *BCLV*, I, 83).

10

Temples and Images

1. The Maurya and the post-Maurya Period

The link between the proto-historic and historical period of India, so far as the activities in the field of arts and crafts are concerned, is not absolutely missing, and the hiatus which is generally supposed to exist between the two may be ascribed to the fact that the intervening Vedic culture did not encourage the construction of religious buildings and cult-images which were the most popular mediums of artistic inspiration and expression. The post-Harappan Chalcolithic cultures and the subsequent stages of their development shows unbroken continuity in the pottery tradition, the changes in technique and design being due to the changing demand of time and regional variations. In the field of terracotta art, specimens of the Maurya-Śuṅga period found at Patna, Buxar, Taxila, Mathura, Ahicchatra, Basarh, Kosambi, Rajghat, Bangarh, Mahasthan, and various other sites show remarkable continuity with the earlier tradition. In fact, in this sphere, a single tradition persists which has remained essentially unchanged by variations of time and space.

The monolithic columns with animal capitals, chiselled out of grey Chunar sandstone and polished lustrously, found at Bakhira, Rampurwa, Lauriya Nandangarh, Rummindei, Saṁkisya, Sarnath, Sanchi and other places are the earliest specimens of Maurya court art. Earlier art historians favoured the idea that these were executed under Achaemenian influence, but closer scrutiny has revealed that there are basic differences in constructional techniques between the Mauryan columns and the Achaemenian ones. In the field of religious architecture, elementry Stūpas, the Caitya halls and the Vihāras began to make an appearance from the Maurya period. The Stūpas were hemispherical structures of brick or stone masonry which emerged as sophisticated forms of the primitive earthen funeral mounds and acquired a special religious significance owing to their association with the relics of the departed saints. The earlier types represented the simple structure of a hemispherical dome (*aṇḍa*) on a low circular base, surmounted by a square box (*harmikā*) and crowned by a parasol (*chatra*). In the course of time these were further decked with embellishment on and around them. The word 'Caitya' is a synonym of Stūpa, but Caitya-halls, meant for prayer and religious assembly, are indeed chapels hewn out of massive rock. They consisted of a long rectangular hall, rounded at the rear and divided internally into a nave or central hall, an apse, i.e., an arched or domed recess containing a Stūpa as the votive object, and two side aisles, separated from the nave by pillars. The Vihāras or Saṅghārāmas were monasteries for housing the monks. They were erected or excavated, or sized when caves were found, at convenient places according to the physical configuration of the rock. Later, elaborate brick structures came into existence.

The incipient stage of the construction of the Stūpas at Sanchi and its vicinity (collectively known as the Bhilsa topes), Bharhut, Manikyala, Amaravati, Bhattiprolu, Jaggayyapeta, Ghantasala, Nagarjunikonda, etc., may be assigned to c. 200 B.C. These were in all probability enclosed by a wooden fence, later replaced by a row of stone baluster with horizontal rails or cross-bars. On the four sides were gateways. The bas-reliefs on the upright pillars and posts of the gates and the railings at Bharhut, Bodh Gaya, Sanchi, Amaravati and other sites appear to have been executed in the first century B.C. Scenes from the Buddha's life, especially the ancedotes of his previous existences as found in the Jātaka stories, have been depicted in the bas-reliefs along with the traditional floral and geometrical designs as also the figures of the Yakṣas, Nāgas and other demi-gods. The Bharhut reliefs contain appropriate labels which are absent in those of Sanchi. In the Bodh Gaya bas-reliefs stories are told more summarily. The reliefs of

Jaggayyapeta, Amaravati, Nagarjunikonda, Goli, Gumadiduru, etc., also depict similar themes.

The Caitya-halls are splendid illustrations of rock-cut architecture, the earliest form of which is represented in the Barabar caves near Gaya. The next stage of evolution was marked by a qualitative change as is observed in Bhaja near Pune in the Western Ghats where twenty-seven pillars distinguish the central hall, the two side ways and the apsidal enclosure. The Caitya-halls at Kondane, Pitalkhora and Ajanta cave no. 10 belong to the same period as Bhaja and may be dated to the first half of the second century B.C. Next followed those of Bedsa, Nasik, Junner and Karle which were marked by a greater elaboration of different components and richer and more variegated ornamentation of the facade. Karle is the ideal example of Caitya-hall; it was completed about the first quarter of the second century A.D. The development of sculptural art on walls and pillars in the form of rock-cut reliefs, which is common to most Caitya-halls, finds perfection in Karle.

Vihāras or Saṅghārāmas or monasteries were attached to the Caitya-hall complex at many places. The Barabar and Nagarjuni groups of caves near Gaya, built for the use of the Ājīvika monks are the earliest examples of rock-cut monasteries. In Western India Bhaja, Bedsa, Ajanta, Kondane, Pitalkhora, Nasik, etc., are sites of Buddhist monasteries as well. The rock-cut Vihāra type in its most decorative form, particularly in the treatment of the facade, pillared verandah and the central hall, is found in Nasik and cave no. 10 of Ajanta. All these may be dated to c. second century A.D. At Karle, we find examples of storied Vihāras. The Jain caves at Udayagiri and Khandagiri near Bhuvaneswar, going back to the time of Khāravela, deserve special mention in this connection. They contain a number of sculptured friezes and panels. The Manchapuri cave relief in Udayagiri and the Anantagumpha reliefs in Khandagiri show an affinity with the art tradition of Sanchi. The long friezes of Rani-gumpha and Gaṇeśa-gumpha, belonging to the second century A.D., reveal some advancement in concept and representation though the workmanship is not subtle.

It is interesting to note that the earlier religious architecture belonged predominantly, if not exclusively, to the non-Brahmanical systems such as Buddhism and Jainism. The same also held good in the case of cult images. This was partly due to the fact that in the Vedic tradition such things were not encouraged. Buddhism and Jainism being monastic in character required buildings for accommodating the monks, halls for religious gatherings and organisational meetings, chapels for worship and so on which led to the construction of magnificent edifices. Even the Stūpa worship was an adaptation of pre-Vedic and non-Vedic religious practices. Buddhism and Jainism, because of their non-commitment to the Vedic tradition, made a compromise with the non-Vedic cults to attract votaries as a result of which the popular cults of Nāga, Yakṣa, Rakṣa, etc., made their way into these systems. The Yakṣa images, plastically round free standing statues of weighty volume, the earlier specimens of which have been found from Didarganj, Parkham, Baroda, Besnagar, Pawaya, Sanchi, Mathura and other places, became models for the Buddhist and Jain images. It should also be remembered that the *bhakti* cults like Vaiṣṇavism and Śaivism were probably inspired to construct *devagṛhas* (houses of gods) and erect *dhvajastambhas* at the instance of the Bhuddhists and the Jains. The latter on their part were influenced by the *arcā* (cult image in which the deity is supposed to reside) concept of the followers of the *bhakti* cults.

In the early bas reliefs of Sanchi or Bharhut, the Buddha is never represented in iconic form. His presence is indicated by means of various symbols. The Gandhara images of the Buddha and the Bodhisattvas began to make their appearance from about the middle of the first century B.C. and the Mathura images some time later. While the former school, owing to its Hellenistic inspiration, attained a sort of perfection in presenting the physique of the images in sophisticated appearance and expression, the latter school, which was closely linked with the existing tradition of image making, was able to uncover the inner sublimity notwithstanding a heavy earthiness in form. The Buddha figures in general are classified under three major types: standing (*sthānaka*), seated (*āsana*) and recumbent (*śayana*). The *mudrās* or hand poses of the seated Buddhas are generally in *abhaya* (protection), *dhyāna* (meditation), *bhūsparśa* (touching the earth) and *dharmacakra* or *vyākhyāna* (palms near the chest as if explaining something). The standing type of the Buddha is usually shown in *abhaya mudrā*, i.e., with the right hand raised in the attitude of protection. In the treatment of hair the Mathura images differ from the Gandhara convention. There are also other differences.

The torso of a nude Jina figure unearthed from Lohanipur in Patna, belonging to the Maurya period, as is indicated by its high polish, strikingly recalls the Harappan tradition. Mention has already been made of some early Jain reliefs in Khandagiri and Udayagiri belonging to the post-Maurya period. Besides a few Jain Stūpas, a number of well-carved Jina images and several votive tablets (*āyāgapaṭa*) with Jina figures in their centre, belonging to the beginning of the Christian era have been found in Mathura. The Jain images of Mathura, like their Buddhist counterparts, are also characterised by a certain heaviness of form, broad masculine chest and shoulders and a firm body. Almost all the seated Jina figures in the Mathura Museum can be dated to the Kuṣāṇa period on the basis of their pedestal inscriptions. The Yakṣas and Yakṣinīs are shown in the traditional composition to the right and left of their respective Jinas. When separately represented they are distinguished by their individual attributes and emblems as well as by the miniature figures of their respective Jinas either on their crown or on the topmost part of the stele.

Vaiṣṇava images belonging to the pre-Christian era are few and far between, as are the shrines. It was probably due to the fact that the earlier *bhakti* cults were not guided by well-knit organisations and that the shrines and images were made of perishable materials like wood or clay. Moreover, *arcā* or *vigraha* (cult image) being one of the principal requirements of the devotee, it was generally not possible for an average individual to make costly images in stone or metal. Images made of clay or wood thus served the purpose of their *vigraha* worship. Some fragmentary specimens obtained from the Mora site are preserved in the Mathura Museum. Some coins and seals of the first/second, century A.D. contain Viṣṇu images. One of the earliest Śaiva sculptures which represents Śiva in human as well as phallic form has been found at Gudimallam near Renigunta in Tamil Nadu. It is of the first century B.C. Śiva images are also found in coins, especially of the Kuṣāṇa period. Some pre-Christian Sūrya figures have been found. In a Bhaja relief the god is depicted in company with Uṣā and Pratyuṣā. The same theme recurs on one of the railing pillars at Bodh Gaya. The Mathura Museum contains a few Sūrya images in red sandstone belonging to the second/third century A.D. Śri or Lakṣmī, either seated or standing on a full-blown lotus and anointed with water by two elephants on either side of her, has been found in early coins and relief carvings.

There was not much scope for secular art, though the Mauryan columns and animal figures were not inconsiderable and gave a good start in a secular direction. The post-Maurya art stands for a different motive and significance based on religious themes, pertaining especially to Buddhism. In the bas-reliefs of Sanchi a rich world of flora and fauna finds a naturalistic expression. The human figure is not absent. At Karle we have the figures of a man and woman standing side by side in a slightly erotic pose. The top section of the pillars contains a sculptured group of a pair each of elephants and horses with riders. The heavy life-size statue of Kaṇiṣka belonging to the Mathura school should also be mentioned as a specimen of secular art. The southern tradition of the Vengi region is manifested in the marble reliefs of Jaggayyapeta and Amaravati; though they deal with a religious theme they can hardly be called religious because of the naturalistic and sensuous presentation. Post-Maurya art was not secular in the real sense of the term, but there was a tendency towards naturalism, a popular impulse towards beauty, a more elastic and elegant treatment in depicting human and animal life and vegetation. The human figure, in every conceivable position and attitude, began to receive greater importance. Free, proud, stately and heroic in the case of the males, and voluptuous with full round breasts and heavy hips, a coquettish and extravagant manner suggestive of warm, living flesh in the case of the females. Elephants, deer, antelopes, lotus-creepers, trees, plants and flowers in the beauty of their form and naturalness provided the background.

2. The Classical Period

From the time of the imperial Guptas there was a steady and multifarious growth in all spheres of art activities. This was the period which saw the amazing growth and culmination of rock-cut architecture. The prolification and elaboration of the Buddhist Caitya-halls and monasteries and the excavation of Jain and Brahmanical caves continued, though erection of the Stūpas received a diminishing importance. Only the Stūpas at Mirpur Khas in Sind and Dhamekh at Sarnath deserve special mention. In fact, the Stūpa, by itself, was no longer held to be important enough to claim the worship of the Buddhist votaries. The Buddha image required to sanctify it, as is evidenced by the addition of the Buddha image on the Stūpa altars at Ajanta and Ellora. This age witnessed the growth of the typical styles of Indian temple architecture. In the field of sculpture, the emphasis was on the human figure. The art of painting found expression in Ajanta, Bagh, Badami, Sittannavasal and a few other sites. Though the contents of the paintings are religious, the spirit is secular and aesthetic, limited to sensory experience.

The most remarkable among the Caitya-halls are those of Ajanta (caves 11 and 26) and Ellora (cave 10). The most significant innovation, noticed in the Caitya-halls of Ajanta, is the wealth of figure sculptures which are made to cover every possible space, both in the exterior facade as well as in the interior. The votive Stūpas in both the halls, which are overloaded with a wealth of carving, each show in front a figure of the Buddha in high relief. At Ellora the votive Stūpa has been completely relegated to the background, allowing space for a colossal image of a seated Buddha flanked by two standing attendants. Cave 19 of Ajanta also contains paintings among which the scene of the Master's return to Kapilavāstu reveals a mastery of style and thematic majesty.

The remaining twenty-seven caves of Ajanta are mostly Saṅghārāmas or Vihāras, planned in the form of rows of cells round a central hall. Cave 11 appears to have been the earliest of the series. Caves 1, 2, 16 and 17 contain paintings based on a variety of themes depicting the Jātakas stories, scences from the Buddha's life like the victory over Māra, the miracles, consecration, return to Kapilavāstu, turning of the wheel of law, scenes of Indra's abode, portrayals of his self and the Bodhisattvas, typical love-scenes, etc. The Vihāra caves at Bagh recall those of Ajanta in general plan and arrangement. Caves 3 and 4 of Bagh contain paintings. The paintings of cave 4 correspond to those of 1 and 2 of Ajanta. Among the twelve rock-cut caves of Aurangabad, only one is a Caitya cave, all the rest being Vihāras. At Ellora, twelve caves starting from the southern end are Buddhist. Most of them differ very little from the monastic caves at Ajanta. Cave 5, known as the Mahanwada, is rather exceptional because of its enormous dimensions. Caves 11 and12, known respectively as Don Thal and Tin Thal, are three-storeyed Besides the Buddhist and Brahmanical caves Ellora also has five Jain caves. There are also two Jain caves at Badmi and Aihole belonging to the middle of seventh century.

The earliest Brahmanical rock-cut shrines are those of Udayagiri near Bhilsa in Madhya Pradesh. The next phase is represented by those at Badami in the Bijapur district. These are provided with an open fore-court, pillared balcony, columned hall and square sanctum cella. The Badami group belongs to the sixth century A.D. In the eastern coast rock-cut architecture of the cave style was introduced by the Pallava kings during the sixth/seventh century A.D. A new style is found in the free-standing monolithic temples of Mamallapuram, which are popularly known as *rathas* and shaped from solid rock. With the exception of Draupadī *ratha*, the others have a pyramidal elevation and storyed arrangement, each storey being provided with a roll cornice decorated with miniature Caitya arches. A few of them with vaulted roofs and apsidal backs structurally resemble the Buddhist Caitya. Among the sixteen Brahmanical rock-cut shrines at Ellora. the Daśāvatāra, Rāvan-ka-khai, Rameśvara, Dhumar Lena and the celebrated Kailāśanātha are the most important. Among other important Brahmanical caves mention may be made of Elephanta, an island near Bombay, and Jogeśvara on the island of Salsette.

But the days of rock-cut construction were numbered. Suitable mountains with spacious solid rock sufficient to provide the required area for magnificent construction were becoming difficult to find. Ideally, the stone should be capable of being smoothly chiselled. That is why we come across many deserted sites where excavation was not possible. Thirldy, rock-cut constructions were enormously time-consuming. Often it took generations to get the work on a cave completed. Lastly, with the growing popularity of what is called Hinduism from the Gupta period onwards, cave excavations were found to be ill-suited for the ritualistic needs connected with the worship of images, and structural temples[9] were required for the enshrinement of the deity.

The structural temples which began to be constructed from the age of the imperial Guptas may be typologically divided into a few categories. To the first category belong those constructions which were modelled after the Caityas and the Stūpas. The Caitya model is found at Ter in the Sholapur district and Chezarla in the Krishna district in which the base is rectangular, the back apsidal and roof barrel vaulted. The Durga temple of Aihole (sixth century A.D.), which has a squat tower (*śikhara*) over the sanctum also belongs to this category though its roof is flat. The *stūpa* model is found in the Maniyar Math at Rajgir in which the base is circular. The second category is that of flat-roofed square temple with a shallow porch in front which is represented by the temples of Sanchi, Tigawa and Eran. The third category, represented by a few temples of Central India and Deccan (Nachna Kuthara, Bhumara, Lad Khan, Kont-Gudi, Meguti temples at Aihole, etc.), is characterised by a flat-roofed square structure with a covered ambulatory passage around the sanctum and a porch in front. The fourth category is characterised by the introduction of *śikhara* or tower that caps the sanctum which may be illustrated with reference to the Daśāvatāra temple at Deogarh in Jhansi district, Mahādeva temple at Nachna Kuthara and the brick temple at Bhitargaon in the Kanpur district. From these elementary categories were evolved the two important styles, Nāgara and Drāvida, which characterised the medieval temples of India.

The sculptural art of this period lays great emphasis on human body. Most sculptures are cult images in which the human figure is elevated to a subtle spirituality. Wood and clay were used for temporary cult images and stones for the permanent ones. Side by side, this age also witnessed the use of metal for making images and other cult objects. The terracotta tradition was continued. It was in the Gaṅgā valley and Bengal, where riverine plains ensured an inexhaustible supply of malleable earth and clay, that this art acquired a greater degree of perfection. Most of the important caves and temples mentioned above contain nice reliefs depicting a variety of Buddhist and Brahmanical legends and concepts. In the reliefs the animal and vegetal patterns of the earlier tradition are omitted from the narrative in which the human figures themselves convey the underlying message of the theme. Regional schools of sculpture also came into existence, among which the Sarnath and Mathura schools predominated in northern India.

Among the Buddha images, the colossal recumbent figure found at Kasia, made by Dinna of Mathura in the early Gupta period, shows a rare type. The Mathura school is also represented by the seated image from Mankuwar of about A.D. 448-49 and a few other images. The Buddha images of the Sarnath school are characterised by curly hair, absence of *urṇā*, greater variety of *mudrās*, robes covering one or both shoulders and an elaborately decorated nimbus. The Sarnath school also produced Bodhisattva images with miniature figures of their respective spiritual fathers, the Dhyānī Buddhas, on their crown. The Khandagiri caves at Bhuvaneswar contain some standing and seated Jina images of the later Gupta period. The northernmost cave, known as Satghara, contains rows of Jain carvings showing the Jinas along with their associates, a few of them signifying association with Brahmanical cults and concepts like Saptamātṛkā, etc.

The Viṣṇu images are divided into three broad classes: the principal Viṣṇu icons (*dhrūva-bera*), the emanatory forms (*vyuha*); and the incarnatory forms (*vibhava*). The first of them (*dhrūva-bera*) is divided into three groups, namely, standing (*sthānaka*), seated (*āsana*) and recumbent (*śayana*). The standing images which are more numerous, are attended on either side by Śrī and Puṣṭi in northern India and Śrī and Būmi in the south. One of the earliest *sthānaka* Viṣṇu images is found carved on the facade of the cave temple at Udayagiri near Bhopal. The *āsana* or seated images are not so numerous, prominent among them being the Yogāsana Viṣṇu of the Curzon Museum at Mathura, the Deogarh temple image seated on serpent coils and the Garuḍāsana image (seated on Garuḍa) found at Lakshmankhati in Barisal district, Bangladesh. An early recumbent type (Viṣṇu lying in the fold of Ādiśeṣa serpent being attended by his spouse), belonging to the Gupta period is found in a relief in the Daśāvatāra temple at Deogarh in Jhansi district. The second category of emanatory forms (*vyūha*), in which the four *vyūhas*—Vāsudeva, Saṅkaraṣaṇa Aniruddha and Pradyuma—are juxtaposed in a four-headed eight-armed figure became popular in a later period, especially in the Kashmir region, and came to be known as Visnu-Caturmūrti. The third category, *vibhava* or incarnatory form (the Avatāras of Viṣṇu) is very frequent and found carved in the rock-cut temples at Udayagiri, Badami and Mamallapuram belonging to the Gupta, early Cālukya and Pallava periods respectively.

One of the earliest *liṅgodbhava-mūrtis* of Śiva (i.e., the column-like phallus being measured by Brahmā on the top and Viṣṇu on the bottom) is found in the Daśāvatāra cave at Ellora. The anthropomorphic figures of Śiva are of various types. An image representing Śiva and Umā standing side by side, belonging to the time of Skandagupta, has been found from Kosam and is now in the Indian Museum, Calcutta. Seated figures of Śiva and Umā, accompanied by their attendants, are found at Ellora. The *ardhanāriśvara* images (composite figure possessing all the iconographic features of Śiva on the right half and those of Umā on the left half) are numerous. The Badami Ardhanārīśvara stone panel is fairly representative. Images showing syncretism of Vaiṣṇavism and Śaivism may be illustrated with reference to Harihara images of Śiva. One of the earliest specimens of this is carved in a panel in the lower cave temple at Badami in which the right half contains Śaivite attributes and emblems and the left half Vaiṣṇavite. The god is attended by both Pārvatī and Lakṣmī as well as by anthropomorphic Nandī and Garuḍa. The syncretism was extended by the inclusion of Brahmā, thus forming the Trinity, the *hari-hara-pitāmaha* images. Individual images of Brahmā also are not rare. One of the earliest brass or bronze images of this god fully in the round found at Mirpur Khas in Sindh is very interesting from iconographic point of view.

The sun cult was popular in the Gupta age and after, and there is no dearth of Sūrya images. The standing Sūrya figures of the Gupta period, discovered in different parts of northern India as well as seated ones from Mathura, reveal certain foreign features. The stone relief of Sūrya in the Bhumara Śiva temple shows the god in Udīcaya-veśa (cf. the garment of Kaṇiṣka in the headless statue from Mathura) as well as in Iranian boots. The south Indian figures of Sūrya have the legs and feet always left bare, and instead of the long coat of northern India we find invariably the *udarabandha* or belt tightening the belly.

The Gupta age also witnessed an expansion of the Śakti cult. The images of the goddess may roughly be grouped under two heads—*ugra* (terrible) and *saumya* (benign). To the former group belongs Durgā killing the buffalo-demon (*mahiṣamardinī*). One of the earliest figures of the goddess is found carved on a facade of the cave temple at Udayagiri where she is twelve-armed. The Bhita reliefs depicting the goddess belong to the Gupta period. Several reliefs in Mamallapuram illustrate in a very interesting manner the different phases of the struggle between the goddess and the demon. The *ugra* forms of the goddess are fewer in number than those of *saumya* or benign form.

Kārttikeya images with peacock vehicle, the deity holding a citron and a spear, belong mostly to the post-Gupta and medieval period. The same holds good in the case of Gaṇeśa images, but there are some specimens belonging to the early Gupta period such as the Mathura sandstone figure or the terracotta plaque from Bhitargaon. Lakṣmī is found on coins and seals and her figure appears in the lintels of Viṣṇu temples at Badami and Aihole. Numerous sculptures of miscellaneous divinities, loosely associated with Brahmanical cults, have been found in different parts of India like those of the Dikpālas or guardians of the eight quarters, Yakṣas, Nāgas, Gandharvas, Vidyādharas, Apsaras, Gaṅgā-Yamunā and others. These originally belonged to the non-Brahmanical cults, but later made their way into Brahmanism, Buddhism and Jainism. From the Gupta age onwards iconism was so deeply rooted that even the emblems and attributes in the hands of the deities were anthropomorphised. The bewildering variety of images belonging to various cults evoked wonder and a feeling of admiration among the people thus helping them to transgress the limits of sectarianism. They created an atmosphere in which even a non-Buddhist could appreciate and show respect to a Buddha image. Iconism thus paved the way for a broader ground on which votaries of different cults could meet.

3. The Early Medieval Period

From the post-Gupta period onwards we come across the distinct formations of the traditional temple styles and their regional distributions. The Nāgara style is almost universal, the fundamental characteristics of which are the cruciform plan and the curvilinear *śikhara* or tower. Of course there are regional variations, since this style is widely distributed over a greater part of India but the two basic features mentioned above are common to every temple. The Drāviḍa style is current in the south. Its outstanding feature is the storeyed arrangement of the tower (*vimāna*) in gradually receding stages, ending in a domical crowning top known as *stūpī* or *stūpikā*. The Vesara style also known as the Cālukyan style, is found in Karnataka and parts of Maharashtra. It is a variation of the Drāviḍa style with some Nāgara influence. It has two principal components: the *vimāna* or a towered structure of storeyed elevation with a dome-shaped top, and the *maṇḍapa* or a flat-roofed structure supported on pillars.

Orissa which contains more temples than those found in the rest of the country put together, represents to a great extent, a pure form of the original Nāgara style. The Orissan temples, especially represented by the Bhuvaneswar group, have two components. A square sanctum, topped by a curvilinear tower, has a buttress-like projection in the middle of each face (popu-lary known as *rekha-deul*) and a porch-hall in front (*jagamohana* or *mukhamaṇḍapa*) with a pyramidal roof (popularly known as *bhadra* or *pīḍha-deul*). The Orissan model influenced the temple architecture of Bengal and Central India. The latter region, vast as it is, also has influences from other parts of the country. Various elaborations of the Nāgara style are found, especially in the workmanship of *śikhara* or the central tower, the minor towers, the pillared porch and ante-chamber. Temples from Sirpur, Gwalior, Kharod, Rewa, Baroli, besides the Amara-kantaka and Khajuraho groups, show between them the varieties of Nāgara style. The Osian group of Rajasthan display both the archaic and the sophisticated types of the Nāgara style. The celebrated group of the Jain temples at Dilwara in Mount Abu are lavish elaborations of the Kumbharia group of Jain temples in southern Rajasthan. In the case of the Gujarat temples the sanctum is usually situated within a covered ambulatory and is surmounted by a pyramidal tower of stepped stages in receding tiers, such as the temples of Kathiawar, the one at Gop being the archetype. In the Deccan, the early Nāgara style, blended with some elements of the Drāviḍa, is found in the temples at Aihole, Pattadakal, Mahākūṭeśvara and Alampur, while later modification of this style is found in some temples of the Khandesh region.

The prototypes of the Drāviḍa style are observed in the rock-cut *rathas* of Mamallapuram. The Drāviḍa style of temples from the period of the Pallava rulers till the end of the Vijayanagara empire may be divided into several well-marked phases. The Kailāsanātha and other temples of Kanchipuram constructed in the Pallava period are representative of the full-fledged Dravidian style of the South. The Deccanese counterpart of this is found in the celebrated rock-cut Kailāsa temple at Ellora which is regarded as the 'world's greatest rock poem'. In the Cola period the Drāviḍa style reached its climax as seen in the Koraṅganātha temple at Srinivāsanallur, the Bṛhadīśvara temple at Tanjore and the like. The hybrid Vesara style is found in Karnataka and parts of Maharashtra, the formative stage of which is represented by the Jain temple at Lakkundi. Some important temples in this category are Kāśiviśveśvara at Lakkundi, Mahādeva at Ittagi, Mallikārjuna at Kuruvatti, Dodda Vasavanna at Dambal, Hoysaleśvara at Halebid, Chenna Keśava at Belur, etc.

In the field of sculpture the development of regionalism became more prominent. The pivot of early medieval sculpture was the human figure in the form of gods and goddesses and their attendants. Mostly cult images, these followed the established canons of iconography. Secular themes were on the increase; a large variety of motifs and subjects decorated the outer walls of temples. Floral and vegetal devices were on the decrease, replaced by scenes of daily life, legendary illustrations, music and dance scenes, *mithuna* couples in a variety of poses, etc. Human figures are represented in the full bloom of youth. Generally, while in the field of architecture there were innovations in that of sculpture there was simple continuation of the earlier tradition. The development of the structural temples was not due to any special artistic inspiration but rested on the progress of engineering skill and conception. And there was no such scope as far as the sculptures were concerned.

In the case of icons there was noticeable proliferation. With the growth of Mahāyāna Buddhism, the images of the Dhyānī Buddhas, their Bodhisattvas, and emanated deities began to be produced in abundance, both in stone and in metal. Among the Bodhisattvas, Avalokiteśvara and Mañjuśrī in their various forms attracted the imagination of the image makers. Among the female Buddhist deities, images of Tārā became more frequent. Other Mahayanic deities, like Jambhala, Hayagrīva, Heruka, Yamāri, Vasudhārā, Parṇaśabarī Prajñāramitā, etc., had elaborate sculptural representation. The Jains also did not lag behind in the making of images of their Tīrthaṃkaras, their Śāsanadevatās and attendant deities. The Dilwara group of marble temples at Mount Abu display some of the finest examples of Jain figure sculpture.

Numerous figures of Śiva of the the post-Gupta age hailing from different parts of India may be subdivided into two principal groups—*saṃhāra* (destructive) and *anugraha* (gracious). Among some of Śiva's terrible forms mention may be made of his *bhairava*, *aghora*, *vīrabhadra* and *virūpākṣa* images and also those illustrating his demon-killing forms like *gajāsurasaṃhāra tripurāntaka*, *andhakavadha*, *Kālāri Kāmantaka*, etc. Among the benign types, sculptures representing the marriage of Śiva and Pārvatī, usually described as *kalyāṇasundara* or *vaivāhika*, are fairly common. The *dakṣiṇā-mūrti* types (god bestowing grace) are principally south Indian in character. The *nṛtya-murtis* or dancing-images of Śiva are also common. The Ellora and Chidambaram temples as well as several other Śaiva shrines in Deccan and south India contain figures of Śiva shown in various dancing poses. The *ardhanārīśvara* type depicting the Śiva-Devī combine is also a favourite theme of the sculptors. The *ekapāda-trimūrti* of Śiva, in which he is shown as standing on one leg, holding his usual attributes in his hands, with four-armed Brahmā and Viṣṇu issuing from his right and left flanks respectively, deserves special mention.

Images of Viṣṇu and his incarnations belonging to the early medieval period are found in large numbers. Apart from the three well-known forms of Viṣṇu images—those belonging to the standing seated and recumbent types—his incarnatory forms are very interesting. Among such forms, the *dattātreya* or *hari-hara-pitāmaha* shows three members of the orthodox Brahmanical triad, namely Brahmā, Viṣṇu and Śiva. Viśvarūpa and Hayagrīva are two other emanatory forms. The former is a twenty-armed deity with various attributes in its respective hands while the latter is a composite form in which the head of a horse is placed on a human body. This iconic type travelled to the countries of the Far East. Of the goddesses associated with Viṣṇu, Lakṣmī and Bhūdevī are the ones most represented in sculpture. Apart from the well-known Gajalakṣmī motif, other varieties of Lakṣmī, two-armed and four-armed, are also frequent.

Numerous Devī or Śakti images belonging to the early medieval period have been found among which a four-armed figure of the Pārvatī type in one of the rock-cut shrines of Ellora deserves special mention. Eight-or ten-armed Mahiśāsuramardinī figures are very common in Eastern India. Mātṛkā, Yoginī and Tantric images are also frequent. Apart from the standing and dancing images of a Gaṇeśa, a particular type is found in southern India in which the god is shown in the company of his consort. A rare type is also found in which the god is shown with five heads and ten arms seated on the back of a roaring lion. The south Indian images of Kārttikeya or Subrahmanya display a multitude of forms. The iconographic representation of Sūrya came to be far more elaborate and several accessories were added.

4. *The Nature and Extent of Patronage*

But for immense financial support from different quarters it would have been impossible to make rock-cut constructions or erect mangificent structural temples which often took more than one generation to complete. The patrons were undoubtedly kings, feudatories, powerful officials, mercantile guilds and other professional organisations, and the amount spent on such projects was fantastic. The earliest patrons of such artistic activities were the Maurya emperors whose purpose was a show of power and majesty and also to earn religious merit. The capitals of the Mauryan columns were crowned with figures of bulls and lions in awe and wonder inspiring forms. The walls of the halls at the rock-cut caves at Barabar and Nagarjuni hills still shine like mirrors, and bear witness to Mauryan splendour. Aśoka is also taken to be the builder of the nucleus around which at a later age, the great Stūpa of Sanchi was built.

The tradition of court art, with the secular purpose to impress and overawe the populace, set up by the Maurya emperors did not continue in the subsequent periods of ancient and early medieval Indian history. Subsequent rulers did partronise artistic activities but not as a part of state policy. They did it for perpetuating their memory and to earn religious merit. The latter purpose eventually became more effective. Heliodorus, the ambassador of the Indo-Greek king Anṭalcidas, erected at Besnagar a *garuḍa-dhvaja*, a column with capital adorned by the figure of Garuḍa, in honour of Lord Vāsudeva in order to earn religious merit. Hiuen Tsang and Al Bīrūnī have recorded legends that refer to the grand monastery built by Kaṇiṣka at Peshawar. Kalhaṇa's *Rājataraṅgiṇī* refers to the successors of Kaṇiṣka who founded many Buddhist establishments styled *maṭha* and *caitya*. An epigraph in a cave in the Nasik hills says that it was excavated during the sovereignty of king Kṛṣṇa of the Sātavāhana family. This does not, however, mean that it was excavated because of the king's desire. An individual might have also been the donor of the cave. Likewise, a votive inscription found on the southern gateway of Sanchi records the gift of Vāsiṣṭhīputra Ānanda, the foreman of the artisans of a Sātavāhana king called Sātakarṇi. Satavāhana Pulumāvi's inscriptions have been found at Nasik, Karle and Amaravati. Yajña Sātakarṇi's name is found in the inscriptions at Nasik and Kanheri. These names, however, are not specially associated with the excavations of the caves. In certain cases kings are directly mentioned as donors. The lower storey of the Manchapuri cave in the Udayagiri hills for example, was excavated by *mahārāja* Vakradeva of the Meghavāhana clan. Khāravela excavated a number of caves in the Kumārī-parvata or the Khandagiri hills. He also built a monastery at a place called Pabhāra.

It appears that kings like Aśoka, Kaṇiṣka or Khāravela, who inclined towards certain religious systems which required monasteries and allied constructions, directly extended their patronge to these. But others, say the Sātavāhanas who were the followers of Brahmanism which did not require such constructions, only provided formal patronage. The Vākāṭaka kings, for instance, were followers of Brahmanism, but some of their names are mentioned in the Ajanta inscriptions. It also appears that the rock-cut constructions were originally started by enthusiastic monks and in the subsequent stages kings, feudatories or men of rank and position came forward with assistance. Even for the maintenance of the monasteries land grants or financial help were offered by willing individuals or groups. A Nasik inscription of the ninth regnal year of the Ābhīra Māṭhariputra Iśvarasena records two investments, one of 1000 *Kārṣāpaṇa* and the other of 500 *Kārṣapaṇa* in trade guilds for the purpose of providing medicines for the sick among the monks dwelling in the monastery on the Nasik hills. The benefactress was a female devotee called Viṣṇudattā of Śaka parentage.

Of the large number of rock-cut shrines and structural temples of the Gupta age very few mention the names of their financiers or patrons. It appears that the Gupta kings were not very interested in architectural activities. Śrī Gupta, the first king of this dynasty, is said to have built a temple for the Chinese pilgrims and endowed it with twenty-four villages. But this information we get only from I-tsing's account. Two of the Udayagiri caves near Bhilsa in Central India bear Gupta dates, but this does not indicate any patronage. Harṣavardhana, notwithstandinig his artistic personality, was not a builder. Rather, the Cālukya prince Maṅgaleṣa constructed a cave temple at Badami and endowed it with the village of Lañjiśvara. The Jain temple of Meguti of Aihole was erected by one Ravikīrti during the reign of Pulkeśin II. The Pallava king Mahendravarman was, however, known as *Cettakāri* or temple-builder. He constructed many rock-cut temples. Such temples are extant in Trichinopoly, Vallam, Mahendravāḍi (near Arkonam) and

Dalavanur. His son Narasiṃhavarman erected the celebrated monolithic shrines called *rathas* in Mamallapuram.

In the following period the names of some royal donors are known. The famous rock-cut Śiva temple at Ellora was constructed under the patronage of the Rāṣṭrakūṭa Kṛṣṇa I. According to the Tibetan chronicles Gopāla of the Pāla dynasty of Bengal and Bihar founded a monastery at Nalanda. His successor Dharmapāla founded the famous Vikramaśīla monastery and also the Somapurī-vihāra in Varendra, the ruins of which have been excavated at Paharpur in the Rajshahi district of Bangladesh. He is also said to have founded the splendid monastery of Odantapurī in Bihar but some scholars give the credit for this achievement to his successor Devapāla. Among the feudatories of the Gurjara-Pratīhāras, the Candella Dhaṅga who later declared independence, erected a number of temples at Khajuraho. The Kalacuri Yuvarāja I of Tripurī was a patron of the Mattamayūra sect and erected several Śiva temples, the most prominent of which is the one at Gurgi, twelve miles east of the Rewa town. His queen Nohalā erected a temple of Śiva at Bilhari in Jabalpur district. The Paramāra Muñja also built a number of temples. Cāmuṇḍa Rāya, minister of the Gaṅga Rācamalla, erected a Jain temple at Sravaṇabelgolā and executed the colossal statue of Gommaṭeśvara which 'in daring conception and gigantic dimensions is without a rival in India.' Among the early Cola kings of the south, Vijayālaya built a Durgā temple at Tanjore while his son Āditya I built a few Śiva temples. Parantaka provided the Naṭarāja shrine at Chidambaram a gold roof. The Pāṇḍya Jaṭilavarman was also a great builder of Śiva and Viṣṇu temples.

Mahīpāla I of the Pāla dynasty of Bengal constructed and repaired a large number of religious buildings in Banaras, Sarnath, Nalanda and Bodh Gaya. Vijayasena of the Sena dynasty built the temple of Pradyumneśvara in the Rajshahi district. The Kalacuri Karṇa built a temple at Banaras. The Paramāra Bhoja also erected a number of temples in honour of Śiva. The Caulukya Jayasiṃha was a devotee of Śiva and built the temple of Rudra Mahākāla at Siddhapura. Two of the four principal temples at Dilwara on Mount Abu were constructed by Vimala and Tejaḥpāla respectively, ministers and feudatories of the Caulukyas. The Western Cālukya king Vikramāditya VI is said to have erected a big temple. The Eastern Gaṅga king Anantavarman Coḍagaṅga founded the magnificent temple of Jagannātha at Puri while the celebrated sun temple at Konarak was built by Narasiṃha I of the same dynasty. The Hoysala Biṭṭiga, a feudatory of the Western Cālukyas, made a grant to the Śiva temple a Maddur, while his general, Gaṅgarāja, is reputed to have restored all the Jain shrines destroyed in the course of Cola invasions. His son Bappa built a Jain shrine at Halebid and had it consecrated by a Jain divine Nayakīrti. The Hoysaleśvara temple at Halebid was due to the patronage of the kings of this line, but it is not known which one. The great Rājarājeṣvara temple at Tanjore was constructed by the Cola emperor Rājarāja the Great. He also erected a temple in honour of Viṣṇu and cooperated in the construction of Cuḍāmaṇivihāra, a Buddhist monastery at Negapatam attributed to the Śailendra king Māravijayatuṅga.

The above survey reveals that although some kings or feudatories erected some temples or donated lands for their maintenance—barring only a few like the Śiva temple of Ellora, the pagodas of Mamallapuram, a few of the Khajuraho temples, the Jagannātha temple of Puri, the sun temple of Konarak, etc.—most of the celebrated temples, rock-cut or structural, were constructed without any specific royal effort. Most of the ruling families had no special inclination for artistic activities. Even the Gupta kings, great though they were in many respects, were not great builders. Even in the dynasties which are known to have patronised artistic activities, it was only some individuals who took the initiative. The celebrated constructions of India, especially the rock-cut ones which took many generations to complete, were rather productions of the masses, as were many structural temples. These were initiated by a few devotees and eventually the people at large were attracted to such constructions and they came forward with money and voluntary labour. The heavy expenditure involved in such projects could never have been any one individual's contribution. Even the royal projects required volutary mass participation and contributions. The maintenance was also provided by peoples belonging to various social ranks as is attested by numerous epigraphical references. The urge was religious and not artistic. The images, artistic though they were, were never considered to be objects of art. They were always regarded as cult objects. Any attempt to connect the constructions with the special economic condition of a given region, or with agricultural or commercial surplus, or the favourable foreign trade balance and other aspects of economic life is also meaningless, because numerous gigantic constructions were made in many regions which were at that time marked by both economic and political decadence.

5. *Erotic Art on Temples*

The presence of the erotic themes in temples has for long been explained according to the personal whims of the viewer. Fanciful interpretations have been devised by the temple guides so as to convey the idea to the inquisitive tourist that these erotic depictions are really meant for mental purification. For instance, that the merit of seeing the idol enshrined in the temple can only be acquired if the individual is able to control his mind after experiencing visually the objects of sexual excitement. This naive interpretation, though absolutely unwarranted, has at least the merit of logical consistency. It is quite another matter when some art historians try to explain these erotic elements in terms of Tantric ideas and practices. They are thus interpreted to be symbolic representations of eternal bliss, or of the creative process, or of the principle of *yuganaddha* suggestive of non-duality, and so forth.

According to H.V. Guenther, the sexual aspects of the Tantras are nothing but a corrective against the one-sided intellectualism and rationalism which is unable to cope with the problems of everyday life. The symbolic *yuganaddha* points to the unique harmony and interpretation of masculinity and feminity. Bisexuality is inherent in all beings and this aspect has to be exercised in order to understand the truth of one's own nature. Sexual partnership is, therefore, the best expression for the most intimate relation between the two opposites. For the man, woman is the material object of concentration, a goddess for meditation and a symbolic truth for comprehension. Such rationalisations of Tantric sexual elements are basically subjective, the interpretations being in all cases largely conditioned by their authors' outlook and approach. No one working on Tantrism can ignore its sexual elements, but the difficulty arises when the entire Tantric tradition is superimposed on these elements. After all, Tantra is not a *kāmaśāstra* (science of erotics), but a *mokṣa-śāstra* (science of liberation).

The course of the evolution of art in India as elsewhere, from the primitive stage to its more advanced forms, depends on the parallel evolution of man's emotional attitude towards the world. But the evolution of this attitude differs very naturally from one section of people to another. While dealing with religious history, we have seen that two sects of beliefs and ideals simultaneously worked in the field of Indian history, one represented by the simpler peoples and the other by the dominant class. Occasionally some of the beliefs and rituals of the former were adopted by the latter, but for a totally different purpose. This may be illustrated with some examples. Among the primitives, art is an illusory technique complementary to the deficiencies of the real techniques. In other words its inspiration is magical. By the symbolical representation of an event, primitive man thought that he could secure the actual occurrence of that event. There are two distinct methods of securing this desired result, the organic and the geometrical. These two types persist all through the history of art. Ritual drawings, very often with pronounced erotic motifs, are quite common in different parts of India. The purpose of this 'ritual art' is entirely different from that of the so-called 'advanced art' although the subject matter may be the same in both cases. For example, a few terracotta specimens from Lower Bengal, emphasising exclusively the copulative aspect of the male-female union, exhibit identity in form and content with some Khajuraho reliefs. But the source of inspiration in both cases is quite different. While the former can be explained in terms of magical fertility rites, the latter admits of a quite different explanation.

It is tempting to connect the sexual depictions on the temples of Khajuraho, Konarak, Puri, Ellora, Halebid, etc., with primitive sex rites and Tantrism but before we do so we must be sure about the real extent of the influence which is supposed to have been exerted on the former by the latter. There was obviously a link between the two, since some of the popular sexual themes first presented in terracotta were later executed in stone. But when these came to reflect the art of the sophisticated, they served a totally different purpose. This difference may be compared with the erotic elements of the Puranic literature meant for the unsophisticated masses, and those found in the erotic Kāvyas meant for the sophisticated. From this point of view, the sculptural extravagance of Khajuraho, Konarak and other temples was mainly the reflection of an underdeveloped urbanism. We can say this because of the fact that the sexual depictions on these temples accord more with the Kāmaśāstra descriptions of sexual acrobatics than with Tantric principles. An example from Khajuraho will make the point clear. A man standing on his head, with legs folded, has a woman sitting in the fold of his legs on his visible organ. The woman's hands rest on the necks of two females standing on either side of her while the man titillates with his hands the sex organs of the two standing nude females. Quite obviously this has nothing to do with the Tantric *Yuganaddha* union.

But why were temples selected for such depictions? Apparently, in ancient India the idea of the holiness of temples differed significantly from that in modern India. It is impossible to say what exactly the temples meant to the worshippers at different ages but the idea of sacredness was, in all probability, not inherent in the temples themselves. There are some reasons to believe that the vivid portrayal of sexual intercourse could only be made on the temple walls and that this was somehow related to the very structure of the temple itself. Functionally, also, the temples provided a logical and appropriate place for them. An inscription of the Gupta period describes a temple as a terrible abode of Ḍākinīs uttering loud and tremendous shouts joy in wild ecstacy. Actual sexual acts were not rare in temples, as is indicated by the custom of maintaining Devadāsīs or temple-girls. A conceptualisation of the temples in sexual terms is also found. There are two major types of temple buildings in Orissa, the Rekha and the Bhadra, which are joined to each other in a very intimate manner. The junction is expressed by a term which literally means a ceremonial knot tied between the garments of the bridegroom and the bride. The Rekha is male and Bhadra female: they are both attached to each other in a state of union. The most important part of the temple is called the *garbha* or womb. The god, in the form of the chief idol, is placed in the womb. Leading up to the *garbha* from the porch is a kind of corridor through which one enters. This sexual design is prevalent in West Asian temples also which were divided into three-parts—porch representing the lower end of the vagina up to the hymen, the hall or the vagina itself, and the inner sanctum or the uterus. Thus, things sexual were not really inconsistent with the supposed holiness of the temple. This alone explains why the sexual depictions on the temple walls, notwithstanding their acrobatic extravagances, were tolerated and given some sort of social sanction by the simpler peoples. This they did partly because they found in those depictions the illusion of a lost reality—the reality of their traditional beliefs and rituals—and partly because they were bound to do so by the pressure of circumstances.

11

Literary Aspects: Some Observations

1. The Primitive Substratum

The contents of the Vedic literature may be divided into three categories, namely ritualistic, mythological and philosophical. A considerable portion of the Vedic literature is concerned with rituals. It is impossible to say, at the present state of our knowledge, what the *yajñas* or rituals really meant to their performers, but it may be said with confidence that these rituals were consistent with the Vedic way of life in its totality. Among the principal characteristics of a ritual, three special aspects deserve attention. The first was *pāriplava ākhyāna* or ancient legends which were recited by the Hotṛ priest before the assembled audience. The second was the miming of certain events or situations by a group of persons. And the third was *sāman* or songs which were of five kinds, namely *hiṅkāra*, *prastāva*, *udgītha*, *pratihāra* and *nidhana*. These were all expressions of a single undifferentiated art, the original purpose of which must have been magical, intended to obtain certain desired results (*apūrva*). In later commentaries it is said that each of the Vedic verses had a distinct application (*viniyoga* or *prayoga*) and that the *sāmans* were to be sung with certain prescribed dancing postures. But, at the same time, it should be remembered that there was a great gulf between the early and later forms of the Vedic rituals. The later forms were highly complicated. This accounts for the growth of an elaborate sacerdotal literature in the post-Ṛgvedic period.

The role of rituals in determining literary norms in the Indian context has never been studied. In the Hellenic context the Graecologists have clearly demonstrated how the ideas evolving out of the primitive rituals gave rise to the epics of Homer and the *Theogony* of Hesiod, in addition to the didactic poems, epigrams and elegies on the one hand and to the chorus, skolion, mónodi and incipient dithyramb on the other, and how the latter became the source of Greek tragedies and comedies. In the Greek context it has also been shown how the various aspects of rituals corresponded to different walks of Greek life. If we use the simile of a tree for the rituals, we can say that it had three main branches. The first was initiation, the major sub-branches of which were the Athenian, Spartan and Cretan education and the minor ones comprised Olympic games, funeral observances and sex rites. The second was social behaviour, the sub-branches of which were birth, marriage, death and professional aspects of life. The third was the mental and intellectual sphere, the lower sub-branches of which were the Elusian, Orphic and Dionysian mysteries while the upper ones were dithyramb and targedy, lenaiya and comedy.

Such developments may be traced also in the Indian context, but it requires prolonged research. There are, however, some clues which point the way. It is ritual which sustains myth outlining the concepts of gods and goddesses and the stories of their life. Myth is that kind of story in which the working of natural phenomenon symbolised by its characters is clearly observed. The Ṛgvedic myth of the slaying of Vṛta by Indra shows how rain is brought by piercing the clouds. To illustrate this point further, reference may be made to a Greek myth which tells that Persephone, daughter of Demeter, was abducted by Pluto, the god of the underworld and that eventually through the mediation of Zeus it was settled that Persephone would stay for six months on the earth with Demeter and for six months under the earth with Pluto. Farnell has shown that this myth was evolved out of agricultural rituals and that Persephone represented the seed-corn when she stayed under the earth and the harvest when she stayed on the earth. One should not fail to recall in this connection that Sītā, the heroine of the *Rāmāyaṇa*, was also originated from the earth, abducted by a Pluto, and after all her adventures she again went back into the earth. Like Demeter or Isis, the etymological meaning of the name Sītā is 'ploughed land' as well as 'harvest'. In this sense the myth of Sītā occurs in *Ṛgveda* IV.57. Sītā with agricultural affiliations occurs in many texts. The name Rāma is derived from the root *ram* meaning to 'plough' and 'to make sexual intercourse'. Conceptually the one is not dissociated from the other. "So intimate", observes E.O. James, "appeared to be the relation between the process of birth and generation and those of fertility in general that the two aspects of the same mystery found very similar modes of ritual expression under prehistoric conditions." It therefore appears that the kernel of the *Ramāyaṇa* was an agricultural myth which was later converted into a great epic by the talented poet Vālmīki. It should be pointed out in this connection that when the natural background of any myth sinks into oblivion, it loses its significance and perspective, develops fabrications and eventually turns into a legend. In the epics and Purāṇas we come across numerous legends (in fact the Purāṇas are collections of legends) the roots of which may be traced to the myths contained in the Vedic literature.

The dramatic elements found in Greek dithyrambs which were evolved from ritualism were the sources of Greek tragedies. The same holds good also in the case of India. We have previously had occasion to say that the miming of events, which was the forerunner of dramatic performance, was an essential feature of the Vedic rituals. In the *Ṛgveda* we come across a number of dialogue-hymns like those between Agastya and Indra (I.165), Agastya and Lopāmudrā (I.179), Viśvāmitra and the rivers (III.33), Indra, Aditi and Vāmadeva (IV.18), Yama and Yamī (X.10), Urvāśī and Purūravas (X.95), Saramā and the Paṇis (X.108), Yama and Kumāra (X.135), etc. Most of the Ṛgvedic hymns were meant to be chanted by one or more priests but these dialogue-hymns were meant to be performed or mimed before a group of persons assembled for a certain purpose. The description of such a dramatic performance is found in the Brāhmaṇa literature in connection with the Aśvamedha ritual. The performance was the chief queen's union with the horse before other priests and queens who exchanged a typical conversation with one another (one is recorded in the *Vājasaneyī Saṃhitā* XXIII.22-31). This dialogue was meant to be part of a ritual act performed by two characters representing the principles of the ritual. The dialogue between Urvaśī and Purūravas, as found in *Ṛgveda* X.95, which apparently reveals the lamentations of a jilted lover was in reality a ritualistic act in which Purūravas was probably sacrificed as is indicated (though not proved) in such phrases as *punar astam (par) ehi* suggestive of sending dead persons to the ancestors. In the speeches of both Urvaśī and Purūravas there are passages with familiar idiomatic circumlocutions for death. In the concluding verse of the dialogue Urvaśī says: "Thus speak these gods to thee, son of Ilā, inasmuch as thou art now doomed to death, thy offspring will offer sacrifice to the gods, but thou thyself rejoice in heaven." That Purūravas was probably killed at a ritual is supported by a tradition recorded in the Brāhmaṇa literature. The *Śatapatha Brāhmaṇa* (XI.5.1 ff), though it does not explain the most obscure feature of the Ṛgvedic hymn, states that Purūravas became a *gandharva* after making himself the upper and lower *araṇis* of *aśvattha* wood from which fire results. Elsewhere in the same text (III.4.1.22) the working of two portions of fire-drill or fire-plough is conceived in terms of human procreation symbolised by Urvaśī and Purūravas. The ritualistic significance of all these is beyond our comprehension; even the writers of the epics and Purāṇas failed to understand the real ritualistic background. In all these texts the legend of Urvaśī and Purūravas occurs as a personalised narrative and its culmination is found in Kālidāsa's celebrated drama *Vikramorvaśī*.

The rise of ruthless state power and class society on the ruins of ancient tribal equality which took place in India at different periods of history was part of an inevitable process of transformation. The forces of injustice and oppression which began to characterise the successive stages of history, with increasing vigour and frequency, could not be arrested notwithstanding abundant goodwill and selfless human endeavour. This frustration is the source of the tragedy in literature. The hero is the symbol of the struggle against injustice and the evil forces of social life while the villain is the personification of the opposite forces and one who always becomes successful through conspiracy and unfair means. The tragic heroes of the imagination are better persons in regard to human qualities but despite their greatness they become victims of unfortunate consequences. Heracles had to face the most cruel fate. The same happened in the life of Svipdag, Beowulf, Hamlet, Sigurd and Siegfrid and in that of the heroes of the Cuchuline-Arthur-Osianic story cycles. The final word in Teutonic mythology is the defeat of light against darkness. The gods are exterminated; the demons become victorious; the rule of *nirṛti,* to use the typical Indian term, prevails and perpetuates. The tone of the Indian *Māhabhārata* and *Rāmāyaṇa*, in which we come across an imaginative victory of *dharma*, the forces of justice, is the same because in reality that did not happen, the *dharmarājya* (the kingdom of justice) did not return. Why otherwise did the victorious Pāṇḍavas renounce the world in frustraction, why did Rāma sacrifice his life in water, why did Kṛṣṇa have an inglorious death, why did everything end in absolute grief and despair?

Ancient Greek and Roman thinkers insisted on the need for tragedy for the sake of the purification of society. A careful student of history will not fail to observe that everywhere in the world tragedy come into existence when ancient moral values faced serious challenge from certain unwarranted forces caused by massive social transformation. Many volumes have been written on the social background of the Greek tragedies. But no such attempt has hitherto been made to analyse the contents of the *Mahābhārata* and the *Rāmāyaṇa* in their real social perspective though there is no dearth of other types of discussions. Apart from these two great epics there is no tragedy in Sanskrit literature; even Bhāsa's *Urubhaṅga* does not fall within this category. Though the externals of tragedy changed over time, the main purpose remains the same which is the ruthless exhibition of the social realities however unbearable their consequences might have been. To the reader or the viewer the sad experience of the inevitable consequence has something to teach. The original purpose of comedy was the same, but it was written in a light vein. But later its purpose was completely changed and it came to be used for the purpose of entertainment of the kings, aristocrats and privileged persons. That is why the writing of tragedy in Sanskrit became a taboo. Sanskrit dramas became 'court-plays', created by efficient hands but on artificial lines.

2. *The Great Epics: Their Influence on Indian Literature*

The two great epics, the *Māhabhārata* and the *Rāmāyaṇa*, in their present forms are the finished products of a prolonged literary activity, the evolution of which took place in no less than 800 years (c. 400 B.C.—A.D. 400) in the case of the former and 400 years (c. 200 B.C.—A.D. 200) in the case of the latter. In point of form, neither of these two epics is a single book, but a whole literature. The structural growth of both the epics is a subject of interesting research on which much work has already been done by well known scholars. The main theme of both is the final triumph of truth and justice over untruth and injustice. The characters are mortal human beings with various sentiments and emotions all of whom, notwithstanding their success or failure in the worldly sense, are tragic victims of the forces of destiny beyond their control. To the main story are added many pieces of ancient bardic poetry, hero legends, various narratives pertaining to the activities of different gods and goddesses, parables and fables which are both entertaining as well as instructive. Apart from these the two epics contain diverse matter on topics such as religion, philosophy, codes of law, science of polity, rules of individual and social behaviour and other aspects of human life.

In the characters described in the *Mahābhārata* and the *Rāmāyaṇa* every Indian finds a reflection of his or her mental image even today. No other literary work in any part of the world has been to able to influence the masses through the ages as has been done by these two great epics. The Buddhist and Jain writers resorted to these great epics, and made their Buddhist and Jain versions for the propagation of their own ideas. A good number of the Buddhist Jātakas were directly influenced by the *Mahābhārata* and the *Rāmāyaṇa*. This also holds good in the case of the Jain *Harivaṃśa*, *Uttarapurāṇa*, *Pāṇḍavapurāṇa*, *Paumacariya*, *Rāmacarita*, etc.

A considerable portion of Sanskrit poetry and drama is based upon either the *Mahābhārata* or the *Rāmāyaṇa*. Among the poetical works based on the *Mahābhārata* are Bhāravi's *Kirātarjunīya*, Māgha's *Siśupālavadha*, Kśemendra's *Mahābhāratamañjarī*, Anantabhaṭṭa's *Bhāratacampu*, Vāsudeva's *Yudhiṣṭhiravijaya*, Amaracandra's *Bālabhārata*, Nītivarman's *Kīcakavadha*, Vastupāla's *Naranārāyaṇānanda*, to name a few. The legend of Nala and Damayantī which is found in the *Mahābhārata* has been utilised by Harṣa, Kṛṣṇānanda, Vāmanabhaṭṭa, Vāsudeva, Trivikramabhaṭṭa, Rāmchandra, Nīlakaṇṭha, Kṣemīśvara and others. Among the Sanskrit dramas based on the *Mahābhārata* we have Bhāsa's *Madhyama*, *Dūta-ghatoṭkaca*, *Pañcarātra*, *Urubhaṅga* and *Karṇabhāra*, Kalidāsa's *Śakuntalā*, Bhaṭṭanārāyaṇa's *Veṇīsaṃhāra*, Rājaśekhara's *Bālabhārata*, Kṣemendra's *Citrabhārata*, Kulaśekharavarman's *Subhadrā-Dhanañjaya* and *Tapatīsaṃbaraṇa*, Prahlādana's *Pārthaparākrama*, Kāñcana's *Dhanañjayavijaya*, etc.

Apart from the traditional *Rāmāyaṇa* a few other *Rāmāyaṇas* were composed based on the same spiritual and philosophical themes and following the outline of the main story. Of these the *Adhyātma*, *Yogavāsiṣṭha*, *Ānanda* and *Adbhuta* deserve special mention. Aśvaghosa's *Buddhacarita* is also modelled on the *Rāmāyaṇa*. Among the poetical works based on the *Rāmāyaṇa* mention may be made of Kālidāsa's *Raghuvaṁśa*, Bhaṭṭi's *Rāvanavadha*, Kumāradāsa's *Janakīharaṇa* Abhinanda's *Rāmacaritra*, Sākalamalla's *Udārarāghava*, Veṅkateśvara's *Citrabandha Rāmāyaṇa* etc. There were also some poetical works in which contents of both the epics were either juxtaposed or the epic theme had been used symbolically to describe another story such as Sandhyākara's *Rāmacarita*, Dhanañjaya's *Rāghava-Pāndavīa*, Harádatta Suri's *Rāghava-Naiṣadhīya*, Cidāmbara's *Rāghva-Paṇḍavīa-Yādavīya*, etc. Among the dramas based on the *Rāmāyaṇa* we may refer to Bhāsa's *Pratimā* and *Abhiṣeka*, Bhavabhūti's *Uttararāmacarita*, Rājaśekhara's *Bāla-Rāmayaṇa*, Damodara Miśra's *Hanumāna-nāṭaka*, Yaśovarman's *Rāmābhyūdaya*, Māyurāja's *Udātta-rāghava*, Murāri's *Anargha-rāghava*, Bhīmaṭa's *Svapnadaśānana*, Jayadeva's *Prasanna-rāghava*, etc.

The list of works based on the two epics cited above is by

no means complete. It is merely a random selection to show the extent of the influence both the epics had on Sanskrit literature. The epic legends travelled beyond the seas and we have also their non-Indian, especially South East Asian versions. Literature in the regional languages of India, as we shall see in a different section of this chapter, also began with translations of these two great epics and independent writings based on their themes. During the Indian Renaissance of the nineteenth century, the *Mahābhārata* and the *Rāmāyaṇa* were reinterpreted by writers to suit the growing demands of Indian nationalism. Michael Madhusudan Dutta was the pioneer, and a host of poets, novelists and dramatists all over India followed him. The best example perhaps is Subrahmanya Bhārati's Tamil poetry *Pañcaliyin Śapatham* which is an expose of the predicament of India under the British rule. Even many Marxist writers of modern times resort to epic legends to impress on their readers the doctrine of class struggle and social change.

3. *The Purāṇas: Literature of the Masses*

The Purāṇas form a considerable portion of Sanskrit literature and are regarded, like the great epics, as the fifth Veda. There is reason to believe that the Purāṇas were originally composed in various Prakrits and that later they were rendered into Sanskrit. The word Purāṇa means "that which is existing from the olden days." Like the great epics, the Purāṇas also contain numerous myths and legends, historical materials, codes of conduct, list of crimes and punishments, aspects of sectarian religions, philosophical doctrines, aspects of physical, chemical and medical sciences, geographical data and so forth. They are so varied in subject matter that is impossible to define or categorise them. Ancient commentators refer to five *lakṣaṇas* or characteristics of the Purāṇas. These are *sarga* (description of the creation of the world), *pratisarga* (description of the dissolution and renovation of the world), *vaṃśa* (dynastic lists of the gods and the sages), *manvantara* (ages of the world under different Manus) and *vaṃśānucarita* (the royal dynasties). Later commentators add five more characteristics, namely, *vṛtti* different means of livelihood), *rakṣā* (facts about the incarnations of God), *mukti* (liberation), *hetu* (unmanifested life) and *apāśraya* (knowledge of *brahman*).

According to tradition there are 18 Mahā-purāṇas (greater Purāṇas) and 18 Upa-purāṇas (lesser Purāṇas) but in fact there are many more of the latter. Among the greater Purāṇas, the *Viṣṇu, Nāradīya, Bhāgavata, Garuḍa, Padma* and *Varāha* are regarded as *sāttvika*, the *Brahma, Vāmana* and *Bhaviṣya* as *rājasika* and the *Matsya, Kūrma, Liṅga, Śiva, Agni* and *Skanda* as *tāmasika*. Modern scholars, however, classify them according to their respective subject matter. To the first category belong *Garuḍa, Agni* and *Nārada* which deal with practical sciences or arts like medicine, grammar, dramatics, music, astrology, etc. To the second category belong *Padma, Skanda*, and *Bhaviṣya* which mainly deal with rituals and places of pilgrimage. The third category comprises *Brahma, Bhāgavata* and *Brahmavaivarta* which have come down to us in their changed Kṛṣṇaite forms. In the fourth category have been placed Purāṇas of historical nature like the *Brahmāṇḍa* and the *Vāyu*. The fifth comprises sectarian Purāṇas like *Liṅga, Vāmana* and *Mārkaṇḍeya* devoted respectively to Śiva, Viṣṇu and Devī. To the sixth belong those which are supposed to have emanated from the incarnations of Viṣṇu like *Varāha, Kūrma* and *Matsya*. The written forms of the Purāṇas were composed between c. A.D. 400 and 1600.

Generally speaking all of them contain a cosmogonical account with the leading sectarian god at the centre who is identified with *brahman*. This supreme being enters into *puruṣa* (the soul element imagined as a male principle) and *prakṛti* (the matter element imagined as a female principle) and creates *mahat* or *buddhi* (principles of intelligence) from which emanate respectively *ahaṃkāra* (egoity), *tanmātras* (five material elements), *indriyas* (sense organs) and *manas* (mind). The Purāṇas divide time into *kapla, manvantara* and *yuga*. The last one is within human comprehension and is divided into four ages: *satya, tretā, dvāpara* and *kali*. The earth is conceived of as comprising seven islands: Jambu, Plakṣa, Śālmalī, Kuśa, Krauñca, Śāka and Puṣkara, each being encircled by one of the seven seas. Bhārata or the Indian subcontinent is a part of the Jambudvīpa having the Himalayan ranges in the north as the *varṣa-parvata* and seven other ranges, Mehendra, Malaya,

Sahya, Suktimat, Rkṣa, Vindhya and Pāripārtra as *kulaparvatas*. Each of the ranges is a source of several rivers, the names and courses of which have also been described.

The dynastic lists of the Purāṇas begin with Vaivasvata Manu. Among his ten sons Ilā was both a man and a woman and as such was the source of two separate dynasties. Dynasties of other sons of Manu have also been described. The length of time from Manu to the Bhārata war is 95 generations. Historical dynasties like those of the Guptas or the Andhras are described in the future tense. In religion, the Purāṇas reveal the incipient form of modern Hinduism. The downfall of the Vedic gods is interesting to observe. The great Vedic deities like Indra, Varuṇa, Uṣas, Aditi, etc., have become insignificant. On the other hand, the minor Vedic gods like Śiva or Viṣṇu have come into the forefront. Buddhism, Jainism and other atheistic systems are condemned. The Puranic religion is monotheistic in character. The Viṣṇuite Purāṇas proclaim Viṣṇu as the only supreme being. The Śaivite and Śākta Purāṇas also uphold the case of Śiva and Śakti. According to the Purāṇas there are four aims in life, namely, *dharma* (laws of individual and social behaviour), *artha* (economic pursuits) *kāma* (propagation of race) and *mokṣa* (liberation). In regard to *dharma* there are references to crimes and punishments, a description of hell, glorification of the places of pilgrimage, description of merits for observances of vows and offering gifts. In regard to *artha* various forms of occupations are mentioned in which connection the science of polity has also been explained. In regard to *kāma*, various forms of marriage, the duties of a wife, some *Kāmasūtra* prescriptions for sex life and allied subjects, are given. So far as *mokṣa* or liberation is concerned various theories have been put forward. It is interesting to note that the Śaivite Purāṇas insist on *yoga*, the disciplining of body and mind, for achieving liberation but the Vaiṣṇavite Purāṇas insist on *bhakti* or pure devotion.

4. *Sophisticated Literature: Some Characteristics*

Sanskrit dramas are mostly court plays dealing with domestic problems of the princes and nobles caused by polygamy. The hero is generally the king, in a good number of cases king

Udayana, who is an ideal *dakṣiṇa-nāyaka* always falling in love with the infamous heroines at the first sight. The king's marriage or courtship with such 'lowly' maidens brings trouble to the royal household, mainly because of the objection of the chief queen who is not ready to tolerate the secret love affairs of her husband. Ultimately it comes to light that the heroine is also a princess and that she is a near or distant cousin of the chief queen, who then withdraws her objection and accepts the bride as her sister. This, or a similar theme, is common to numerous Sanskrit dramas.

In the *Svapnavāsavadattā*, attributed to Bhāsa (third century A.D.) the king's polygamy is supported on political grounds. Here, however, the hero is a serious lover and both the heroines are endowed with some sort of personality. By contrast the hero of Harṣa's (seventh century A.D.) *Ratnāvalī* and *Priyadarśika* is a gay and courtly lover and other characters are marked by artificiality and absurdity. These dramas are similar, being for most part an imitation of Kālidāsa's *Mālavikāgnimitra.* In Kālidāsa's *Abhijñānaśakuntala* the hypocrisy of a king who takes advantage of the simplicity of a poor girl giving her false assurances is nicely depicted. The drama is based upon the *Mahābhārata* story, but Kālidāsa has breathed quite a new and vital spirit into it by introducing several slight but effective changes. The curse of Durvāsā, the loss of the ring, the scene of the fisherman, the charming picture of the working of love in the heart of a young innocent maiden, all charm the audience by creating alternately an atmosphere of suspense and relief. The drama, however, ends with the union of the hero and the heroine, according to the existing convention of Sanskrit drama, but this portion is an artificial addition. The intensity of undisciplined passion has been revealed in Kālidāsa's *Vikramorvaśīya* and also in Bhavabhūti's *Mālatimādhava*, but much of the talk of love and grief in these works is unconvincing and superficial. These dramas were intended for a selected audience and their authors did not care to plumb the depths of the human mind.

The *Uttararāmacarita* of Bhavabhūti shows a better and none realistic treatment of love; the sentiments are homely, real and human. Bhavabhūti is said to have surpassed Kālidāsa in depicting tender (*karuṇa*) sentiments. His works abound in descriptive passages and compounds out of proportion, but he excels himself when he treats of pathos. The love he treats of is spiritual rather than sensuous. Bhavabhūti's insistence on conjugal love must be taken as a sharp protest against the ugliness of the existing licentious society. The inglorious condition of the wife is also depicted well in Śūdraka's *Mṛcchakaṭika* in which the wife of Cārudatta appears occasionally as a grim embodiment of sadness. The *Mṛcchakaṭika* is, however, a realistic work, a drama of actual life in which characters are living men and women drawn from different grades of society.

The prose romances, especially those with a strong story-element, like the *Daśakumāracarita*, *Kathāsaritsāgara*, *Śukasaptati*, *Vetālapañcaviṃśati*, *Dvātriṃśatputtalikā*, etc., are very lively because men and women belonging to different walks of life, often from unconventional backgrounds, dominate the scenes with their uniqueness of character. In Daṇḍin's *Daśakumāracarita*, the hero and his nine companions, who were separated and passed through strange vicissitudes of fortune, on being reunited again relate their experiences. Daṇḍin shows in this work great power of characterisation while depicting the different types of men and women belonging to all classes of society and in different walks of life and draws realistic scenes from life with wit and humour. By contrast, works like Subandhu's *Vāsavadattā* or Bāṇa's *Kādambarī* have many elements artistically displayed by their authors but since in both the cases the subject matter is very poor and the authors resort only to sentimental imagination; the realities of life are seldom reflected in them. Such works were intended for a select group of readers whose interest lay in glamour and not literary merit. This glamour was displayed by fantastic description, unrestricted imagination and the bombastic use of rhetoric. Long involved constructions, unusual words, the use of epithet after epithet with the verb held back for pages together, unusually long compounds and a fondness for details and descriptions, even to the neglect of the main narrative and action, are the defects with which Bāṇa is often charged.

In classical Sanskrit poetry there are two important elements—description of nature and erotic imagery. These two elements take the form of elegant and finished miniatures that are grafted into the main body of the narrative. Erotic is presented as a definite feeling of sensation with a direct appeal to the female body. Interestingly enough, the physical charms of men are seldom described but those of women are emphatically described in the minutest detail. In the *Kumārasambhava* Kālidāsa imagines that Pārvatī was created by an assemblage of all the beautiful objects, set assiduously in their proper places as if the creator was desirous of seeing beauty concentrated in one place. The sentiment is repeated in the *Mālatimādhava* in describing Mālati's beauty. The Sanskrit poets prefer a gracefully slim but developed figure. A complexion of pure gold is generally appreciated, although *śyāmā* is favoured by Kālidāsa. A mass of jet black hair, often set with flowers, is admired but some prefer curls (*kuntālaka*) playing over the forehead. The eyes, as well as the glances, are compared to those of the deer and the brows are imagined in thes hape of a bow. Lips are usually imagined as red; the nose, ears and cheeks are seldom directly described but rows of well-formed teeth, jasmine-white and like the seeds of the pomegranate, are praised. Full-orbed bosoms, inadequately borne by slender limbs, are very much appreciated, and are frequently compared to a pair of golden pitchers. Heavy and prominent hips and buttocks are always taken as mark of beauty. The abdomen and the navel region are also elaborately described and so also the legs and thighs which are compared to different natural objects.

In Sanskrit poetry, as also in the dramas and prose romances, different types of lovers, male and female, are classified according to their rank, character, temperament and the different shades of their feelings and gestures. The hero is classified into the faithful (*anukula*), gallant (*dakṣiṇa*), the sly (*śaṭha*) and the saucy (*dhūrta*). In the same way, the heroine, in relation to the hero, may be his wife (*svīyā*), or belonging to another (*parakīyā*), or common to all (*sāmānyā*). They are subdivided again into *mugdhā* (adolescent and inexperienced), *madhyā* (youthful and partly experienced) and *pragalbhā* (mature and fully experienced). The *parakīyā* or another man's wife is the most popular type of heroine. The *sāmānyā* heroine is only of one kind, the *gaṇikā* or the courtesan. These types are further arranged according to the eight-fold diversity of the situation in relation to her lover: *svādhīna-patikā* (the heroine who has her lover under absolute control), *utkā* (the heroine disappointed in her assignation through the involuntary absence of her lover), *vāsaka-sajjā* (the heroine in full dress waiting for her lover), *vipralabdhā* (the heroine deceived), *kalahāntaritā* (the heroine separated by a quarrel), *khaṇḍitā* (the heroine outraged by signs of unfaithfulness in her lover), *abhisārikā* (the heroine who ventures out to meet her lover) and *proṣita-patikā* (the heroine pining for the absence of her lover).

In the narrative poetry emphasis is mainly laid on the theme, the events and the characters. The main purpose is to tell the story. The poets own subjective comments have a secondary role. But in the case of powerful poets the latter aspect becomes a factor which can not be ignored. In the *Kumārasambhava* Kalīdāsa has displayed considerable skill in delineating the main characters through following the Puranic tradition faithfully, but at the same time his own romanticism runs parallel in several passages of enchanting beauty. For instance, in the laments of Rati, the description of Pārvatī's body, the sudden arrival of spring, etc., in which the presence of the poet's mind is strongly felt. A loving sympathy with nature forms the background of his works. He has complete mastery in delineating sentiments, in characterisation, in construction of the plots and in creating dramatic situations. *Meghadūta* is also a singular testimony to the endless creativity of the poet's imagination. Here he gives to the airy nothing of a cloud any number of forms and functions, making the cloud a partner and participant in all sorts of human experiences fancied by a love-laden mind. But such a combination is rare. With the exception perhaps of the *Meghadūta* and the *Gītagovinda*, Sanskrit romanticism usually takes the form, not of a systematic well-knit poem, but of single stanzas in which a single emotion is depicted. It is probable that these stanzas were originally composed independently rather than in a particular context and were collected together as *śatakas*, each consisting of one hundred such stanzas. These *śatakas* have varied subject matter but the viewpoint of the composer permeates them all. For our purpose, the *Amaruśataka* is most important. It is rich not only in metrical variety but also in its romantic approach. However, Amaru depicts only the playful moods of love and is reluctant to touch the deeper chord, the note of sorrow and tragedy. In contrast, Bhartṛhari, though less exacting than Amaru in intensity, range and delicacy of expression, shows a great deal of genuine emotion which lends his verse a peculiar charm.

5. *Regional Literature*

The peoples of ancient India, barring those of certain southern territories, spoke in various forms of Prakrit which belonged to the Indo-European family. Sanskrit was never a spoken language. It was a refined transformation (*saṃskṛta*) of the existing languages and was evolved through scholarly efforts intended for communicating higher forms of thoughts and literary persuits and for maintaining the cultural tradition of the elitists. Likewise, Pali was an artificial language meant for the composition of the Buddhist texts. Some scholars hold that Pali was formed out of the regional Prakrit of the Magadha region while others ascribe its formation to the Prakrit of Kosambi or the Avanti region. In the beginning of the Christian era four types of Prakrit were widely prevalent: Ardhamāgadhī, Māgadhī, Śaurasenī and Mahārāṣṭrī. The regional languages of northern India and upper Deccan were derived mostly from these four forms of Prakrit.

In the South, Tamil came into existence from the Dravidian speech family. The earliest period of Tamil literature is known as the Saṅgam age, the span of which has been ascribed tentatively between 500 B.C. and A.D. 500. Among the surviving compositions of this age mention may be made of the grammatical work called *Tolkappiyam* and the poetical collections known as *Patthuppattu*, *Ettuthokkoi* and *Padinenkikkanaku*. The twin epics *Śilappadikāram* and *Maṇimakalai* were composed in the second century A.D. The Śaiva Nāyānars and the Vaiṣṇava Āḷvārs flourished between the seventh and the ninth centuries A.D. and we have already had occasion to refer to their devotional songs which are masterpieces not only in Tamil literature but in Indian literature as a whole.

From the eleventh century A.D., the horizon of Tamil literature began to expand and the writers became interested in the vast treasure house of Sanskrit literature. A good number of Sanskrit works were translated into Tamil. In the twelfth century Kamban, Ottakuttan and Pugalandi brought about a qualitative change in Tamil literature. Kamban's *Rāmāyaṇa*, in six cantos, was adapted from the work of Vālmīki and is a classic in itself. Ottakuttan's poetical works comprised a new version of the seventh canto of the *Rāmāyaṇa* and numerous hero legends. Pugalandi wrote on various episodes of the *Rāmāyaṇa* and the *Mahābhārata*. From the eleventh century onwards the Śaiva Siddhānta doctrine found its best expression in Tamil. The Vaiṣṇavas also did not lag behind. The *Mahābhārata* and a few Purāṇas were translated in the thirteenth century. This period marked the beginning of secular literature.

Kannaḍa is also a language of the Dravidian family which is widespread in modern Karnataka and in parts of Maharashtra. The Kannaḍa script is similar to that of Tamil. The grammatical rules are also similar in both the languages. From epigraphic evidence it appears that the Kannaḍa language began to reveal its characteristics from the fourth century A.D., though the earliest literary work in this language was not produced untill A.D. 850. It was *Kavirājamārga*, a book on poetics and literary criticism composed by the Rāṣṭrakūṭa king Amoghavarṣa or Nṛpatuṅga. In the tenth century Pampa, Ponna and Ranna enriched Kannaḍa literature. They wrote on the lives of the Jain Tīrthaṃkaras. One of the most celebrated works of Pampa was *Vikramārjuna-vijaya* or *Pampabhārata* which was based on the *Mahābhārata*. In the twelfth century Kannaḍa literature received a great fillip from the Vīraśaiva movement. There were 213 poets belonging to this faith ; their verses were called *vacanas*. Vasava, the founder of this sect composed as many as 700 *vacanas*. Among other Vīraśaiva poets, Prabhūdeva or Allama Prabhu and Harihara were famous. In the twelfth and thirteenth centuries Jain writers like Abhinavapampa, Nemicandra, etc., enriched Kannaḍa literature. In the middle of thirteenth century Mallikārjuna brought out a collection of Kannaḍa poems known as *Suktisudhārṇava*.

Telugu is the language of the Andhra region. The name probably was a corruption of Triliṅga. Compared to Tamil and Kannaḍa, Telugu is a more recent language. There are two types of Telugu—Deśī and Mārgī—the former being the language of the masses. The folk songs are in Deśī. Three types of such songs have been discerned: *lalipatalu* or songs for children, *jabalulu* or love-songs, and *udupupatalu* or songs of harvest. Mārgī Telugu is more Sanskritised. Nannia began to compose the *Mahābhārata* in this language in the eleventh century and it was completed in the thirteenth century by Tikkanna and Errapragada. These three poets were collectively called *Kavitraya*. In the twelfth century the Vīraśaiva faith influenced some Telugu writers, prominent among whom was Somanātha. In the same century Nannacoḍa composed *Kumārasambhava*; it should be noted that it was not an imitation of Kālidāsa's work of the same name. Two versions of the *Rāmāyaṇa* were composed in the thirteenth century. One was done by Raṅganātha and the other by four poets. Dandi's *Daśkumāracarita* was translated into Telugu by Ketana in the thirteenth century.

Malayalam was regional development of Tamil, but in the course of time it assumed a distinct character. The word *malai* means mountain. Malayalam-speakers claim Kamban's *Rāmāyaṇa* as the first work in their language. Owing to the influence of the Nambudri Brahmins Sanskrit words were introduced in the local Tamil of the Kerala region which was an important factor in the distinctive growth of Malayalam. Political isolation, regional disputes, the influence of the Christians and the Muslims were some of the other factors responsible for this transformation. The earliest Malayalam work was *Rāmacaritam*, based on the *Rāmāyaṇa*, which was composed in the fourteenth century.

The northern languages were evolved from different existing Prakrits through an intermediary stage known as Apabhraṃśa. The position of Apabhraṃśa is somewhat anomalous in the literary history of India. In some cases it was merly a transitory stage while in many other cases it became a medium of literary expression, complete in every respect. According to Patañjali Apabhraṃśa is a regional form of 'a pure word'. In Bharata's *Nātyaśāstra* it is stated that the Prakrits have three forms—Samāna, Vibhraṣṭa and Deśī the last form being divided into seven regional categories namely, Māgadhī, Avantī, Prācya, Śaurasenī, Ardhamāgadhī, Bāhlika and Dākṣiṇātya. Bhāmaha and Daṇḍi acknowledged the importance of Apabhraṃśa. From an inscription of the sixth century we know that the Valabhī king Guhasena wrote poems in Apabhraṃśa. Rudraṭa in the ninth century recognises Apabhraṃśa as a distinct medium of literary works. There is no dearth of Apabhraṃśa poetry, short-stories and even epics. The Jain writers depended on Apabhraṃśa even in the twelfth century. Thus it may be concluded that there were two streams in Apabhraṃśa, one of which was channelised into a distinctive literary language while other served as a link in the transition from Prakrit into regional languages.

The Marathi language was the transformation of western Prakrit and became a medium of literary expression between A.D. 1000 and 1300. The Nātha religious community began to exert its influence on Maharashtra from the tenth century. The *Gorakṣa-Amaranātha-Saṃvāda* was the first prose work in Marathi which belonged to the Nātha sect. Jñānadeva, the celebrated author of *Jñāneśvarī* and the composer of numerous poems in *abhaṅga* metre, also belonged to the Nātha tradition. Mukundarāja's *Vivekasindhu* composed about A.D. 1190. was the first work of a distinct Marathi character. In the thirteenth century a *bhakti* movement was launched in Maharashtra by Cakradhara whose followers had made a vigorous literary campaign for propagation. The verses of Nāmadeva, Tukāram and Janābāi contributed immensely to the development of the Vaiṣṇava *bhakti* movement. Marathi poetical literature drew its main impulses from the *Rāmāyaṇa* and the *Mahābhārata*. Bhāskarabhaṭṭa composed *Uddhavagītā* which was a commentary on the eleventh *skandha* of the *Bhāgavatapurāṇa*.

The older Rajasthani hero legends were composed in a form of Marwari language which was little different from Gujarati. The Jain polymath Hemacandra (1088-1173) collected a good number of Apabhraṁśa verses which have been claimed by historians to be the forerunners of Gujarati, Marwari and Hindi literature. Gujarati which was evolved from western Prakrit became the medium of literary expression from about the tenth century A.D. owing to the efforts of the Jain scholars and saints. Among the early non-Jain and secular writings mention should be made of *Vasantavilāsa*, *Raṇamallachanda*, *Uṣāharaṇa*, *Sītāharaṇa* and *Prabandhacintāmaṇi*. A few old Gujarati poems of the twelfth century that are available to us were composed in the *rāsa* form which was a semi-lyrical, semi-narrative form of literary expression. The Parsis of Gujarat translated their scriptures into Gujarati in the fourteenth century. The Sindhi language evolved from an Apabhraṃśa called Brãcaḍa. The Sindhi *Mahābhārata* was composed about A.D. 1000. In spite of this vigorous start, practically nothing was composed in Sindhi, except some love songs and hero legends, till the beginning of the seventeenth century.

So far as the Hindi group of dialects is concerned, the western Hindi groups were evolved between A.D. 1000 and 1300. from different existing Apabhraṃśas. The one emanating from Śaurasenī Apabhraṃśa bacame prominent. The eastern, Hindi, also known as Kosali or Awadhi, was likewise a conglomeration of various dialects in one of which was composed a book in the twelfth century. It was Dāmodara Paṇḍita's *Ukti-vyakti-parkaraṇa* meant for teaching Sanskrit in the local medium. Modern Hindi, which is the state language of India, is based on the Khariboli dialect which did not exist before A.D. 1800.

The evolution of Maithili began to take place from the thirteenth century A.D. The first work in Maithili was Jyotirīśvara's *Varṇaratnākara* which was composed at the beginning of the fourteenth century A.D. Maithili and Magahi, represented a sort of central Magadhan speech, while Bhojpuri was western Magadhan.

Bengali, Assamese and Oriya formed a very closely connected group and these languages showed the greatest amount of agreement among themselves. The earliest literary specimens of these languages are the *Caryāpadas* composed in the tenth century by the Buddhist Siddhācāryas in an eastern Apabhraṃśa known to them as *sandhyābhāṣā* or twilight language. The *Mādalāpāñjī* is a form of Oriya temple-records composed towards the end of the twelfth century. Oriya literature matured in the fourteenth century owing to the development of the *bhakti* movement. The main poets were Sāralādāsa and Markaṇḍadāsa. The former composed *Caṇḍīpurāṇa* and *Rāmāyaṇa* and made an abridged version of the *Mahābhārata*. The latter composed *Mahābhāṣya* and *Kesava-Koidhi* which were based on the Rāma and Kṛṣṇa legends respectively. The first notable poet in Assamese was Hema Sarasvatī who composed *Prahlādacarita* on the lines of Viṣṇupurāṇa. In the beginning of the fourteenth century Harihara Vipra and Kaviratna Sarasvati rendered some of the episodes of the *Mahābhārata* into Assamese. The greatest poet of the fourteenth century was Mādhava Kandalī who composed the Assamese *Rāmāyaṇa.*

6. Indian Literature Abroad

India's contact with the outside world was established in remote antiquity and developed through successive ages. Trade and maritime enterprises marked the beginning of this contact which was further strengthened by cultural relations. This intercourse resulted in a wide range of Indian literature—religious, philosophical, scientific, poetic, fictional, etc.—finding its way to regions both near and distant.

Among the neighbouring countries Indian literature had a natural access to Nepal, the valley of which "was never regarded as outside India's sphere of influence." As early as in 1824, B.H. Hodgson had discovered and collected from Nepal 423 volumes of Sanskrit manuscripts and distributed them to different research organisations. Notwithstanding subsequent collections and dispersions, Nepal is still a storehouse of ancient and medieval Indian manuscripts of Brahmanical and Buddhist traditions. The Mithila region served as the link of Nepal's cultural communication with the rest of India. The Maithili scholars were invited to the Nepalese courts. During the Muslim rule a good number of Indian scholars made their permanent residence in Nepal. The Malla kings of Nepal of the late medieval period were patrons of Sanskrit, Maithili and Bengali language.

Indian literature reached Tibet and Mongolia due to the spread of Buddhism. Over 4500 works of the Indian Buddhists, the Indian originals of which are largely lost, survive in meticulous Tibetan translation. These are contained in the great Tibetan collections called the *Kanjur* and the *Tanjur*, broadly meaning the collection of the words of the Buddha and of the expository treatises by the Ācāryas. Besides the canonical and exegetical texts of Buddhism, a large number of secular texts also have been translated and preserved in these collections. These texts pertain to various branches of Sanskrit literature like poetry, drama, rhetoric, grammar, astrology, medicine, etc. Among the writers whose works have been translated mention may be made of Pāṇini, Kālidāsa, Daṇḍin, Śrīharṣa, Vararuci and others. Buddhism and its literature in Tibetan translations reached Mongolia through Tibetan missionaries during the second half of the twelfth century A.D. A large number of the Indian texts were rendered into Mongolian. The Avadāna stories from Sanskrit and Jātaka stories from Pali were also translated into Mongolian in two collections, namely, *Uligarun-dalai* and *Altan-garal.* Mongolia has its own version of the *Rāmāyaṇa*, *Dvātriṃśatputtalikā*, *Pañcatantra*, *Subhāṣitaratnasaṃgraha*, etc.

From different sites of Central Asia numerous Buddhist manuscripts in Sanskrit, Prakrit, Uigur, Tokharian, Khotanese, Kuchean, Sogdian and also in other dialects have been found. Apart from the Buddhist missionaries, the Kuṣāṇa empire, which extended over a considerable part of Central Asia, was also responsible for the spread of Buddhism and Buddhist literature. It is also interesting to note that both Kharosthi and Brahmi scripts were used for writing Prakrit in some parts of Central Asia. In Chinese Central Asia, Brahmi was used for writing not only Sanskrit, but also Kuchean, Agnean, and Saka-Khotanese. Sanskrit was introduced into Central Asia by the Sarvāstivāda school which flourished in Kashmir, north western India and Afghanistan. The Sūtra Piṭaka of Central Asia included Āgamas corresponding to the Nikāyas of the Pali Tripiṭaka. Mahāyānic texts like *Saddharmapuṇḍarīka*, *Suvarṇaparbhāsa*, *Vajracchedikā*, etc., various *Prajñāpāramitās* and *Dhāraṇis*, as also commentarial works, have been found. Manuscripts of the non-canonical texts like Aśvaghoṣa's *Buddhaacrita* and *Saundarānanda*, Kumaralāta's *Kalpanāmaṇḍitikā*, Ārya Śūra's *Jātakamālā*, etc., should also be mentioned in this connection.

India's literary contact with China, Korea and Japan was also through Buddhism. The first Indian missionaries to China were Kaśyapa Matanga and Dharmarakṣa who translated a number of Buddhist works into Chinese. The visits of Chinese pilgrims to India was also reponsible for the spread of Indian Buddhist literature in China. The Chinese Buddhist canon forms a large collection of Sūtra or Āgama, Abhidharma or Śāstra and Vinaya texts of various sects. Texts of Mahāyāna and Tantric Buddhism are also numerous. In the field of secular literature Indian texts on astronomy, mathematics and medicine have Chinese versions. In Korea Indian Buddhist literature went through Chinese translations. A few Indian monks went to Korea and Korean monks frequently visited the Indian Buddhist monasteries and had training in Sanskrit. The Korean Hanggul script has Sanskrit influence. Buddhism was officially introduced in Japan from Korea about the middle of the sixth century A.D. The study of Sanskrit Buddhist scriptures became extensive in Japan. The discovery of ancient Sanskrit manuscripts in old Brahmi characters preserved at Horyuji and other monasteries deserves special mention. These manuscripts mostly belong to the Mahayanic stream.

According to tradition Buddhism was introduced in Śrīlaṅka during the reign of Tissa (247-207 B.C.) by Aśoka's son Mahendra. The Theravāda form which based itself squarely on Pali language become predominant there. In fact the complete Pali canon was first recovered from Śrīlaṅkā in the last century. A typical Śrīlaṅkān Pali also came into existence in which numerous commentaries were composed and transmitted to Southeast Asian countries. Apart from Theravāda other sects of Buddhism also went to Śrīlaṅkā and were responsible for the introduction of Sanskrit there. Numerous Sanskrit texts—religious, philosophical and secular—besides texts of Mahāyāna Buddhism, went to Śrīlaṅkā. Moreover, throughout the known period of ancient and early medieval Indian history there is ample evidence to show that south India was intimately connected with Śrīlaṅkā, both politically and culturally. Hinduism and Tamil culture had a deep impact on Śrīlaṅkan literary development.

Theravāda as well as Sanskrit Buddhism were preached in Burma as a result of which texts and commentaries belonging to both the traditions are found there in abundance. The impact of Pali on Burmese language is profound and Brahmanical culture as well as Brahmanical religio-philosophical, legal and secular literature had been significant in Burmese life. The Brāhmaṇas attached to the royal courts of Burma exerted their influence on the royal patrons. Inscriptions in Sanskrit or in mixed Pali-Sanskrit, medieval writings in Nagari and proto-Bengali scripts have been found. The Kalyani inscription dated A.D. 1442. mentions names of Sanskrit texts.

In Kambuja (earlier Fu-nan, modern Cambodia or Kampuchia) Sanskrit and Brahmanical culture played a vital role. Sanskrit inscriptions found there refer to the study of Pāṇini's grammar, Mīmāṃsā, Nyāya, the Purānas and Dharmaśāstras. Many of the rulers were accomplished Sanskrit scholars. We know there were Brahmanical settlements because a number of Sanskrit inscriptions refer to individual Brāhmaṇa scholars and the special lines of their study. All the six systems of Hindu philosophy were seriously studied in Kampuchia. Several inscriptions refer to extracts from the *Manusmṛti*. The kings were Śaivas with Tantric orientation. Vaiṣṇavism was also popular. The *Mahābhārata*, *Rāmāyaṇa* and *Harivaṃśa* were regularly recited in Kampuchian temples. The inscriptions of Yaśovarman refer to Sanskrit authors like Vatsyāyana, Guṇādhya, Bhāravi and Mayura. Buddhism, especially the Hīnayāna form, was preached in this region as well. The Pali canon and its commentaries are also integral part of the cultural life of Kampuchia.

Campā (south Annam, now under Vietnam) was also influenced by Brahmanical and then by Buddhist culture. More than one hundred Sanskritic inscriptions found there show that in this small region, the Vedas, Sanskrit grammar, the Dharmaśāstras, the six branches of Hindu philosophy, the Purāṇas and the two great epics were meticulously studied. Buddhism and Buddhist texts subsequently went to this region. When in A.D. 605 the Chinese general sacked Campā he is said to have taken way 1350 Buddhist texts. In Thailand also Brahmanical culture was succeeded by Buddhist culture. Like Burma, Thailand based its society on a revised version of the code of Manu. There is also a Thai version of *Rāmāyaṇa*. The Buddhist Jātaka stories and Aṭṭhakathā or commercial literature characterise the later literary structure of Thailand and Laos.

In Malaysia the *Rāmāyaṇa*, *Mahābhārata*, Jātakas and Kathā literature, as well as the Puranic legends, have been popular through the ages. Sanskrit culture had the maximum influence in Indonesia. The Vedas were studied in Java, so also were the Purāṇas. A prose and versified recension of the *Brahmāṇḍa Purāṇa* has been found in Java. The Indo-Javanese language took literary shape between A.D. 650 and 850. Between A.D. 925 and 1400 Java and Bali witnessed an elaborate growth of Āgamas (basically Śaiva with Tantric orientation), Dharmaśāstras (texts of individual and social behaviour), Nīti (ethics), Śāsana (law), Kāṇḍa (technical literature) and Itihāsa (epic works best represented by the Javanese *Mahābhārata* and *Rāmāyaṇa* and works based on them, the *Smradahana* dealing with the burning of Kāma by Śiva's wrath, *Kṛṣṇavijaya*, *Rāmavijaya*, *Bhomakāvya* etc.). Works like *Tantri Kāmandaka* are based upon the stories found in the *Pañcatantra* and *Hitopadeśa*.

"Mother of wisdom, India gave her mythology to her neighbours who went to teach it to the whole world. Mother of law and philosophy, she gave to three quarters of Asia a god, a religion, a doctrine, an art. She carried her scared language, her literature, her institutions into Indonesia, to the limits of the known world, and from there they spread back to Madagascar and perhaps to the coast of Africa, where the present flow of Indian immigrants seems to follow the faint traces of the past" (Coedes, 1968, XVI). There is evidence of the existence of Brāhmaṇa philosophers at Alexandria during the Kuṣāṇa period. We have to remember, however, that India's historical and cultural ties with Egypt did not bring the former into direct contact with genuine African culture and civilization, as Egypt during the time of Aśoka was Hellenized and thereafter it was successively dominated by the Jewish, Persian and Arabic powers. The only African country with which India's cultural contact is known to us is Ethiopia. But there is very little evidence to show that apart from a few loan-words and some influence on the script that Ethiopia owes something to India.

Some Vedic gods were worshipped in West Asia as early as the fourteenth century B.C. which is proved by the Boghaz Köi inscriptions. In subsequent centuries, some forms of Brahmanical religion prevailed in different parts of West Asia. The influence of Buddhist and other forms of Indian liteature upon West Asian religious systems was by no means insignificant. A Manichaean treatise written in the form of a Sūtra speaks of Mani as Tathāgata and mentions Buddha and Bodhisattva. The story of the Great Renunciation of Buddha occurs in a book called *Kitab Bilawhar wa Yudasaf*. From Arabic it was rendered into Georgian and then into other European languages including Greek and Latin. A Manichaean version of this legend was discovered by the Le Coq from Turfan on the basis of which

P. Alfaric tried to show that Indian Buddhist legends reached Europe about third century A.D. through the Manichaeans.

The Sassanian king of Iran, Khusru Anushirwan (A.D. 531-79), was interested in Indian medicine. Interest was similarly shown by the Abbasid Caliphs of Arabia. The medical treatises translated into Arabic included such famous works as the *Caraka*, *Suśruta*, *Nidāna* and *Aṣṭāṅga*. A tenth century Sanskrit text by one Rai was also translated. Among the Indian visitors to Abbasid Baghdad, mention may be made of Sabeh, a physician; Dhan, translator of Indian sciences into Arabic; Shanuk, author of a number of scientific treatises on poison, astrology and astronomy, morals and veterinary science; and Kan-kah, writer of four books on 'age', 'secret of birth', 'cycles of the year' and 'beginning of the year'. Alrazi or Rhazes of the ninth-tenth century A.D. incorporated Indian medical science in his *Kitab-al-hawi* known to medieval Europe as *Liber Continess* through the Latin translation by Moses Farachi.

Indian philosophical treatises, including the *Bhagavadgītā*, were directly introduced in the Islamic world by Al Bīrūnī. Under the patronage of several Muslim rulers of India many Sanskrit texts were translated into Persian. Zain-ul-Abedin, ruler of Kashmir, got the *Mahābhārata* translated into Persian in the fourteenth century. A number of scholars of Akbar's court were commissioned to translate into Persian the *Atharvaveda*, *Mahābhārata*, *Harivaṃśa*, *Bhagavadgītā*, *Yogavāsiṣṭha*, *Viṣṇupurāṇa*, *Bhāgavatapurāṇa*, etc. Such Persian translations of Sanskrit religious literature were produced under the Muslim rulers in other parts of India also. Among the works transtated, the following deserve special mention: the *Brahmavaivartapurāṇa*, *Adhyātma Rāmāyaṇa*, *Vrajamhātmya*, *Gayāmāhatmya* and *Kāśīkhaṇḍa*.

Ibn Ibrahim Alfazari translated towards the close of the eighth century an Indian astronomical work in Arabic. Subsequently the *Brahmasphūṭa-siddhānta* and *Khaṇḍakhādyaka* of Brahmagupta were translated. Alkhwarizmi's work on the Hindu method of calculation was translated into Latin under the title *De Numero Indico*. Other mathematical ideas, including the *sūlva* theorem, solutions to indeterminate equations as found by Brahmagupta and Bhaskara II, and the introduction of sine and cosine functions in trigonometry were of Indian origin and went to Europe through Arabia. Al-Bīrūnī's *Qanural-Mas'udi* was largely based upon Indian astronomical ideas. He also translated the *Sūryasiddhānta* of Varāhamihira.

The *Pañcatantra*, the famous book of fables in Sanskrit, was translated into Pahlavi by Barzoi at the command of Khusru Anushirwan (A.D. 531-79). The Syriac translation of this book was made by Bud in A.D. 570. It was translated into Arabic about the middle of the eighth century by Ibn-i-Maqaffa. There is also a later Syriac version (A.D. 1000), a later Persian version (A.D. 1130) and a Hebrew version (A.D. 1250). A number of Buddhist Jātakas were also translated into Arabic. Aśvaghosa's *Buddhacarita* was edited and modified by the Arab writers. The *Śukasaptati* had two Persian translations.

Greece was the first European country to come in close cultural contact with India. Indian contribution to European philosophy, medical science, mathematics and astronomy has long been recognised and commented on by scholars. The Indian epics, particularly the *Mahābhārata*, were well known to the Greeks in the first century A.D. as is evident from the statement of the Greek rhetorician Dio Chrysostom. The *Barlaam and Josaphat* written in Greek by John of Damascus is a Christianised version of Buddha's renunciation. It was also translated in many other European languages. The same holds good in the case of *Pañcatantra* which had Greek, Latin, Spanish German, Italian and English versions. "In the whole field of world literature" writes V. Raghavan, "there has been no work more remarkable than the Sanskrit *Pañcatantra* of which 200 versions arose in more than fifty languages, three-fourths of which are non-Indian."

Select Bibliography

Since the present work is meant for non-specialists, only names of some representative and easily available books and periodicals are given here. As the readers must have noticed, instead of footnotes, when something is quoted from any book, reference has been given when the quotation ends, either after the surname of the author or after the initials of the title. Such books are also mentioned in this bibliography and the readers will not be in any difficulty to find them.

Chapter One

For the books, reports and articles on Indian archaeology see *Annual Bibliography of Indian Archaeology* (Leiden), *Ancient India* and *Annual Report of the Archaeological Survey of India, Indian Archaeology: A Review* (Delhi), *Antiquity* (Cambridge), *American Anthropologist* (Chicago), *World Archaeology* (London), *Ancient Pakistan* (Peshawar), etc.

D.P. Agarwal, *Archaeology in India* (1982); F.R. and B. Allchin, *Birth of Civilization: South Asia* (1983); B. Subbarao, *The Personality of India* (1958); V.D. Krishnaswami 'Progress in Prehistory' in *Ancient India* No. 9 (1952), 53-79. 'Neolithic Pattern of India' (1965) ; *ibid.*, No. 16 (1960), 24-64; N.R. Banerjee, *Iron Age in India* (1965); D.K. Chakravarti, 'The Aryan Hypothesis in Indian Archaeology' in *Indian Studies Past and Present* (1968), IX. 343-358; R.E.M. Wheeler, *The Indus Civilization* (1968); W.A. Fairservis (Jr.), *The Roots of Ancient India* (1971); B.K. Thapar, 'The Aryans : A Reapprisal of the Problems' in *Vivekanada Commemoration Volume* (197), 147-164; H.D. Sankalia. *Prehistory and Protohistory of India and Pakistan* (1974); D.H. Gordon, *Prehistoric Background of Indian Culture* (1971).

Chapter Two

English translations of the Vedic texts: *Ṛgveda*, R.T.H. Griffith 1896-97; in parts F. Max Müller in *SBE* XXXII (1891) and H. Oldenberg in *SBE*, XLVI (1897); *Atharvaveda*, W.D. Whitney (1905), M. Bloomfield in *SBE*, XLII, (1897); *Aitareya* and *Kauṣītaki Brāhmaṇa*, A.B. Keith, *HOS* XXV, 1920; *Śatapatha Brāhmaṇa*, J. Eggeling in *SBE*, XII, XXVI, XLI, XLIII, XLIV (1882-1900); *Aitareya* and *Śāṅkhyāyana Āraṅyaka*, A.B. Keith (1909) Principal Upaniṣads; F. Max Müller in *SBE* I and XV; R.A. Hume, *Thirteen Principal Upaniṣads* (1921); Principal Dharmsūtras, G. Bühler in *SBE* II and XIV; Gṛhyasūtras, H. Olderberg in *SBE* XXIX and XXX.

M. Winternitz, *History of Indian Literature* I, (1927); A.A. Macdonell and A.B. Keith, *Vedic Index*, 2 Vols (1912); A.B. Keith, *Religion and Philosophy of the Veda and Upaniṣads*, 2 Vols (1925); P. Basu, *Indo-Aryan Polity* (1925); J. Jolly, *Recht und Sitte* (Eng. trans. B.K. Ghosh 1928); N.N. Bhattacharyya, *History of Indian Cosmogonical Ideas* (1971); R.C. Majumdar (ed.), *The Vedic Age* (1951); J. Muir, *Original Sanskrit Texts* (1872-74); D.P. Chattopadhayaya, *Lokāyata* (1959).

Chapter Three

E.J. Rapson (ed), *Cambridge History of India* I (1922); H.C. Raychaudhuri, *Political History of Ancient India* (1950); R.C. Majumdar (ed.), *Age of Imperial Unity* (1951), *The Classical Age* (1954), *Age of Imperial Kanauj* (1955), *Struggle for Empire* (1957); H.C. Ray, *Dynastic History of Northern India*, 2 Vols (1931, 1936); R.G. Basak, *History of North Eastern India* (1934); A.S. Altekar, *Rāṣtrakūṭas and Their Times* (1934); R.C. Majumdar (ed.), *History of Bengal* (1943); R.S. Tripathi, *History of Kanauj* (1937); K.A.N. Sastri, *History of South India* (1955), *The Colas* (1955), *Comprehensive History of India* (ed.) II (1957); G. Yazdani (ed.), *Early History of Deccan* (1960); Romila Thapar, *From Lineage to State* (1984).

Chapter Four

R. Shamastry, Eng. trans. of Kauṭilya's *Arthaśāstra* (1929), Eng. trans. R.P. Kangle (1960-65); G. Jha, *Manusmṛti*. Eng.

trans. with Notes, 5 Vols (1922-29); T.W. Rhys Davids and H. Oldenberg, *Vinaya Piṭaka*, Eng. trans. in SBE (1881-85); T.W. Rhys Davids, *Dīgha Nikāya*, Eng. trans. *Dialogues of the Buddha*, 3 Vols. (1899, 1910, 1921); R.L. Mitra, *Kāmandakīya Nītīsāra*, rep. by S.K. Mitra (1982); N.N. Bhattacharyya, *Ancient Indian Rituals and Their Social Contents* (1975); P.V. Kane, *History of Dharmaśāstra*, 5 Vols (1930-62); N.C. Bandyopadhyaya, *Development of Hindu Polity and Political Theory*, ed N.N. Bhattacharyya (1980); Beni Prasad, *The State in Ancient India* (1928), *Theory of Government in Ancient India* (1927); K.P. Jayaswal, *Hindu Polity* (1924); O. Stein, *Megasthenes Und Kauṭilya* (1921); R.S. Sharma, *Aspects of Political Ideas and Institutions in Ancient India* (1959), *Indian Feudalism* (1980); B.N.S. Yadava, *Society and Culture in Northern India in the Twelfth Century* (1973); D.C. Sircar, *Landlordism and Tenancy in Ancient and Medieval India* (1960), ed. *Land System and Feudalism in Ancient India* (1965); R. Thapar, *Ancient Indian Social History* (1978).

Chapter Five

P.C. Aggarwal, *Caste, Religion and Power: An Indian Case Study* (1971); Imtiaz Ahmed (ed.), *Caste and Social Stratification Among the Muslims* (1973); A. Aiyappan. and L.K. Bala Ratnam (ed.), *Society in India* (1956); F.G, Baily, *Caste and Economic Frontier* (1957); J.N. Bhattacharyya, *Hindu Castes and Sects* (1896); E.A.H. Blunt, *The Caste System of Northern India* (1931); L. Dumont, *Homo Hierarchicus* (1970); N.K. Dutt, *Origin and Growth of Caste in India* (1931, 1933); R. Fick, *Social Organisation of North India in Buddha's Time* (1920); G.S. Ghurye, *Caste, Class and Occupation* (1961); E.W. Hopkins, *Mutual Relation of the Four Castes in Manu* (1881); J.H. Hutton, *Caste in India* (1969); S. Jaiswal, 'Studies in Early Indian Society: Trends and Possibilities', *Indian Historical Review*, VI (1979-80); P.V. Kane, *History of Dharmaśāstra*, II (1974 ed.); I. Karve, *Hindu Society: An Interpretation* (1961); S.V. Ketkar, *History of Caste in India* (1909-11); K.C. and J. Panchanadikar, *Determinants of Social Structure and Social Change in India* (1970); P.H. Prabhu, *Hindu Social Origanisation* (1958); H.V. Rao, *Indian Caste System* (1931); E.

Senart, *Caste in India* (1936); R.S. Sharma, *Śūdras in Ancient India* (1958); S. Sinha, *Caste in India: Its Structural Pattern and Socio-Caltural Integration* (1967); M.N. Srinivas, 'Caste: A Trend Report and Bibliography', *Current Sociology*, VIII, (1959); M. Singer and B.S. Cohn (ed.), *Structure and Change in Indian Society* (1968); E. Westermarck, *Origin and Development of Moral Ideas* (1921).

Chapter Six

S. Ratnagar, *Encounters: The Westerly Trade of Harappa Civilization* (1981); B.D. Chattopadhyay, 'Trade and Urban Centres in Early Medieval North India' in *Indian Historical Review*, I (1974), 203-19; L.G. Possehl (ed.), *Ancient Cities on the Indus* (1979); J. Rai, *Rural-Urban Economy and Social Changes in Ancient India* (1974); V.K. Thakur, *Urbanisation in Ancient India* (1981); N.K. Wagle, *Society at the Time of the Buddha* (1966); E.H. Warmington, *Commerce between India and the Roman Empire* (1928); R.G. Basak, *Gāthā Saptaśatī* (1956); S.C. Upadhyaya, *Kāmasūtra of Vatsyāyana* (1961); W.H. Schoff, *The Periplus of the Erythrean Sea* (1912); A. Ghosh, *City in Early Medieval India.*

Chapter Seven

J.W. McCrindle, *Ancient India as described by Megasthenes and Arrian* (1877); T.W. Rhys-Davids, *Buddhist India* (1903); S. Beal, *Si-yu-ki, Buddhist Record of the Western World*, 2 Vols. (1906); *Life of Hiuen Tsang* (1911); T. Watters, *On Yuan Chwang's Travels in India*, 2 Vols. (1904-05); H.M. Elliot and J. Dowson, *History of India as told by Its Own Historians*, I-II (1866-70); G. Jha, *Manubhāṣya of Medhātithi* Eng. trans. (1922-29); J.J. Meyer, *Kuṭṭanīmata und Samaymātṛkā*, German trans. (1903); R. Schmidt, *Kalāvilāsa*, German trans. (1914); G.K. Shrigondakar, *Mānasollāsa*, 2 Vols. (GOS, 1925, 1939); H. Yule and H. Cordier, *The Book of Ser Marco Polo*. 2 Vols. (1920).

Chapter Eight

S. Sanghvi, *Advanced Studies in Indian Logic and Metaphysics* (1961); D.P. Chattopadhyaya, *Indian Atheism* (1960), *Science and Society in India* (1977); N.N. Bhattacharyya, *History of Indian Cosmogonical Ideas* (1971); P.C. Ray, *History of Chemistry in Ancient and Medieval India* (1956); S.N. Dasgupta, *History of Indian Philosophy* (1922); S. Radhakrishnan, *Indian Philosophy* (1923, 1927)

Chapter Nine

J.N. Banerjea, *Pauranic and Tantric Religion* (1966); N.N. Bhattacharyya, *Jain Philosophy: Historical Outline* (1976), *History of Researches on Indian Buddhism* (1981), *History of the Tantrik Religion* (1982); J.M.S. Hooper, *Hymns of the Āḷvārs* (1929); P. Kingsbury and G.E. Phillips, *Hymns of the Tamil Saivite Saints* (1921); G.E. Pope, *The Tiruvācakagm* (1900); R.G. Bhandarkar, *Vaiṣṇavism, Śaivism and Minor Religious Systems* (1913), J.N. Farquhar, *Outline of Religious Literature of India* (1920); D.R. Bhandarkar (ed.), *B C. Law Volume* (1945), S.B. Dasgupta. *An Introduction to Tantric Buddhism* (1950).

Chapter Ten

A.K. Coomaraswamy, *History of Indian Art* (1927); J. Fergusson and J. Burgess, *Cave Temples of India* (1880); P. Brown, *Indian Architecture* (1940); S Kramrisch, *Indian Sculpture* (1973); N.R. Ray, *Maurya and Sunga Art* (1945); N.K. Bose, *Canons of Orissan Architecture* (1932); S.K. Saraswati, *Survey of Indian Sculpture* (1958); B. Rowland, *Art and Architecture of India* (1953); H. Zimmer, *Art of Indian Asia* 2 Vols (1955); J.N Banerjea, *Development of Hindu Iconography* (1956); D. Desai, *Erotic Sculpture of India* (1975).

Chapter Eleven

M. Winternitz, *History of Indian Literature* 2 Vols. (1927, 1933); J.N. Farquhar, *An Outline of the Religious Literature of India* (1920); A.B. Keith, *Sanskrit Drama* (1924); S.N. Dasgupta and S.K. De (ed), *History of Sanskrit Literature* (1947); G. Coedes, *The Making of South East Asia* (1966); V. Raghavan, *Sanskrit: Essays on the Value of the Language and the Literature* (1972); A.D. Pusalkar, *Studies in the Epics and Puranas of India* (1955); for histories of regional literature see the Sahitya Akademi publications.

Index

ābhāsavāda 262
Ābhīras 65, 75
administration : formative stage in the Vedic age 32-34, 110-14, Mauryan 117-18, 200, measures suggested by Kauṭilya 119-21, post-Mauryan 121-23, Gupta and post-Gupta 128-32, economic basis of 133-36, officials 117-20, 128-29, 193-94, royal titles 121-22, village administration 183-84, administrative units 190-93, municipal administration 193-94
advaita 241-44
Āgamānta Śaivism 260-61
Agnimitra 55
Ajanta caves 274-75
Ajātaśatru 49, 50
Ājīvikism 264, 249, 270
Al-Biruni, his views on Indian civilization 214-18
Alexander 49-51
Āḷupas 84
Amravati : stūpa 261
scenes from 273
Amoghavarṣa 92-93
Ānandas 76
Anantavarman Coḍagaṅga 96
Antalcidas 56
Apabhraṁśa 308-09
Arab accounts 206-09
architecture 269-81, see under caityas, monuments, saṅghārāmas, stūpas, rock-cut and structural temples
Ārjunāyanas 63-64
Aryanism : development of the myth 19-20, hypothetical theories regarding Aryan homeland 20-23, supposed migration associated with archaeological sites 23-26
Āṣādhasena 65
Assamese, genesis of language and literature 310
Aśoka 51-54
Aulikaras 64
Aurangabad caves 275
Azes I and II 57-58
Azilises 57

Bādarāyana 241
Bagh caves 275
Bauls 267
Bhadraka 55
bhakti cult 241, 245, 247-51, 253-55, stages of 260, image worship in 271, 273
Bhāskara, expounder of dualism 259
Bhāskaravarman 79
Bhoja : dynasty 75, Pratihāra 91, Paramāra 107-08
Bhūmaka 61
Bhūmimitra 55
Bimbisāra 49, 50
Bindusāra 51
Bodhgaya : stūpa 269
pillar 273
Brahma image 278
brahman : transformation and transfiguration of 241-42, 259, relation with the world 242-45, Gauḍapāda and Saṅkara on 242-44, theistic interpretation 244-45, of

Rāmānuja, Madhva and Nimbārka 258-63, influence on Buddhist Mādhyamika and Yogācāra 242-43, *saguṇā brahman* and *māyā* 243-44, creative process as the self expression of 258, identification of *brahman* with the supreme being of the sectarian systems 260-63

Brahma sect 260

Bṛhasvātimitra 55

Bṛhatphalayanas 65

Buddhism : political ideals of 114-17, on caste system 152-54, Hiuen Tsang's account of 205-06, common features with Hindu way of life 251, no social code 251, historical development of 246-47, rise of Mahāyānism 247, monuments 247-48, iconic types 247, 250, 271-72, 277, 282, image worship 249, monasteries 270, influence on Vedānta 242, female principle in 252, metamorphosis of 263-67, influence on Nātha, Dharma and Pīr cults 267. See under Hinayāna, Mahāyāna and Vajrayāna

Buddhist sects : Sthavira and other Hīnayāna sects 247, Sarvāstivāda 250, Vaibhāsika and Sautrāntika 250, Mādhyamika and Yogācāra 250, Mahāsaṅghikas 247, Vājrayāna 264-65

Budhagupta 71-72

Burials : Late Stone Age 5, pre-Harappan 8, Harappan 12-13, graves and wares associated with the Iron Age 17-19

Caitya halls : description 269, evolution of style and sites of 270, of the Gupta and post-Gupta period 274-75

Cahamanas 84, 94, 106-08

Cālukyas : of Badami 80-81, Pulakesin II 82-83, 85, rivalry with the Pallavas 84-86, Eastern Cālukyas 97, Western Cālukyas 98-99, under Somesvara and Vikramāditya VI 100-102

Candellas 94-95, 108

Candragupta : Maurya 50-51, Gupta I and II 65-66, 68-69

Caste system : genesis and development in the Vedic age 34-40, consequence of detribalisation 34-40, modern views on 143-44, material basis of 145-46, in Dharmasūtras and Dharmaśāstras 146-50, hybrid castes 148-50, inconsistencies in *varṇasaṅkara* theory 150-52, Buddhist views on 152-54, Jainism on 154, medieval reformers on 154-55, the Viraśaiva transformation of 155-56, among Muslims and Christians 156-57, hierarchy and social position 157-60, the first caste vis-a-vis the dominant caste 158-60, Brahmanas not a homogeneous social groups 160-61, lower clan Brāhmaṇas 161-63, ambivalence in the concept of Brāhmaṇahood 164-65 untouchability 165-68, subcastes 168-69, theories on 170-71, caste and slavery 171-75, seven castes of Megasthenes 200, Hiuen Tsang's description of Indian castes 203, Medhātithi's interpretation of 211-12

Caulukyas 94, 106-08

Cemetery 12, 14, 17-18

Ceras 63, 85

Cities : Harappan 8-14, 178, various types of 176-77, Maurya, Kuṣāṇa and Gupta 176, economic life, ports and market towns 185-87, life of urban elites 187-90, post-Gupta cities 193-94, municipal administration 193-94, administration of the Maurya cities 199,

cities as described by Hiuen Tsang 303, paucity of cities in India as told by the Arab writers 207
Coins: cult images inscribed on 272-73, Lakṣmī on 280
Colas: Karikāla 63, of Uraiyur and Renaṇḍu 81, Pallava subjugation 85, under Rājarāja and Rājendra 99-100, Āditya to Rājarāja 98, rivalry with the Cālukyas 100-01
Copper hoard cultures 17

Darius 49
Demitrius 56
Devagupta 78
Devahuti 55
Devapāla 89-90
Dharmāditya 74
Dharma cult 267
Dharmapāla 88-89
Dhruva 87-89
drama 301-03
dvāita school 260
dvaitādvaita school 259

Eastern Gaṅgas 77, 85, 97
Economy: prehistoric 4, pre-Harappan 5-6, Harappan 10-12, Vedic 40-42, perspective 133-36, evidence of Bhddhist literature 180-82, of the *Periplus* 1985-86, foreign accounts 194-96, Megasthenes on 198-99, Hiuen Tsang's evaluation 202-03, Arab accounts of 206-09, Marco Polo on 221-25
Ellora caves 275, 278, 282, 285
epic literature: their influence and works based on them 291-99, in regional languages 306-11, Indian epics abroad 313-16
erotic: sculpture 288-90, literature 303-04
Eucretides 56

Female Principle: pre-Harappan 8, Harappan 12, post-Harappan 16-17, of secondary importance in the Vedas 43, conception of *yoni* and *prakṛti* as cosmic principle 45, 47, mother goddess as *śakti* 249, 252, 258, in Vaisnavism 258-60, in Śaivism 260-62, in Buddhism 252, 264-66, in Sahajiyā tradition 266-67
Feudalism: some question on King's land right 123-26, vassals and feudatories: their position and categories 129-30, differences with European feudalism 137, the caste question 138, Sharma's thesis of feudalistic 'formations' 138-39, Yadava's views 139-40 Sircar's contradictory statements 140-41, *amaranāyakas* of Vijayanagara and *ḍāmars* of Kashmir 141-42, clan-feudalism among the Rajputs 142
Feudatories: post-Mauryan 54-56, Kuṣāṇa and post Kuṣāṇa 64-65, of the Śakas and Sātavahanas 64-65, of the Guptas 72-74, of the Pratihāras 95-96, clan leaders 56-58, 142, of the Cālukyas 84-85, account, position and historical role of 102-05, position and categories 129-30, their patronage to art and architecture 286-88
Foreign invasions: Persian and Greek 49-50, later Greeks 56-57, Śakas and Pahlavas 57-58, Kuṣāṇas 58-60, Huṇas 70-72, Turkish 106-10

Gāhaḍavālas 106
Gajalakṣmī 283
Gāṇapatya 263
Gandhāra images 271-72
Gauḍas 78-79, 83

Gauḍapāda 242
Gautamīputra Sātakarṇi 61-62
God: see under Iśvara
Gondophernes 57
Gopacandra 74
Govinda III 89, 92
Grahavarman 78, 87
Guhilas 87, 94, 107
Gujarati literature: genesis and development 309
Guptas: early history 65-66, Candragupta I 66, Samudragupta 66-68, Candragupta II 68-69, Kumāragupta 69-70, Skandagupta and his successors 70-72, later Guptas 73, 77-78, 86
Gurjaras: of Broach 82, Pratihāras under their earlier Kings 87-89, under Bhoja and his successors 91, feudatories of 94-95, resistance of Arab invasions 87, 106

Harappa civilization: beginnings 8-9, area and sites 9, town planning 9-10, metallurgy 10-11, productions 11, cultural uniformity 11-12, religion 12, disposal of the dead 12-13, date 13, end 13-14
Harṣvardhana 61, 81-84
Haryaṅkas 49
Hīnayāna: Sthavira and other sects 247, Sarvāstivāda 250, Vaibhāṣika and Sautrantika 250
Hindi language: genesis 310
Hinduism: in the making 249-52, catholicity and spirit of tolerance 249-50, epico-puranic contribution to its shaping 251, 253, new theistic orientation 258-63, five major cults of 263, popular cults 246-252, 265
Hiuen Tsang 83-84, account of his travels 200-01, his description of India 202-06
horse trade 196
Hoysalas 99, 109-10
Huviṣka 60

Icons, iconography: Buddhist 247, 250, 271-72, 277, Dhyani Buddhas 282, images from Gandhāra and Mathura 271-72, depiction of the Jātaka stories in Bharhut, Sanchi and other places 269-70, cult images 271, on coins 272-73, Jain images 248, 272, Brahma image 278, Gajalakṣmī 273, Lakṣmi on coins 280, Vaiṣṇava, Śaiva, Sākta and Saura images 272-73, 279-83, Viṣṇu 277-78 Siva 278-79, syncretistic icons 263
Ikṣvākus 65
Indrāgnimitra 55
Iron Age: beginnings 17-18, Gandhara grave culture 18, sites 18-19, PGW and NBP connection 18, black-and-red ware connection 18-19, southern megaliths 19
Iśānavarman 73-74
Iśvara, as the first cause 45, Nyaya-Vaiśeṣika defence of the concept 232-36, Jain and Mīmāṃsaka arguments for refuting the concept 233-36, growth of theism 239-42, Vedantic concept of 243, theistic interpretors of Vedanta 259-60

Jaimini, on king's land right 123-26
Jainism: political ideals of 115, on caste system 154, logicians 250-51, common features with the Hindu way of life 257, identity maintenance 251-52, social codes 252, religion of the merchants 255-58, progress of 250-51, patronage 255-56, centres and history 256-58, concept of charity 257, causes of survival 263-69, introduction of image worship 247-49, images 277, 282, from Mathura 272, monuments 250-

57, monasteries 270, stūpas 272, temples 281

Kacchapaghātas 107
Kadambas 84
Kākatiyas 99
Kaḷabhras 85
Kālacakrayāna 264-65
Kalachris: early rulers 79-80, of Tripuri 94, 106, 108
Kaliṅgas: Khāravela 62-63, Cālukya feudatories 85, Salodbhavas, Bhauma-Karas Bhanjas, Sulkis, Somavaṃsis 95, Anantavarman Coḍagaṅga 95-96, 106
Kāmarūpa: early rulers of 79, after Bhāskaravarman 95, Ahom occupation 109
Kaṇiṣka 59-60
Kannaḍa literature: genesis 307
Kārdamakas 62
Karikāla 63
Kārkotakas 93-94
Karma, doctrine of 237-39, 241
Kauṭilya: on detribalisation 38, on state system 119-21, on slavery 173
Khāravela 62-63
Kosalas 85
Kṛṣna III 93, 98
Kujula Kadphises 58-59
Kumāragupta 69-70
Kṣemendra 213-14

Lakṣmanasena 109
Lalitāditya 93-94
Liṅgāyatas 261-62
Literature: drama 301-03, epics 297-99, 306-11, 313-16 erotic 303-04, Indian literature abroad 310-17, Pali and Prakrit 306, 309, poetry 304-06, Purāṇas 299-301, primitive substratum of 292-97, regional literature 306-10, ritual significance of 293-94, romances 303-04, Vedic 27-30
Loharas 94

Madhusudana 244
Madhva 244-45, on *brahman* 241, doctrines of 260
Mādhyamika 242-43
Magadhi language 310
Mahāsaṅghikas 247
Mahāsenagupta 78
Mahāyāna 242-43, 247, 264
concept of *śakti* in 252-58, sexual dualism 264-66, influence on Vedanta 242
Mahendravarman 85
Mahīpāla, Pāla 90, Pratihara 91
Maīthili language 310
Maitrakas 77, 82-83
Mālavas 64
Malayalam literature, genesis 309
Mānas 79
Maṇḍana 244
Manu: socio-political ideas 126-28, on caste 148-52, on untouchability and Kulluka's interpretation 167-68, on slavery 173-74, Medhātithi's commentary on 209-13
Marathi literature: genesis 309
Māṭharipuira Iśvarasena 65
Mathura images 271-72
Maues 57
Maukharis 73-74, 77
Mauryas 51-54, of Konkan 84
Mauryan columns 268-69, 273
māyā: concept of 243-45, as *śakti* of *brahman* 258, as material cause of the world 260-61, transformatory aspects of 263
Megaliths 19
Megasthenes, account of India, 198-200
Menander 56
Mithradates 57
Monuments: Buddhist 247-48, 250, 252, 269-72, Jain 248, 256-57, Jain caves and stūpas 270, 272, 275, Vaisnava and Saiva 248
Mother Goddess: pre-Harappan 8, Harappan 12, post-Harappan

16-17, *yoni* 47, as *śakti* 249, 252, 258. See under Female Principle
Myekandadeva 260

Nāgas 246, 271
Nāgabhaṭa I 87-88, II 89
Nāgarjuna 242, 247, 250
Nahapāna 61
Nalas 79
Nandas 50-51
Narasiṃhagupta 71-73
Narasiṃhavarman 85
Nārāyaṇa 55
Nātha Siddhas 267
Naval trade 179, 181, 185-86, 194-96, 223-24
Neḍuñjaḷiyan 63
Neolithic-Chalcolithic; problems 2-3, 5-6, pre-Harappan settlements 5-8, of Baluchistan 6-8, post-Harappan Gujarat, Rajasthan, Sind and Punjab 14, Central India 15, Maharashtra 15-16, South India 16, transition in eastern India 16-17
Nimbārka 245, 260
Nirgrantha 246, see under Jainism
Noḷambas 97

Occupations 40-42, 146-50, 180-82
officers: see under administration
Oriya literature: genesis 310
overland routes 180

Padmapāda 243
paintings 274-75
Pālas: rise 88, under Dharmapāla and his successors 89-90, bid for mastery over Kanauj 88, decline and downfall 96
Pali and Prakrit 306, 309
Pallavas: early rulers 81, rivalry with the Cālukyas 84-86, decline 97-98
Pañcopāsanā 263
Pāṇḍyas: early history 63, 81, subsequent history 98, last phase 110, Marco Polo on 223-25
Paramaras 87, 106-08
Patronage, of art and architecture, 248-49, 252, 255-56, 283-88
Philosophy: Vedic beginnings 43-45, first principles of creation 45-46, sources of later tradition 47-48, the concept of god: see under Iśvara, epistemology 226-27, conflict between empiric and *a priori* ideas 228, atomism 233-34, doctrine of *karma* 47, 237-39
Pir cult, Buddhist influence on 267
poetry 304-06
popular cults 246, institutionalisation 248-49, within the Hindu fold 251-52, presided over by Śivā 265
Prakāśānanda 244
Pravarasena I 65
prostitution: Vātsyāyana on 189-90, Dāmodara and Kṣemendra on 213-14
Pulakeśin II 82-85
Purānas: classification and contents 299-301
Purugupta 72
Puṣrabhūtis 77-84, 205
Puṣyamitra 55

Rājaraja 99
Rajasthani literature: genesis 309
Rājendra I, 99-100
Rājyavardhana 78
Rāmacandra, Yādava 109
Rāmānuja: 244, on *brahman* and *māyā* 244-45, doctrines of 258-59
Rāṣṭrakūṭas 76, Dantidurga and his successors 87, Govinda III and his successors 92-93, north Indian invasions 87, 92, 97, victory over Colas 98
religion: pre- and protohistoric 5, 8, 12-13, Vedic 43-48, see under Vaiṣṇavism, Śaivism, Śāktism,

Buddhism, Jainism, popular cults, non-formal approach and rise of institutionalism 240-41, 244-45, 252-53, non-theistic sects 249, patronage 248-49, 252 255, toleration 249-50, concept of God' 232-36, theistic transformations 246-49, supreme being identified with sectarian deities 249, 253, Al-Biruni on Indian religion 215-16
rock-cut and structural shrines: 270-71, stūpas, *devagṛha* and *dhvajastambha* 211, of Gupta period 274-75, brahmanical shrines 275-76, Pallava 275, structural 276-77
Romances 303-04
Rṣabhadatta 61
Rudradaman 61, 62, 64

Sahajayāna 266-67
Sailodbhavas 95
Saindhavas 94
Saisunāgas 50
Saivism, 246, 248-49, 251, 253, 260-62, images 272-73, 278, 282, female principle in 252, Nāyanars 253-54, 260, Saivite interpretation of Vedānta 260-62, Śaiva Siddhānta 260, Agamānta 260-61, Virasaiva 261-62, Kashmir 262, absorption of Mahāyānic elements 265
Śakti 249, 258, basic Sākta viewpoint 262-63, of Viṣṇu 259-60, of Śiva 260-62, *prakāśa* and *vimarśa* aspects 262-63, in Buddhist and Sahajiyā cults 264-66, icons 279-80, 283
Sālaṅkāyanas 76
Samācāradeva 74
Samudragupta 65-68, 76-77
Sanaka sect 259-60
Sanchi, stūpa 269, bas-reliefs 271
Saṅghārāma, description of 269, the rites 270, of Gupta and post-Gupta period 274-75
Śaṅkarācārya 241-44
Sarvajña 244
Śaśaṅka 78, 83
Sātavahanas: Gautamīputra and his successors 61-62
Sauras 263
Science: anatomy 231-32, Arabic translation of medical texts 209, 315-16, Al-Biruni on Indian science 216-17, ambivalent attitude towards science 228-32, chemical sciences 231, mathematics 231-32
sculpture: secular 273, emphasis on human figure 274, of Ajanta caves 275, growth of regional schools 276-77, further developments of 281-83, erotic 288-90
Seleucus 51
Senas 96, 108-09
sexo-yogic practices 264-66
Sindhi literature: genesis 309-10
Skandagupta 70-71
slavery: outside India 171, no slavery in Vedic civilization 171-72, view of Megasthenes 172-73, 200, Kauṭilya's classification of 173, law-givers on 173-74, divergence in injunction and social practice 174-75
Smārta-Puranic way 251-52
social life: prehistoric 3-8, Harappan 11-17, post-Harappan 11-17, Vedic 34-40, in Manu 126-28, influence of the caste system 144-75, village society 182-85, urban society 187-90, Megasthenes on 199-200, Hiuen Tsang on 203-03, Arab accounts of 206-09, norms set by Medhātithi 209-12, darker sides of: Damodarās and Kṣemendra's account 213-14, Al-Biruni on 217-18, account of Somesvara 220-21, Marco Polo on 222-25
Solar images 278-79, 283

Someśvara, Cālukya 98, 100-01
Somavaṃśis 80, 95, 97
Srivaiṣṇava sect 258-60
state system: Vedic ideals of sovereignty 110-14, the Buddhist concept of state 114-17, Mauryan centralisation 117-18, Kauṭilyan state 119-21, ideals in *Manusmṛti* 126-28, state in post-Maurya and Gupta periods 121-23, 128-32, view of Kāmandakī 132-33, economic basis of 133-36
Sthaviravāda 247
Stone Age cultures 2-5, problems 2-3, sites and characteristics of Early, Middle and Late 3-5
Stūpas: structural developments of 269, description and sites 269-70, Votive stūpas of Ajanta and Ellora 274
Suṅgas 55-56
Śūnyavāda 240-43, 250
Sureśvara 244
Suśarman 55

Tamil literature: genesis 306-07
Tantrism 260-62, in Buddhism 264-67, question of sexuality 288-90
Telugu literature: genesis 308-09
Terracotta art 268, 276-77
theism 240-45
Tomaras 94
trade: Harappan 11-12, guilds 180-81, routes 180, naval 179, 181, 185-86, crafts and professions 182, ports and maritime trade 194-96, Marco Polo on 221-25
Traikutakas 75-76
tribal settlements: Vedic 30-32, of the early historical period 50, of the pre-Gupta period 63-65

Uneven development 1-3, 176-78
Untouchability: no scriptural sanction 165, aparthied practised by European nations 165-66, question of impurity 166-67, causes of its growth 167-68
Urbanism: Harappan 8-14, 178, uneven developments of 176-78, Childe's definition of 176, nature of 178-80, Mauryan, Kuṣāṇa and Gupta 179, commercial association 180-82, ports and markets 185-87, elitism 187-90, post-Gupta developments 193-94
Utpalas 94
Uttamabhadras 64

Vācaspati 244
Vaidumbas 97
Vaiṣṇavism: 246, 248-49, 251-53, female principle in 252, Āḷvar saints 253-55, Viṣṇu identified with *brahman* 258-60, absorption of Buddhist Sahajayāna elements 266, concept of Rādhā-Kṛiṣṇa combine 266, the southern *ācāryas* 258-60, icons 272
Vajrayāna 264-65
Vākāṭakas 65, 74-75, 79
Vāsiska 60
Vāsudeva, Kāṇva 55, Kusāṇa 60
Vatsaraja 88
Vātsyāyana 187-90
Vedic civilization: literature and tradition 27-30, early t[illegible] settlements 30-31, post-Ṛgved[illegible] developments 31-32, rise of [illegible] power 32-33, kingship 33-[illegible] tribal disintegration 34-40, caste system 34-40, pastoral economy 40-42, social division and patriarchy 42, religion and worldview 43-48, popular sanction of sovereignty 111-14, Aśvamedha 112, Rājasūya 112, Vājapeya 113, the *dāsas* 171-72
Vedānta: view of Bādarāyana 241, of Śaṅkara 241-43, of Gauḍapāda 242, *advaita* school of 243-44, theistic interpretation of

Rāmānuja, Madhva and Nimbārka 244-45
Vidyāsaṇya 244
Vijayasena 96
Vijñānavāda 242-43, 250, 252
Vikramāditya VI 101-02
Villages: causes of ruralism 176-77, Vedic 178, economic life 181-82, glimpses of rural life 190-93, administration 183-84
Vima Kadphises 59
Vindhyaśakti 65
Viraśaivas 261-62
Viśiṣṭadvaitavāda 258-59, 263
Viṣṇu images 277-78, 283
Viṣṇukuṇḍins 76, 80
Viṣṇuvardhana 109-10
Vyāsatirtha 244

Warfare 105, 117, 121, 141-42, 155
Western Gaṅgas 81, 84
Women 42, 184-85, 187, 189-90, 212-14

Yādavas 99, 107, 109-10
Yakṣa 246, images of 269, 271
Yogācāra 242-43
Yaśodharman 64, 72, 73
Yaśovarman 86
Yaudheyas 64